OXFORD MONOGRAPHS IN
PRIVATE INTERNATIONAL LAW

GENERAL EDITOR: P. B. CARTER QC
Emeritus Fellow of
Wadham College, Oxford

FOREIGN LAW IN ENGLISH COURTS

OXFORD MONOGRAPHS IN
PRIVATE INTERNATIONAL LAW

The aim of the series is to publish work of high quality and originality in a number of important areas of private international law. The series is intended for both scholarly and practitioner readers.

ALSO IN THIS SERIES

Declining Jurisdiction in Private International Law
JAMES J. FAWCETT

FORTHCOMING TITLES INCLUDE

Insolvency in Private International Law
IAN FLETCHER

Autonomy in International Contracts
PETER NYGH

Intellectual Property and Private International Law
JAMES J. FAWCETT and PAUL TORREMANS

FOREIGN LAW IN ENGLISH COURTS

Pleading, Proof and Choice of Law

RICHARD FENTIMAN

Fellow of Queens' College, Cambridge
Lecturer in Law in the University of Cambridge

OXFORD UNIVERSITY PRESS · OXFORD
1998

Oxford University Press, Great Clarendon Street, Oxford OX2 6DP
Oxford New York
Athens Auckland Bangkok Bogotá Buenos Aires Calcutta
Cape Town Chennai Dar es Salaam Delhi Florence Hong Kong Istanbul
Karachi Kuala Lumpur Madras Madrid Melbourne Mexico City Mumbai
Nairobi Paris São Paolo Singapore Taipei Tokyo Toronto Warsaw
and associated companies in
Berlin Ibadan

Oxford is a trade mark of Oxford University Press

Published in the United States
by Oxford University Press Inc., New York

© Richard Fentiman 1998

First published 1998

All rights reserved. No part of this publication may be reproduced,
stored in a retrieval system, or transmitted, in any form or by any means,
without the prior permission in writing of Oxford University Press.
Within the UK, exceptions are allowed in respect of any fair dealing for the
purpose of research or private study, or criticism or review, as permitted
under the Copyright, Designs and Patents Act 1988, or in the case of
reprographic reproduction in accordance with the terms of the licences
issued by the Copyright Licensing Agency. Enquiries concerning
reproduction outside these terms and in other countries should be
sent to the Rights Department, Oxford University Press,
at the address above

British Library Cataloguing in Publication Data
Data available

Library of Congress Cataloging in Publication Data
Fentiman, Richard.
Foreign law in English courts: pleading, proof, and choice of law/
Richard Fentiman.
p. cm.—(Oxford monographs in private international law)
Includes bibliographical references and index.
1. Foreign law, Pleading and proof of—Great Britain.
2. Conflict of laws—Great Britain. I. Title. II. Series.
KD7508.P74F46 1998 340.9'0942—dc21 97–51513
ISBN 0–19–825878–X

1 3 5 7 9 10 8 6 4 2

Typeset by Hope Services (Abingdon) Ltd.
Printed in Great Britain
on acid-free paper by
Bookcraft Ltd., Midsomer Norton, Somerset

For Alicia

General Editor's Preface

This volume is the second contribution to the series, *Oxford Monographs in Private International Law*. The aim of this series is to publish works of originality and quality on a number of important and developing areas of private international law. Contemporary private international law is a subject characterized by a marked interaction between scholarly and practitioner interests. The series is designed to accommodate this.

In England ascertainment of the rules governing pleading and proof of foreign law has traditionally been regarded as involving no more than the provision of simple answers to a few apparently simple questions. Is foreign law to be treated as law or as fact? If fact, who decides it, judge or jury? If judge, may he take judicial notice of it? If not, may he rely upon all relevant evidence? Where does the burden of proof lie? What standard of proof is required? What is the position if the content of foreign law is neither judicially noticed nor proved? The present author, however, reveals a more complex, and more sophisticated, underlying pattern. Moreover, he sees the issues involved in the wider context of the whole choice of law process. He not only investigates doctrinal implications of pleading and proof of foreign law, but he also explains and demonstrates its importance in practice. This volume can indeed be seen as a good example of the achievement of the aim of the series, *Oxford Monographs in Private International Law*.

Wadham College, Oxford P. B. CARTER
1 November, 1997

Preface

When and how foreign law is applied is, in many jurisdictions, a matter of urgent concern, prompting a large and vibrant literature. Yet in England the pleading and proof of foreign law are generally relegated to subsidiary chapters in the standard commentaries, attracting little critical comment. This book attempts to make good that imbalance. It offers an account of English law's handling of foreign law, depicting the law afresh and suggesting why the English approach may be more sophisticated, and more defensible, than is sometimes supposed. But the focus of the following discussion is broader than this implies. Although concerned with the law of civil procedure, this is as much, or more, an essay in private international law. It is an extended reflection on the choice of law process as its nature is revealed in the pleading and proof of foreign law. It is, more especially, concerned with the special status of the *lex fori* in the conflicts process, and with the extent of party autonomy in choice of law. For, in the end, whether foreign law must be established is a choice of law matter, concerning how far litigants may choose to apply English law by omitting to plead another. The procedures for establishing foreign law, the day-to-day practicalities of evidence and argument, also have a special significance for conflicts lawyers. Indeed, far from being a procedural adjunct to the subject's real concerns, they lie at its heart. For, unless the content of the applicable law can be effectively determined, the choice of law process must be counted a pointless exercise.

But this is also a more limited book than it might have been. It draws freely on the laws of other jurisdictions and the writing of commentators abroad. But it does so merely to illuminate the English experience. It is not a systematic comparative survey of the terrain. Nor has it been possible to explore completely every theoretical avenue suggested by the topic. Such matters as the role of party autonomy in choice of law, and the distinctive claims of the *lex fori* to be applied in transnational disputes, are important in the present context. But they have implications for the conflicts process beyond the scope of this work.

Many friends and colleagues have contributed to this book, perhaps unwittingly, although none is responsible for the faults which remain. Some commented on work in progress. Other suggested (or discouraged) lines of enquiry. Others shared their practical knowledge and experience. Others put my arguments to the best of tests by disagreeing with me. I need especially to thank: John Allison, Jack Beatson, Jack Barcelo, Stuart Bridge, Ruth Collard, John Correa, Gerhard Dannemann, Brian

Davenport, Clive Gringrass, Michael Hwang, Ian Karsten, Masahiko Ohmura, David Parsons, Pippa Rogerson, Robert Summers, John Tiley and Peter Trooboff. I am particularly grateful to John Collier and Erik Jayme, who read substantial portions of the manuscript in draft. I also benefited from the opportunity to develop my views at seminars arranged by Allen & Overy, the British Institute of International and Comparative Law, Cornell Law School, Chuo University, and the International Law Association, British Branch. I am grateful to Jill Watson of the American Society of International Law who made available some otherwise inaccessible material. To the staff of the Squire Law Library in Cambridge I owe a special debt for their tireless efficiency.

This book has also been shaped by my association with different institutions. There can be few more rewarding places to be a lawyer than Cambridge and I owe much to the stimulating company of my colleagues and students in the Faculty of Law. No less am I indebted to the Fellows of Queens' College (legal and otherwise) who, by providing, in matchless surroundings, an environment at once scholarly and congenial, made the task of writing an easier one. But this book is also infused with lessons taught elsewhere, by Peter Birks, Hugh Collins and John Davies at Brasenose College, Oxford. I can but hope that it is as questioning, but also as principled and as constructive as they would expect.

I am especially indebted to Takeshi Kojima, at whose prompting I first explored this topic and began to appreciate its significance. I also owe much to Trevor Hartley, whose insight has made this a better book. To Kurt Lipstein I owe a special debt, for his advice, for his enthusiasm about this project, but especially for the example of his scholarship. Particular thanks are also due to Richard Hart and his successor at Oxford University Press, Chris Rycroft, for their forbearance in the face of ever-dissolving deadlines. Above all, I am indebted to Peter Carter, who quickly realised that this would be a larger project than he or I first imagined, and responded with much patience and encouragement.

Queens' College, Cambridge   RICHARD FENTIMAN
1 November, 1997

Contents

General Editor's Preface		vii
Preface		ix
Table of Cases		xiii
Table of Legislation		xxvii
Table of Conventions		xxxi
Table of Abbreviations		xxxiii
I	Introduction	1
II	The Role of Foreign Law	23
III	Party Choice and Foreign Law	60
IV	Party Choice and Proof	142
V	Exercising Party Choice	159
VI	Proof by Experts	173
VII	Improving Expert Proof	203
VIII	Replacing Party Experts	219
IX	Comparative Excursus	265
X	Principle, Policy, and Reform	286
Select Bibliography		316
Index		325

Table of Cases

Page references given in **bold type** indicate that a case is considered in the body of the text

Australia

BP Exploration Co. (Libya) Ltd. v. Hunt [1980] 1 NSWLR 496........**150, 153**
France v. Hutchinson (1891) 17 VLR 471...147
Lazarus v. Deutsche Lufthansa A.G. [1985] 1 NSWLR 188..............102, 123
Walker v. WA Pickles [1980] 2 NSWLR 123
Waterhouse v. Australian Broadcasting Corporation (1989)
   86 ACTR 1..39
Waung v. Subbotovsky [1968] 3 NSWR 261 189

England

A.-G. of New Zealand v. Ortiz [1984] AC 1 (CA), [1984]
   1 AC 41 (HL)..191, 201, 202, 246, **249–250**, 262
Abbey National Mortgages plc v. Key Surveyors Nationwide Ltd.
   [1996] 3 All ER 97...212, 213, 233, 234, 235, **237, 300**
Abbot v. Abbot and Godoy 4 SW & TR 254...181
Abbott v. Abbott (1860) 29 LJPM & A 57 180
Abidin Daver, The [1984] AC 398..51
Abu Dhabi National Tanker Co. v. Product Star Shipping Ltd.
   [1991] 2 Lloyd's Rep. 508 241
Adams v. Cape Industries plc. [1990] 2 WLR 657................................192, **247**
Ajami v. Comptroller of Customs [1954] 1 WLR 1405 ....179, 181, 192
Al Battani, The [1993] 2 Lloyd's Rep. 219..51
Albaforth, The [1984] 2 Lloyd's Rep. 91 28
Alcock v. Smith [1892] 1 Ch. 238 130
Alfred Dunhill Ltd. v. Sunoptic SA [1979] FSR 337 103
Aluminium Industrie Vaassen BV v. Romalpa Aluminium Ltd.
   [1976] 1 WLR 676 ....**159–160, 166–168**
Amand, Re [1941] 2 KB 239 200
Amand, Re (No 2) [1942] 1 KB 445..200
Amin Rasheed Corpn. v. Kuwait Insurance. Co. [1984] AC 51 ....191, 249
Ann and Mary, The (1843) 2 Wm. Rob. 189..212, 233
Annesley, Re [1926] Ch. 692..192
Anon. (1610) 2 Bro. & Goulds 16 ....216, **234**

Anziani, Re [1930] 1 Ch. 407..161
Arkwright Mutual Insurance Co. v. Bryanston Insurance Co. Ltd. [1990]
    2 QB 649..29, 46, 55
Armagas Ltd. v. Mundogas SA [1976] AC 717..105
Armour v.Walker (1883) 25 Ch. D 678...211
Armour v. Thyssen Edelstahlwerke AG [1991] 2 AC 339..................159, 167
Arton, Re [1896] 1 Q B 509...204, 205
Ascherberg, Hopwood & Crew Ltd. v. Casa Musicale Sonzogno [1971] 1
    WLR 173..3, 65, 66, 182
Associated Shipping Services Ltd. v. Department of Private Affairs
    of H. H. Sheikh Zayed Bin Sultan Al-Nahayan, The Financial Times, 31
    July 1990..8, 181, 196, 198, **230–231**
Assyrian, The (1890) 63 LT 91...212, 233

Badische Anilin und Soda Fabrik v. Basle Chemical Works [1898]
    AC 200..33, 161
Badische Anilin und Soda Fabrik v. Levinstein (1883) 24 Ch. D 156......233
Baker's Trusts, Re (1871) LR 13 Eq. 168...**259, 260**, 261
Baldwin and Francis v. Patents Appeal Tribunal [1959] AC 663.....233, 305
Banca Populare di Novara v. John Livanos & Sons Ltd. [1965]
    2 Lloyd's Rep. 149...131
Banco Atlantico SA v. British Bank of the Middle East [1990]
    2 Lloyd's Rep. 504..52, 130, 207
Bank of Baroda v. Vysya Bank [1994] 2 Lloyd's Rep. 87..........................125
Bankers and Shippers Trust of New York v. Liverpool Marine and
    General insurance Co. Ltd. (1926) 24 Ll LR 85 ....60, 173, 192
Banque des Marchands de Moscou, Re [1958] Ch. 182..............196, 197, **199**
Barlow's Will, Re (1887) 36 Ch. D 287..260, 261
Baron de Bode's Case (1845) 8 QB 208...173, 258
Bater v. Bater [1907] P 333...114
Batra v. Ebrahim [1982] 2 Lloyd's Rep. 10 ....107, 108, 109
Beatty v. Beatty [1924] 1 KB 807 ......**4**, **154**, 155, 187, 192, 193, **260**, 261, 262
Berisford (S & W) plc. v. New Hampshire Insurance Co. [1990]
    2 QB 631..46
Blackburn Union v. Brooks (1878) 7 Ch. D 68 206
Bonelli, In the Goods of (1875) 1 PD 69 179
Bonhote v. Bonhote [1920] WN 142 ....225, **260**, 261
Boys v. Chaplin [1971] AC 356 ....31, 35, 39, 100, **104**, **105**
Brailey v. Rhodesia Consolidated Ltd. [1910] 2 Ch. D 95 ....179, 180
Breen v. Breen [1964] P 144 191
Bremer v. Freeman (1857)10 Moo. PC 306 ....192, 200
Bristow v. Sequeville (1850) 5 Exch. 275..179, 180
Brown v. Brown (1917)116 LT 702.......................................154, 187, 224, 228

Table of Cases

Brown v. Gracey (1821) Dow. & Ry. NP 41n 182
Brunswick (Duke) v. Hanover (King) (1844) Beav. 1 66
Buckland v. Buckland [1968] P 296 .... 117, 160
Buerger v. New York Life Assurance Co. (1927)
   96 LJKB 930 .... 177, 187, 196, **197**, **198**, 199, **257**, 262
Bumper Development Corpn. v. Commissioner of Police for the Metropolis [1991] 1 WLR 1362 .... 3, 4, 5, 8, 68, 147, 173, 183,
                     188, 189, 193, 196, **199**, 200, 201, 230, 231, 258, 287
Burford v. Burford [1918] P 140 180
Buttes Gas and Oil Co. v. Hammer (No 2) [1975] QB 557 .... 102, 231

Calgar v. Billingham [1996] STC (SCD) 150 204
Callwood v. Callwood [1960] AC 659 .... 193, 204, 205
Caltex Singapore Pte. Ltd. v. BP Shipping Ltd [1996]
   1 Lloyd's Rep. 286 .... **86**, 88
Camille and Henry Dreyfus Foundation Inc. v. IRC [1954] Ch. 672 198
Cammell v. Sewell (1860) 5 H & N 728 .... 160, 161
Cap Blanco, The [1913] P 130 45
Carr v. Fracis Times & Co. [1902] AC 176 102
Cartwright v. Cartwight and Anderson (1878) 26 WR 694 180
Casey v. Casey [1949] P 420 .... **118**, 147, 149, 183
Castrique v. Imre (1870) LR 4 HL 414 173
Chad, The [1965] 2 Lloyd's Rep. 1 .... 212, 233
Charm Maritime Inc. v. Kyriakou [1987] 1 Lloyd's Rep. 433 46
Chase Manhattan Bank NA v. Israel-British Bank (London) Ltd.
   [1981] Ch. 105 .... 37, 41
Chattanay v. Brazilian Co. [1891] 1 QB 79 245
Church of Scientology v. Commissioner of Police for the Metropolis
   (1976) SJ 690 .... 101, 102, 105
Clark (Inspector of Taxes) v. Oceanic Contractors Inc. [1983]
   2 AC 130 151
Cliff, Re [1892] 2 Ch. 229 226
Cohn, Re [1945] Ch. 5 .... 4, 12, 221, **260**, 261
Coin Controls Ltd. v. Suzo International (UK) Ltd. [1997]
   3 All ER 45 50
Coles v. Home and Colonial Stores Ltd. [1904] AC 179 233
Colorado, The [1923] P 102 .... 146, 149, 183
Commonwealth Shipping Representative v. P & O Branch Service
   [1923] AC 191 248
Concha v. Murietta (1889) 40 Ch D 543 .... 187, 188, 200
Cooper v. Cooper (1888) 13 App. Cas. 88 202
Cooper v. Stuart (1889) 14 App. Cas. 286 245
Cooper-King v. Cooper-King [1900] P 65 .... 114, 180, 181

Corocraft Ltd. v. Pan American Airways Inc. [1969] 1 QB 616...................86
Coupland v. Arabian Gulf Oil Co. [1983] 1 WLR 1136 105
Czarnikow Ltd. v. Koufos [1969] 1 AC 350..160

Dalmia Dairy Industries Ltd. v. National Bank of Pakistan [1978]
    2 Lloyd's Rep. 223......................................4, 49, 173, 194, **201**, 261, 262, 287
Dalrymple v. Dalrymple (1811) 2 Hagg. Con. 54..200
De Beeche v. South American Stores [1935] AC 148 181
De Dampierre v. De Dampierre [1988] AC 92..51, 55
De Reneville v. De Reneville [1948] P 100................................**117–118**, 156
De Thoren v. Att.-Gen. (1896) 1 App. Cas. 686..202
De Wutz v. Hendricks (1824) Bing. 314..107, 108
Def Lepp Music v. Stuart-Brown [1986] RPC 273................................35, 162
Derby & Co. Ltd. v. Weldon (No.9), 18 October 1990 154
Devaux v. Steele (1840) 6 Bing. NC 360..200
Di Sora v. Phillipps (1863)10 HLC 624; (1863) LJ Ch. 129.......5, 68, **136–138**,
                                            148, 173, 189, 197, **247**, 252, 258, **259**
Dobell v. Steamship Rossmore Co. [1895] 2 QB 408...................................**252**
Dormoy, Re (1832) 3 Hagg. Ecc. 767 222
Dost Aly Khan's Goods, Re (1880) 6 PD 6...181
Du Pont de Nemours v. Agnew [1987] 1 Lloyd's Rep. 585 ....46, **49**
Dubai Bank Ltd. v. Galadari, The Times, 20 June 1990....171, 182, 200, 230,
                                                                                                 231–232
Duke of Wellington, Re [1947] Ch 506...180, 191, 200
Dynamit AG v. Rio Tinto Co. [1918] AC 260..............146, **149–150**, 182, 183

Earldom of Perth, The (1846) 2 HLC 865...173
Easterbrook v. Easterbook [1944] 1 All ER 90.....................................117, 160
Entry Clearance Officer, Dhaka v. Ranu Begum [1986] Imm. A R 461...249
Edmeades v. Thames Board Mills Ltd. [1969] 2 QB 67 ....69, 154, 241
Eglington v. Lamb (1867)15 LT 657.............................134, 135, 136, 138, 239
El Ajou v. Dollar Land Holdings plc [1993] 3 All ER 717 ....4, 8, **220**, **250**,
                                                                                                 258, 288
Eleftheria, The [1969] 1 Lloyd's Rep. 237 ....45, 47, 48, 310
Elliot v. Joicey [1935] AC 209 ....202, 246
Eras EIL Actions, The [1992] 1 Lloyd's Rep. 570...248

Finske Anfartygs A/B v. Baring, (1937) 54 TLR 147..................................225
Forsikringsaktieselskapet Vesta v. Butcher [1989] AC 852.......................191
Forum Craftsman, The [1984] 2 Lloyd's Rep. 102; [1985]
    1 Lloyd's Rep. 291 (CA) **46**, 206, 207
Foster v. Driscoll [1929] 1 KB 47 ....107, 108, 111
Fothergill v. Monarch Airlines [1981] AC 251..193

Table of Cases

Foubert v. Cresseron (1698) Show. PC 194 234
Frank Pais, The [1986] 1 Lloyd's Rep. 529 .... 124, 125
Fraser, Re [1891] P 285 226
Fremoult v. Dedire (1718)1 P Wms. 429 225
Fuld's Estate, Re [1968] P 675 .... **39, 40**, 192, 200

Ganer v. Lanesborough (1790) Peake 25 3
Glenbank, The [1959] 1 Lloyd's Rep. 133; [1960] 1 Lloyd's
 Rep. 178 (CA), [1961] 1 Lloyd's Rep. 231 (HL) 137, **252, 254–255**
Gossage v. Gossage and Heaton (1934) 78 SJ 551 181
Grupo Torras SA v. Sheikh Fahad Mohammed Al Sabah [1995]
 1 Lloyd's Rep. 375; [1995] ILPr. 667 (CA) 13, **55–58**, 128, 156,
                                                               157, 188, 201, 206, 208, 209
Guaranty Trust Co. of New York v. Hannay & Co. [1918]
 2 KB 623 .... 173, 182, 193, 200
Guepratte v. Young (1851) 4 De G & Sm. 217 .... 147, 185
Gulf Bank v. Mitsubishi Heavy Industries Ltd. [1994]
 1 Lloyd's Rep. 323 46
Gulf Consolidated Co. v. Credit Suisse First Boston Ltd. [1992]
 2 Lloyd's Rep. 301 192

Halket v. Dudley [1907] 1 Ch 590 226
Hamlet, The [1924] P 224 255
Hansen v. Dixon (1906) 96 LT 32 180
Harris v. Quine (1869) LR 4 QB 653 38
Harrods (Buenos Aires) Ltd., Re [1992] Ch. 72 .... 28, 51
Hartmann v. Konig (1933) 50 TLR 114 .... 137, 149, 182, **250**
Helbert Wagg's Claim, Re [1956] Ch. 323 .... 164, **246**
Hellenes (King) v. Brostrom (1923) Ll L R 200
Helmsing Schiffarts GmbH & Co. KG v. Malta Drydocks Corporation
 [1977] 2 Lloyd's Rep. 444 .... **39**
Henaff v. Henaff [1966] 1 WLR 598 .... 114, 228
Henson v. Ashby [1896] 2 Ch. 1 233
Hinds v. LTE [1979] RTR. 103 .... 176, 177
Hollandia, The [1982] QB 872, 883 (CA); [1983] 1 AC 565
 (HL) 86, 108
Holman v. Johnson (1775) Cowp. 34 106
Hutter v. Hutter [1944] P 95 117

Ichard v. Frangoulis [1977] 1 WLR 1 99
Ikarian Reefer, The [1995] 1 Lloyd's Rep. 455 (CA) 176
Intercontex v. Schmidt [1988] FSR 575 103
Iran Vojdan, The [1984] 2 Lloyd's Rep. 380 .... 1, 124

Jabbour, F & K v. Custodian of Israeli Absentee Property [1954]
1 WLR 139..12, 178, 183, 195, 221, **260**, 261, 262
Jasciewicz v. Jasciewicz [1962] 1 WLR 1426........................154, 195, 223, 224, 228, **249**, 250
Jones v. NCB [1957] 2 QB 55..236, 300

K (A Minor), Re, The Times, 6 April 1995..233, 234
Kalinowska v. Kalinowski (1964)108 SJ 260...116, 120
Kennard v. Aslam (1894)10 TLR 213...233
Kent v. Kent and Aysseh (1962)106 SJ 16..224, 227
King of Spain v. Machado (1827) 4 Russ. 225...................................3, 178, 245
Kirby Hall, The (1883) 8 PD 71 ....212, 233
Klingemann, In the Goods of (1863) 32 LJP 16...222
Koechlin & Cie. v. Kestenbaum [1927] 1 KB 616.......................................196
Krajina v. Tass Agency [1949] 2 All ER 274 ....222, **230**, **261**
Kruppstahl AG v. Quittmann Products Ltd. [1982] IRLM 551 167
Kursell v. Timber Operators and Contractors Ltd. [1927]
1 KB 299..33, 161

L. v. L. (1919)36TLR 148...225, 260
Lacon v. Higgins, 3 Stark 178...181
Lawrence v. Lawrence [1985] Fam 106...119, 120
Lawson v. Vacuum Brake Co. (1876)1 PD 107 211
Lazard Bros. & Co. v. Midland Bank Ltd. [1933] AC 289 ....**179**, 188, 192, 196, 200, 223, **250**, **257**, 258, 260
Leroux v. Brown (1852) 12 CB 801 ....**40**
Limerick v. Limerick (1863) 4 Sw. & Tr. 252..245
Lindo v. Belisario (1795) 1 Hagg. Con. 216...**234**
Lipkin Gorman v. Karpnale Ltd. [1991] 2 AC 548 34
Lloyd v. Guibert (1865) LR 1 QB 115 ....149, 173, 182
Lloyd, ex. parte (1822) Mont. At. 72n. 300
Lord v. Colvin (1860) 1 Dr. & Sm. 24 ....135, 239
Luckett v. Wood (1908) 24 TLR 617 106

Machado v. Fontes [1897] 2 QB 231 102
Mackender v. Feldia AG [1967] 2 QB 590...110, 124
Macmillan Inc. v. Bishopsgate Investment Trust plc (No. 3) [1995]
1 WLR 978..34, **156**, **157**, 182, 192, 301, 307
MacShannon v. Rockware Glass Ltd. [1978] AC 297.........................202, 246
Magnum, The [1989] 1 Lloyd's Rep. 47 ....52, 207
Mahadervan v. Mahadervan [1964] P 233 ....39, 116, 195
Maharanee of Baroda v. Wildenstein [1972] 2 QB 283 28
Maldonado, Re [1954] P 223..1

Male v. Roberts (1799) 3 Esp. 163 ....**113**
Markes v. Markes (1955) 106 LJ 75 203
Marshall, Re [1957] Ch. 507 261
McCabe v. McCabe, The Independent, 3 September 1993 180
McDermid v. Nash Dredging and Reclamation Co. Ltd. [1987] AC 906....99
Mecklermedia Corporation v. D C Congress GmbH [1997]
 3 WLR 479 ....54, 55, 57
Medway Packaging Ltd. v. Meurer Maschinen GmbH [1990] 1 Lloyd's
 Rep. 383 54
Memec plc v. Inland Revenue Commissioners [1996] STC 1336 203
Merak, The [1964] 2 Lloyd's Rep. 527 ....137, 253
Metall und Rohstoff AG v. Donaldson Lulkin Jenrette [1990]
 1 QB 391 ....28, 124
Montage GmbH v. Irvani [1990] 1 WLR 667 ....**190**, 191, 201
Monterrosso Shipping Co. Ltd. v. International Transport Workers
 Federation [1982] 3 All ER 841 ....**40**
Morgan v. London General Omnibus Co. (1884) 13 QBD 832 248
Mosovitch, Re (1927) 138 LT 183 180
Mostyn v. Fabrigas (1774) 1 Cowp. 161 ....3, 5, 60, 66, 173, 216, 289
Mother Bertha Music Ltd. v. Bourne Music Ltd.,
 31 July 1997 ....147, **151–152**
Moulis v. Owen [1907] 1 KB 746 ....196, 219
Muduroglu Ltd. v. TC Ziraat Bankasi [1986]
 3 WLR 606 ....23, 34, **45**, **51**, **304**, **310**

National Shipping Corpn. v. Arab [1971] 2 Lloyd's Rep. 363 ....147, 183,
                                                               185, 204, 206, 209
Nelson v. Bridport (1845) 8 Beav. 527 ....30, 60, 173, 188, 189, **194**, **196**,
                                                        197, 200, 258, **259**, 288, 289, **304**
Neptun v. Humber Conservancy Board (1937) 59 Ll L R 107 ....212, 233
Nesbitt, Re (1844)14 LJMC 30 245
Nile Rhapsody, The [1992] 2 Lloyd's Rep. 399 ....**45**, **47**, **190**, 193
Noble Julius Ofori (1994) CR. APP. R. 223 79
Nouvelle Banque de l'Union v. Ayton (1891) 7 TLR 377 ....149, 182

Oldenburg, In the Goods of (1884) 9 PD 234 222
Österreichische Länderbank v. S'Elite Ltd. [1981]
 1 QB 565 ....**131–132**, 144, 147, **151**, 183, 184, 186
Ottoman Bank of Nicosia v. Chakarian (No. 2) [1938] AC 260 ....60, 173

Pagnan & Fratelli v. Corbisa Industrial Agropacuaria Limitada [1971]
 1 All ER 165 160
Paley (Princess Olga) v. Weisz [1929] 1 KB 718 200

Palmer v. Crone [1927] 1 KB 804 248
Panayiotou v. Sony Music Entertainment (UK) Ltd. [1994]
  Ch. 142 241–242
Papadopoulos v. Papadopoulos [1930] P 55 ...... 195, 224
Parana Plantations Ltd., Re [1946] 2 All ER 214 ...... 137, 149, 182
Parchim, The [1918] AC 157 ...... 146, 183
Parkasho v. Singh [1968] P 233 ...... 4, 9, 173, 194, 201, 220, 287
Parouth, The [1982] 2 Lloyd's Rep. 351 124
Partington and Son v. Tameside Metropolitan Borough Council
  (1985) 32 BLR 150 233
Pearce v. Ove Arup Ltd. [1997] 3 All ER 31 50
Perkins v. Slater (1876)1 Ch. D 83 206
Perrini v. Perrini [1979] Fam 84 ...... 119, 120
Pfeiffer Weinkellerai-Weineinkauf GmbH v. Arbuthnot Factors Ltd.
  [1988] 1 WLR 150 165
Phillips v. Copping [1935] 1 KB 21 ...... 106, 111
Phillips v. Eyre (1869) LR 4 QB 225 ...... 31, 35, **100, 101, 102, 104, 105**
Piers v. Piers (1849) 2 HL Cas. 331 229
Planeta, The, 18 January 1993 46
Plastus Kreativ AB v. Minnesota Mining and Manufacturing Co.
  [1995] RPC 438 50
Polessk, The [1996] 2 Lloyd's Rep. 40 ...... 51, 185, **208–209**
Polly Peck International plc v. Citibank NA [1994] I L Pr 71 ...... **55–58**
Port Sudan Cotton Co. v. Govindaswamy Chettiar & Sons [1977]
  1 Lloyd's Rep. 166 249
Pritchard v. Pritchard (1920) 37 TLR 104 228
Prowse v. European and American Shipping Co. (1860) 13 Moo.
  PC 484 ...... 195, 196
Prudential Assurance Co. v. Page Ltd. [1991] 1 WLR 756 154

Queen Mary, The (1947) 80 Lloyd's Rep. 609 232

R v. Aspinall (1876) 2 QBD 48 248
R v. Brampton (1808) 1OEast282 180
R v. Governor of Brixton Prison, ex parte Shuter [1960]
  2 QB 89 ...... 154, 224, 228
R v. Immigration Appeal Tribunal, ex parte Rafika Bibi [1989]
  Imm. AR 1 249
R v. Lindsay (1902) 66 JP 505 79
R v. Neguib [1917] 1 KB 359 ...... 79, 180
R v. Povey (1852) Dears CC 32 79
R v. Savage (1876) 13 Cox CC 178 79
R v. Turner [1975] 1 QB 834 177

R v. West Yorkshire Coroner, ex parte Smith [1983] QB 335 151
Radwan v. Radwan (No. 2) [1973] Fam 35...................................116, 120, 229
Ralli Bros. v. Compania Naviera Sota y Aznar [1920] 2 KB 287 109–110
Red Sea Insurance Co. Ltd. v. Bouygues SA [1995]
  1 AC 190 ....31, 35, 100, **104**, **105–106**, 162
Regazzoni v. K.C. Sethia (1944) Ltd. [1958] AC 301 ....107, **108–111**
Reid v. Margison, 1 Camp. 469 225
Reynolds v. Llanelly Associated Tinplate Co. Ltd. [1948]
  1 All ER 410...248
Richardson v. Redpath, Brown & Co. Ltd. [1944] AC 62..........................233
Roberta, The [1937] 58 Lloyd's Rep. 159..37
Roberts v. Brennan [1902] P 143 228
Roe v. Roe (1916)115 LT 792..225, 260
Rohmann v. Rohmann (1908) 25 TLR 78...228
Rossano v. Manufacturers Life Insurance Co. Ltd. [1963]
  2 QB 352...176, 177, 180, 192, 196, 197, 198
Rouyer Guillet & Cie. v. Rouyer Guillet & Co. Ltd. [1949]
  1 All ER 244..178, 245
Rover International Ltd. v. Cannon Film Sales Ltd. [1987]
  1 WLR 1597 203
Royal Boskalis NV v. Mountain [1997] 2 All ER 929 ....**146**, **183**, **184**
Russell v. Att.-Gen. [1949] P 391..116
Russian Commercial Bank v. Comptoir d'Escompte de Mulhouse
  [1925] AC 112 ....188, 200

Sarrio SA v. Kuwait Investment Authority [1996]
  1 Lloyd's Rep. 650..207, 210
Saudi Prince, The [1988] 1 Lloyd's Rep. 1 ....4, 201
Saxby v. Fulton [1909] 2 KB 208..4, 195, **248**
Saxton, Re [1962] 1 WLR 968..213, 233, 235, 237
Schneider v. Eisovitch [1960] QB 430..99, 160
Seasconsar Far East Ltd. v. Bank Markazi Jomhouri Islami Iran [1994]
  1 AC 438 ....124, 204
Sebba, Re [1959] Ch. 166 ....223, 261
Settlement Corp. v. Hochschild [1966] Ch. 10 45
Sharab v. Salfiti, The Times, 13 February 1997....................................107, **112**
Sharif v. Azad [1967] 1 QB 605..196, 314
Shepherd, Re [1904] 1 Ch. 456...229
Singh Batra v. Ebrahim [1982] 2 Lloyd's Rep. 11 86
Snell v. Unity Finance Ltd. [1964] 2 QB 203...106
Spiliada Maritime Corpn. v. Cansulex Ltd. [1987]
  AC 460 ....28, 44, 46, 51
Spivack v. Spivack (1930) 46 TLR 243...116

Stafford Allen & Sons Ltd. v. Pacific Steam Navigation Co. [1956]
  1 Lloyd's Rep. 105..........................12, **50**, **137**, 143, 148, 155, 160, **166**, 222,
                                                                  251, **253**, **254**, 255, **256**, **261**
Standard Steamship P & I Ltd. v. Gann [1992] 2 Lloyd's Rep. 528............**46**
State of Norway's Application, Re [1989] 1 All ER 661......................**154–155**
Stolt Sydness, The [1997] 1 Lloyd's Rep. 273......................137, **253**, **255–256**
Suisse Atlantique Societe d'Armement SA v. NV Rotterdamsche Kolen
  Centrale [1967] 1 AC 21 160
Sussex Peerage Case, The (1844) 11 Cl. & Fin. 85...............173, 180, 181, 258
Szalatany-Stacho v. Fink [1947] KB 1..31
Szechter v. Szechter [1971] P 286..**117**, 149, 186

Tallina Laevauhisus, A/S v. Estonian State Steamship Line (1947)
  80 Ll L R 99 ....60, 173, 177, 178, **194**, 196, 198, 200, 258, 288
Tank of Oslo (A/S), Re [1940] 1 All ER 40 ....149, 182
Tay Bok Choon v. Tahansan Bank [1987] 1 WLR 413................................143
Taylor v. Caldwell (1863) 32 LJQB 164 288
Taylor v. Taylor [1923] WN 65..224
Terrell v. Secretary of State for the Colonies [1953] 2 QB 482 245
Thermawear Ltd. v. Linton, 17 October 1995 174
Tolten, The [1946] P 135 ....**247**
Topham v. Portland (Duke) (1863) 1 DJ & S 517...............................134, 239
Toprak v. Finagrain [1979] 2 Lloyd's Rep. 98 110
Torni, The [1932] P 78...195, 196
Trendtex Trading Corpn. v. Central Bank [1976] 3 All ER 437;
  [1977] QB 529 (CA) 181, 222
Trimbey v. Vignier (1834)1 Bing. N.C. 151...200
Trotter v. Trotter (1828) 4 Bli. (NS) 502..178, 245
Turner, Re [1906] WN 27 ....**248**
Tweney v. Tweney [1946] P 180 229
Tyburn Productions v. Conan Doyle [1991] Ch. 75 ....35, 50

UCM v. Royal Bank of Canada [1983] AC 168 ....86, **107–108**
University of Glasgow v. The Economist [1997]
  EMLR 495...8, 43, 66, 103, 144, **145–146**, 162

Valentine's Settlement, Re [1965] Ch. 831 ....198, 204, 205, 206
Vander Donckt v. Thelluson (1849) 8 CB 812 ....179, 181
Varna, The [1994] 2 Lloyd's Rep. 41...45, 46
Victory, The, 2 July 1996 233
Viswalingham v. Viswalingham [1979] 1 FLR 15 226

Waddle v. Wallsend Shipping Co. Ltd. [1952] Lloyd's Rep. 105.............158

Table of Cases xxiii

Walpole v. Ewer (1789) Ridg. temp. H 276n...192
Ward v. Dey (1849) 1 Rob. Ecc. 759...182, 228
Waterfield v. Waterfield (1929) 73 SJ 300...224
Wellington (Duke), Re [1947] Ch. 506...180
Western National Bank of New York v. Perez, Triana & Co. (1890)
  6 TLR 366...147, 206
Westlake v. Westlake [1910] P 167 ....114, 205, 222, 228
Whitehouse v. Jordan [1981] 1 WLR 246...176
Whitelegg's Goods, Re [1889] P 267...180
Wilson v. Wilson [1903] P 157...114, 180, 181
Wilson, Smithett & Cope Ltd. v. Terruzzi [1976] Q.B. 683 261
Winkworth v. Hubbard [1960] 1 WLR 150 ....99, 160
Winmill v. Winmill (1934) 78 SJ 536...228

X AG v. A Bank [1983] 2 All ER 464...181

Yorke v. British & Continental Steamship Co. Ltd. (1945)
  79 Lloyd's Rep. 181...103

Zanelli v. Zanelli (1948) 64 TLR 556...10, 114
Zapita v. Act Group plc, 11 February 1993...**129**

European Court of Justice

Custom Made Commercial Ltd. v. Stawa Metallbau GmbH,
  Case 288/92 [1994] ECR 1-2913 53
De Bloos v. Bouyer, Case 14/76 [1976] ECR 1497...53
Effer v. Kantner, Case 38/81 [1982] ECR 825 123
Elefanten Schuh GmbH v. Jacqmain, Case 150/80 [1981]
  ECR 1671 ....53, 124
Ivenal v. Schwab, Case 138/81 [1982] ECR 1891...53
Kongress Agentur Hagen GmbH v. Zeehaghe BV, Case 365/88 [1990]
  ECR 1-1845...127
Mulox IBC Ltd. v. Geels, Case 125/92 [1993] ECR 1-4075, [1994]
  1 IRLR 422...53
Tessili v. Dunlop, Case 12/76 [1976] ECR 1471.................................54, 124, **125**
Zelger v. Salinitri, Case 129/83 [1984] ECR 2397 55

Canada

Allen v. Hay (1922) 69 DLR 193...196
Berthiaume v. Dastous [1930] AC 79 ....1, 114

Direct Winters Transport v. Duplate Canada (1962) 32 DLR (2d.) 278 181
Elter v. Kertesz (1960) DLR (2nd) 209 196
Purdom v. Pavey (1896) 26 SCR 412 ....147, 185
Reinblatt v. Gold (1928) Que. R 45 KB 136..180
Tolofson v. Jensen [1994] 3 SCR 1022..71

France

Cass. civ., 12 May 1959...169
Cass. civ., 2 March 1960 271
Cass. civ., 19 October 1971...279
Cass. civ., 25 November 1986..267, 285
Cass. civ., 25 May 1987...267, 285
Cass. civ., 11 and 18 October 1988..267, 285
Cass. civ., 4 December 1990...113, 267, 269, 272, 285
Cass. civ., 8 January 1991...267, 281
Cass. civ., 10 December 1991...267
Cass. civ., 5 October 1994...271, 272

Germany

BGH 10 August 1975...278
BGH 26 March 1964..268
BGH 23 December 1981 281
BGH 15 January 1986 284
BGH 18 January 1988 284
BGH 21 January 1991 ....279, 284

Hong Kong

Adhiguna Meranti, The [1988] 1 Lloyd's Rep. 384 ....51, **52**, 186, 190, 206, **207, 209**

Ireland

Macnamara v. Hatteras [1933] IR 675 196
O'Callaghan v. O'Sullivan [1925] 1 IR 90 ....196, 200

The Netherlands

Hoge Raad, 19 November 1993 ....268, 271

New Zealand

Williamson v. Auckland Electric Tramways Co. (1912) 31 NZLR 161 ...229

Scotland

Credit Chemique v. James Scott Engineering Group Ltd., 1982
  SLT 131 ....**45, 49**
Deutz Engines Ltd. v. Terex Ltd., 1984 SLT 273..159
Emerald Stainless Steel Ltd. v. South Side Distribution Ltd., 1983
  SLT 162 ....159, 160
MacDougall v. Chittinaris, 1937 SC 390 ....135, 239
MacKinnon v. Iberia Shipping Co., 1955 SC 20..................................**103–104**
McElroy v. McAllister, 1949 SC 110 ....104, 145, **150**
Mitchell v. McCulloch, 1976 SC 1 39
Prawdziclazarska v. Prawdziclazarski, 1954 SC 98 117
Zahnrad Fabrik Passau GmbH v. Terex Ltd., 1986 SLT 845.....................167

Singapore

Eng Liat Kiang v. Eng Bak Hern [1995] SLR 407...48
Vishva Apurna, The [1992] 2 SLR 175 45

South Africa

Bank of Lisbon v. Optichem Kunismus Bpk., 1970 (1) SA 447 (W).........130
Schapiro v. Schapiro [1904] TS 673...182
Schnaider v. Jaffe (1916) 7 CPD 696 ....147, 185

United States

Bartsch v. Metro-Goldwyn-Mayer, Inc., 391 F. 2d. 150, 155 n3
  (2d. Cir. 1968) 271

Burnett v. Trans World Airlines, Inc., 368 F. Supp. 1152
(DC N Mex. 1973) 257, 280
Camporese v. Port Authority of New York and New Jersey,
415 NYS 2d. 28 (1979) 99
Crosby v. Cuba Railroad Co., 222 US 473 (1912)...........................68, 74, 265
Fotochrome, Inc., Re, 377 F. Supp. 26, 29 (DCNY 1974)...................257, 280
Kalmich v. Bruno 553 F.2d 549, 555 n4 (7th Cir. 1977) 280
Kleartex (U.S.A.), Inc. v. Kleartex, SDN BHD, 1994 WL 733688,
at *15 n.5 (SDNY June 9, 1994) 271
London Film Productions Ltd. v. Intercontinental Communications Inc.,
580 F. Supp. 47 (1984) **48**, 50
Milwaukee Cheese Co. v. Olaffson, 40 Wis. 2d 581 (1968) 47
Ramirez v. Autobuses Blancos Flecha Roja, 486 F.2d. 493, 497
(5th Cir. 1973) 257, 280
Ramsay v. Boeing Company, 432 F.2d 592, 600 (5th Cir. 1970) 280
Vishipco Line v. Chase Manhattan Bank, NA., 660 F.2d 854, 860
(2d Cir. 1981) 271
Walton v. Arabian American Oil Co., 233 F.2d. 541
(2d Cir. 1956) 68, 265

Table of Legislation

Australia

Rules of the Supreme Court of New South Wales Part 10, r. 5 153

France

Code of Civil Procedure
   Article 12(3) 273
   Article 232 279

Germany

Code of Civil Procedure
   § 293 .... 269, 273, 278–279
   § 404(4) 278

Switzerland

Law on Private International Law 1987 272–273
   Article 16(1) 273
   Article 16(2) 273
   Article 132 .... 268, 272, 273

United Kingdom

Bills of Exchange Act 1882 .... 130–132, 296
   s. 29(2) 132, 151
   s. 30(2) 132, 151
   s. 72 130–132
Bretton Woods Agreement Act 1945
   Article VII(2)(b) 107, 108
British Law Ascertainment Act 1859 .... 4, 134–135, 136, 139, 141, 238–239, 314
   s. 1 238–239
   s. 3 239
Civil Evidence Act 1968 232

s. 2 228
s. 4 228
Civil Evidence Act 1972 314
    s. 2 231
    s. 4(1) 179–180, 231
    s. 4(2) 4, 9, 66, 193, 223, 247, 287
    s. 4(3) 223
    s. 4(4) 223
    s. 4(5) 223
Civil Evidence Act 1995 202
Civil Jurisdiction and Judgments Act 1982
    s. 2 88
    s. 11 226
    s. 41 ....126, 127
    s. 42(7) 54
    Sch. I *see* 1968 Brussels Convention on Jurisdiction and the
        Enforcement of Judgments
Carriage of Goods by Road Act 1965 25
Carriage of Goods by Sea Act 1971 ....25, 108
Carriage of Passengers by Road Act 1974 25
Colonial Laws Validity Act 1865 259
    s. 6 224
Contracts (Applicable Law) Act 1990 169
    s. 2(1) 86, 88
    Sch. I *see* 1980 Rome Convention on the Law Applicable to
        Contractual Obligations
Criminal Justice Act 1993
    s. 6 79
Evidence Act 1851 ....225, 226
    s. 7 225
Evidence (Colonial Statutes) Act 1907 ....154, 224–225, 228, 229, 259, 314
    s. 1(1) 224
Evidence (Foreign, Dominion and Colonial Documents)
    Act 1933 ....227, 228
    s. 1(2) 225
Family Proceedings Rules (1991)
    r. 2.6(2) 114, 226
    r. 10.14 ....114, 116, 118, 227, 229
Foreign Law Ascertainment Act 1861 141
Foreign Limitation Periods Act 1984 ....37, 129–130, 139, 296
    s. 1 ....38, 129
    s. 1(4) 38
    s. 4 130

Foreign Marriage Act 1892
  s. 1 228
  s. 18(2) 228
International Transport Conventions Act 1983 25
  s. 12 228
Maintenance Orders Act 1950
  s. 22(2) 4, 246
Marriage Act 1949
  Preamble 115
Matrimonial Causes Act 1973
  s. 1(3) 115
Merchant Shipping Act 1979 25
Non Contentious Probate Rules (1987)
  Rule 19 179
Oaths and Evidence (Overseas Authorities and Countries)
  Act 1963 228
  s. 5(1) 225
Private International Law (Miscellaneous Provisions)
  Act 1995 .... 15, 76, 97, 102, 140, 162, 169, 296
  s. 9(1) 98
  s. 9(5) 35
  s. 11 .... 1, 97
  s. 11(1) 30, 35
  s. 12 97
  s. 13 .... 35, 97, 100
  s. 13(3)(b) 99
  s. 14(2) 98
  s. 14(4) 98
Recognition of Trusts Act 1987 .... 133–134, 167
  Sch. *see* 1984 Hague Convention on the Law Applicable to Trusts
    and their Recognition
Registration of Births, Deaths, and Marriages (Scotland) Act 1965 228
Rules of the Supreme Court (1965) (SI 1965 No 1776)
  Order 11 28
    r. 1(1)(d) 123
    r. 1(1)(e) 123, 124
    r. 1(1)(f) 124
    r. 2 129
  Order 18 65
  Order 33
    r. 6 .... 158, 212
  Order 38
    r. 3 155

    r. 4...157
    r. 8...214
    r. 11...214
    r. 36..203, 204
    r. 37..157, 307
    r. 38..157, 307
    r. 41...203–204
  Order 39 ....27, 241
    r. 2...210
    r. 3...210
  Order 40 ....212, 232–238
Supreme Court Act 1981
  s. 69(5)..4, 239, 287, 314
  s. 70 212
Theft Act 1968
  s. 24(1)...79
Unfair Contract Terms Act 1977
  s. 27 31
Variation of Trusts Act 1958...133
Wills Act 1963...132–133

United States

Federal Rules of Civil Procedure
  Rule 44.1 ....175, 268, 271, 279–280, 291, 315
Federal Rules of Evidence
  Rule 706 280
New York Civil Practice Law
  Rule 451(b) 271

Table of Conventions

Brussels Convention on Jurisdiction and the Enforcement of
Judgments in civil and commercial matters 1968 28,52
    Article 2 54
    Article 4 128
    Article 5(1) 53, 54, 123, 125
    Article 5(3) 30, 53, 128
    Article 14 96
    Article 16 128
    Article 16(1) 30, 53, 123
    Article 17 .... 53, 123, 124
    Article 20 .... 90, 122
    Article 21 .... 54, 55, 90
    Article 22 55
    Article 52 .... 54, 55, 125–129, 296
Hague Convention on the Conflicts of Law Relating to the Form of
Testamentary Dispositions 1961 133
Hague Convention on the Law Applicable to Trusts and their Recognition 1984 133–134
    Article 6 133
    Article 7 133
    Article 10 133
    Article 15 133
London Convention on Information on Foreign Law 1968 239–244
    Article 2 240
    Article 3 240
    Article 4 240
    Article 5 240
    Article 6 240
    Article 7 240
    Article 8 240
    Article 14 240
    Article 15 240
Lugano Convention on Jurisdiction and the Enforcement of
Judgments in civil and commercial matters 1988 .... 28, 52
    Article 21 55–57
    Protocol 2, Article 1 57
Rome Convention on the Law Applicable to Contractual
Obligations 1980 .... 108, 125
    Article 1 80
    Article 1(1) 88, 90

Article 1(2)(c)	130
Article 1(2)(h)	91
Article 3	1, 80, 81
Article 3(1)	95, 170
Article 3(2)	83, 84, 93, 95, 163
Article 3(3)	80, 84, 85, 89, 90, 93
Article 4	80, 81, 170
Article 5	81, 84, 87, 89, 90, 93, 94, 95, 96, 295
Article 6	81, 84, 87, 89, 90, 93, 95, 295
Article 7(2)	85, 109, 110
Article 8(2)	81
Article 9(6)	81, 84, 91, 93, 95
Article 10	252
Article 10(1)(c)	36
Article 10(1)(d)	36, 38
Article 10(2)	109
Article 12(2)	84, 91, 93
Article 14	36, 37
Article 16	109, 110
Article 18	89, 90, 92

Table of Abbreviations

A number of frequently cited works are identified in the following shortened form in the text. Other principal works referred to in the text are listed in the Select Bibliography.

Cheshire and North	*Private International Law*, 12th edn. (London, 1992), by P. M. North and J. J. Fawcett
Dicey and Morris	*The Conflict of Laws*, 12th edn. (London, 1993), by Lawrence Collins with specialist editors
Hodgkinson	*Expert Evidence: Law and Practice* (London, 1993), by Tristram Hodgkinson
Morris	*The Conflict of Laws*, 14th edn. (London, 1993), by J. D. Mclean
O'Malley and Layton	*European Civil Practice*, (London, 1989), by Stephen O'Malley and Alexander Layton

I
Introduction

How foreign law is pleaded and proved is the crux of the conflict of laws. Suppose that a Californian and a German agree a contract, a contract submitted expressly to the law of Germany. One sues the other in England for breach, liability turning on German law.[1] Or suppose that a defendant injures a plaintiff by a tort committed in France, proceedings being in England but subject to French law.[2] Suppose, again, that a testator dies domiciled in Italy, succession to his movable property turning on contested points of Italian law.[3] In numerous ways such disputes—the examples could be multiplied—are shaped and animated, the parties' thinking informed, by the pleading and proof of foreign law. Imagine, finally, that the parties to a contract, marriage, or other legal relationship, arrange their affairs with a view to its being governed by a given country's laws, perhaps by expressly so providing. Suppose that a marriage is celebrated somewhere so as to enjoy the benefit of the law prevailing there,[4] or that the parties to a commercial contract assume that its performance is regulated by a particular law,[5] or agree a jurisdiction clause in contemplation of its validity under a given country's rules.[6] Such choices of law are meaningful, the participants' arrangements only secure, if means exist whereby their chosen law may be accurately and effectively applied. In this important sense the prospective planning of legal relationships lacks all point, its purpose is subverted, without an adequate regime whereby foreign law can be pleaded and proved.

Nor should we suppose, beguiled by the procedural, adjectival nature of pleading and proof, that this is a topic of small importance. Its practical significance is manifest, such matters often controlling the conduct of conflicts disputes, begging pressing questions of strategy and practice for litigants. Need foreign law be pleaded at all in a given case, the cost and inconvenience of doing so often outweighing any advantages such pleading might yield? If foreign law is pleaded, how is its proof to be effected most expeditiously and most favourably from each parties' perspective? Above all, does the presence of a foreign element, and the problems of

---

[1] 1980 Rome Convention on the Law Applicable to Contractual Obligations, Article 3.
[2] Private International Law (Miscellaneous Provisions) Act 1995, section 11.
[3] *Re Maldonado* [1954] P 223 (CA).   [4] *Berthiaume* v. *Dastous* [1930] AC 79.
[5] 1980 Rome Convention on the Law Applicable to Contractual Obligations, Article 3.
[6] *The Iran Vojdan* [1984] 2 Lloyd's Rep. 380.

proof it might entail, tip the balance sufficiently that a claim is not worth pursuing at all?

The handling of foreign law also has implications in a wider context of policy. At a time when English civil procedure is the subject of extensive debate as to its efficacy and purpose an examination of the handling of foreign law throws a host of urgent questions into sharp relief.[7] Is the voluntary pleading of foreign law a feature of the overly passive posture of English courts in regulating the conduct of civil disputes? Is the proof of foreign law by party-led experts, the standard means of such proof, a needlessly burdensome and expensive technique? Should courts take the initiative by appointing their own, single expert to resolve foreign law questions?

Such reflections also have a deeper significance, bearing on nothing less than the future of private international law. Does the difficulty and expense of proving foreign law argue that the application of the *lex fori* is preferable to the operation of choice of law rules which might lead to the application of foreign law? Do such practical considerations imperil the choice of law process as it is conventionally understood? The search for the most appropriate governing law has long been the focus of academic study and refinement. Must it now be counted no more than an experiment which has failed, wrecked by an inadequate procedural infrastructure? Again, does the difficulty of proving foreign law, and the fact that some countries regard the pleading of foreign law as voluntary, undermine attempts to harmonize the private international law of different countries? Does this imply that the harmonization of domestic private law, or no harmonization at all, are the only viable options? Does it suggest that uniformity in the rules of civil procedure is a precondition of effective harmonization in the conflict of laws?

But in the end there is theory. For the treatment of foreign law lies at the conceptual core of private international law, central to a proper grasp of the conflicts process, its meaning and scope. In an obvious sense, the *proof* of foreign law represents the conceptual terminus of that process, underwriting the rules for choice of law, lending them point by providing the means whereby a foreign applicable law can be applied. But the *pleading* of foreign law is of equal, or greater, importance. Consider, for example, the deeper implications of the familiar principle that the introduction of foreign law is generally at the parties' motion. No mere rule of procedure, it gives the conflict of laws in England its distinctive status. It ensures that many cases with foreign elements are resolved in English courts as purely

---

[7] For the terms of the debate see, Lord Woolf, *Access to Justice, Interim Report to the Lord Chancellor on the Civil Justice System* (London, HMSO, 1995); *Final Report* (London, HMSO, 1996); Zuckerman and Cranston, eds., *Reform of Civil Procedure, Essays on 'Access to Justice'*, (Oxford, 1996).

domestic matters, English law applying by default where foreign law is not relied upon. It means, strikingly, that the conflict of laws, or that part of it which concerns choice of law, is largely a voluntary body of law, whether a case is a conflicts case depending not on the existence of a foreign element, but upon the parties' choice. As this suggests, the principle that the introduction of foreign law is generally voluntary, at the instance of those who would rely upon it, so far from being axiomatic, begs arresting questions about the nature of the choice of law process. Does it reflect an unstated assumption about the dynamics of that process? Does it imply that we should envisage the application of foreign law as an exception to a basic rule whereby English law should normally govern? In so far as an omission to plead foreign law amounts to a choice of English law, are litigants always free to choose the law applicable to their dispute? What are the proper limits to party autonomy in choice of law? When, if ever, should the law require the application of the *lex causae*, objectively determined? Should it make a difference that the law which the parties have chosen, by an omission to plead any other, is that of the forum, as distinct from foreign law? When, in short, should choice of law rules be mandatory?

1. FOUR PRINCIPLES

Given the topic's importance, English law's treatment of foreign law is straightforward, even simplistic. As traditionally conceived, its approach may be expressed in four principles.[8] The first, from which the others follow, is that foreign laws are facts not laws.[9] As such, they are beyond the scope of judicial notice, being unknown and unknowable to the judge. Secondly, being facts, foreign laws must be formally proved, generally by expert evidence, for a judge is unaware of their content.[10] Thirdly, being facts, foreign laws are subject to such principles of pleading as govern other facts.[11] This means that one who relies upon foreign law must

---

[8] For the principal textbook accounts of the subject see, Dicey and Morris, Ch. 9; Cheshire and North, Ch. 7; Morris, Ch. 3; Collier, Ch. 4; O'Malley and Layton, Ch. 9; Hodgkinson, Ch. 16; Hill, *The Law Relating to International Disputes* (London,1994), Ch. 23. See also, Anton, *Private International Law*, 3rd edn. (Edinburgh, 1990), Castel, *Canadian Conflict of Laws* (Toronto and Vancouver, 1994), Ch. 6; Forsyth, *Private International Law*, 3rd edn. (1996), Ch. 4; Nygh, *Conflict of Laws in Australia*, 4th edn. (Sydney, 1995), Ch. 17; Sykes and Pryles, *Australian Private International Law*, 3rd edn. (Sydney, 1991), 267–278; Tetley, *International Conflict of Laws* (Montreal, 1994) , Ch. XXII.

[9] *Mostyn* v. *Fabrigas* (1774) 1 Cowp. 161, 174 (*per* Lord Mansfield); *Bumper Development Corpn.* v. *Comr. of Police* [1991] 1 WLR 1362, 1368 (CA).

[10] *Ganer* v. *Lanesborough* (1790) Peake 25; *Bumper Development Corpn.* v. *Comr. of Police*, op. cit., 1368.

[11] *King of Spain* v. *Machado* (1827) 4 Russ. 225, 239; *Ascherberg, Hopwood & Crew Ltd.* v. *Casa Musicale Sonzogno* [1971] 1 WLR 173, 1128 (CA).

expressly plead it, but, equally, one who does not so rely need not do so. Fourthly, if foreign law is not pleaded, or is pleaded but not adequately proved, a court will apply English law instead,[12] for knowing only English law it presumes foreign law to be the same.

But it is generally recognized that each of these principles must be qualified. First, although formally factual in character, points of foreign law are subject to appeal much as if they are issues of law.[13] Similarly, although few civil cases are of this type, questions of foreign law are for a judge alone in those cases before a judge and jury.[14] Secondly, there are exceptions to the principle that foreign law must be formally proved. This is probably not required when the law in question is notorious,[15] and certainly not when statute confers judicial notice of particular laws.[16] Nor is it necessary if the parties agree otherwise,[17] or if it is possible to establish foreign law merely from reading foreign legal materials.[18] There are also situations in which the proof of foreign law by expert evidence may not be required. The British Law Ascertainment Act 1859[19] offers a means of remitting (in effect) questions of Commonwealth law to the courts of the country concerned. The European Convention on Information on Foreign Law provides a procedure for obtaining foreign official assistance in foreign law matters, although the Convention has not been expressly implemented in English law.[20] The proof of foreign law may also be expedited where an English court has already decided a given point of foreign law, in which case there is a rebuttable presumption that the law is to that effect.[21] Thirdly, although the introduction of foreign law is generally voluntary, a court might introduce foreign law of its own motion in cases within the British Law Ascertainment Act 1859,[22] although this is so unlikely as to be a fanciful suggestion.

All four principles reflect the reality that judges are generally unaware of the content of foreign law. It is for this reason that foreign laws are equated with other facts because, like other facts, they are outside a court's knowledge. Again, because courts are unaware of foreign law, they cannot know its content unless it is pleaded and explained by a qualified expert. Nor can a court do anything but apply English law when the proof

[12] *Bumper Development Corpn.* v. *Comr. of Police*, above n. 9, 1368.
[13] *Parkasho* v. *Singh* [1968] P 233, 250; *Dalmia Dairy Industries Ltd.* v. *National Bank of Pakistan* [1978] 2 Lloyd's Rep. 223, 286 (CA); *Bumper Development Corpn.* v. *Comr. of Police*, above n. 9, 1368 (CA); *The Saudi Prince* [1988] 1 Lloyd's Rep. 1, 3 (CA).
[14] Supreme Court Act 1980, s. 69(5).
[15] *Saxby* v. *Fulton* [1909] 2 KB 208, 211 (CA); but see *El Ajou* v. *Dollar Land Holdings plc* [1993] 3 All ER 717, 736.
[16] The Maintenance Orders Act 1950, s. 22(2) is a rare example.
[17] *Beatty* v. *Beatty* [1924] 1 KB 807 (CA).   [18] *Re Cohn* [1945] Ch. 5.
[19] Below, pp. 238–239.
[20] Below, pp. 239–244.   [21] Civil Evidence Act 1972, s. 4(2).
[22] Below, pp. 134–135.

Introduction

of foreign has failed, being ignorant of its content and knowing only English law. Certainly, a court's lack of notice of foreign law ensures that it cannot properly undertake its own researches so as to establish foreign law itself.[23] But this is not to say that the English approach follows merely from a court's lack of notice of foreign law, nor even from the bare designation of foreign laws as facts. For what matters is not that foreign laws are facts, but what this implies in English law. It is not inevitable, for example, that a court should apply English law when the proof of foreign law has failed. English law could as easily have responded by insisting that such a defective claim or defence should simply be dismissed.[24] Again, the picture might have been different had English law committed itself to the principle *iura novit curia*,[25] or to the application of the *lex causae* as a matter of *ordre public*, or to a doctrine of parity between local and foreign laws,[26] or to a style of adjudication more interventionist than adversarial in which courts may introduce issues *ex officio*.[27] But English law did not do so. Instead its approach to foreign law owes everything to the fact that, at the time when it became increasingly necessary for courts to consider foreign law, it had already adopted the position that the doctrine of judicial notice extended only to English law.[28] By that time the only way to allow the introduction of foreign laws at all was by treating them as facts.[29] Indeed, it should not be forgotten than the purpose of designating foreign laws as facts is to help not to hinder their application.

But the implications of the fact doctrine are ambiguous. Is it that foreign laws are always deemed to be facts, such that they will not be applied in the absence of express pleading and formal proof of their content? Or is it that they should be treated as such only in so far as they actually resemble other facts, implying that they deserve different treatment where there is no such resemblance? Whether or not foreign laws are facts, for example, the circumstances in which they should be applied are defined by the rules of private international law. As such, if a given choice of law rule is mandatory, it might be expected that foreign law should be applied (if the *lex causae*), whether or not the parties wish to plead and prove it. What, then, is the status of facts which the law ordains should be established and applied? This begs a question of classification. Is the pleading of foreign

---

[23] *Di Sora v. Phillipps* (1863) 10 HLC. 624, 640; *Bumper Development Corpn. v. Comr. of Police* [1991] 1 WLR 1362, 1368 (CA).
[24] Kahn Freund, *General Problems of Private International Law*, 2nd. edn., (1976), 278.
[25] As commonly understood, implying a knowledge of all laws: Sass, (1968) 16 *Am Jl Comp L* 332, 347–351. Where the principle extends to foreign law it is not to be taken literally, implying merely that a court is required to research foreign law so as to supply the knowledge expected of it.
[26] Savigny, VIII *System des heutigen Romischen Rechts*, (Berlin, 1849); Sass, op. cit., 357–359.
[27] Pollock, *Expansion of the Common Law*, (1904), 33–34.
[28] Sass, above n. 25, 337.   [29] As in *Mostyn v. Fabrigas* (1774) 1 Cowp. 161.

law procedural, involving no more than the pleading of fact? Or, in so far as it concerns the introduction of the applicable law, is it a substantive matter of private international law?[30] Again, what if a given rule of foreign law is common knowledge, or what if a judge is able to determine its content merely by reading a foreign statute? Are foreign laws to be proved like facts only when they are actually unknown or unknowable to an English court; or are foreign laws always deemed to be beyond a judge's notice because technically they are facts? Such questions, and the ambiguity they disclose, are of recurring concern in the following chapters. As we shall see, the case law is divided between those decisions in which the fact doctrine has been strictly enforced, foreign laws being treated merely as facts, and those where the legal character of foreign law has been recognized.[31] Indeed, as this implies, and as the following discussion confirms, English law's approach to foreign law cannot adequately be described by reference simply to the four principles which are its basis. Certainly, it is wholly misleading simply to intone that foreign laws are facts.

2. A PUZZLING TENSION

The pleading and proof of foreign law are at the fulcrum of private international law, pivotal concerns of the subject at a number of levels, practical, theoretical, and in terms of policy. Despite its importance, however, there is a puzzling tension in the English experience between the topic's centrality and its neglect, in terms of comment and scrutiny, by commentators and practitioners alike. Although an account of the subject is a feature of the leading works on private international law,[32] sustained, critical treatment of the topic is almost entirely lacking in the English literature.[33] As the authors of a leading Australian work observe:

> Proof of foreign law is often treated as a procedural matter of little importance. In fact its importance can hardly be overstated. The choice of law rules, and the underlying purpose of private international law, can only be effectively implemented if the applicable foreign law can be adequately proved or otherwise ascertained.[34]

Several factors explain, if they do not justify, the surprising tendency to ignore the importance of foreign law's pleading and proof. The dearth of decided cases involving foreign law, still more the lack of those which

---

[30] Below, pp. 70–74.
[31] The tension is described by Hodgkinson, 306–309.   [32] Above, n. 8.
[33] See further, Fentiman, (1992) 108 *LQR* 142; North, *Essays in Private International Law* (Oxford, 1993), 179–181; Hartley, (1996) 45 *ICLQ* 271; Rodger and van Doorn, (1996) 46 *ICLQ* 151.
[34] Sykes and Pryles, above n. 8, 278.

discuss directly the law surrounding its pleading and proof, is one explanation for its neglect. Although a misleading guide to the subject's importance, given the frequency with which disputes are settled before trial and the infrequency with which those which do so are reported, the lack of authority inevitably diminishes its prominence. The tendency in England to treat questions of evidence and procedure as practical matters of little scholarly account may also explain the lack of attention paid to the foreign law problem.[35] So does the connected fact that academic study of the conflict of laws has always focused squarely on the design of rules for choice of law, relegating other matters, especially those of a procedural sort, to a lesser role. Such scholarly emphasis, neglectful of procedural questions, deprives the foreign law problem of the critical exposure necessary to give it a visible academic profile.

Another prominent reason for the topic's marginalisation may be the tendency for commentators and practitioners alike to take the perceived state of the law for granted, to regard it as so settled as to require no further discussion. This is partly because the lack of reported cases, noted already, both reduces the topic's apparent importance and lends the law a spurious air of stability. It is also, no doubt, because, more than most legal subjects, English private international law is informed by a pervasive and potent conventional wisdom.[36] Perhaps because cases are relatively few, or because of the subject's conceptual difficulty, there is a tendency to assume that the standard view is the correct view, to believe that what is done is what ought to be done. Certainly, what the law is may depend less on authority or principle than on what it is perceived to be. Part of the prevailing *opinio juris* is that foreign laws are facts and must be treated strictly as such, allowing no deviation from the principle that the pleading of foreign law is voluntary, its proof always to be effected by expert evidence. Certainly, few lawyers would readily depart from conventional practice, either in this context or otherwise, for fear that such innovation may cost the client an advantage it might otherwise enjoy or might itself become the subject of dispute. Nor is this necessarily a matter for criticism, given that no legal system could operate unless certain matters (rightly or wrongly) are taken for granted.

But there is also a tendency to prefer the traditional image to any other, obscuring the existence of other approaches, with the consequence that the conventional wisdom casts the topic in a mould which is misleadingly

---

[35] This tendency was always subject to exceptions, as the distinguished work of Professor Jolowicz and Sir Jack Jacob attests. It is also less marked than it was. See, e.g. Andrews, *Principles of Civil Procedure* (London, 1994); Collins, *Essays in International Litigation and the Conflict of Laws* (Oxford, 1994).

[36] Fentiman, 'Legal Reasoning in the Conflict of Laws', Krawietz, MacCormick and von Wright, eds, *Prescriptive Formality and Normative Rationality in Modern Legal Systems, Festschrift for Robert S. Summers* (Berlin, 1994).

familiar and unexceptional. Certainly, costly as it is to operate, the traditional model, whereby the pleading of foreign law is voluntary and the introduction of evidence is the responsibility of litigants, is comfortingly party-led, underwriting its appeal to practitioners. So too, for all its expense, proof by the oral examination of party experts may have practical attractions. Despite the existence of other mechanisms, such proof is standardly regarded as the only means of establishing foreign law, perhaps because it allows each party considerable control over the presentation of their case. Proof by expert testimony may also attract practitioners in so far as it requires of them, not a skill in foreign law which they clearly lack, but an expertise in advocacy which they possess.

The lack of attention paid to foreign law's pleading and proof also owes much to the fact that the law in this area, superficially at least, is so much a reflection of general principles. It might be thought that there is nothing to say about the pleading and proof of foreign law other than to recite that foreign laws are treated as facts in English law. Provided one knows how facts are pleaded and proved there is nothing further to be added concerning foreign law in particular. Judges are generally unaware of facts, so foreign law must be pleaded; the proof of specialised facts normally depends on expert testimony, so the proof of foreign law is usually by experts. But the notion that English law's treatment of foreign law is settled, and follows simply from the status of foreign law as fact, is misplaced. In reality, as it is the burden of the following discussion to show, the law is less settled than is sometimes supposed. It is open to question whether the subject's cardinal assumptions—that the pleading of foreign law is voluntary, its proof possible only by reference to expert testimony—are strictly justified. It is also far from true that the law in this area is clear, a number of recent cases begging fundamental questions of a controversial nature. Is the pleading—and proof—of foreign law mandatory in cases involving defamatory publications abroad?[37] May foreign laws be treated as notorious facts?[38] What are a judge's powers in assessing documentary evidence of foreign law?[39] How may the existence of a foreign corporation be established?[40] Such recent cases are testimony to the subject's importance and continuing difficulty, each turning on how foreign law should be pleaded or proved. Arrestingly, however, few have been fully reported.

Not only is it more controversial than sometimes appears, the law regarding foreign law is also more distinguishable from that which gov-

---

[37] *University of Glasgow* v. *The Economist* [1997] EMLR 495.
[38] *El Ajou* v. *Dollar Land Holdings plc*, above n. 15, 736.
[39] *Bumper Development Corpn.* v. *Comr. of Police*, above n. 23.
[40] *Associated Shipping Services Ltd.* v. *Department of Private Affairs of HH Sheikh Zayed Bin Sultan Al-Nahayan, The Financial Times*, 31 July 1990.

erns other facts than the common perception implies. Indeed, in ways which are often but dimly appreciated, the proof of foreign law differs materially from the proof of such other facts as depend upon expert testimony. Foreign laws are unlike other facts for the telling, if self-evident, reason that, in effect if not in theory, they govern the legal basis on which a case is argued and decided, affecting the legal rights and obligations of those involved. Moreover, judges have a technical expertise in law, albeit not foreign law, which is inescapably different from the likely state of their knowledge of, say, medical or scientific matters. Truly, foreign laws are facts 'of a peculiar kind'.[41] Indeed, their hybrid status in English courts— foreign laws are laws treated as facts—is highlighted by the alacrity with which judges resolve even the most complex issues of foreign law.[42] It shows itself also in the principle that appeals on points of foreign law are permissible, notwithstanding their factual status,[43] and the possibility that the courts' previous findings as to foreign law are presumptively binding in later cases.[44] Significantly, it is also revealed in the distinctive appropriateness of proving foreign law by reference to competing expert testimony, a process which, whatever the faults of expert proof in other areas, uniquely captures the dialectical nature of legal reasoning.[45] Decisive as they are, however, such dissimilarities between foreign laws and other facts are not always recognized, too ready an equation between them diminishing foreign law's distinctiveness and distracting attention from its specialized nature.

But the relative obscurity of the treatment of foreign law may also owe something to a prevalent assumption about the nature of private international law. It might be thought unsurprising by some that the pleading and proof of foreign law should be neglected, given, so it might be said, that the choice of law process, which stimulates the application of foreign law, is of declining importance.[46] Indeed, some may say that the attention paid to choice of law questions has never been realistic, reflecting more the preoccupations and interests of scholars than the business of the courts. Much turns on this perception, which receives closer scrutiny in the next chapter. For now, we need only notice that several factors feed the belief that the choice of law process is—or has become—relatively unimportant. One is the fact that so many disputes with foreign elements in English courts concern matters of jurisdiction, not choice of law. Another is the English court's ability to stay proceedings which they are otherwise competent to adjudicate, which reduces the number of conflicts disputes before the courts. A third factor may be the tendency for litigants to settle

[41] *Parkasho* v. *Singh* [1968] P 233, 250.
[42] Below, pp. 186–187, 190–191.
[43] Below, p. 201.
[44] Civil Evidence Act 1972, section 4(2).
[45] Below, pp. 299–300.
[46] At least in relative terms: Dicey and Morris, xvi.

their differences before trial, a phenomenon accentuated in English practice by the existence of institutions which encourage compromise, such as extensive pre-trial discovery and wide-ranging interim relief. A fourth reason is that several matters which in other legal systems might beg choice of law questions, leading potentially to foreign law's application, are governed in England by the *lex fori*. Divorce proceedings, for example, are invariably subject to English law,[47] as are many aspects of the law affecting children.[48] In practice there is also a tendency for disputes of a commercial nature to be governed by English law, not least because English law is likely to be applicable in the type of proceedings which come before English courts.

It is intriguing to speculate as to whether the tendency in conflicts scholarship to focus on major issues such as liability in tort, for example, or for breach of contract, or the validity of marriage, ever reflected reality. Indeed, it is tempting to see such an emphasis merely as a reflection of those issues which were, and are, prominent in domestic law. Certainly, the subject's founders were substantive private lawyers, not proceduralists, explaining their focus. And private international law in England borrowed much at its inception from American scholarship,[49] substantive conflicts of law being a pre-eminent problem in the United States context. If, however, judged by modern practice, this concern with substantive issues is an unbalanced perspective, it should not be inferred that the study of private international law should focus instead on matters of procedure and jurisdiction, important as they are. Still less should it be thought that choice of law issues and the application of foreign law are of no significance. The true lesson may be that the map of private international law must be redrawn to reflect changed perceptions of the subject's true morphology, partly to reflect the importance of jurisdictional questions, but also to emphasise the less obvious ways in which it is necessary to consider the role of foreign law in English courts. For, as we shall see in Chapter II, foreign law is significant not only in those relatively few situations in which the direct application of foreign law is required at trial. The difficulty of proving foreign law features significantly in jurisdictional disputes, affecting the courts' determination of questions of *forum non conveniens*.[50] So too, the existence of a foreign element and the relevance of foreign law, inform the preparation of cases, by conditioning the strategic thinking of lawyers, even for those disputes which never reach court at all.[51] Indeed, it may be in the preparation of cases for trial, rather than in court, that the problem of foreign law is most significant. Certainly, even if a case never reaches trial, the parties and their advisers will surely

---

[47] *Zanelli* v. *Zanelli* (1948) 64 TLR 556 (CA).   [48] Morris, 41–42.
[49] Dicey, *Law and Opinion in England*, 2nd edn., (London, 1914), 365.
[50] Below, pp. 44–52.   [51] Below, pp. 42–44.

conduct themselves as if it might, the consideration of its foreign elements included.

As this implies, to disparage the overemphasis of traditional conflicts scholarship on choice of law matters is to risk over-emphasis of a different sort by ignoring that the foreign law question arises in contexts other than the choice of law process at trial. It is to fall into error by supposing that proceedings at trial are the core of legal experience, and that the measure of a subject's vitality is the number of decided cases. But to do so is also to risk error in a different sense. For, as Chapter II suggests, far from suffering a reduction in importance in recent years, the choice of law process has to some extent been revitalised, and with it the importance of foreign law.

3. A REAPPRAISAL

Against this background a fresh appraisal of the pleading and proof of foreign law is warranted for several reasons. First, given its neglect, it is necessary to highlight the topic's true importance. Indeed, the treatment of foreign law in this work amounts to an extended demonstration of its true role, both practically and conceptually. Secondly, the foreign law problem has never received extended, critical examination in English legal writing,[52] although it has been explored with great insight and sophistication elsewhere.[53] Thirdly, accuracy demands that the law should be restated. Re-inspection of the material shows the law to be altogether more complex, more flexible, and more interesting in its implications than is often supposed. Indeed, it may be somewhat different, in form and in practice, from the picture normally presented. As we shall see, it is not at all clear, as is commonly thought, that the pleading of foreign law is always a

---

[52] Aspects of the subject have received critical scrutiny. See especially, Wolff, *Private International Law*, 2nd edn. (Oxford, 1950), Ch. XVII; Kahn-Freund, *General Problems of Private International Law*, above n. 24, 276–280; O'Malley & Layton, Ch. 9; Hodgkinson, Ch. 16; and articles cited above, n. 33.

[53] For a seminal study of the theoretical background to the introduction of foreign law see, De Boer, 'Facultative Choice of Law', (1996) *Recueil des Cours*, vol. 257, 227. Particularly suggestive essays are those of Lando, (1995) *Maastricht Journal* 359, 367–371, and Satjay, (1973) *CILSA* 245. Many sources in English are American in origin. See Sommerich and Busch, *Foreign Law* (New York, 1959) and, for materials on American practice in a comparative context, Schlesinger, Baade, Damaska, and Herzog, *Comparative Law*, 5th edn. (Mineola, 1988), 43–228. References to the extensive American periodical literature are given in Wright and Miller, *Federal Practice and Procedure: Civil 2d* S 2441. See especially: Miller, (1967) 65 *Mich L Rev*. 613; Sass, (1968) 16 *Am Jl Comp L* 333; Schlesinger, (1973) 59 *Cornell L R* 1; The Second Sokol Symposium on Private International Law, (1978) 18 *Virginia Jl of Intl L*, Number 4; Pollack, (1978) 26 *Am Jl Comp L* 470; Sass, (1981) 29 *Am Jl Comp L* 97; Spranking and Lanyi, (1995) 19 *Stan Jl of Intl L* 3. The conceptual relationship between foreign law and the law of the forum was famously delineated by Currie, (1958) 58 *Col L Rev* 964, and Ehrenzweig, (1960) 58 *Mich L Rev* 638; (1965) 18 *Oklahoma L Rev* 340.

voluntary matter for the parties.[54] Nor is it true, as traditionally supposed, that the proof of foreign law by party-led expert testimony is the only—or the most effective—mode of proof.[55] Nor, again, is it certain that the familiar presumption of similarity—whereby, absent contrary proof, English and foreign law are deemed to be the same—has the scope or the support that is commonly claimed for it.[56]

A re-assessment of the topic is particularly important for two reasons. First, a proper understanding of English law's approach to foreign law may influence the behaviour and practice of litigants and their advisers, lessening the cost and delay associated with the process at a time when such considerations have become paramount. Secondly, such an understanding bears in important ways on the current debate about the future of private international law and strategies for its reform. These considerations require elaboration before proceeding, each lending particular urgency to the task of re-appraising English law's approach to foreign law.

(a) EFFECTIVE PRACTICE

The neglect of foreign law is of more than academic interest, having unfortunate practical consequences. It means that the law is often misunderstood, its sophistication frequently ignored, its potential under-exploited. In consequence the law's true merits and faults pass unnoticed. Such misunderstanding of the topic has implications for litigation practice, two of them of special importance. First, to oversimplify the proof of foreign law denies litigants in English proceedings a proper choice between the range of optional modes of establishing foreign law which are, in truth, at their disposal. This is unfortunate because it is a strength of the English approach to foreign law that it offers litigants a variety of evidential techniques, of varying cost and effectiveness, allowing them to weigh the difficulty and importance of each mode of proof against its cost. There may be occasions, for example, when the parties may wish to save time and costs by establishing foreign law without expert testimony. They might do so in a contractual dispute by asking the court to treat the issue of foreign law as one of construction. This allows the court to determine foreign law merely by asking itself what the parties must have intended foreign law to be.[57] Again, the task might be expedited by asking the court to determine foreign law solely by reference to foreign legal texts.[58] But, despite such

[54] Below, Chapter III.　　　　　　　　　　　　　　　　　[55] Below, Chapter VIII.
[56] Below, pp. 62–63, 146–153, 183–188.
[57] *Stafford Allen & Sons Ltd.* v. *Pacific Steam Navigation Co.* [1956] 1 Lloyd's Rep. 105.
[58] e.g. *Re Cohn* [1945] Ch. 5; *F & K Jabbour* v. *Custodian of Israeli Absentee Property* [1954] 1 WLR 139. Conversely, litigants may wish the judge to adopt a more elaborate mode of proof than is usual. It has been known, for example, for the parties to a jurisdictional dispute to introduce oral testimony as to particularly important issues of foreign law, although such

variety and flexibility in the English approach, there is a tendency to assume that the relatively expensive, unpredictable proof of foreign law by party-led expert testimony is the only means of effecting such proof. The range of choice in establishing foreign law is wider, however, the possibility of effecting savings in time and cost greater, than might be supposed. This is not to say that such alternative mechanisms, and the savings they might bring, will always be appropriate. Proof by expert testimony may be the only effective means to prove complex matters of foreign law. But at a time when the cost and delay of civil proceedings is a matter of concern, it is important to highlight any means whereby litigants might select the most cost- and time-efficient mode of proving foreign law.

Secondly, that the subtlety of English law in this context, the range of modes of proof it offers, is sometimes not appreciated has some potentially damaging consequences. It encourages litigants to overstate, and so misjudge, the difficulty of establishing foreign law, its cost and inconvenience. As such, their legitimate aversion to introducing foreign law into proceedings, for reasons of delay and economy, may be exaggerated. It also persuades the courts, more readily than might always be justified, that the difficulty of proving foreign law is a near-decisive reason to deny that an English court is the appropriate forum in which to try matters of foreign law.[59] As such it tends to distort the way in which English courts determine which cases they should hear. This is not to deny that the proof of foreign law will not sometimes be difficult and costly, especially where party-led expert testimony is required, nor that any case involving foreign law is likely to be more cumbersome and expensive than one which does not. Nor does it prevent an English court from treating as a persuasive indicator of the *forum conveniens* that English would need to be proved abroad. It may, however, be easier and cheaper than is sometimes supposed to prove foreign law in England. The courts especially might do well to be sceptical of arguments which take for granted that the cost of proving foreign law is always prohibitive.

(b) Foreign Law and Law Reform

In several important ways the future of private international law, and strategies for its reform, are matters of debate. And in important ways the debate centres on the viability of proving foreign law. This partly concerns the prospects for harmonizing the rules of private international law. Some would argue that international harmonization in choice of law requires uniformity in national approaches to foreign law's pleading and proof.

---

matters are normally handled in writing in preliminary proceedings: *Grupo Torras S.A. v. Sheikh Fahad Mohammed Al Sabah* [1995] 1 Lloyd's Rep. 375.

[59] Below, pp. 44–52.

They would see the latter as a pre-requisite of the former. But others would question whether such harmonization is feasible at all, given the difficulties of applying one country's laws in another's courts. They would see the harmonization of substantive private law as the only effective strategy for controlling the problem of diversity between the worlds legal systems. But there is also debate at a local level about the appropriate course for law reform. It is possible that the choice of law process is fatally undermined by inescapable deficiencies in the application of foreign law, such that application of the *lex fori* is the only practical alternative. If so, this implies that legislation should seek to minimize the choice of law process, not to introduce new choice of law rules.

Arguably, any movement towards wider harmonization in private international law implies the need for uniformity in the rules concerning foreign law's pleading and proof, in so far as those rules may allow for the different application of a given applicable law in different countries. Certainly, the harmonization of European private international law, represented most obviously by the 1980 Rome Convention on the Law Applicable to Contractual Obligations, brings into sharp focus national differences in the matter of pleading and proving foreign law.[60] Is it legitimate, for example, that the parties to contractual proceedings in England may have a choice whether to plead foreign law at all, the effect of their not doing so being to oust the Rome Convention's rules and to invite the application of English law as the *lex fori*? Is it tolerable that different techniques of proof in different countries may lead to the content of a contract's applicable law being differently understood and applied depending on the forum in which proceedings are brought? Such questions are pressing. They suggest the importance of examining whether harmonization in the proof of foreign law is possible. But, more importantly, they make it necessary to enquire whether existing techniques for establishing foreign law are truly as defective as is commonly thought.

More radically, the harmonization of private international law might be depicted as a fruitless exercise, given the difficulty of applying foreign law effectively. Some might cite in support of this view the failure of such attempts as have been made to harmonize national procedural rules, including those concerning foreign law,[61] which may condemn any common conflicts rules to potential inconsistency in their application. Others might regard the application of foreign law as inherently a hopeless task, however much its pleading and proof is improved and harmonized, simply because no court applies a law better than it does its own. Certainly, it is now widely accepted in the European context that the inherent weak-

---

[60] Below, p. 82.
[61] See, for example, the so far abortive attempt to harmonize the civil procedural rules of European Union states.

ness of the conflicts process dictates that future initiatives for harmonization within Member States of the European Union should be directed at the institutions of domestic private law.[62] Professor Lando has argued strongly for such an approach.[63] He would point to the inherent difficulty of proving foreign law effectively and efficiently, whatever method is adopted, and to the resulting injustice of applying the same law differently in different countries. Such difficulties in applying foreign law ensure that 'the conflict of laws is a weak tool for legal integration'.[64] Such loss of faith in the conflicts process offers a challenge to private international law, questioning its purpose and utility. Yet it is far from clear that such misgivings are justified, or could not be assuaged if the proof of foreign law were made more effective, or itself harmonized. Certainly, it is essential to investigate the workings of the English approach to foreign law to test the grounds for such disquiet.

At a local level, the choice of law process also faces a potentially destructive challenge, this time from the argument that situations should be discouraged in which the proof of foreign law is necessary, with all the difficulty and expense such proof entails. Some would prefer the simple application of the *lex fori* in cases with international elements for this very reason, the abolition of the choice of law process being the logical consequence. The implications of this position are striking, amounting to nothing less than a loss of confidence in the choice of law process as traditionally conceived, and an argument for its abolition. Radical as it is, however, this argument is not far-fetched. It underlies a prevalent objection to the recent Private International Law (Miscellaneous Provisions) Act 1995, a statute which invites the application of foreign law in cases involving foreign torts in so far as the law which governs is the *lex loci delicti*. As some commentators have observed, such a rule increases the situations in which foreign law may have to be applied, attracting all the familiar problems associated with proving foreign law.[65]

---

[62] As reflected in the work of the European Commission on Contract Law; on which see, Lando and Beale, eds., *Principles of European Contract Law, Performance, Non-performance and Remedies* (PECL, 1995). Contrast the discussion of policy which begins the Report on the 1980 Rome Convention on the Law Applicable to Contractual Relations by Professors Giuliano and Lagarde, (Report on the Convention, OJ 1980, No. C282/1), with the resolution of the European Parliament endorsing the move towards the harmonization of private law: OJ 1989 No. C158/400; cf. OJ 1922 No. C102/24. See generally, Stein, ed., *Il Futuro Codice Europeo dei Contratti* (Milan, 1993).

[63] 'European Contract Law', Sarcevic, ed., *International Contracts and Conflicts of Law* (1990); Hay, Lando and Rotunda, 'Conflict of Laws as a Technique for Legal Integration', Cappelletti, Seccombe and Weiler eds., *Integration Through Law*, 170; Lando, (1995) 2 *Maastricht Journal* 359, 367–371.

[64] 'European Contract Law', op.cit., 5.

[65] *Private International Law (Miscellaneous Provisions) Act 1995, Proceedings of the Special Public Bill Committee*, HL Paper 36, (1995), 48.

The pleading and proof of foreign law, therefore, are central to the discussion of such matters of policy, principle and reform. Upon the effectiveness of the treatment of foreign law may depend the future of the harmonization of private international law, for, if the choice of law process is hobbled by the foreign law problem, the harmonization of domestic law, or no harmonization at all, may be the inevitable consequence. Upon that issue depends also the future of the choice of law process itself, for, if the proof of foreign law is inherently defective, so too is the choice of law process, a conclusion which argues inescapably for invariable resort to the *lex fori*. Such questions are arresting, requiring a proper understanding and assessment of the ascertainment and application of foreign law in different jurisdictions. But they are especially urgent for two reasons. First, they have particular significance in the context of English law, given the widespread perception that its techniques for proving foreign law are particularly cumbersome and, possibly, ineffective. Secondly, they demand attention because, however flawed the application of foreign law may be, however compelling the argument for harmonization in domestic private law, the need to apply foreign law will always be with us, and the strategy of harmonizing will never completely answer the problem. Certainly, the experience of international harmonization suggests that it works best either in narrow areas, or when it sets minimum standards, or establishes general principles. It may limit, but is unlikely to remove, the need to apply foreign law.

4. ORGANIZATION AND ASSUMPTIONS

Against this background, the present work revisits afresh the issue of foreign law in English courts. Its thesis is that the law in this area is altogether more complex, more subtle and, arguably, more defensible that is commonly supposed. Chapter II continues the direction of this Introduction by placing English law's treatment of foreign law more firmly in context. It locates the practical role of foreign law in the English experience. Its conclusion is that foreign law problems are of greater significance than is misleadingly implied by the dearth of decided cases involving the application of foreign law at trial. Indeed, the distinctive rule of foreign law is as much in the pre-trial preparation of cases, and in interlocutory proceedings, especially those under the doctrine of *forum non conveniens*.

Chapters III and IV explore the principle of voluntarism which underpins the English approach to foreign law. They consider the extent to which litigants are at liberty to control whether and how foreign law is established. Chapter III is concerned with those cases in which litigants may be required to rely upon foreign law. It examines the possibility that rules for choice of law might be mandatory in character, compelling litigants to establish foreign law, if only in exceptional cases. Its conclusion is that this possibility is of greater importance than might be supposed. Chapter IV highlights a different but related problem, concerning the degree of control which courts may exert in regulating the manner and quality of foreign law's proof. It focuses in particular on whether a party who relies upon foreign law, through choice or because compelled to do so by a mandatory choice of law rule, may avoid having to prove its content. In doing so it considers the scope of the familiar but questionable presumption that English and foreign law are similar, which, on inspection, may be ill-founded in authority.

Chapter V adopts a more behavioural approach, examining what reasons litigants may have in practice for introducing (or not) questions involving foreign law. It excavates, in so doing, at least some of the practical and strategic factors which, more than legal doctrine, determine the occurrence of foreign law disputes in England, and thus the shape and dimensions of English private international law. Such factors also suggest why there may be good reasons in principle to allow litigants considerable freedom to seek the application of the *lex fori*, thus avoiding the proof of foreign law.

Chapters VI, VII and VIII amount to an extended examination of the available means of establishing foreign law. As they reveal, although proof by the oral examination of experts is the characteristic means of establishing foreign law in England, other techniques are available, some of them cheaper and more efficient. Indeed, given the legal nature of foreign law, the province of the court in this area may be greater than is usual in connection with matters of fact. Chapter VI pays particular attention to the manner in which courts weigh expert evidence as to foreign law, exploring the limits of their freedom to re-assess defective evidence and emphasizing the sometimes surprising facility—and alacrity—with which difficult matters of foreign law are resolved. Chapter VII assesses a number of means of improving the proof of foreign law on the basis of expert evidence. Principally, it considers the possibility of resorting to court-appointed advisers, such as experts or assessors, although this may have less to commend it than superficially appears. Chapter VIII examines whether foreign law may be determined without relying upon expert opinion. It argues that the range of techniques available for establishing foreign law is wider than is commonly supposed in so far as foreign law might be established without the need for formal proof, and thus without expert evidence.

With Chapter IX the argument adopts a comparative perspective, attempting to relate the English approach to its counterparts abroad. It shows that approach to be closer to those found in other jurisdictions than might be expected, in practice if not in principle. Such radical differences as exist reflect not so much contrasting approaches to foreign law as to private international law and civil procedure.

Chapter X completes the discussion by examining whether the law is in need of reform. It offers substantial justification for the English approach, while identifying areas in which improvement is required. It suggests that difficulty lies not so much in the law itself as in how it is perceived. It reinforces the theme, disclosed in earlier chapters, that proof by expert testimony, whatever its deficiencies in other areas, is uniquely suited to proving foreign law. This is not because such evidence is inherently superior in all cases, but because of the special nature of the foreign law problem. But Chapter X also argues that the strength of the English approach is that it offers a range of other techniques whereby foreign law might be established less formally. This allows a properly proportionate response depending on the case. Finally, Chapter X suggests that English laws predominantly voluntarist approach to the introduction of foreign law is also justified. It reflects the importance of party autonomy in the choice of law process. And it captures the distinctive advantages of applying English law in English proceedings.

As this suggests, the present discussion is more concerned with the conflict of laws than with the law of civil procedure. Certainly, its focus, and its thesis, is that foreign laws, if facts, are treated in special ways, even for evidential purposes. But the topic should not be seen in isolation. In particular, it must be set in the context of the movement to re-imagine the civil justice system and its most basic assumptions. If, however, English law is beginning to adopt a less adversarial approach to litigation, with considerations of cost, efficiency, and access to justice to the fore,[66] the effects upon the treatment of foreign law should not be exaggerated. It should not make it any more likely that a court will, say, request or require the introduction of foreign law, or seek better evidence of its content. For, however the assumptions of litigators will change in future, nothing alters the status of foreign laws as facts, nor the principle that facts must generally be pleaded. Indeed, the impetus for change in the civil justice system is a desire to reduce the cost and delay of civil justice, objectives which may not be served by making disputes with foreign elements more complex than they are by introducing foreign law where the parties do not wish it. Again, if such reform is designed to make English courts more interventionist in approach, this stops far short of requiring them to examine a dispute's foreign elements of their own motion. Its objective is certainly not to introduce the principle *iura novit curia* into English law. Nor is it to alter aspects of English private international law, the question whether

---

[66] See further the material cited above, n. 7.

foreign law should be pleaded and proved being at root a conflicts issue. The reform of the law of civil procedure is not concerned with whether litigants may select the law of the forum as the applicable law. Admittedly, the revolution in civil justice may impact more on the proof of foreign law. Courts might be more astute in future to appoint independent experts, in establishing foreign law as elsewhere. But the oral examination of the parties' experts is so often the most effective means of proving foreign law, that little amendment to current practice is likely. Indeed, as we shall see, there are particular disadvantages in employing court advisers in establishing foreign law. There is also a growing awareness that legal procedures should be proportionate in their scale and cost to the difficulty of any given dispute. But, as we shall see in Chapter X, English law already provides a range of means of establishing foreign law, each offering a suitably proportionate response depending on the case. And the use of party experts, if a costly approach, is nonetheless, in most cases, appropriately cost-effective and just. Certainly, the content and even the form of the current rules of civil procedure are transforming. And some areas of civil practice will be significantly affected. But the impact of such reforms on the practice of pleading and proving foreign law may not be substantial.

5. A BROADER PERSPECTIVE

The clue to the general lies always in the particular. So it is with law, and with the discussion which follows. For although the present work comes to close quarters with a narrowly defined subject matter—foreign law's pleading and proof in English courts—the themes which it implicates are broader, its boundaries wider. Certainly, proper exposition of English law's handling of foreign law requires repeated attention to issues of general significance, just as such general themes are illuminated by the subject's intricacies. What residual powers do courts enjoy, for example, in regulating their procedure? What are the proper limits of a court's inherent knowledge and expertise, such that evidence of certain matters is not always required? To what extent may litigants waive the application of foreign laws which render their acts illegal, or which affect their personal status, or which are protective in nature? When are they free to select the *lex fori* as the applicable law?

Nor can a study such as this confine itself to the explication of doctrine. For legal doctrine, its rules and principles derived from statutes and decided cases, is but part of law. Of equal, perhaps greater, importance in explaining legal experience is the behaviour of those—the lawyers, courts, and commentators—whose actions and assumptions define the law's contours in practice and shape how we imagine it. The following discussion, then, is as much about the behaviour and attitudes of lawyers and the courts as it is about the law itself. Why, for example, is the proof of foreign law by party experts so much favoured, given its expense and protractedness? Why have commentators paid such scant attention to foreign law's treatment in English law? Why, above all, do litigants so often not plead foreign law at all, such that English law applies instead?

The themes of the present study also resonate at a deeper level of theory. For, in considering what to expect of the proof of foreign law a fundamental question is begged: what does it take to establish the 'truth' of a legal proposition? When may a rule or principle be treated as established with sufficient certainty that it may fairly govern the rights and liabilities of litigants? What evidence is required, what decision-making process must be complied with? Necessarily, the present discussion cannot engage at length with such jurisprudential issues.[67] They are, however, of recurring importance in what follows. Not least, they suggest how suitable the use of party-led experts may be in proving foreign law, given how the conflicting nature of such evidence replicates the essentially dialectical, rhetorical nature of legal reasoning. For resolving questions of law, whether local or foreign, is a process of argument, not of discovery.

Such fundamental questions also remind us that we should not expect more of the proof of foreign law than of the determination of issues of domestic law. Nor should we demand more of a local court in applying foreign law than of a foreign court in determining its own law. Indeed, we should not be tempted to assume that the proof of foreign law is necessarily a less stable means of resolving legal disputes than adjudication in the relevant foreign court. Such adjudication may be as fallible, as dependant on the vicissitudes of litigation and legal argument, not to say the capability of the judge, as the proof of foreign law elsewhere. Indeed, to suppose that some objectively correct solution is uniquely available in a foreign court is to adopt the jurisprudentially suspect view that questions of law can ever yield a right answer. As this implies, the true measure of any technique for proving foreign law is not its capacity to excavate objective legal truth. It consists merely in its ability to reproduce the circumstances in which law is determined in the foreign jurisdiction whose law is in dispute. We need not expect the proof of foreign law to produce a correct result, any more than the process of adjudication ever does so. But we may insist that the process be authentic, capturing the assumptions, reasoning and idiom of the foreign forum.

---

[67] The literature on the topic is extensive. See especially MacCormick, *Legal Reasoning and Legal Theory* (Oxford, 1978); Dworkin, *Taking Rights Seriously* (London, 1977), Ch. 4; *A Matter of Principle* (Cambridge, 1985), Part II; Perelman, *Justice, Law and Argument* (Dordrecht, 1980); Perelman and Olbrechts-Tyteca, *The New Rhetoric* (Notre Dame, 1969).

Nor should we necessarily suppose that the possible inaccuracy of establishing foreign law in an alien forum counts against the enterprise. Certainly, there may be cases where the importance of the issue makes such a risk unacceptable.[68] But the effective application of foreign law is not the only interest which the proof of foreign law may serve. In the majority of cases, any inaccuracy in the process of proof must be set against the interests and expectations of litigants. Any imprecision must be weighed against the fact that the parties may regard the process as a fair and acceptable component in the resolution of their differences. It may be preferable, for example, that a court should establish foreign law, however imperfectly, than stay its proceedings on the ground that the issue should be litigated, with further delay and expense, in the relevant foreign forum. Again, whatever charge may be laid against the effectiveness of proving foreign law by party experts, the process allows litigants the fullest opportunity to put their case, thus contributing to the fairness of the process and enhancing the respect in which it is held. As this suggests, the success of any procedural institution should not be narrowly judged. Certainly, objective correctness in the proof of foreign law may be less important than the overall contribution which the process makes to the fair and expeditious resolution of disputes.

In the end, however, the heart of the following discussion is the choice of law process itself. Indeed, little illuminates the dynamics of its operation better than the problem of how and when foreign law applies. It is commonly supposed, for example, that all choice of law rules are optional, in the sense that the application of foreign law can always be prevented if neither party pleads it. In reality, as we shall see, rules of private international law may be mandatory, as much as any legal rule may be mandatory. There is therefore no reason why the choice of law process should not obligate a court to apply foreign law, and the parties to allege it. And when this occurs, so far from undermining the process, the principle of voluntary pleading is simply suspended. Again, it is a familiar principle that, in the absence of contrary evidence, English law and foreign law are treated as the same. But is it really true, as this unlikely fiction assumes, that a foreign *lex causae* somehow 'applies' in cases where it is neither pleaded nor proved? Inspection suggests that this mistakes the logic of the choice of law process. Certainly, if it is assumed that the *lex fori* generally applies in English law, unless the contrary is alleged and successfully proved, it is difficult to see how the presumption of similarity can be justified. More fundamentally, a recurring theme in the following discussion is that the central issue in the choice of law process is not so much 'does foreign law apply?' It is whether it is necessary to pose that question at all, given that

---

[68] Below, p. 49.

the law of the forum may be applicable instead. When and how the *lex fori* governs, thus disabling the choice of law process, is a matter of general concern. And more direct means exist for ousting foreign law, such as the doctrine of public policy, or deployment of mandatory legal rules. But none is so commonplace, none has such everyday significance for litigants, as the freedom to exclude foreign law by not pleading it at all.

Finally, the following pages are animated by another, more general concern. It is that, however practical a topic may be, however shaped and honed in litigation, there is a role for scholarly reflection beyond merely reporting that practice. What happens in the law and why is a crucial ingredient in depicting legal experience. But the commentator's task is to challenge the law's conceptual limits, to discern and to test its logic, mindful that the benchmark is not what is done but what is possible. This task is of particular importance in the conflict of laws. Much influenced in England by a powerful and enduring conventional wisdom, there is a tendency to take much of the subject for granted. Indeed, given the relative infrequency of decided cases, even its most fundamental propositions may be based on scant evidence, or on the licence of jurists. Certainly, in extreme cases courts may tend more towards the reproduction of orthodoxy than to an examination of policy and principle. And, given the relative sparseness of the case law, the subject may be denied the constant testing in practice on which its health and maturity so much depends. This gives critical, scholarly reflection an unusually significant role in developing the law and ensuring its conceptual integrity.[69]

As such considerations suggest, this book is only partly concerned with technical rules for the pleading and proof of foreign law—although it is about such rules. It is as much about the conflict of laws itself, its nature, purpose and, ultimately, its future. Its theme is the conflict of laws, viewed in terms of the two operations which give it definition and meaning—the proof of foreign law which governs how foreign law is applied, and the pleading of foreign law which determines whether conflicts issues arise at all.

---

[69] See further, Fentiman, 'Legal Reasoning in the Conflict of Laws', above n. 36, 457–460.

II
The Role of Foreign Law

The previous chapter began the work of locating the foreign law problem in its proper context. The present chapter completes the task by identifying when the problem becomes an issue in practice. This occurs most obviously in the process of applying the governing law at trial. Once identified through the choice of law process as being foreign, its content must be established by proof. In some cases this will not be contested, although satisfactory evidence will be needed if foreign law is to be applied. In others, the content of foreign law may be disputed. But the application of the *lex causae* at trial is far from being the most frequent, or the most significant, context in which the pleading and proof of foreign law become issues in practice. In reality, the foreign law problem is important in less familiar ways, and not necessarily in the context of substantive proceedings. As we shall see, of equal—or greater—significance is the role of foreign law in jurisdictional contests, and in informing the strategic thinking and pre-trial preparation of litigants and their lawyers. The important truth is that the frequency of substantive choice of law disputes is no barometer of the significance of foreign law questions in English proceedings. Indeed, the foreign elements in a dispute may have less to do with what law is eventually applied than with where proceedings are brought—or whether they are brought at all.

But this is not to say that English courts are hostile to the conflicts process, or to the application of foreign law.[1] Nor is it to endorse the fashionable view that substantive choice of law issues are of dwindling importance. True, they are relatively less significant than is commonly

[1] But (a different matter) they may be inclined to prefer the application of English law in certain cases. This may be no cause for criticism, however, if the parties' expectations, or those connections which caused the dispute to be litigated in England, warrant such a result. Moreover, the English court's approach seems unaffected by any notion that the application of foreign law may involve a 'surrender' of English law's control, still less any concern that the proof of foreign law is necessarily a flawed exercise: see the remarks of Mustill LJ in *Muduroglu Ltd.* v. *TC Ziraat Bankasi* [1986] 3 WLR 606, 625, given, below, p. 45. Some legal systems may be more hostile to foreign law. This may be because the principle *iura novit curia* might require the application of foreign law against the parties' wishes, a result generally excluded in English law by the principle of voluntary pleading. Or it may be that cases too often arise where the accurate determination of foreign law is difficult, a result discouraged in England by operation of the doctrine of *forum non conveniens*. See, further, Lando, (1995) 2 *Maastricht Journal* 359, 371; Hay, Lando and Rotunda, 'Conflict of Laws as a Technique for Legal Integration', Cappelletti, Seccombe and Weiler, eds., *Integration Through Law*, 170 ff.

supposed. And several features of English civil practice operate to diminish the scale and importance of conflicts issues, reducing the number of cases in which foreign law need be applied. But others suggest that choice of law issues remain of the first importance in English private international law, indeed may be more frequent today than previously. As we shall see, the advent of new choice of law rules in tort, and the gradual increase in matters which English courts regard as substantive rather than procedural, serve to increase the range of cases in which the choice of law process is relevant, and with it the application of foreign law.

In establishing the role of foreign law in English courts, its nature and scale, three elements require particular consideration. First, there are those factors which diminish the relevance of the choice of law process, or, at least, reduce the number of cases where the application of foreign law is ultimately required. Secondly, there are those which suggest how choice of law disputes may be more common in future than has recently been the case. Thirdly, there are those respects in which the application, or potential application, of foreign law may be significant other than in cases which go to trial.

1. DIMINISHING FOREIGN LAW

It is easy to suppose that every case with a foreign element begs a choice of law question. But the reality is otherwise.[2] Four features of English conflicts practice tend to diminish the importance of the choice of law process, and of the foreign law problem: first, the uniformity of national laws; secondly, the tendency of litigants to settle their differences before trial; thirdly, the possibility that an English court might decline to entertain proceedings, notwithstanding that it has jurisdiction; and, fourthly, the existence of a distinct homeward trend which ensures that English law often applies to the exclusion of any other. Each of these factors ensures that the incidence of choice of law disputes, and thus of cases in which foreign law might be applied, is relatively less than might be expected. Certainly, it is less than the total of cases with foreign elements. But, as we shall see, none makes the foreign law problem irrelevant or uninteresting. They merely put it in its place.

(a) The Trend Towards Uniformity

Self-evidently, the greater the uniformity between national legal systems, the fewer choice of law problems arise. As harmonization proceeds, so all

[2] Dicey and Morris, xvi.

conflicts become false conflicts. In some areas the trend towards harmonization has been marked, as in connection with international transport[3] or in the large range of matters which are the subject of European Directives. In others, progress has been slow, as typically is the case when the wholesale harmonization of the major departments of private law is contemplated.[4] But, however obvious the competition between harmonization and choice of law, the importance of the former should not be exaggerated. In the English context, for example, the Vienna Convention on the International Sale of Goods, pre-eminent amongst international harmonizing measures, has not been ratified. And even in those areas where harmonization is most conspicuous its effect may not be to introduce complete uniformity. Important examples are the principal international conventions concerning intellectual property which, in general, merely establish a framework for local legislation.[5] Again, European Directives tend only to establish minimum standards of legal protection, leaving open the possibility that Member States may differ in their implementation of their provisions.[6] Moreover, whatever degree of harmonization such Directives achieve within the European Union, their effect is often to create still further disparities between the laws of Member States and non-Member States which, as between such states, accentuate the importance of the conflicts process.[7] If the gradual erosion of the conflicts process through substantive harmonization is thus undeniable its effect will often be incomplete in practice.

Nor should it be supposed that harmonization of the world's legal systems represents an inevitable evolution towards a natural state of affairs, or that its virtues are self-evident.[8] Uniformity may serve specific and

---

[3] See e.g. the Carriage of Goods by Sea Act 1971, embodying the Hague Rules for carriage by sea. Other English legislation implementing similar international conventions includes the Carriage of Goods by Road Act 1965, the Carriage of Passengers by Road Act 1974, the Merchant Shipping Act 1979, the International Transport Conventions Act 1983.

[4] See the work of the Commission on European Contract Law. See, Lando and Beale, eds., *Principles of European Contract Law, Performance, Non-performance and Remedies* (PECL, 1995), and the discussions reported in Stein, ed., *Il Futuro Codice Europeo dei Contratti* (Milan, 1993). For other examples of harmonization see the 1964 Uniform Law on the International Sale of Goods, and the 1964 Uniform Law on the Formation of International Sales of Goods, embodied in the Uniform Laws on International Sales Act 1967.

[5] e.g. the 1861 Berne Convention for the Protection of Literary and Artistic Works and its successor treaties in the field of copyright.

[6] See e.g. the differences in national approaches contemplated by the European Directive on Products Liability; Kelly and Attree, eds. *European Products Liability* (London, 1992), 523–556.

[7] An example is the difference between the protective rules of the emerging Community intellectual property regime and that of other countries, such as the United States: Heymann, (1994) 2 *Intl. Computer Lawyer* 15.

[8] For critiques of the harmonization process see, Hobhouse (1990) 106 *LQR* 530; Mann, (1991) 107 *LQR* 353; Fentiman, 'Il problema dell'armonizzazione nell'ottica di un internazionalprivatista', *Il futuro codice europeo dei contratti*, above n. 4.

identifiable goals. To harmonize the contract law of European states may, for instance, facilitate trade within the single European market.[9] But such goals must be identified, and it must be clear that harmonization would achieve them. They must also be weighed against the disadvantages of harmonization, not least the uncertainty it engenders and the risk that the final form of international instruments may owe as much to compromise as sound policy. The virtues of harmonization must also be set against the positive attributes of diversity between systems. Amongst these may be the desirability of allowing national laws to operate in a way which is sensitive to local conditions, and the need to allow individual states to prosecute their distinctive interests and policies. As this implies, a mature approach to harmonization should reflect, not competition between harmonization and the conflicts process, but a balance between those alternative approaches to legal diversity. Certainly, it may be as undesirable as it is unlikely that the choice of law process will soon become redundant.

(b) The Tendency to Settle

It is a truism that most legal disputes settle before trial, making the application of foreign law as irrelevant in such cases as any other substantive issue. Indeed, the very existence of a foreign element ensures that this is more likely in such cases than otherwise. The difficulty of proving foreign law and of obtaining evidence abroad, for example, or the possibility of a protracted contest about the English court's international jurisdiction may add extra, expensive elements to such proceedings. But other general features of international litigation practice in English law also encourage pre-trial settlement. Three may be of particular importance, each providing a watershed in proceedings at which the parties frequently reconsider their chances of success and calculate the cost of continuing as against the possibility of victory.

The first concerns the manner in which jurisdictional disputes are handled in English law, especially the examination of a dispute's legal context involved in determining the *forum conveniens*.[10] The effect of the court's enquiry into the question which forum—that in England or abroad—is most appropriate for trial, is often to expose a number of matters, especially regarding the procedural aspects of proceedings, which distinguish the English court from the other, rendering one more advantageous than the other for the respective parties. More sharply, the effect of determining the most appropriate forum is to resolve, in effect, where any proceedings are to be heard. Litigants are thus made aware of the rules of

---

[9] Lando, above, n. 1, 374–375.

[10] For accounts of the doctrine's operation see, Dicey and Morris, Ch. 12; Cheshire and North, Ch. 12.

procedure, the rules of private international law and, to a degree, the remedial law, which will govern their dispute, bringing into focus the relative strength or weakness of their respective positions. Such information, combined with the cost and delay already incurred in determining the *forum conveniens*, will often encourage compromise or capitulation. Secondly, the extensive pre-trial discovery of documents permitted in English procedure may encourage settlement in several ways.[11] The cost and duration of the process may discourage the parties from embarking upon it at all. And the fear of what might be disclosed may, exceptionally, compel one party to settle rather than submit to such exposure. Most commonly, the information revealed by the examination of documents may so sharpen and define the factual basis of the dispute as to enable the parties to assess the relative strength and weakness of their respective positions. Thirdly, the strategic effectiveness of such interlocutory remedies as Mareva injunctions and Anton Piller orders may so affect the balance of strength between the parties as to encourage compromise or retreat.[12] It is a familiar truth that the battle to obtain such interlocutory relief is often the real focus of the parties' dispute, the outcome effectively determining the ultimate victor and loser. Apart from such procedural watersheds in the pre-trial timetable the readiness of litigants to settle out of court in international disputes may be encouraged, in particular, by the evidential burden of contesting matters with foreign elements. As we shall see, the cost of proving foreign law, at least by the customary means of employing expert witnesses, is a significant burden. So too the cost and inconvenience of obtaining non-expert evidence located abroad might encourage the settlement of international disputes, typically because of the relative delay and expense involved in the examination of foreign witnesses.

It must be emphasised, however, that the tendency of litigants to settle their differences out of court does not—or does not significantly—reduce the importance of foreign law in English proceedings. It merely reduces the number of cases which go to trial concerning foreign law, and so the number of reported decisions. As we shall see, depending on the moment at which proceedings terminate, much thought may have been given by the parties to choice of law questions, much expense incurred in obtaining and assessing expert evidence as to foreign law. Indeed, the tendency of litigants to settle international disputes may itself highlight the importance of the foreign law question, in so far as the difficulty and cost of proving foreign law may contribute to their readiness to compromise.

---

[11] RSC Order 39; O'Malley and Layton, Ch. 8.
[12] Gee, *Mareva Injunctions and Anton Piller Relief*, 3rd ed. (London, 1995).

(c) Declining Proceedings

English courts will, or may, decline outright to entertain proceedings with foreign elements in three types of case, concerning respectively, the Brussels and Lugano Conventions, the doctrine of *forum non conveniens*, and the non-justiciability of certain types of claim, such as those amounting to an abuse of process.[13] Of these exclusionary mechanisms, the doctrine of *forum non conveniens* has a distinctive role in controlling the admission of cases involving foreign elements. It allows the courts to decline to entertain proceedings far more readily than most legal systems permit, giving them the power to do so whenever they consider that the most appropriate forum for trial lies elsewhere.[14] True, this is partly but a response to the readiness with which English courts might otherwise assume jurisdiction, especially over defendants with only a transitory connection with England.[15] But the fact remains that English courts are prepared to decline a hearing even to those claimants who otherwise may have a right to sue in England. Indeed, they are prepared to exclude even those disputes over which they enjoy jurisdiction by virtue of the apparently mandatory jurisdictional rules of the 1968 Brussels Convention, giving the doctrine a range which many would regard as exorbitant.[16]

It is not merely that the possibility that an English court may employ *forum non conveniens* suggests in principle that fewer international disputes of a substantive nature may occur in England than might be expected. The practical operation of the doctrine tends to ensure that cases with foreign elements are those which are most likely to be rejected. None of these examples should be understood as disclosing immutable rules. And the doctrine of *forum non conveniens* is inoperable *vis à vis* other contracting states to the Brussels or Lugano Conventions.[17] It is possible, however, that English courts may tend to decline proceedings in several commonly occurring situations having foreign elements. These include such important situations as those involving torts committed, or substantially committed, abroad[18] and those involving the application of foreign

---

[13] See further, Dicey and Morris, Ch. 8.
[14] *Spiliada Maritime Corpn. v. Cansulex Ltd.* [1987] AC 460 (HL).
[15] The doctrine compensates for the English court's power to assume jurisdiction based on mere presence in England: *Maharanee of Baroda v. Wildenstein* [1972] 2 QB 283 (CA). It also controls their exorbitant jurisdiction over foreign parties pursuant to RSC Order 11: *Spiliada Maritime Corpn. v. Cansulex Ltd.* op cit. The effect of the doctrine, as presently applied, is to render it relatively easier—by comparison with previous authority—for an English court to deny proceedings.
[16] *Re Harrods (Buenos Aires) Ltd.* [1992] Ch. 72 (CA); Fentiman, (1993) 26 *Cornell Intl. LJ* 60.
[17] *Re Harrods (Buenos Aires) Ltd.*, op. cit.
[18] *The Albaforth* [1984] 2 Lloyd's Rep. 91; *Metall und Rohstoff AG v. Donaldson Lufkin Jenrette* [1990] 1 QB 391 (CA).

law, at least where complex questions of foreign law are in dispute.[19] Trial in England may also be denied in cases involving witnesses located abroad whose evidence cannot be—or cannot easily be—introduced by way of witness statements at trial, oral examination being necessary.[20] The relatively commonplace nature of such features of international disputes ensures that there will be, at the least, a serious possibility that an English court might decline to entertain proceedings in very many cases in which a foreign element exists, in which a choice of law question might arise, and in which the application of foreign law might be anticipated. Indeed, whether or not an English court would decline a hearing in a case exhibiting such features, the very fact that a serious issue as to the *forum conveniens* might arise because of the court's approach to such matters may incline the parties to settle their differences without contesting the point, or persuade a plaintiff that its claim is not worth pursuing in England.

But it should be underlined again that the fact that such proceedings may be rejected does not diminish, or does not much diminish, the importance of the choice of law process, nor of issues of foreign law. Such considerations may figure centrally in the parties' willingness to embark on proceedings at all, whatever the likelihood of their being rejected. Moreover, as we have seen, questions involving foreign law may be important in determining the location of the *forum conveniens*. Once again, the lesson is that the application of foreign law may be less common than might be thought, but the possibility that it might be applied nonetheless looms large in international litigation practice.

(d) THE HOMEWARD TREND

The homeward trend in English conflicts law, the tendency to apply English law in English proceedings, removing any question of applying foreign law, is visible in several ways. First, the importance of choice of law issues may be reduced by the relative size of the category of matters which, being classified as procedural in character, are submitted automatically to English law, no conflicts question arising.[21] The scope of the procedural category is the result of two different elements. One is the growth, especially in recent years, in the number of mechanisms of a clearly procedural character in the area of international litigation. The burgeoning doctrine of *forum non conveniens* and the importance attached to pre-trial Mareva injunctions, both considered above, are prime examples of the procedural focus of such litigation. A further reason for the importance of procedure in English law is the traditional tendency to define as

---

[19] Below, pp. 44–50.
[20] e.g. *Arkwright Mutual Insurance Co.* v. *Bryanston Insurance Co. Ltd.* [1990] 2 QB 649.
[21] See further, Dicey and Morris, Ch. 8.

procedural matters which in many jurisdictions would be treated as substantive. These factors confirm the particular importance of the procedural category in English private international law. But it would be an error to suppose that this necessarily diminishes the importance of substantive choice of law questions. Although the doctrine of *forum non conveniens*, and the availability of effective interlocutory relief, may reduce the number of choice of law questions which go to trial, this does not alter the importance of a case's foreign element in the planning and preparation. Not least, the application of *forum non conveniens* may involve consideration of questions of foreign law. Again, however true it might have been that English law has traditionally viewed a large range of issues as procedural, there is evidence that this trend is being reversed, a matter to which we shall return below.

A second feature of the homeward trend in private international law is more obvious. English law may be the substantive governing law in a given case. This occurs for several reasons. English law will often be properly identified as the *lex causae* by the operation of general rules for choice of law. This will be common, especially because, in proceedings before an English court, English law is likely to be one of the laws which the court is asked to apply. Especially where a contractual submission to jurisdiction exists, the parties may have chosen to proceed in England precisely because it is the applicable law—or, indeed, *vice versa*. Moreover, despite the conceptual distinction between jurisdiction and choice of law there will often be congruence between *lex fori* and *lex causae*, especially where jurisdiction is assumed in respect of the subject matter of the claim, rather than over the defendant *in personam*. This is likely where, for example, jurisdiction is assumed in connection with a tort committed in the territory of the forum,[22] or over immovable property located there.[23] In either case the governing law is likely to be the *lex fori* because those connections which establish the courts competence equally suggest which law has the strongest interest in being applied.[24]

In other cases, however, the relevant rule of private international law may in its structure favour the application of English law.[25] This occurs because of the homeward-tending nature of particular choice of law rules, whereby particular issues are not submitted to the choice of law process at all, the *lex fori* invariably applying. Such rules are relatively common, English law's traditional posture being to regard the choice of law process,

---

[22] e.g. pursuant to the 1968 Brussels Convention, Article 5(3).
[23] e.g. pursuant to the 1968 Brussels Convention, Article 16(1).
[24] In tortious proceedings the governing law is likely to be that of the place of the wrong: Private International Law (Miscellaneous Provisions) Act 1995, s. 11(1). In cases concerning title to land it will be the *lex situs*: Nelson v. Bridport (1845) 8 Beav. 527.
[25] Carter, (1995) 54 *CLJ* 38, 41.

and the application of foreign law, as exceptional. Matrimonial matters, for example, concerning divorce, legal separation, and maintenance, are governed exclusively by English law, no conflicts question arising.[26] So too, most matters concerning children, their adoption and issues of guardianship, disclose no conflicts issue, English law governing automatically.[27] Again, it was for many years the case that English law was the only law which could apply in English proceedings involving foreign torts, although this is no longer so.[28] Certainly, whatever the position with regard to foreign torts, proceedings founded on torts committed in England could at one time be governed only by English law, no conflicts question arising.[29] The immediate application of English law, enshrined in such homeward-tending rules, considerably modifies the nature of the conflicts process, reducing the number of cases in which reference to foreign law is necessary. Such matters being removed from the domain of the regular choice of law process, a significant number of cases, which might otherwise involve the application of foreign law, simply never arise.

Alternatively, a choice of law rule may govern a given case but the application of foreign law may be excluded in the interests of public policy. There is considerable hostility to the use of public policy in English law generally, and to its use in private international law in particular. But if its role should not be overstated, public policy may have a greater influence in conflicts disputes than is sometimes supposed.[30] In other situations a choice of law issue may arise but the application of foreign law may be displaced by the operation of specific mandatory rule. English law does not provide clear guidance as to what constitutes a mandatory rule of a type which will be applied irrespective of the normal rules of private international law. But there are numerous examples, some statutory, some not, of situations in which an English statute has been given such an effect.[31] In the present context, however, the exclusion of foreign law must be put in its place, for, although the application of mandatory law and public policy may, in marginal cases, reduce the number of situations in which foreign law is actually applied, it does not reduce those in which it may have to be pleaded and proved. This is for the obvious reason that it is only once a court has decided that foreign law is prima facie applicable that a question

[26] Cheshire and North, 639–642, 730. It is more controversial whether English law applies invariably in nullity proceedings; ibid., 642–655.

[27] Ibid., 745–746.

[28] *Phillips* v. *Eyre* (1869) LR 4 QB 225. It is unclear whether this ceased to be the case with the decision in *Boys* v. *Chaplin* [1971] AC 356 (HL), or in *Red Sea Insurance Co. Ltd.* v. *Bouygues SA* [1995] 1 AC 190 (PC); see now Private International Law (Miscellaneous Provisions) Act 1995, Part III.

[29] *Szalatany-Stacho* v. *Fink* [1947] KB 1.   [30] Carter, (1985) BYIL 111.

[31] Section 27 of the Unfair Contract Terms Act 1977; Section 153(5) of the Employment Protection (Consolidation) Act 1978; Hartley, (1979) 4 *ELR* 236; Diamond, (1986) IV *Hague Recueil*, Ch. IV; Fawcett, [1990] 40 *CLJ* 44; Cheshire and North, 496–504.

of its exclusion by public policy arises, and only once its content has been proved that the question of its compatibility with English policy becomes relevant. Indeed, so far from being an exception to the choice of law process, the exclusion of foreign law is in truth an integral part of its operation.

A third aspect of the homeward trend in English law is central to our present theme. Whether foreign law is relevant to a given dispute, indeed whether a dispute is a conflicts dispute at all, may be determined by English law's voluntarist treatment of foreign law. As we shall see in Chapter III, English law starts from the position that the pleading of foreign law is voluntary. It is for the parties in dispute to decide whether they wish to plead foreign law, thereby introducing a foreign element into the proceedings, a decision which may itself be affected by the difficulty and expense of proving foreign law. The important consequence if they elect not to do so is that the court will treat the case as one with no foreign dimension, requiring merely the application of English domestic law. In principle, it might be preferable to describe the application of the *lex fori* by this means as an aspect of the choice of law process. English law, it might be said, allows litigants to select the *lex fori* without formality merely by omitting to plead foreign law. But in practice an omission to plead foreign law does not merely render the application of foreign law unnecessary, it has the effect of excluding any choice-of-law question that might otherwise have arisen. For, if foreign law is not pleaded, foreign law is irrelevant. And if foreign law is irrelevant, so, crucially, is any issue touching the choice of applicable law.

English law's permissive attitude towards the pleading of foreign law is visible in numerous decisions having conspicuous foreign elements, in which the possibility that a choice of law issue might be involved, and with it the application of foreign law, was never canvassed, neither party having pleaded foreign law. Although this possibility is the subject of extended treatment in Chapter V, it is important to notice immediately that the parties' freedom not to plead foreign law may have one of two consequences. First, it may exclude the application of foreign law in individual cases in which it might have governed. Secondly, and more arrestingly, the principle of voluntary pleading may impede the development of any choice of law rules at all in certain areas of law, thus extinguishing the possibility that foreign law might ever be applied in those areas. In such cases the application of the *lex fori* as a *de facto* choice of law rule is brought about not by judicial decision, still less as a result of any consideration of the principles involved, but simply by the consistent failure of litigants to plead foreign law in the type of case in question.

One instance of the way in which a *de facto* choice of law rule is created by an omission to plead foreign law concerns the practice whereby English law invariably applies in matters involving the annulment of marriage on the grounds of lack of consent and physical incapacity.[32] Another example concerns title to property under contracts for the sale of goods. In principle, such a question of title should be referred to the *lex situs* of the goods at the time of contracting.[33] Certainly, an important question of choice of law is begged in such a situation. In many cases, however, where goods were located abroad at the moment of sale but the contract was expressly governed by English law, neither the parties nor the court has questioned that English law should govern the issue of title, despite the important distinction between the contractual and proprietary aspects of the transfer.[34] In similar fashion, foreign law is rarely pleaded, issues of choice of law seldom raised, in cases involving contracts between English buyers and English sellers concerning goods located elsewhere at the moment of sale.[35] So also, there is a tendency for litigants not to introduce issues concerning foreign law in disputes concerning contractual retention of title provisions, even where such contracts are governed by foreign law or the goods were located abroad at the time of sale.[36] While it may be overstating the matter to say that the *lex fori* has effectively become the governing law in all such cases it is undeniably true the omission to introduce foreign law has insulated an important area of law from any discussion of its choice of law aspects. Certainly, as this confirms, the principle of voluntary pleading ensures that some departments of English law are not subject to choice of law rules at all, thus confirming the homeward trend in such areas.

2. THE EXPANSION OF CHOICE OF LAW

Despite those factors which diminish the scale and importance of the conflicts process it would be seriously misleading to leave matters there. As we have seen, that cases involving the application of foreign law at trial arise relatively seldom does not mean that issues involving foreign law cannot arise in other ways. But nor should we assume, because they are less frequent than might be supposed, that disputes involving foreign law do not arise at all, still less that they are of no difficulty or interest when they occur. As one judge has expressed it:

... many actions are brought each year in which some aspect of the relationship between the parties is governed by foreign law. This is so particularly in the

---

[32] Below, p. 161.   [33] Below, p. 161.
[34] *Badische Anilin und Soda Fabrik* v. *Basle Chemical Works* [1898] AC 200, 204; *Kursell* v. *Timber Operators and Contractors Ltd.* [1927] 1 KB 299, 312.
[35] Sassoon, *Cif and Fob Contracts*, 4th edn., (London, 1995), para. 404.
[36] Below, p. 160.

Commercial Court because of the large proportion of foreign litigants who choose or are brought to appear before the court . . . So far as my experience has shown most of these cases are decided solely in accordance with English law not so much because the court has applied the presumption that foreign law is the same as English law but because in so many practical respects there is insufficient difference between the commercial laws of one trading nation and another to make it worthwhile asserting and proving a difference. There does however remain a residue of cases where foreign law is hotly in dispute.[37]

But, if disputes involving foreign law have always arisen, their number may be expected to increase in future. Particular instances of the continuing vitality of the choice of law process could no doubt be multiplied. One example is the growing importance of transnational restitutionary claims.[38] A variety of factors have coalesced to bring this about, not least the recognition that the law of restitution is an independent department of English law,[39] the increasing incidence of insolvency amongst multinational corporations, and an apparent growth in transnational fraud. Similarly, there has been a marked increase in the incidence of cases in which it is necessary to determine the validity of a foreign adoption.[40] More significantly perhaps, although not yet reflected in the case law, the increasing globalization of information technology begs many important questions concerning the conflicts treatment of intellectual property rights.[41] Less obviously, there is also some evidence that English courts are increasingly aware that different issues within a single cause of action should, in principle, have their own governing law, a process of fragmentation which, if pursued, would increase the number of conflicts questions raised in a given case.[42] But two more general illustrations might be offered, both representing significant recent developments, each having the effect of making the application of foreign law potentially more important than ever. One concerns the newly enacted choice of rules in tort which make it possible to sue in England on foreign torts where before this was pointless. The other concerns the gradual expansion of the category of issues which English courts regard as substantive rather than procedural.

(a) CHOICE OF LAW IN TORT

English law's choice of law rules in tort have been transformed.[43] The Privy Council has ruled that the *lex loci delicti* may govern foreign torts,

---

[37] *Muduroglu Ltd. v. TC Ziraat Bankasi* [1986] 3 WLR 606, 625 (per Mustill LJ), (CA).
[38] See generally, Rose, ed., *Restitution and the Conflict of Laws*, (Oxford, 1995).
[39] *Lipkin Gorman* v. *Karpnale Ltd.* [1991] 2 AC 548.   [40] Cheshire and North, 746.
[41] See, e.g., Commission of the European Communities, *Green Paper on Copyright and Related Rights in the Information Society*, (Brussels, 1995), 38–43.
[42] *Macmillan Inc.* v. *Bishopsgate Investment Trust Plc* (No.3) [1995] 1 WLR 978.
[43] See generally, Dicey and Morris, Third Supplement to the 12th Edition, Ch. 35.

notwithstanding that the wrong is not actionable under English law.[44] More dramatically, statute now ensures that even torts committed in England may be subject to foreign law,[45] and that the *lex loci delicti* may be applied to those committed abroad.[46] At first sight, the effect of these changes is obvious—foreign law may be applied where before it could not. In reality, the implications are more subtle. In the case of English torts, for example, it is indeed the case that the pleading and proof of foreign law may matter where before it did not. This is because a choice of law problem arises where before none existed, English law alone being relevant. In the case of foreign torts, however, the effect is different. True, the *lex loci delicti* may be applied where before this was impossible. But even under the previous rules it may still have been necessary to plead and prove foreign law in such cases, if only to establish (as was then required) whether the wrong was actionable where it was committed. In that sense, the pleading and proof of foreign law was always relevant, albeit that foreign law could not be applied. In such cases the importance of the new law on the incidence of foreign law disputes is somewhat different. It is that, for as long as the old double-actionability rule was in place it was pointless to sue in England on a foreign tort unless the wrong was actionable under English law. But now that this inhibition has been removed a potentially large category of cases may be brought before the English courts which before were effectively non-justiciable. These are those in which the wrong is actionable under the *lex loci delicti* but not under English law.[47] For that important reason it is possible that the number of cases concerning foreign torts will increase and with it the number of cases requiring the application of foreign law.

(b) Foreign Law and Procedural Law

A familiar mechanism for reducing the significance of the conflicts process, thus avoiding the application of foreign law, is to classify the

---

[44] *Red Sea Insurance Co. Ltd.* v. *Bouygues SA*, above n. 28; actionability under both the *lex fori* and the *lex loci delicti* was previously required, subject to an exception in certain cases of non-actionability under the latter: *Phillips* v. *Eyre*, above n. 28; *Boys* v. *Chaplin* , above n. 28.

[45] Private International Law (Miscellaneous Provisions) Act, s. 9(5); the Act does not apply to proceedings in defamation which are now governed by the *Red Sea Insurance* decision: s. 13.

[46] Section 11(1).

[47] This may become especially important in the area of intellectual property. Hitherto it was always supposed that a claim based upon the infringement abroad of a foreign intellectual property right, although actionable under the *lex loci delicti*, would fail. It would not have been actionable under English law which extends only to infringements of English intellectual property rights in England: *Def Lepp Music* v. *Stuart-Brown* [1986] RPC 273; *Tyburn Productions* v. *Conan Doyle* [1991] Ch. 75; Arnold, (1990) 7 EIPR 254; Carter, (1990) 61 BYIL 400. The inhibition imposed by the double actionability rule is now removed, although such claims may remain non-justiciable on jurisdictional grounds: *Private International Law (Miscellaneous Provisions) Bill, Proceedings of the Special Public Bill Committee* (1995), 61.

issue in dispute as procedural, at once attracting the *lex fori*.[48] But a phenomenon in recent years has been the trend towards subjecting an increasing number of issues to the substantive law which governs the matter in dispute between the parties. This deserves some scrutiny partly because its effect is to increase the number of cases in which conflicts of law arise, and in which the pleading and proof of foreign law may be required. But it is also noteworthy because a tendency to treat issues as procedural is so often given as a reason why choice of law issues have reduced importance in English law.[49]

This subtle but significant development may be animated by the realisation that if the procedural category is too widely drawn the application of the substantive law might be frustrated, the choice of law process thereby subverted.[50] Suppose that a contract is governed by French law but a question arises as to the burden of proving liability for breach. If the issue of the burden of proof is characterized as procedural by an English court, English law will determine what that burden should be, with the consequence that the proper application of French law might be impeded. Only by treating the question as substantive, thereby subjecting it to French law, will the question of liability truly and comprehensively be determined by French law. Although the proper characterization of the burden of proof itself remains in doubt,[51] there are two prominent statutory examples of this growing, if gradual, trend away from too expansive a concept of substance. One concerns proceedings in contract, the other (more generally) the limitation of actions. More fundamentally, there has been a perceptible shift in the approach of the courts, which may be more inclined than previously to classify issues as substantive in nature.

(i) PROCEEDINGS IN CONTRACT

The 1980 Rome Convention on the Law Applicable to Contractual Obligations[52] is particularly important in reducing the forum's control of procedural matters. It ensures that such issues as the burden of proof,[53] the limitation of actions,[54] and, it seems, the availability of remedies[55] are subject to a contract's substantive applicable law. Although the limitation of

[48] Dicey and Morris, 169–170; Dicey, *Conflict of Laws* (1896), 712
[49] Dicey, op. cit.; Lando, above n. 1, 363.
[50] As has been said: 'So intimate is the connection between substance and procedure, that to treat an English rule as procedural may defeat the policy which demands the application of a foreign substantive law': Cheshire and North, 75.
[51] Ibid., 84–85; see now the 1980 Rome Convention on the Law Applicable to Contractual Obligations, Article 14.
[52] Enacted by the Contracts (Applicable Law) Act 1990.
[53] Rome Convention, Article 14.   [54] Article 10(1)(d).
[55] Article 10(1)(c); foreign remedies need be applied only 'within the limits of the powers conferred on the court by its procedural law'.

actions is now similarly treated under English law apart from the Convention,[56] the burden of proof and the availability of remedies are not so regarded, the Convention representing an important departure from existing practice.

The Rome Convention's treatment of such procedural matters has particular significance for the proof of foreign law. This is because, as has been noted, the application of foreign law is rare in contractual disputes before the English courts, not least because of the similarity between the contract law of the major trading nations. Given the procedural character of the matters now subjected to the *lex causae* by the Rome Convention, however, and given the relatively greater dissimilarity between the procedural laws of different countries, such matters are likely to represent an important and novel source of disputes concerning the application of foreign law. It may be, indeed, at least with regard to contractual disputes, that the number of disputes concerning the proof of foreign adjectival law will increase in future.

An example will highlight the potential importance of this change and the increasing likelihood of such quasi-procedural or adjectival disputes. Suppose a dispute in the English courts concerns a contract governed by Ruritanian law. One party sues the other for breach, the latter having refused performance in anticipation of the former not making payment. Under English law, the burden is upon the defendant to show that it was beyond doubt that the plaintiff would not make payment. But under Ruritanian law, the plaintiff would have to show that it was ready, willing and able to pay in order to succeed in its claim. Prior to the Rome Convention it is likely that the requirements of proof would have been governed by English law.[57] Since the Convention, they are governed by Ruritanian law,[58] posing a question for foreign law where before there was none. It is likely, moreover, that the proof of Ruritanian law in our example could give rise to complex evidential problems. Not only would it be necessary to establish the position under Ruritanian law, it might be necessary to show, if challenged, that the relevant rule is itself regarded as a substantive matter in Ruritanian law, thereby involving a potentially complex dispute concerning characterization in Ruritanian law.[59] This is because, as Ruritanian law governs the burden of proof *qua* the contract's substantive governing law, any rule of Ruritanian law which is procedural, not substantive, is irrelevant and inapplicable. Furthermore, a dispute may arise between the parties as to whether the Ruritanian rule in

---

[56] Foreign Limitation Periods Act 1984; below, p. 129.
[57] *The Roberta* [1937] 58 Lloyd's Rep. 159; Dicey and Morris, 183. [58] Article 14.
[59] Cf. *Chase Manhattan Bank NA* v. *Israel-British Bank (London) Ltd.* [1981] Ch. 105, 122; Cheshire and North, 79.

question is part of that country's law of contract, a requirement imposed by the language of the Rome Convention.

Although merely one instance of how questions of foreign law may arise in connection with procedural matters, this example prompts two important reflections: it shows how novel questions of foreign law may arise in future concerning, not liability, but subsidiary matters of a quasi-procedural sort; and it shows how difficult such questions may be to resolve, not least because it will always be necessary to prove under foreign law how the foreign system concerned would itself classify the issue, a profoundly controversial matter in many jurisdictions.

(ii) THE LIMITATION OF ACTIONS

The limitation of actions was formerly treated as procedural in English law. Since 1984, however, the limitation period applied in English courts will generally be that imposed by the law which governs the substantive claim between the parties.[60] Although there were always some cases in which a limitation period was regarded as substantive—where a foreign time bar had the effect of extinguishing a claim altogether[61]—English law's change of approach is significant. But this is not in quite the fashion that might be supposed. For, although it makes foreign law more relevant than before it is unlikely to increase the number of cases in which foreign law need be applied. More probably, it will simply prevent potential claimants from proceeding at all once the defendant has resisted the proceedings by reference to a foreign limitation period, and once it is clear that the claim is time-barred. Certainly, the relative ease with which the length of a foreign limitation period may be ascertained makes it unlikely that the issue will be disputed, except perhaps where the foreign limitation law imports an element of discretion into the imposition of a time-bar.[62] Once again it seems, the presence of a foreign element in a case may be felt less at trial, than in how a case is presented, or in deciding whether to proceed at all.

(iii) FROM PROCEDURE TO SUBSTANCE

Such statutory examples aside, the trend towards widening the category of substantive matters, enhancing the potential relevance of foreign law, is discernible in other ways. Many commentators, for example, advocate a method of classification which departs from the more formalistic

---

[60] Foreign Limitation Periods Act 1984, s. 1; 1980 Rome Convention, Article 10(1)(d); Carter (1985) 101 *LQR* 68.
[61] *Harris* v. *Quine* (1869) LR 4 QB 653, 656.
[62] Foreign Limitation Periods Act 1984, s. 1(4).

approaches of the past and avoids equating what is procedural in domestic law with what is procedural in private international law.[63] Such a flexible approach, sensitive to the purposes of particular rules and the need not to undermine the conflicts process by too liberal a use of the procedural category, is likely to increase the number of matters which are regarded as substantive. But there is also growing awareness in the courts of the need to treat such classification flexibly, usually with the result that the issue in question is treated as substantive. This often takes the form of a sense that issues cannot be classified in the abstract, but only in the circumstances in which they arise. As Scarman J observed:

When is a question one of substantive law? When is a question merely one of evidence or procedure? I attempt no general answer to these questions; for answer can only be made after an analysis of the specific questions calling for decision, its legal background and factual content.[64]

An instance of the courts' increasingly flexible, substantivist approach is the shift in judicial opinion over the question whether the *lex fori* or the *lex causae* governs the rate of interest payable on awards of damages. At least one judge has departed from the conventional view that the former applies. Thus, in *Helmsing Schiffarts GmbH & Co. KG v. Malta Drydocks Corporation*,[65] Kerr J argued that the policy of upholding the parties' choice of law favoured treating the issue as substantive in cases involving contractual claims. In doing so he emphasised the importance of giving effect to the parties' expectations in contractual dealings and the difficulty that, by regarding a matter as procedural, a court is effectively rewarding a plaintiff for his choice of forum.[66] Both factors reflect considerations of policy which, if more generally applied, would favour treating particular issues as substantive.

To the same effect, the courts have, in recent years, consistently favoured treating as substantive the question whether a particular head of damage exists in claims concerning foreign torts. Despite some well-known dicta to the contrary[67] it is now apparent that issues such as whether a claim lies for exemplary damages,[68] and whether damages are recoverable for pain and suffering,[69] and for pure economic loss,[70] are

---

[63] *Mahadervan v. Mahadervan* [1964] P 233, 245; *Re Fuld's Estate* [1968] P 675, 695; Cook, *Logical and Legal Bases of the Conflict of Laws* (1942), 166; Lorenzen, *Selected Articles on the Conflict of Laws* (1947), 134; Cheshire and North, 74–79.

[64] *Re Fuld's Estate (No. 3)*, op. cit., 695.   [65] [1977] 2 Lloyd's Rep. 444.

[66] Ibid., at 450; Kerr J's views have not, however, been generally accepted: Cheshire and North, 97; Law Commission Report No. 124 (1983), paras. 3.55–3.56.

[67] e.g. *Boys v. Chaplin*, above n. 28, 381–383 (per Lord Guest), 383 (per Lord Donovan); Carter, (1971) BYIL 232, 233–234.

[68] Cf. *Waterhouse v. Australian Broadcasting Corporation* (1989) 86 ACTR 1.

[69] *Boys v. Chaplin*, above n. 28, 379 (per Lord Hodson), 392–393 (per Lord Wilberforce).

[70] Cf. *Mitchell v. McCulloch* 1976 SC 1.

substantive. The Court of Appeal has also displayed flexibility in assessing of the status of a statutory presumption. In *Monterrosso Shipping Co. Ltd. v. International Transport Workers Federation*[71] the question was whether a collective labour agreement was governed by English or Spanish law. Under English law, by virtue of section 18 of the Trade Union and Labour Relations Act 1974, the agreement was presumed unenforceable in the absence of a written stipulation. But this was only relevant if English law applied, as it would if the presumption were procedural in character. This was seemingly governed by the well-known decision in *Leroux v. Brown*,[72] which held that the non-enforceability of oral agreements for the sale of land under the Statute of Frauds was procedural. But the Court of Appeal distinguished *Leroux* deciding that unenforceability under section 18 was substantive. It concerned not simply the remedies available for enforcing an agreement, but its very existence, a matter which was necessarily one of substance. In doing so, the court further expanded the category of what is substantive, encouraging a flexible approach by deprecating the traditional tendency to treat all presumptions as to an agreement's legal effect as procedural.[73]

An apparent exception to the trend towards treating adjectival issues as substantive may be Scarman J's insistence in *Re Fuld's Estate (No. 3)*[74] that the burden of proof must be governed by the *lex fori*. But it is important to notice that even Scarman J's seemingly unequivocal view that an English court 'must in all matters of burden of proof follow scrupulously its own *lex fori*'[75] is not quite what it seems. On inspection, it becomes apparent that he intended to support the application of the *lex fori* only where policy and principle so required. In cases concerning probate, such as *Fuld*, it was essential that an English court should satisfy itself whether a testamentary instrument properly reflected the testator's intentions.[76] As such, in its sensitivity to the policy implications of individual cases, the decision argues for a flexible approach to classification, with its promise that the *lex causae* may govern where appropriate.[77]

But it is not merely that the expansion, gradual as it is, of what English law treats as substantive increases the number of cases in which foreign law may become relevant. It may engender a particular type of foreign law problem, concerning whether a foreign rule of law is regarded as substantive or procedural under foreign law. This is so because, even if an English court regards a given matter as substantive, subjecting it to foreign law,

---

[71] [1982] 3 All ER 841 (CA).   [72] (1852) 12 CB 801.
[73] See especially 846 (per Denning MR), 848–849 (per May LJ). Interestingly, no attempt was apparently made to argue that, even if substantive, section 18 was a mandatory rule of the forum.
[74] [1968] P 675.   [75] At 697.   [76] At 698–699.
[77] Indeed, as much is implied by Scarman J's insistence that the substance-procedure distinction should be applied on a case-by-case basis; ibid., 695.

the foreign rule in question will not be applicable in England if it is regarded as procedural as a matter of foreign law.[78] The importance of this possibility is that, if the question whether an issue is substantive or procedural as a matter of English is controversial, it may be equally controversial under foreign law. It is not simply, therefore, that the effect of classifying issues as substantive or procedural for English purposes bears on whether a question of foreign law arises at all; the difficulty of classifying a foreign rule as belonging to one class or the other may itself be a difficult question of foreign law.

In sum, there is a discernible trend, fuelled by statutory change but reflected also in the case law, towards treating an increasing number of issues as substantive rather than procedural. The consequence is that the choice of law process and the application of foreign law acquires enhanced importance. This is not to say that everything that was once procedural in English private international law is now substantive. But there is increasing reluctance to treat as procedural for conflicts purposes everything that might be so treated in domestic law. Although the effect is to broaden significantly the category of cases in which foreign law is relevant this expansion is important as much for the nature of the issues thus affected, as for their number. It is a truism that the world's legal systems, especially concerning core issues in the law of obligations, are more alike than not, at least in the results they achieve if not in idiom or doctrine. But there can be considerable differences between the procedural laws of the world's legal systems, differences reflecting fundamentally distinct philosophies and approaches. To regard such adjectival matters as substantive is to create a category of cases in which real conflicts of law arise, and in which the proof of foreign law is likely to be critical.

3. FOREIGN LAW WITHOUT TRIAL

As the foregoing discussion suggests, the application of foreign law in substantive proceedings may occur less often than might be supposed. But, as we have seen, this is not to say that when and how foreign law is applied are matters of no account. One reason is that the number of cases involving a choice of foreign law might be expected to increase in future. But another, the concern of the remainder of this Chapter, is that the existence of a foreign legal element shapes and informs even those situations in which the substantive liability of the parties is never disputed, or is disputed but is never tried. It does so in three senses. First, how foreign law

---

[78] *Chase Manhattan Bank N.A.* v. *Israel-British Bank (London) Ltd.* above n. 59, 122, 127; Cheshire and North, 79

is treated forms the background to any planned relationship with transnational aspects, even one which is never the cause of litigation, underwriting any choice the parties make of the law to which they are subject. Secondly, foreign law has a significant role in shaping and informing those disputes—the vast majority—which never come before a judge at all. Indeed, given that most disputes are of this type, there are grounds for supposing that foreign law's principal practical role is in the extra-curial context. Certainly, whether or not a court ever addresses a point of foreign law, the parties may have done so, having obtained expert evidence, thought through the choice of law issues involved, and formulated their case accordingly. Thirdly, however rarely foreign law is applied in substantive proceedings, whether and how foreign law is applied has a sometimes decisive role in the resolution of preliminary disputes concerning jurisdiction. This is a matter of considerable importance, given the prominence of such disputes in transnational proceedings in the English courts.

(a) Non-Contentious Matters

The significance of the foreign law problem is not confined to contentious matters. If contracting parties agree to submit their affairs to the governance of a particular law their assumption in doing so, no doubt as unstated as it is obvious, is that there exists some reliable means for ascertaining the content of the applicable law: a choice of law becomes pointless unless the chosen law can be applied. Unlikely as it is that contracting parties will consider the matter in such technical terms, it is the proof of foreign law which makes their choice meaningful. Again, in a rather different fashion, the difficulty and unreliability of proving foreign law may inform the parties' choice of applicable law by persuading them not to select a law different from that of any forum which they might also select. The need for congruence between forum and governing law in drafting international commercial documentation, familiar to any practitioner, is caused in large part by the difficulty of applying foreign law in a court which is unfamiliar with it.

(b) Pre-Trial Planning

Foreign law's introduction and application is important even to those cases which never come to court at all. It may affect the parties' prospective planning of their dispute, influencing both the strategy they employ and, indeed, their decision whether to sue (or defend) at all. It looms large in the strategic thinking of litigants and their lawyers, influencing, first, their decision whether or not to issue, or to defend, proceedings; secondly, their choice of a forum in which to do so; and, thirdly, their preparedness to capitulate or settle.

Take, first, the matter of forum-shopping, the process whereby each party selects its preferred court. No litigant favours trial where the court is required to apply a law other than its own, with the additional inconvenience, uncertainty, and cost that the proof of foreign law entails, and with the attendant risk that foreign law will be wrongly, or unfavourably, applied. True, a well-funded party, hoping to engineer capitulation or compromise, might try to exploit such difficulties by litigating where its weaker opponent finds the proof of foreign law burdensome. Generally speaking, however, litigants prefer courts to apply their own domestic law. Then there is the role of foreign law in forcing or encouraging settlement, and in determining whether proceedings are brought at all. The difficulty of proving foreign law, its expense and the time it takes, might lead the parties, or the less well-funded party, to compromise. More starkly, it might also discourage claimants from proceeding at all, at least in cases where victory might be possible in one country by applying the law of another. Indeed, so troublesome, so unpredictable, so costly is the proof of foreign law perceived to be that practitioners often regard it as the single most obstructive obstacle to successful international litigation.[79]

Of particular strategic importance is the English rule whereby foreign law is deemed to be the same as foreign law unless the contrary is proved. As we shall see, the scope and status of this presumption is controversial, more so perhaps than is often supposed.[80] But its effect, if it exists in its commonly accepted form, is that a claimant in English proceedings may frame its action in foreign law yet call no evidence of its content, relying on the presumption of similarity. The effect is to impose upon the other party the burden of rebutting the presumption. That party then has the difficulty of deciding whether or not to call evidence as to foreign law, itself a matter requiring resort to foreign lawyers and, possibly, foreign experts. It is true that the claimant's bluff may easily be called, requiring the claimant either to admit any allegations by the other party as to foreign law, or to call expert evidence of its own. But, even so, the claimant will be no worse off than if it had called expert evidence initially and may, indeed, have succeeded either in delaying proceedings, which might be to its benefit, or in forcing the other party to compromise rather than prove foreign law. Although not a commonplace occurrence, the strategy of relying upon foreign law without also proving it is visible in a number of cases concerning defamatory statements published abroad.[81] The technique is particularly effective because such statements may have been published in

---

[79] *Private International Law (Miscellaneous Provisions) Bill, Proceedings of the Special Public Bill Committee, Written Evidence*, at 48 (evidence of Norton Rose).
[80] Below, pp. 146–153.   [81] *University of Glasgow* v. *The Economist* [1997] EMLR 495.

several foreign countries, each of them representing a distinct *lex loci delicti*, each of which might be alleged to be the same as English law, each of which a defendant would have show is not the same as English law.[82]

But, whatever strategy the parties adopt, there is an important practical reason why the infrequency with which foreign law is applied in substantive proceedings does not diminish, or does not much diminish, the significance of foreign law. For, whether or not a case comes to trial, the parties' advisers are bound to act as if it will. Suppose that a case settles before it is heard. By then it is likely that each party will have prepared to such a degree, and in such a way, that issues of foreign law will already have arisen and been considered. Each will have decided whether to introduce foreign law and, if so, each will have obtained the necessary expert evidence. Each will have incurred costs and made strategic decisions on the assumption that foreign law is relevant, each will have considered the nature of the foreign rules in question, and such related matters as the means of effecting proof and the availability of an appropriate expert witness.

(c) Jurisdiction and Foreign Law

Whether and how foreign law is applied may be highly significant at the jurisdictional stage of proceedings. Such proceedings are very frequent in English practice, far more so than substantive trial proceedings, and issues concerning the proof of foreign law may be critical to their outcome. Indeed, the role of foreign law in such disputes is of the first importance in understanding the context in which foreign law operates. It is necessary to elaborate in some detail how this is so. In different ways the legal treatment of foreign law affects both the traditional doctrine of *forum non conveniens*, and the European conventions on jurisdiction.

(i) forum non conveniens

Whether an English court will entertain proceedings at all in a given case is a matter of obvious importance. This is often subject to the court's discretion in matters of jurisdiction, as crystalised in the doctrine of *forum non conveniens*.[83] This allows a judge to stay proceedings commenced against defendants within the jurisdiction, and to decline jurisdiction over those abroad, on the basis that the English court is not the most appropriate forum in the interests of the parties and of justice.[84] Within the framework of *forum non conveniens* a foreign legal element may acquire a special significance and sometimes a decisive role. That an issue is governed by

---

[82] Below, pp. 146–153.   [83] See generally, Dicey and Morris, Ch. 12.
[84] *Spiliada Maritime Corpn.* v. *Cansulex Ltd.*, above n. 14.

foreign law may be significant in two respects. First, the difficulty of proving foreign law may incline a court to treat a foreign forum as more natural. Secondly, the conduct and likely outcome of proceedings in the alternative forum, matters themselves requiring proof, may bear on the justice of staying a particular action. The latter involves directly the introduction and proof of foreign law in jurisdictional proceedings; the former concerns how foreign law is to be applied at trial—and whether it can be established at all.

(i) The Difficulty of Proof

Whatever the merits of the English approach to the proof of foreign law it is likely that a case involving such proof will be harder and more expensive to resolve than one where it is not required. As one judge has said of the role of foreign law in English proceedings:

> ... the issue has to be fought on expert evidence, with the help of written materials, in the light of jurisprudential concepts and procedural systems markedly different from our own. It is part of the stock-in-trade of the practitioner and judge in the Commercial Court to deal with this kind of dispute, and the volume of business in this court would give the lie to any suggestion that the court is seen by its users as incapable of dealing with any but characteristically English disputes. At the same time, it would be unrealistic not to acknowledge that the trial of an issue of foreign law must be more complicated and expensive here than in the court to which the law belongs....[85]

As these remarks imply the difficulty of proving foreign law represents at least two different but associated problems. One concerns the inconvenience and expense involved. The other is that the effective determination of foreign law may depend so much on the principles and assumptions underlying a foreign legal system that an English judge could never apply it accurately. The first issue goes straightforwardly to the utility of litigating in England rather than abroad. But the second is not merely a matter of efficiency. It touches the heart of the doctrine of *forum non conveniens* for, as has been said: 'To reach a wrong conclusion would not be in the best interests of the parties nor would it best serve the interests of justice'.[86]

More commonly, it is the first of these problems which bears on the determination of the appropriate forum. So great can be the difficulty of proving foreign law that English judges may prefer to see it more expeditiously applied by courts familiar with it.[87] It is sometimes assumed that

---

[85] *Muduroglu Ltd v. T. C. Ziraat Bankasi*, above n. 1, 625. See also, *The Cap Blanco* [1913] P 130, 136; *Settlement Corp. v. Hochschild* [1966] Ch. 10, 18; *The Eleftheria* [1969] 1 Lloyd's Rep. 237, 246; *The Vishva Apurna* [1992] 2 SLR 175, 188–189.

[86] *Credit Chemique v. James Scott Engineering Group Ltd.* 1982 SLT 131, 136 (per Lord Jauncey).

[87] *Muduroglu Ltd v. T. C. Ziraat Bankasi*, above n. 1; *The Nile Rhapsody* [1992] 2 Lloyd's Rep. 399, 411; *The Varna* [1994] 2 Lloyd's Rep. 41, 48.

foreign law is *inevitably* best applied in the relevant foreign forum.[88] But courts generally adopt a more sensitive approach, considering, sometimes at length, whether the issues of foreign law involved are truly so complex that the proof of foreign law in England would be less efficient than the determination of such issues abroad. In *The Forum Craftsman*,[89] for example, Sheen J concluded that, although contested points of Japanese law arose, they were not hard to resolve. The defendants, having failed to secure a stay of the English proceedings, appealed partly on the ground that the issues of Japanese law were indeed of such difficulty that significant savings in time and costs would be achieved were they determined in Japan. After lengthy consideration the Court of Appeal agreed with Sheen J that those issues were not so challenging as to make Japan the better forum.[90]

The dis-utility of courts applying laws other than their own is underscored in those cases where an English court can more appropriately apply English law than one abroad. As a judge has said, in a complex case concerning a contract of reinsurance, courts in London and San Diego being the alternatives:

... serious questions of law will arise as to the relationship of principal, agent and sub-agent, vis-à-vis the plaintiff. These questions will turn both on issues of principle and upon the construction of the relevant documents. The construction of the documentary material ... is, as the authorities plainly show, best undertaken by the English courts employing English law canons of construction. If, on the other hand, this task were to be undertaken in San Diego, the Court, in applying English law, will need to rely on expert evidence of English lawyers brought to California at considerable expense. This is a serious disadvantage.[91]

Cost and inconvenience are not, however, the only factors which bear upon the appropriateness of applying one country's laws in the courts of another. It is apparent that English judges are sometimes, if less often, impressed by the difficulty they might experience in applying foreign

---

[88] *The Varna*, op. cit., 48.   [89] [1984] 2 Lloyd's Rep. 102, 108.
[90] [1985] 1 Lloyd's Rep. 291, 299 (CA). In a striking sequel to *The Forum Craftsman* the same point of Japanese law, concerning a shipowner's tortious liability under a time charter, arose in Hong Kong proceedings in *The Planeta* (unreported), 18 January 1993 (HKHC, Admir. Juris.), comment by Margolis [1994] *LMCLQ*. 30. Barnett J found that the shipowner's expert's evidence in the earlier case was 'tentative and weak' and stayed the proceedings on the basis that the issue was sufficiently difficult that it was best decided in Japan.
[91] *Standard Steamship P & I Ltd.* v. *Gann* [1992] 2 Lloyd's Rep. 528, 536; see also *Spiliada Maritime Corpn.* v. *Cansulex Ltd.*, above n. 14, 486; *Charm Maritime Inc.* v. *Kyriakou* [1987] 1 Lloyd's Rep. 433, 448, 451; *Du Pont de Nemours* v. *Agnew* [1987] 1 Lloyd's Rep. 585, 594–595 (CA); *S & W Berisford plc.* v. *New Hampshire Insurance Co.* [1990] 2 QB 631, 647–648; *Arkwright Insurance Co.* v. *Bryanston Insurance Co. Ltd.*, above n. 20, 664–665; *Gulf Bank* v. *Mitsubishi Heavy Industries Ltd.* [1994] 1 Lloyd's Rep. 323, 329. How easily a foreign court can determine English law is itself a matter of foreign law, requiring evidence of the relevant foreign rules of evidence and procedure.

rules where their proper application depends too greatly on an expertise in foreign law which they cannot hope to acquire. In one case, for example, it was recognized how the complex interplay of civil law and Islamic law, academic writing and *jurisprudence* made questions of Egyptian law singularly difficult for English courts to determine.[92] Here the objection to proceeding in England is not that it would be expensive and time-consuming but that the meaningful application of foreign law would be unlikely or impossible. The rationale is that some questions of foreign law depend so much on an intimate familiarity with a foreign legal culture, with the principles and habits of thought employed, as to be beyond meaningful proof.

As we shall see, such reluctance to entertain proceedings in which the true application of foreign law is at risk is an important and desirable aspect of English practice.[93] But how does a court know whether an issue of foreign law is effectively beyond proof? The view has sometimes been expressed that all, or most, cases involving foreign law may fall into this category. As a distinguished judge expressed it:

> ... in general, and other things being equal, it is more satisfactory for the law of a foreign country to be decided by the Courts of that country. Moreover, by more satisfactory I mean more satisfactory from the point of view of ensuring that justice is done.[94]

This view is echoed by a distinguished commentator:

> The judge applying foreign law is a dilettante, a beginner. The judge applying the lex fori is a learned expert, he is sovereign. On the whole the judicial process has a lower quality when the judge applies foreign law than when he applies the lex fori.[95]

It is doubtful, however, that such pessimism is always warranted or that the proof of foreign law is so inherently suspect.[96] Certainly, the English courts tend not to doubt the general efficacy of their procedures

---

[92] *The Nile Rhapsody* [1992] 2 Lloyd's Rep. 399, 411; cf. *Milwaukee Cheese Co.* v. *Olafsson*, 40 Wis. 2d at 581, 162 NW 2d, 613 (Wisconsin Supreme Court). American writers have been especially concerned that the local context of foreign law may render its content impossible to determine accurately: 'There are very few points [of foreign law] which lend themselves to ... simple treatment ... [W]e must know the sources of the foreign law as they are recognized in the foreign country: we must be able to locate and evaluate these sources, whether or not written, indexed or digested'; Stern, (1957) 45 *Cal L Rev* 23; Schmertz, (1978) 18 *Virginia Jl Intl L* 697, 698–699.

[93] See below, Chapter X. It also echoes, if unconsciously, an important theoretical account of how hard cases are decided: see, Dworkin, *A Matter of Principle*, (London, 1985), Chs. 5, 6, 7; *Law's Empire* (London, 1986). Although expressed in a different idiom in different works, Dworkin's general position is that the correctness of a legal decision must be measured by its conformity to the underlying principles and assumptions of the area of law and the legal system in question.

[94] *The Eleftheria*, above n. 85, 246, per Brandon J.

[95] Zweigert, (1973) 44 *Colorado L R* 283, 293.

[96] Above, p. 20.

for establishing foreign law, although they are rightly aware that extreme cases may prove so intractable that proceedings should be stayed.[97] They may also be sensitive to the sometimes undesirable consequences of staying proceedings in such circumstances, thereby effectively postponing the case for determination in the alternative forum. The delay and expense that might be entailed by commencing or continuing proceedings abroad, given that the English court will already have tried the question of jurisdiction, may outweigh the difficulty of proving foreign law in England. Indeed, in extreme cases litigational convenience may outweigh the risk that an English court is unlikely to reach a correct result in establishing foreign law. It is in the nature of the doctrine of *forum non conveniens* that each element in the equation must be weighed against the others. Even the likelihood that an English court might apply foreign law inexpertly might thus be outweighed by other factors. In a leading American case it was argued that a court in New York was an inappropriate forum in which to try a number of related disputes involving the copyright laws of several South American countries.[98] In rejecting that argument the court decided that, even if a court in such a country 'would afford greater expertise in applying relevant legal principles' this was outweighed by the greater practical convenience of litigating in New York.[99] Such an approach is consistent with principle. But it also reflects the important truth that accuracy in the application of foreign law is not an end in itself. It is but part of the process of resolving disputes fairly, efficiently and economically.

Particular doubt concerning the accuracy and effectiveness of proving foreign law surrounds its treatment on appeal. It has been suggested that issues of foreign law can never be handled on appeal in England as successfully as in the country concerned.[100] Being treated as issues of fact, the fear is that the possibility of appeal might be restricted as a result. But such concerns pre-date the increased readiness of the Court of Appeal to recognize the legal character of questions of foreign law.[101] This is not to deny that some cases are likely to be harder to resolve on appeal than others. The more a point turns upon radical differences of expert opinion, and the less it depends merely on the construction of documents, the harder an appellate court's task will be. More precisely, the possibility of serious review is less the more an appellate court must rely on the written evi-

---

[97] Arguably, English courts have become less reticent about accepting cases involving foreign law since it has become clear that, although questions of fact, questions of foreign law are subject to appeal much like questions of law.

[98] *London Film Productions Ltd.* v. *Intercontinental Communications Inc.*, 580 F.Supp.47 (1984).

[99] At 50.

[100] *The Eleftheria*, above n. 85, 246. See also, *Eng Liat Kiang* v. *Eng Bak Hern* [1995] SLR 407, 587.

[101] See below, p. 201.

dence of the parties' experts. Indeed, it may in many cases be significantly harder to determine foreign law on appeal than at trial, where the judge may hear and see the witnesses.[102] As this suggests, the difficulty is not that questions of foreign law are unappealable. Nor is the possibility of appeal a decisive factor against entertaining proceedings. But the nature of any possible appeal may be a matter of legitimate enquiry in determining the *forum conveniens*.

The handling of foreign law on appeal is but one aspect of assessing the viability of hearing cases involving foreign law. A more general problem concerns how to segregate those cases in which the proof of foreign law is effectively impossible from those in which it is merely costly and inconvenient. It has been said that this turns on whether the risk of a court's reaching a wrong conclusion is 'by no means remote'.[103] But it is unclear what this means in practice. As we have seen, the distinctiveness of the method of legal reasoning employed in a foreign system may be decisive. But the effective proof of foreign law may also be rendered impossible by the nature of the issue in dispute. This is most obvious where questions of foreign public policy are involved. Depending on a judge's intimate understanding of local mores or the national interest it is hard to imagine an issue less suitable for determination by a court elsewhere. Certainly, it is hard to conceive how the machinery for proving foreign law could adequately equip a judge for such a task. The problem was highlighted by the approach of the Court of Appeal in *Du Pont de Nemours* v. *Agnew*,[104] which concerned the appropriateness of applying the English doctrine of public policy in Illinois.[105] As Bingham LJ said, speaking of the effect of one party's right to indemnity against legal liability under insurance policies governed by English law:

This Court is necessarily better placed than any other to rule on that question.... There is no decided authority in English law which denies them an indemnity. If English public policy is to be held to deny the right to indemnity in these circumstances, then this Court and no other must so hold. I do not regard this as a question capable of fair resolution in any foreign court, however distinguished and well instructed.... The primary question ... is a question which I do not think any foreign judge could conscientiously resolve with any confidence that he was reaching a correct answer.[106]

---

[102] *Dalmia Dairy Industries* v. *National Bank of Pakistan* [1978] 2 Lloyd's Rep. 223, 286 (CA).
[103] *Credit Chemique* v. *James Scott Engineering Group Ltd.* 1982 SLT 131, 136 (per Lord Jauncey).
[104] [1987] 2 Lloyd's Rep. 585. Bingham LJ would apparently distinguish the proof of foreign law in ordinary cases from those circumstances in which what are required are 'fine rulings of principle': ibid., 594.
[105] The same principles would presumably govern the application of foreign law in England.
[106] At 595–596.

But, as this suggests, it is not merely that English courts should defer to the unique expertise of those abroad. The mere risk of error, inherent in proving foreign law, argues for a stay where another country has a justified interest in the outcome. One case, for example, concerned the status in US law of the port of Cristobal in the Panama Canal Zone.[107] The decision predated the modern law of *forum non conveniens*, and the issue went to trial. But, by insisting that the question should be referred to the US Government for an authoritative answer,[108] the judge implicitly recognized that it was beyond resolution by an English court, at least by normal means. English courts have also shown particular hesitation in determining matters which depend on the grant of a monopoly power by a foreign state, as is the case with regard to foreign rights in intellectual property.[109] The denial of jurisdiction in the latter case is normally expressed in terms of a mandatory exclusionary rule, and the English court's reluctance to usurp what may be seen as the sovereignty of foreign state agencies underlies their approach. But the risk of inaccuracy in handling such sensitive matters may also be a factor. American courts faced with the same problem have been impressed by the inappropriateness of a court in one country determining inexpertly matters affecting monopoly rights under foreign law.[110] And, as a matter of principle, any concern that foreign sovereignty might be infringed would presumably disappear, or be eased, if it were thought that an English court could resolve such issues as competently as a foreign court.

In important ways, therefore, the appropriateness of hearing a case in England may turn on the likely difficulty and effectiveness of proving foreign law. Such proof may be straightforward. Or it may be complicated, expensive, but still feasible. Or it may simply be impossible. English courts in jurisdictional proceedings may thus devote much time and effort to assessing the true nature and difficulty of such issues of foreign law as may be in dispute. Indeed, it may not be an exaggeration to say that the characteristic role of foreign law in English litigation is as much (or more) in identifying the *forum conveniens* as in determining the parties' substantive rights and duties.

---

[107] *Stafford Allen & Sons Ltd.* v. *Pacific Steam Navigation Co.* [1956] 1 Lloyd's Rep. 104, where Sellers J was asked to determine the 'momentous question' whether the port of Cristobal was in the United States: '... if he (the judge) said that it was, and the United States Government said that it was not, the position would be very unsatisfactory'; op.cit., 114.

[108] At 119.

[109] *Tyburn Productions Ltd.* v. *Conan Doyle* [1991] Ch. 75; *Plastus Kreativ AB* v. *Minnesota Mining and Manufacturing Co.* [1995] RPC 438; *Coin Controls Ltd.* v. *Suzo International (UK) Ltd.* [1997] 3 All ER 45; *Pearce* v. *Ove Arup Ltd.* [1997] 3 All ER 31.

[110] *London Film Productions Ltd.* v. *Intercontinental Communications Inc.*, above n. 98, 49; cf. *Packard Instrument Co.* v. *Beckman Instruments Inc.*, 346 F Supp. 408, 410 (1972).

(ii) Establishing Foreign Law[111]

There are also occasions in which the proof of foreign law is directly required as an aid in identifying the *forum conveniens*. Here it is not that the proof of foreign law at trial may be difficult; it is that such proof is actually required in order to establish the most appropriate forum. Typically, this occurs when a plaintiff in English proceedings argues that it would suffer a disadvantage under the foreign law applied in a foreign court were it compelled to litigate there, as it might be so compelled were the foreign court found to be the *forum conveniens*.[112] Commonly, this involves consideration of the procedures in place in the alternative foreign forum.

Such allegations, involving a consideration of foreign law, form an important part of such jurisdictional disputes. Indeed, they may represent the most frequent occasions on which an English court is required to determine—if not to apply—foreign law. If their importance is considerable, however, it should be emphasised that a court in such cases may not be in a position to resolve such issues of foreign law conclusively. This is because foreign law is generally proved in such proceedings on the basis of affidavit evidence.[113] Indeed, however important interlocutory disputes about foreign law may be, courts generally refuse to allow the oral examination of the parties' experts,[114] thereby restricting the possible scale of such disputes. Although there may be good reasons of efficiency for this stance, it is perhaps curious that such critical questions of foreign law, which may (in effect) determine the outcome of the parties dispute, should be resolved on the basis of abbreviated evidence.

Although English courts are wary of comparing foreign procedures with their own[115] it is regarded as legitimate to examine whether, for example, an action would be time-barred in the foreign court,[116] or whether a plaintiff would obtain an effective remedy there.[117] In such cases, involving nothing less than a claimant's access to (effective) justice, evidence of foreign law is required. It may also be relevant to consider the likely outcome of foreign proceedings, which requires proof of the law to be applied in the court concerned. In one case the Court of Appeal refused to stay English proceedings, having heard evidence that the courts of Sharjah, the alternative forum, would not apply the disputed contract's

---

[111] How foreign law is proved in jurisdictional disputes is considered below at p. 204 ff.
[112] *Spiliada Maritime Corpn.* v. *Cansulex Ltd.*, above n. 14, 478, 482–483.
[113] Below, p. 204.   [114] See, e.g. *The Polessk* [1996] 2 Lloyd's Rep. 40, 43–44.
[115] *The Abidin Daver* [1984] AC 398, 410 (HL) but see *Muduroglu Ltd.* v. *T. C. Ziraat Bankasi*, above n. 1, 1248 '. . . there are other parts of the world where things are badly wrong.'
[116] *Spiliada Maritime Corpn.* v. *Cansulex Ltd.*, above n. 14, 482; *The Al Battani* [1993] 2 Lloyd's Rep. 219, 223.
[117] *De Dampierre* v. *De Dampierre* [1988] AC 92, 102, 110 (HL); *Re Harrods (Buenos Aires) Ltd. (No. 2)* [1991] 4 WLR 379 (CA); *The Adhiguna Meranti* [1988] 1 Lloyd's Rep. 384, 395 (CA Hong Kong).

governing law but would enforce their own, the claim being subject to summary dismissal under that law.[118] In a similar case the Court of Appeal found the courts in England, not Spain, were more appropriate, given that the plaintiff would be denied recovery in Spain by reason of public policy.[119]

How foreign law is proved is a matter for another chapter.[120] But for now it is important to notice how the very difficulty of establishing foreign law at the preliminary stage may affect a court's readiness to entertain substantive proceedings. The evidence, if provided only in writing,[121] may be so inconclusive that a court may be forced to conclude simply that the position under foreign law, based on such abbreviated evidence, is uncertain. In *The Adhiguna Meranti*,[122] for example, the limitation of a shipowner's liability in Indonesian law fell to be assessed by reference to the conflicting affidavits of the parties' experts. The Hong Kong Court of Appeal, conscious of the difficulty of resolving such issues on unclear evidence, felt itself able only to find that Indonesian law might limit liability to as little as $2,541, although recognizing that the amount could be higher. This was considerably lower than the $1.27 million which the plaintiff would certainly obtain in Hong Kong. As such it would have been unjust to deprive the plaintiff of an action in Hong Kong, the law of Indonesia limiting liability in a way which was 'at best uncertain, and at worst derisory'.[123] The very uncertainty of foreign law, as revealed by truncated evidence, set against the certainty of the *lex fori*, may thus disadvantage a plaintiff if deprived of the opportunity to litigate under the latter law. At the very least it restricts what a party may allege with certainty about the law in force in a foreign court.

(ii) FOREIGN LAW AND THE EUROPEAN CONVENTIONS

The United Kingdom is a party to both the Brussels and Lugano Conventions on Jurisdiction and the Enforcement of Judgments.[124] The former, whose provisions the latter mirrors in cases involving states within the European Economic Area, is designed to facilitate the enforcement of judgments between European Union countries and, in the service of that objective, to avoid the risk of inconsistent judgments by preventing concurrent proceedings in more than one Member State. Taking precedence, within their sphere of operation, over national jurisdictional rules

---

[118] *Banco Atlantico S.A. v. British Bank of the Middle East* [1990] 2 Lloyd's Rep. 504 (CA).
[119] *The Magnum* [1989] 1 Lloyd's Rep. 47 (CA). [120] Below, pp. 204–210.
[121] Below, p. 204. [122] [1988] 1 Lloyd's Rep. 384 (H.K. Ct.). [123] At 396.
[124] The 1968 Brussels Convention on Jurisdiction and the Enforcement of Judgments in Civil and Commercial Matters, OJ 1989 L 285/1 (amended version); the 1988 Lugano Convention on Jurisdiction and the Enforcement of Judgments in Civil and Commercial Matters, OJ 1988 No. L319/9. See generally: Cheshire and North, Ch. 14.

the Conventions may affect the nature and incidence of foreign law problems in several ways.

In some respects the problems of foreign law engendered by the Conventions are less than they might be. This is because, in the interests of uniformity, the European Court of Justice has consistently ruled that many of the Brussels Convention's more important provisions should bear an autonomous, community interpretation. In such cases, the Court of Justice having supplied a general community definition of a given term, it is for a Member State's courts to apply it without reference to national law.[125] A prominent example of the way in which the Convention may oust national rules of private international law is the rule that the formal validity of a jurisdiction agreement—although not, of course, of the contract which contains it—is a matter to be resolved solely by reference to the conditions imposed by Article 17, no reference to the contract's applicable law being permitted.[126] Another reason why disputes involving foreign law might be reduced under the Brussels Convention is that the Court of Justice might be taken to have suggested that the desirability of ensuring congruence between *lex fori* and *lex causae* is a factor to be considered in interpreting its provisions.[127] It is true that, although the doctrine of *forum non conveniens* is inapplicable as between Contracting States, the process of interpreting the Convention allows some flexibility in ensuring that cases are heard in the appropriate forum. The Convention may also encourage congruence between *lex fori* and *lex causae* by conferring jurisdiction on courts whose substantive law, because of its connection with the issue, is likely to be applied.[128] Article 5(3), conferring jurisdiction on the courts where a tort occurs, is one example. Another is Article 16(1) which gives exclusive competence to the courts of the *lex situs* in matters concerning immovable property. It is unclear, however, whether encouraging such congruence is a general policy objective of the Convention, and its status as a factor in interpreting the Convention has been doubted.[129] Finally, it should be recalled that not every question which a foreign court may face in applying the European Conventions is one of foreign law. Where an issue arises concerning how a foreign court would interpret the meaning

---

[125] e.g. the definition of 'obligation in question' in Article 5(1); Case 14/76 *De Bloos* v. *Bouyer* [1976] ECR 1497.

[126] Case 150/80 *Elefanten Schuh GmbH* v. *Jacqmain* [1981] ECR 1671. Whether the same is true of essential validity is more controversial; see the opinion of Advocate General Lenz in *Custom Made Commercial Ltd.* v. *Stawa Metallbau GmbH* [1994] I L Pr 516; see further Cheshire and North, 316, and works there cited.

[127] Case 133/81, *Ivenal* v. *Schwab* [1982] ECR 1891, para. 15 (ECJ); Case 125/92, *Mulox IBC Ltd.* v. *Geels* [1994] IRLR 422, 427 (per Advocate General Jacobs).

[128] Lando, above n. 1, 361–367.

[129] Case 125/92, *Mulox IBC Ltd.* v. *Geels* [1994] IRLR 422, 427 (per Advocate General Jacobs); Lando, above n. 1, 366.

and purpose of the Conventions the question ceases to be one of foreign law and becomes a community matter. As such, an English judge may resolve it without evidence, subject only to the supervisory jurisdiction of the European Court of Justice.[130]

But it is far from being the case that the proof of foreign law is unnecessary in applying the Conventions. Most obviously, the Conventions themselves may require the application of foreign law in novel circumstances. Article 52, for example, requires an English court to determine whether an individual is domiciled in another Contracting State by reference to the law of that state.[131] That it may do so even in cases where neither party has expressly pleaded foreign law may ensure that the role of foreign law in such cases cannot easily be avoided. Again, there are matters which the Court of Justice has decided should be subject to national conflicts rules, inviting the application of foreign law. An example concerns identifying the place of performance of the 'obligation in question' for the purposes of Article 5(1), the courts of that place having jurisdiction in actions for that obligation's non-performance. In the course of proceedings under Article 5(1) it may be necessary to determine such disparate matters as whether a claim to compensation amounts to an independent obligation,[132] or whether a term specifying the place of performance is valid.[133] Such questions are to be answered by reference to the law applicable to the contract, ascertained under the choice of law rules of the forum, which may involve the proof of foreign law.

But of the novel problems of foreign law engendered by the European Conventions the most important concerns the need to ensure uniformity in matters involving concurrent proceedings. This stems from the fact that both Conventions require an English court to decline jurisdiction in situations in which the Conventions confer paramount jurisdiction on another Contracting State's courts. This occurs, typically, if another country's court is that of the defendant's domicile,[134] or is the court first seised.[135] In addition to such mandatory grounds of dismissal an English court has a discretion to stay its proceedings where another Contracting State's court is already seised of related proceedings.[136] It is essential in such a regime to know whether another Contracting State has paramount jurisdiction,

---

[130] *Mecklermedia Corporation* v. *D C Congress GmbH* [1997] 3 WLR 479.

[131] See below, p. 126.

[132] *Medway Packaging Ltd.* v. *Meurer Maschinen GmbH* [1990] 1 Lloyd's Rep. 383, 389 (Hobhouse J).

[133] Case 12/76 *Tessili* v. *Dunlop* [1976] ECR 1473, 1485.

[134] Article 2. The Convention explicitly refers the question whether a person is domiciled in another Contracting State to the laws of that state: Article 52; Civil Jurisdiction and Judgments Act 1982, section 42(7).

[135] Article 21. [136] Article 22.

such that English proceedings should be stayed or dismissed,[137] a question which depends on the local law of the state concerned.[138] This not merely creates a new situation in which the application of foreign law is required. It has created a new type of foreign law problem. This is because the overriding importance of avoiding parallel proceedings in different Contracting States requires an English court to know with a high degree of certainty whether any other court is competent. This necessitates more than usual accuracy in ascertaining foreign law. Indeed, it ensures that the very success of the Conventions rests on how effectively foreign law can be proved.

An illustration of the important role given to the proof of foreign law under the Conventions is *Grupo Torras SA* v. *Al Sabah*,[139] concerning whether the Spanish courts had prior jurisdiction under Articles 21 or 22 of the Brussels Convention. Mance J, whose approach occasioned no comment on appeal, departed from the usual practice whereby the proof of foreign law in jurisdictional disputes is effected without the oral examination of experts. Although with some reluctance, he accepted both parties' view that in such cases 'the Court must have a higher level of assurance about the basis and appropriateness of its exercise of jurisdiction'.[140] The effect, as Mance J regretfully noted, was to involve the court in ten days of cross-examination of Spanish legal experts. As this implies, the special obligations placed on a court under the Brussels Convention does not simply create new varieties of foreign law problem. It introduces the possibility, however necessary, of protracted, costly investigations into foreign law at the jurisdictional stage.

But the effect of the Conventions is not necessarily to create new situations in which English courts must determine foreign law. Indeed, it may be the opposite, as is suggested by Vinelott J's striking decision in *Polly Peck International plc* v. *Citibank NA*.[141] The question was whether the Swiss courts were already seised of the same matter pursuant to Article 21 of the Lugano Convention. It was pressed upon Vinelott J that he should follow the normal practice in such cases and resolve the issue on the available evidence of Swiss law. But he declined to do so, preferring to adjourn the

---

[137] No such difficulty arises at common law when a court is invited to stay proceedings (partly) on the basis that parallel proceedings are in progress elsewhere. There the question is not whether, in law, the foreign court is seised, but whether in fact the proceedings are sufficiently advanced that English proceedings would be undesirable: *De Dampierre* v. *De Dampierre* above n. 117; *Arkwright Mutual Insurance Co.* v. *Bryanston Insurance Co. Ltd.*, above n. 20, 665.

[138] Whether a defendant is domiciled in another Contracting State depends on the law of that state: Article 52. Whether, and when, a court is seised depends equally on the local law of the court in question: Case 129/83, *Zelger* v. *Salinitri* [1984] ECR 2397 (ECJ).

[139] [1995] 1 Lloyd's Rep. 374, affirmed [1995] I L Pr 667 (CA). See also *Mecklermedia Corporation* v. *DC Congress GmbH*, above n. 130.

[140] At 378.   [141] [1994] I L Pr 71.

proceedings so that the issue might be resolved by the Swiss courts. He relied partly on the mandatory words of Article 21 which require the court second seised to stay proceedings until the jurisdiction of the court first seised is established. But, of greater significance it seems, Vinelott J considered that an English court should not address whether a foreign court is seised when it is inevitable that the foreign court would subsequently do so.[142] Comity was one reason. Another was that conflicting answers to the same question in both courts could only be avoided, given that a foreign court cannot be stopped from answering such a question itself, were the English court to abstain from asking it. But this is not to say that an English court should never determine a foreign court's status upon proof. Vinelott J would have permitted this course had both parties been content and had no application been made for an adjournment.[143]

At first sight the approach adopted in *Polly Peck* is novel, even revolutionary. It is also one which, in a sense, removes one type of foreign law problem from the purview of the English courts. Admittedly, it reflects the relatively discernible principle that some matters of foreign law are too important, or too localised, to be addressed by another country's courts.[144] It is also sustained by the logic of the Lugano Convention and the policy of avoiding parallel proceedings by ensuring consistency in its application. But it is far from clear that the decision is well-founded and it has been described as presenting a 'nightmare scenario'.[145] Certainly, Article 21 itself supplies no justification for adjourning the question whether a foreign court is seised. It operates only once the question whether one court or another is first seised has been resolved. It says nothing about how a court should behave in addressing that issue. Nor is it certain that the considerations of policy and principle enunciated by Vinelott J are decisive. The decision in *Polly Peck* encourages delay and expense, which is hardly desirable. Its effect is also to place an obstacle in the way of plaintiffs which the Convention itself does not contemplate. By allowing defendants, in effect, a novel ground for staying English proceedings it provides them with a tactical weapon of considerable power. Even before the technical requirements of Article 21 are satisfied it enables them to stop such proceedings in their tracks and divert the case to a forum which is for them (no doubt) more congenial and convenient. Indeed, it is doubtful that the Convention permits the creation of what amounts to an additional ground for challenging the competence of national courts to entertain proceedings which is independent of Article 21 itself.

But *Polly Peck* conceals an ambiguity. Was the case concerned with a question of Swiss law, or with the interpretation of the Lugano Convention? Only if the former was a question of foreign law involved,

[142] At 80.   [143] Ibid.   [144] Above, p. 49.   [145] Briggs, [1994] *LMCLQ* 470, 472.

the Convention being an aspect of the domestic law of each signatory state, a matter of law not evidence.[146] If the latter, the somewhat unusual course adopted in *Polly Peck* is explained, and the decision may be distinguished from that in *Grupo Torras*. At one level, as we have seen, the issue clearly concerned identifying when the Swiss court had become seised of the dispute, a matter of Swiss law. But this depended on the effect of Article 21 on pre-existing Swiss legislation, a matter concerning the meaning of the Convention. Admittedly, the judgment tends to conflate these issues and the question is sometimes referred to as one of Swiss law.[147] But there are also passages which suggest the opposite.[148] More telling, it appears that Vinelott J was emboldened to adjourn the English proceedings because the European Court of Justice lacked jurisdiction over the Lugano Convention, which meant that the only way to avoid inconsistent results in England and in Switzerland was for the English court to abjure from answering the question at all.[149] Such reasoning only makes sense on the basis that a 'community' issue was involved, over which the Court might have had jurisdiction had the case concerned the Brussels Convention. Moreover, viewed as a decision concerning the interpretation of the Lugano Convention, *Polly Peck* has much to commend it. In principle, such questions of interpretation, being as much questions of English law as of Swiss law, would have been justiciable as much by the English court as by that in Switzerland. But, in the absence of the unifying control of the Court of Justice, this might have led to inconsistent interpretations of the Convention in each of the courts concerned. Given that the Swiss courts would have been obliged to take 'due account' of any pronouncements of the English court,[150] this would have placed them in the undesirable position of having to respect a foreign court's ruling on a matter concerning the effect of the Convention on their own law. But, given that they would not strictly have been bound by the English court's ruling, and might have arrived at a different conclusion, only by adjourning the question could Vinelott J have ensured a uniform interpretation of the Convention.

As this suggests, the better view of *Polly Peck* may be that it does not concern foreign law at all. But it stands as a reminder of the importance of distinguishing, as is uniquely necessary in cases involving such Conventions, between foreign law on the one hand, and the common law of signatory states on the other. In that sense the proper operation of the European Conventions turns on precisely identifying the role of foreign law. Moreover, even if *Polly Peck's* otherwise dramatic implications disappear, *Grupo Torras* remains as an example of English law's increasingly flexible

---

[146] *Mecklermedia Corporation v. DC Congress GmbH*, above n. 130.
[147] At para. 29.
[148] At para.27.
[149] At para. 30.
[150] 1980 Lugano Convention, Protocol No. 2, Article 1.

approach to foreign law, at least in proceedings involving the European Conventions. Certainly, the decisive importance of avoiding parallel proceedings within the framework of the Conventions may justify some leniency in applying the principle that affidavit evidence is sufficient in interlocutory proceedings. Indeed, the European Conventions may have created a new role for the proof of foreign law, one in which the very success of the Conventions may turn on the efficacy of the available techniques of proof.

4. CONCLUSION

The application of foreign law is a topic of pervasive practical importance within English private international law. It informs, to a greater or lesser degree, any dispute involving a foreign element, whether it comes to trial or not. Indeed, it provides the invisible background to many international legal relationships by underwriting the parties' selection, implied or express, of the governing law. And in important ways the treatment of foreign law gives international litigation in England its distinctive stamp, in so far as the voluntary nature of the pleading of foreign law allows parties to dispense with the conflicts process altogether by subjecting their dispute to English law by default. Above all, perhaps, the complexity and cost of proof bears significantly upon whether a court will entertain proceedings involving foreign law. It may even determine the parties' decision whether to litigate at all.

Against this background, matters of foreign law have acquired new significance in several important ways. English law's new rules governing choice of law in tort promise an increase in litigation involving foreign-related torts. Similarly, the weakening of the unstated assumption that adjectival matters should generally be classified as procedural has led to an expansion in the range of issues which may be classified as substantive. This increases the number of cases in which a choice of law issue, and the proof of foreign law, may be relevant. Finally, the central place of foreign law in determining the *forum conveniens*, and the enhanced importance of the proof of foreign law in cases under the Brussels and Lugano Conventions, ensures that foreign law can have a decisive role in preliminary disputes concerning jurisdiction.

Thus depicted, the role of foreign law is clarified. But so are the problems which the pleading and proof of foreign law may occasion. Certainly, it is not simply that effective means must be found to prove foreign law at trial. It appears, for example, that special difficulty surrounds the proof of foreign law in interlocutory proceedings. The normal practice of excluding oral testimony in such cases, reducing the effectiveness of the evidential process, is at odds with the importance of such proceedings in practice. It may certainly be inapt where nothing less is at stake than the purposes underlying the Brussels and Lugano Conventions. Again, the overall efficacy of the evidential process bears in important ways on the willingness of litigants to proceed under foreign law—or, indeed, to sue at all. This has the potential to deny such litigants access to justice or, at least, to justice applied on the correct legal basis. Indeed, it is as much in its effect on litigation strategy, and in its tendency to discourage the application of foreign law, that the proof of foreign law gives cause for concern. But the previous discussion also carries a more general message. Rumours of the death of choice of law are, it seems, exaggerated. Certainly, the presence of a foreign element remains important in shaping the course of litigation, whether or not proceedings come to court, and whether or not the direct application of foreign law is required. Indeed, as the examples previously examined suggest, the foreign law problem is, if anything, more significant than ever.

III
Party Choice and Foreign Law

It is often said that the pleading and proof of foreign law are voluntary. Foreign laws are facts in English doctrine and the pleading and proof of facts are at the parties' motion.[1] This chapter and the next are concerned with the scope of that principle, and with the extent to which the pleading and proof of foreign law are truly within the parties' untrammelled control. The present chapter identifies several situations in which the application of foreign law is required, and in which the content of foreign law must therefore be established. Chapter IV develops the theme by addressing several matters concerned specifically with the proof of foreign law. It examines in particular the parties' freedom to rely upon foreign law without also proving it by invoking the familiar, if troublesome, presumption that English law and foreign law are treated as similar unless the contrary is shown. But, although both chapters are thus concerned with the circumstances in which foreign law must be pleaded and proved, their subject matter is different in an important sense. The present chapter is concerned with those relatively rare cases in which reliance upon foreign law is required by the relevant rules for choice of law. But the obligation to prove foreign law whenever it is relied upon assumes no such pre-existing duty. It arises even if a claimant introduces foreign law voluntarily, the relevant choice of law rule being optional in character. It rests on the general principle that one who relies upon a fact must establish it by proper evidence.

But this chapter is not so much concerned with the pleading and proof of foreign law as those terms are properly understood. Nor is it directly concerned with how the content of foreign law is pleaded and proved but with whether foreign law must be established at all in certain cases. Nor does it address at length the manner and form in which such pleading and proof must be effected. It engages instead with a question of private international law. To what extent may litigants avoid the law which in principle applies to their dispute by virtue of the relevant rules for choice of law? In particular, to what extent may they implicitly choose the *lex fori* as the

[1] *Fremoult* v. *Dedire* (1718) 1 P. Wms. 429; *Mostyn* v. *Fabrigas* (1774) 1 Cowp. 161, 174; *Nelson* v. *Bridport* (1845) 8 Heav. 527; *Bankers and Shippers Trust of New York* v. *Liverpool Marine and General Insurance Co. Ltd.* (1926) 24 Ll L R 85, 93 (HL); *Ottoman Bank of Nicosia* v. *Chakarian (No. 2)* [1938] AC 260, 279 (PC); *A/S Tallina Laevauhisus* v. *Estonian State Steamship Line* (1947) 80 Ll L R 99, 107, 113 (CA).

governing law by omitting to plead and prove any other? As this implies, such an omission to plead and prove foreign law is not, as might be imagined, a procedural issue. It goes to choice of law. It is but one aspect of a more general question—to what extent are litigants free to select the law applicable to their dispute, whether it is English or foreign? As such this chapter concerns the extent to which particular choice of law rules may be mandatory, in the sense of being unwaivable by agreement, such that the governing law must be applied whatever the parties' wishes.

But this is not to deny that the mandatory character of any given conflicts rule may not affect the pleading and proof of foreign law in the conventional sense. For, if a claimant is duty-bound to rely upon foreign law by virtue of such a rule, this entails an obligation to plead and to prove its content. This point deserves particular emphasis because it might be supposed that such a duty implies no such obligation. It might be thought that a plaintiff should indeed be required to plead, for example, that a defamatory publication is actionable under the *lex loci delicti* by virtue of the double actionability rule which applies in such cases. But could not such a claimant avoid introducing evidence in support of this contention by invoking the presumption that English law and foreign law are deemed to be the same unless the contrary is shown?[2] If this were so there would certainly be little point in pursuing the theme of this chapter by identifying those situations in which the application of foreign law might be mandatory. But the assumption that even a mandatory choice of law may be defeated by the presumption of similarity may be mistaken for two reasons. First, it ignores the true nature of the duty which arises when a choice of law rule is mandatory. It is not merely that a claimant must rely on foreign law, perhaps by alleging merely that the applicable law is foreign. It is that foreign law must in some cases be applied. But if foreign law must be applied in a given case it is hard to see how such a duty could be meaningful unless it also entails an obligation to establish the content of foreign law. Secondly, to allow a claimant who relies upon foreign law to avoid establishing its content may be to set too much store by the presumption of similarity. As we shall see in the following chapter, it is doubtful that such a presumption relieves one who introduces foreign law from the obligation to establish its content. Such an obligation affects even a claimant who elects to rely upon foreign law without legal compulsion. *A fortiori*, one who is obliged to rely upon foreign law because its application is compulsory should plead particulars of that law and prove its content by proper evidence.

As this implies, some fine distinctions must be made, and some issues of terminology resolved, before proceeding. Strictly, to plead foreign law

---

[2] Dicey and Morris, 1514; see below, pp. 143–146.

is to allege that the content of foreign law is to a certain effect, which involves giving appropriate particulars of the relevant foreign rules in the statement of claim or defence. What is pleaded is not that foreign law governs a given issue, but the fact that the legal system in question contains a particular rule. The pleading of foreign law in this sense must be distinguished from the inevitably connected allegation that the law which governs a given case is foreign. To make such an allegation does not involve pleading a fact but stating a proposition of law—of private international law. These distinct operations must themselves be distinguished from the steps taken to prove the content of foreign law once it has been pleaded, which is a matter of evidence. Such conceptual distinctions are important. Indeed, it is possible in theory, if unlikely in practice, that a claimant might wish to rely upon foreign law without pleading its content, or plead foreign law without seeking to prove it. But such distinctions are regularly obscured in common speech. When lawyers speak of pleading foreign law this often comprehends both the allegation that foreign law applies and the claim that it is to a given effect. Indeed, this elision is inevitable, given that litigants invariably plead the identity of the governing law in their statement of claim or defence. Generally only matters of fact not law are pleaded. But the identity of the governing law depends necessarily on the facts of a case. And it is, in any event, proper to raise in the pleadings such points of law as define the terms of a dispute.

Ambiguity also surrounds what it means to say that the introduction of foreign law may be mandatory in certain cases, because a given choice of law rule so requires. Does this mean that the relevant choice of law rule is mandatory, such that the court and the parties must seek to identify the applicable law? Or does it mean that the application of that law, if foreign, is required? The answer is that both are necessary, for this is a distinction without a difference. To say that a given choice of law rule requires the application of the governing law necessarily involves consideration of the identity of that law. Conversely, to say that a given conflicts rule is mandatory normally means that the law which is applicable thereunder must be applied.

Another preliminary matter concerns, once again, the presumption that, in the absence of contrary proof, English law and foreign law are deemed to be the same. It might be supposed that it can never matter if a given choice of law rule is mandatory because all that litigants need do is to invoke the presumption. But this is to mistake its legal status, which, as we have seen, is less secure than might be thought. It is also to ignore the fact that it has never been an invariable rule, as this chapter and the next reveal. If it operates at all it does so only when the application of foreign law is not otherwise obligatory.

But even if it is possible to think of this chapter and the next as being concerned with the scope of the presumption of similarity, that would be to distort the enquiry. For the presumption may apply in three quite different situations: where foreign law is not relied upon; where it is relied upon but not pleaded and proved; and where it is inadequately proved. It is clear, however, that the question how such cases should be handled cannot be answered merely by reference to whether, and to what extent, such a presumption exists. Whether foreign law must be invoked in a given case, whether if invoked it must be proved, and whether the proper response to unsatisfactory proof is to apply English law or to dismiss the claim are quite distinct issues. Their separateness is merely obscured by supposing that the application of foreign law is governed by a single presumption. And so is the true nature of the issues involved. For the problem is not whether English law and foreign law are similar. It is whether litigants are always free to circumvent the foreign element in proceedings. The question is not whether it is plausible to equate English law with foreign laws which are unlikely to be similar—the foreign system might, for example, belong to the civil law tradition, or the equivalent English rules might be statutory, or might otherwise be unique.[3] It is whether the relevant rules for choice of law are mandatory in character. For these reasons these distinct issues are treated, respectively, in the present chapter, in Chapter IV, and in Chapter VI.

Nor are we mainly concerned, perhaps surprisingly, with the extent to which English courts may intervene in the shape and progress of litigation. Certainly, it is important that English courts have traditionally adopted a passive posture towards fact-finding, and even towards regulating the legal basis of proceedings.[4] But this chapter is concerned with identifying mandatory rules for choice of law. As such it is concerned with situations in which, in principle, the choice of law aspects of a dispute must be considered, and a foreign applicable law applied. In such cases, whatever their role elsewhere, English courts are in principle obliged to enforce the relevant conflicts rule, perhaps by dismissing the claim or defence of one who fails to rely upon foreign law. Certainly, the relationship between court and litigant in such cases is not explained by examining the boundaries of an adversarial system of justice. It is a matter of identifying their respective duties under private international law.

But, such technical matters aside, the question with which the chapter is concerned may be simply stated: when is the application of foreign law required? The answer, as we shall see, is that courts have, in principle, a greater freedom to police whether foreign law is relied upon, pleaded and proved than appears at first sight. Resort to the relevant choice of law rules is not as such *d'ordre public* in English law. But English law may exceptionally require the application of foreign law. Specific rules of private

[3] See below, p. 147.
[4] See further, Andrews, *Principles of Civil Procedure*, (London, 1994), 51–52.

international law sometimes provide that the governing law (English or foreign) must be applied, legally requiring its introduction and proof. This is seldom the case. But the familiar freedom of litigants to ignore foreign law is clearly less than might be thought.

1. VOLUNTARY CHOICE OF LAW

This chapter is largely concerned with those exceptional cases in which the application of foreign law is required. But what of the far more common situations in which it is not? Although such cases are more numerous the law which governs them is far more simply stated. They are subject to the principle of party choice, whereby litigants are largely free to determine how a claim or defence should be expressed, both factually and legally. In this respect it is indeed true to say that foreign laws are treated like ordinary facts.

The key to the English position is its restrictive doctrine of judicial notice. It lies in two principles: facts are generally excluded from judicial purview, and foreign laws are facts.[5] The effect is that courts do not know the *content* of foreign law. But this is not to say that a judge does not know that foreign law, or an issue of choice of law, may be relevant in a given case. For the introduction of foreign law has a legal as well as factual dimension. Whether foreign law is to a particular effect is an issue of fact. Whether foreign law applies at all, however, is a matter of private international law, turning on the application of the relevant choice of law rule. Being a question of law there is no doubt that an English court has judicial notice of English rules for choice of law, just as it has notice of every other aspect of English law. But there are several reasons why a court's constructive knowledge of the potential relevance of foreign law does not affect the parties' freedom to rely upon on foreign law in the majority of cases. Whatever a court's suspicions it is unlikely, save in the easiest cases, that it could know for certain the identity of the applicable law. Cases involving contractual choice of law clauses might be an exception, but even they are not without difficulty. It is certainly unlikely that a court would intervene to request (still less require) that the parties argue any choice of law issue that might be relevant, with the object of identifying the applicable law. Courts normally abstain from intervening in how parties put their case, although the powers of a court in shaping the legal basis of proceedings is a matter of debate.[6] It is clear that a court has notice of all

---

[5] Sass, (1968) 16 *Am Jl Comp L* 332, 335–347 (1968); Eggleston, *Evidence, Proof and Probability* (London, 1978), Ch. 10; Keane, *The Modern Law of Evidence*, 2nd. edn. (London, 1989), 479–484.

[6] Andrews, above, n. 4, 47–50.

rules of English law, which suggests that it might address a point which the parties have not taken. But the adversarial principle implies that a court should not do so, or should not do so without allowing the party concerned to argue the point.

In the end, however, English courts are generally powerless to compel reliance upon foreign law. Not only are they unaware of the content of foreign law, they are, as we shall see, unable to discover it *ex officio*. Their power of intervention is thus confined to those rare cases where a claim based upon English law may be dismissed. This is, of course, possible if English law is inapplicable. The relevant English rule may be territorially limited to acts or events occurring in England, thus preventing its application to a case with foreign elements. More importantly, the relevant choice of law rule may be mandatory, requiring a court to penalise an omission to plead foreign law by dismissing the claim in question.

But this is not to say that the pleading of foreign law is entirely free of technical requirements. *How* foreign law is pleaded is regulated by the normal rules of pleading. No technical rules govern such pleading specifically, although a recognized practice has developed based upon general principles and on what is required to give effect to the purpose of pleadings generally.[7] Any pleading must be full and precise, thereby serving three important purposes. The other party is not taken by surprise by matters raised at trial. A court is fully acquainted with the nature of the dispute, an increasingly important matter as courts adopt a more pro-active role in case management. And the dispute's foundations are exposed such that the parties are able to judge their respective strengths and weaknesses and perhaps settle their differences on that basis. Where a party wishes to allege that foreign law governs a given issue both the relevant foreign law and the issue to which it applies must be identified in the statement of claim or the defence. Full particulars of its content must be given, and the relevant foreign authorities—typically statutory provisions or judicial decisions—must be specified.[8] It is fundamental that only facts are pleaded and not the evidence by which those facts are to be proved.[9] It may be appropriate, however, to elaborate on foreign law by referring in the pleading to an affidavit or an expert's report, thereby incorporating such sources in the pleadings by reference.[10]

---

[7] Jacobs and Goldrein, eds., Bullen & Leake & Jacobs, *Precedents of Pleadings*, 13th edn, (London, 1990), 421, 423, 1169–1171. See RSC Order 18, rule 7(1):

Subject to the provisions of this rule ... every pleading must contain, and contain only, a statement in summary form of the material facts on which the party pleading relies for his claim or defence, as the case may be, but not the evidence by which those facts are to be proved, and the statement must be as brief as the nature of the case admits.

[8] RSC Order 18, para. 8/8/7.   [9] RSC Order 18, r. 7(1).
[10] *Ascherberg Hopwood & Crew Ltd. v. Casa Muscale Sonzogno* [1971] 1 WLR 1128, 1131 (CA).

It is insufficient merely to allege that foreign law is to a particular effect, for example by alleging that an instrument is void under the law concerned.[11] Where this occurs a court may order that the pleadings be amended accordingly. The pleading must also be sufficiently full. Where a party intends to rely on a special sense in which foreign law, or a provision in a document, is to be understood such special matters must be pleaded.[12] Were such matters of construction not pleaded it might unfairly surprise the other party at trial were they relied upon. So as to give the other party early warning of the fact it is conventional, but not obligatory, for a party who wishes to rely on a previous English decision on a point of foreign law by way of evidence to give the necessary notice[13] in the statement of claim or defence.

2. MANDATORY CHOICE OF LAW

It is undeniable that foreign laws are treated as facts in English doctrine. But this is less illuminating than might be supposed. We should not imagine, in particular, merely because English law treats foreign laws as facts for some purposes, that it does so for all purposes. Nor should the familiarity of the doctrine blind us to its strangeness. Why should we treat something legal, against intuition, as if it were factual? In reality, it is not so much that foreign laws are facts (although technically they are), but that they are laws which cannot, for practical reasons, be treated exactly like domestic laws.[14] Because, in a practical sense, courts lack (actual) notice of foreign laws, they tend to be treated as facts, of which courts also lack notice. And, as with other facts, the courts' lack of knowledge is compensated for by accommodating foreign law within the normal rules of evidence. As Lord Mansfield said, in a telling phrase which implies that the status of foreign law in English practice owes more to practicality than doctrine, the 'way of knowing foreign laws is by admitting them as facts'.[15]

This rationale for equating foreign law with fact also implies an important limitation on that doctrine. Foreign laws are facts because otherwise a court cannot know their content. But this implies that foreign laws should be treated as facts only where this is necessary, that is to say only where this enables a court's ignorance of the content of foreign law to be cured.

---

[11] *Duke of Brunswick* v. *King of Hanover* (1844) Beav. 1; see, however, *University of Glasgow* v. *The Economist* [1997] EMLR 495 (Popplewell J), below, p. 145.

[12] *Ascherberg Hopwood & Crew Ltd.* v. *Casa Musicale Sonzogno*, above n. 10.

[13] Civil Evidence Act 1972, s. 4(2)–(5).

[14] Wolff would go further in repudiating the fact doctrine, denying that foreign law is anything but foreign law; *Private International Law*, (Oxford, 1950), 216–221.

[15] *Mostyn* v. *Fabrigas*, above n. 1, 174 (italics added).

This suggests that they should be treated as such only for evidential purposes. Indeed, the fact doctrine might only mean that foreign law must be established by evidence by one who relies on it. But this need not entail that whether foreign law is relied upon should be entirely a matter for such a party, which is the case with other facts. The fact doctrine may have little or nothing to do with whether foreign law must be introduced in a given case. It concerns how foreign law is established, but not whether it must be established at all.

This is not to deny that such scepticism about the fact doctrine also has implications for the proof of foreign law. It indicates that foreign laws should be subject to strict proof only when a court lacks the knowledge or competence to ascertain them. But in the present context it means that litigants may not have the freedom in pleading, or not pleading, foreign law which they may enjoy in connection with other facts. It would hardly be surprising if such constraints exist. Unlike other questions of fact, which fix the background to the dispute, issues of foreign law go directly to the parties' rights and liabilities, affecting the just determination of disputes. This is not to deny that a proper determination of other facts is a prerequisite of justice. But the question whether foreign law can properly be omitted from proceedings goes directly to whether litigants may waive their legal rights and duties. Furthermore, foreign law is identified and made applicable by the rules of the conflict of laws. As such, we might expect that whether it should be applied in any case is properly a matter for those rules, not for the principles of pleading and practice.

Against this background, the argument of this chapter is that the freedom of litigants not to rely upon foreign law may be qualified. This is because the rules of private international law are sometimes, if exceptionally, mandatory. There are circumstances in which litigants are not free to select the applicable law, whether it is English or foreign. They cannot waive by agreement whichever law is applicable under the relevant choice of law rule, objectively judged. The effect of such restrictions on party autonomy is not confined to whether foreign law must be introduced in English proceedings. They might equally limit the parties' choice of foreign law. But it has a particular effect in the former context. It overrides the general rule, expressed by the principle of voluntary pleading, that litigants may generally select the *lex fori* as the governing law. Differently expressed, it qualifies the scope of any presumption to the effect that English and foreign law are similar.

But this perspective forces us to address three issues which would not otherwise intrude. The first concerns what happens when a party who is obliged to plead foreign law does not do so. Will a court direct a defaulting party to do so? Or will the court establish foreign law by itself? The second issue goes to the heart of the relationship between the voluntary pleading principle and the choice of law process. It concerns how to analyse a situation where the introduction of foreign law is required. Is it that the normal rule of pleading is overridden or, being a procedural matter and governed by the *lex fori*, is the pleading of foreign law always voluntary, whether or not the relevant choice of law rule is peremptory? Indeed, is the pleading of foreign law procedural or substantive? The third issue is perhaps of most pressing concern. If it is possible that conflicts rules may be mandatory, requiring the introduction of a foreign applicable law, how are such rules to be identified?

(a) FAILURE TO INTRODUCE FOREIGN LAW

We must be clear about the consequences of a failure to plead foreign law where this is required by the relevant conflicts rule. Does the defaulting litigant pay the price of such a breach of duty in the form of dismissal of the claim or defence? Or is the court responsible for introducing the missing law *ex officio*? Principle ordains a straightforward answer. Faced with a defective pleading, a court will not introduce and establish foreign law on its own motion. To do so might infringe the rule that a court may not undertake its own researches into foreign law.[16] It is also unclear by what means a court could determine foreign law alone, were it permitted to do so. One solution, which may escape the rule that a court may not research foreign law itself, might be the appointment of a court expert. But this is an unlikely possibility in practice.[17] Intervention may also be prevented by the principle which, ultimately, may disable a court from introducing and applying foreign law *sua sponte*. English courts have neither the power, nor the duty to obtain evidence.[18] More accurately, their investigatory responsibility is confined to what they know, and what they know is English law. As such, despite foreign law's 'legal' character it is not the court's duty, but that of one whose case depends on it, to establish foreign law.[19] Rather than cure a defective claim or defence itself, therefore, a court has but one option—to dismiss it.[20] Nor will a court instruct an unwilling

---

[16] *Di Sora* v. *Phillipps* (1863) HLC 624, 640; *Bumper Development Corp.* v. *Comr. of Police* [1991] 1 WLR 1362, 1369 (CA).

[17] See below, p. 158.

[18] As Pollock famously expressed it: '... the court will have nothing to do with making enquiries to find things out for itself. It is not there to inquire, or to do anything of its own motion, but to hear and determine between parties according to the proofs which the parties can bring forward.' *Expansion of the Common Law* (1904), 33–34.

[19] Contrast the position in Germany: below, p. 269.

[20] The practice of dismissing such defective claims once had distinguished support in the United States, notably in the opinion of Mr Justice Holmes in *Crosby* v. *Cuba Railroad Co.*, 222 US 473 (1912); see also, *Walton* v. *Arabian American Oil Co.*, 233 F.2d. 541 (2d Cir.), cert denied, 352 US 872 (1956). But it has been discredited, partly because it rested on a strict application of the vested rights theory, which is itself no longer favoured, and partly because it was

party whose claim depends upon it to plead foreign law. To do so carries the implication that such a party would be in contempt for failure to comply, which is not the appropriate sanction when a party fails to establish its case.[21] The proper and unexceptional response is that a party who does not plead and prove foreign law where this is necessary does not establish its case. The penalty is that the claim or defence simply fails.

But it might be objected that a court will seldom if ever be in a position to know whether a party has failed in its duty to rely upon foreign law. If foreign law has not been pleaded, how does a court know that foreign law is relevant at all? This objection is not well-founded. In some cases the other party might argue that the claim or defence should be dismissed for incompleteness. Or, if the claimant relies upon the presumption of similarity, the other party might reply by arguing that the pleading and proof of foreign law are mandatory. Indeed, the problem is not so much that both parties will ignore entirely the foreign elements in a case. It is that one party will rely upon foreign law without attempting to prove it. But, whether or not foreign law is introduced, it may be apparent from such facts as have been pleaded that a case has a foreign element, such that a mandatory choice of law rule is implicated. How could a plaintiff proceed in tort without indicating the *locus delicti*; how could an action for breach of contract arise without the residence of the parties or the place of performance being mentioned? But it might be further objected that it may not be clear whether the law of a particular foreign country is definitely applicable, although the facts may disclose sufficient foreign elements that a choice of law issue clearly arises. Indeed, some may detect circularity in the suggestion that the application of foreign law is mandatory—how can we know that the law of Utopia must apply unless the applicable law has been identified? But this criticism is misplaced. The basic premise is not so much that the law applicable to a given matter must be applied. It is that the relevant choice of law rule is mandatory, which in turn requires that the governing law must be applied (whether foreign or not). If the relevant choice of law rule is mandatory this implies that a court must hear argument as to the identity of the applicable law. Otherwise the rule's mandatory status would be meaningless. Certainly, if the introduction of foreign law is in principle mandatory, it follows that the party who would have to plead it must show why it does not apply or face dismissal of its case. This would amount to arguing that English law is the applicable law.

assumed that it was proper in all cases involving foreign law: Ehrenzweig, (1960) 58 *Mich L Rev* 637, 678–679; Schlesinger, (1973) 59 *Cornell L Rev* 1, 3–12. In effect, the former US practice assumed that all choice of law rules were mandatory by virtue of the vested rights theory, which may be to distort the nature of particular rules, and is to make their status depend on a theoretical construct which may have little purpose or merit. It is as extreme as suggesting that choice of law rules are never imperative.

[21] *Edmeades v. Thames Board Mills Ltd.* [1969] 2 QB 67, 72–73.

In this way, of course, the obligation to introduce foreign law connotes more than a duty to rely upon foreign law. It implies a requirement that a case should be fought as a conflicts case and its choice of law implications examined. This has a bearing on the cost and protractedness of disputes which might explain why examples of mandatory choice of law rules are so rare. Certainly, as we shall see, it is unlikely that an English court would regard a given choice of law rule as a serious candidate for mandatory status unless it is of such a type that it is relatively straightforward to identify the applicable law. But the fact that dismissal is the consequence of a failure to plead and prove foreign law where this is required need not force a claimant to do so. Claimants who wish to avoid the application of foreign law can do so by arguing that English law governs the point in issue. Indeed, the practical consequence of the fact that the application of foreign law may sometimes be required is not so much that foreign law must be applied. It is that the identity of the applicable law must be discovered.

(b) Pleading and Choice of Law[22]

That reliance upon foreign law may be required in some cases begs a question of classification. Indeed, we must be careful to avoid a potentially damaging error in this connection. The problem is that English lawyers commonly regard the pleading of foreign law as a procedural matter.[23] In a sense, of course, it is. The manner and form in which such pleading occurs in a statement of claim or defence are clearly procedural issues, as much as the methods whereby foreign law is proved. But this does not mean that *whether* foreign law must be introduced in a given case (and thus pleaded) is also a matter of procedure. Indeed, whether the introduction of foreign law is required at all concerns the proper identification of the applicable law and is presumably a choice of law issue. As such it is a substantive matter which must be referred to the relevant choice of law rule.

There is certainly no doubt that the introduction of foreign law is generally voluntary. More precisely, English law normally allows litigants to select the *lex fori* as the applicable law. This choice may apparently be effected without express agreement by a simple omission to plead any other law. But such a choice of the *lex fori* is not always permitted. The principle of voluntary pleading is always subject to what the prevailing conflicts rule requires. It means that the parties' choice of that law may be subject to whatever limits are placed on their freedom to choose the applicable law.

---

[22] See generally, North, *Essays in Private International Law* (Oxford, 1993), Ch. 7.
[23] e.g. Dicey and Morris, 229.

If support were needed for this analysis one need only cite the principle that the classification of matters as substantive or procedural should be purposive not dogmatic.[24] Apart from the juridical character of an institution its classification should depend on what is required in order to give effect to the substantive law governing the case in question. But it hardly respects a rule requiring the mandatory application of foreign law to invoke the principle that the pleading of foreign law is procedural. Indeed, if that were so, there could never be a situation in which the introduction of foreign law is mandatory in English law, a view which is not supported in the authorities. The difficulty is strikingly illustrated by reference to the 1980 Rome Convention on the Law Applicable to Contractual Obligations, to which we shall return.[25] There seems little doubt that the Convention contains a number of mandatory choice of law rules which may require the application of foreign law. But it was not intended to affect a forum's procedural law.[26] We might assume that whether foreign law should be introduced in a given case is a procedural issue in English law, governed by the principle of voluntary pleading. But, if so, it would be possible to evade the law which is compulsorily applicable under the Convention merely by omitting to plead it.

It might be objected that the parties' ability to secure the application of English law, by pleading no other, does not necessarily amount to a choice of law in the true sense. It might be said that English law properly treats the question whether English law may govern as a matter outside the normal choice of law process, a matter of procedure not of private international law. But this resistance to adopting a choice of law analysis is puzzling. It might be suggested that an omission to plead foreign law is not a choice of law at all. Perhaps it implies a lack of any such choice. But it is unclear why a choice is not a choice merely because it is implicit, or because it is effected procedurally. Such a view also fails to account for the fact that, whether or not the *lex fori* has been 'chosen', the question whether it should be applied concerns what the applicable law should be. It is certainly curious that a question concerning the identity of the applicable law should not be treated as a matter within the remit of the rules of private international law.

It is also unclear why a choice of English law should be regarded differently from the choice of any other law. Certainly, there are important respects in which an indirect selection of the *lex fori* differs from any other choice of law. There are sound reasons of convenience why disputes in

---

[24] See above, p. 36.
[25] Merely to view an omission to plead foreign law as a choice of the *lex fori* is no solution. Is the scope of that choice defined by the relevant rules of procedure, or is it substantive, governed by the rules of private international law? See, e.g. *Tolofson* v. *Jensen* [1994] 3 SCR 1022, 1053.
[26] Article 1(2)(h).

English courts should be fought under English law. It might also be fairer and more just, in so far as it might be better to decide a case accurately under English law than inaccurately under foreign law. For the same reason it may better prosecute the purposes of the conflicts process, which is to encourage the accurate application of the governing law. There is also a sense in which, merely because an English court has jurisdiction in a matter, it may have some interest in regulating the law which is applied. But, despite their force, it might be thought that such factors properly concern the question of jurisdiction rather than choice of law, at least where the doctrine of *forum non conveniens* is available.[27] More importantly, they suggest why the freedom to choose the law of the forum should be wider than the freedom to choose any other law. But they do not mean that party autonomy should never be restricted where a choice of the *lex fori* is concerned.

It must also be recalled that English law may be relatively generous in allowing litigants to choose the governing law, and not merely in contractual matters. Only rarely does it confer mandatory status upon its conflicts rules, thus limiting the range of party choice.[28] It is unclear whether those factors which argue for the application of English law in an English court should override the particularly strong grounds which would have been required to render obligatory the application of the objectively applicable law. More importantly, to treat the freedom of litigants to ignore the foreign elements in proceedings as a choice of law matter does not mean that any special reasons for applying the *lex fori* need be ignored. English law implicitly recognizes the advantages in applying English law in English proceedings by permitting voluntary pleading in the majority of cases. There is also no reason why such advantages should not be considered in those rare situations in which a court is required to assess whether a given choice of law rule is mandatory. They might appropriately be weighed in the balance in determining, for example, the meaning and purpose of a statutory choice of law rule. The question in such a case is not whether a given choice of law rule is mandatory but whether it is mandatory, given that the parties have implicitly chosen English law.

In the end, therefore, no purpose might be served by denying that the introduction of foreign law is in English law a choice of law matter. But scholars in some civil law jurisdictions advocate detaching the freedom of litigants to select the *lex fori* from the ordinary choice of law process.[29] Their position mirrors and defends the traditional English view that the pleading of foreign law is voluntary. They would see the freedom to avoid

---

[27] See above, pp. 44–50.   [28] North, above n. 22.
[29] Flessner, 'Fakultatives Kollisionsrecht', *Rabels Zeitschrift*, 1970, 547; *Interessenjurisprudenz im internationalen Privatrecht*, (Tübingen, 1990), 119 ff.; De Boer, 'Facultative Choice of Law', (1996) *Hague Recueil*, vol. 257, 227.

the application of foreign law as a procedural matter, as an aspect of the parties' freedom to regulate the basis upon which their dispute is litigated. On such a view, even if the rules for choice of law are mandatory, the parties may elect to treat the case as purely domestic. But it is unclear that this theory of 'facultative choice of law' would necessarily achieve results very different from those described in this chapter. For, just as English law sometimes insists that particular choice of law rules are mandatory, so supporters of the theory would presumably accept that certain choice of law rules must have the character of *ordre public*, and thus be unwaivable in any circumstances. And, just as the theory calls attention to the advantages of allowing an indirect choice of the *lex fori*, so does English law, not least because they should be considered when determining the mandatory status of any particular choice of law rule. Moreover, the theory of facultative choice has developed because in many civil law systems most conflicts rules are in principle mandatory. As such, greater flexibility can only be won, and the advantages of applying the *lex fori* secured, by denying that the introduction of foreign law is a choice of law matter. But the position in English law is different. What is required is not a theory which allows greater flexibility against a background of conflicts rules which are generally mandatory. What is needed is a theory which explains the limits of party autonomy against a background of conflicts rules which are generally optional. This can only be supplied by supposing that choice of law rules may be mandatory, even to the extent of preventing selection of English law by procedural means.

But in English law it is unusual to treat the introduction of foreign law as anything but voluntary, normally by treating it as procedural. Several factors may explain this reluctance. One explanation may be the persistence of the idea that English and foreign law are presumed to be similar. As we shall see, such a view has never been unqualified, and its conceptual basis is insecure. Certainly, there is no firm foundation for the view that the applicable law may be relied upon yet not pleaded and proved.[30] But at first sight the presumption might be taken to excuse litigants from having to rely upon foreign law even when the relevant choice of law rule is mandatory. Another explanation may lie in history, in the vested rights theory, whereby courts are perceived not as applying foreign law *per se*, but only rights acquired thereunder.[31] This precise, if somewhat technical, distinction may have been responsible for enhancing the role of the fact doctrine and giving it significance beyond the law of evidence. Certainly, it lends support to the idea that foreign laws, or rights acquired under

[30] See below, p. 152.
[31] Dicey, *Conflicts of Law*, 2nd edn., (1908), 23; Beale, *Conflict of Laws* (1935), 1663–1664; Cheshire and North, 27–30; Ehrenzweig, (1960) 58 *Mich L Rev* 191, 661–669; Kahn-Freund, (1974) *Hague Receuil* 147, 464–465.

foreign law, are not laws but facts. And if it teaches that foreign law is never really applied at all it is understandable why the application of foreign law is not considered mandatory. Alternatively, the problem may lie more generally in the lack, in English law, of a developed taxonomy of mandatory rules, whether in private international law or elsewhere. Given the novelty of the notion that even the rules of internal private law are mandatory, it is unsurprising that it is so seldom recognized that rules for choice of law may also have this character. Again, the reluctance to view certain choice of law rules as mandatory may have a more subtle cause. It may lie in concern about the consequences of conferring mandatory effect upon such rules. Certainly, there has been strong resistance to any suggestion that a party who fails to plead or prove foreign law will invariably face dismissal of the claim, which is the result of doing so.[32]

Alternatively, the tendency to assume that all English conflicts rules are voluntary might owe its origins to an oversimplification. It might be thought that the choice of law rules of any legal system must either be entirely optional or entirely compulsory. If so, the particular advantages in applying the *lex fori*, or in respecting party autonomy, might be thought to favour the former approach. As we have seen, however, there is no reason why some rules might have one character, other rules another. The question is not whether, but when the rules for choice of law are mandatory.

Finally, the tendency to treat the application of foreign law as purely an evidential or procedural matter (and thus invariably voluntary) inevitably owes much to the designation of foreign laws as facts. For, if facts, how else can they be handled except as matters requiring evidence?[33] And it may also owe something to the ambiguous relationship between the procedural and the substantive in English law.[34] For, although it is readily accepted that the purpose of procedural law is to serve the purposes of substantive law,[35] this is tempered by a powerful strain of proceduralism in the English experience. There is certainly a willingness to accept that the scope of substantive rights may properly depend on what is procedurally possible, rather than to insist that procedures should give effect to substantive rights. It is particularly arresting that it is so widely assumed that litigants in England can generally select the *lex fori* as the *lex causae*—a proposition of substantive private international law—because *as a matter of procedure* the pleading of foreign law is not required.[36] It might have been expected that what must be pleaded and proved should depend on the relevant choice of law rule, not the opposite.

[32] Ehrenzweig, above n. 20, 678–679; *Crosby* v. *Cuba Railroad Co.*, above n. 20.
[33] Schlesinger, above n. 20, 5.
[34] See generally, Jolowicz, 'On the Nature and Purposes of Civil Procedural Law', *International Perspectives on Civil Justice*, ed. Scott, (1990).
[35] Bentham, *Principles of Judicial Procedure*, (1843), 5.　　[36] e.g. Dicey and Morris, 229.

(c) Mandatory Conflicts Rules

There is no reason why the introduction of a foreign governing law should not be required in English private international law. Whether it may be obligatory depends in principle simply upon whether a substantive rule exists to that effect. But it is often unclear whether this is the case. English law is generally ambivalent about whether its rules are mandatory, lacking the precise account of norms which is familiar in some legal systems.[37] This is as true of whether its conflicts rules are mandatory as of whether its local law has this effect. But the position in the present context is made more difficult because it is not generally recognized that conflicts rules—as distinct from domestic rules—may be compulsory. As such no practice has developed concerning how their mandatory status might be determined. But principle suggests how an approach to that question might be designed. The natural starting point is that the *lex fori* should govern in English proceedings unless the contrary is established. This would certainly follow if we were to endorse the view famously associated with Currie and Ehrenzweig that application of the *lex fori* is the basic rule in the conflict of laws.[38] But it is unnecessary to avow that position to recognize that English law begins with the assumption that the *lex fori* applies unless the contrary is shown. Indeed, we need not proceed in an *a priori* fashion but by inferring the principle from the English practice. The presumptive application of the *lex fori* reflects and rationalises the normal practice whereby the introduction of foreign law is voluntary, for the freedom not to plead foreign law amounts to a freedom to select the law of the forum. It also conforms to the principle that, if foreign law is not relied upon, or is relied upon but not adequately proved, English law applies. It also reflects the total absence in English law of any suggestion that the rules for choice of law should in general be mandatory. Indeed, the assumption is the opposite. On that basis, as common sense confirms, the mandatory application of foreign law may be regarded as exceptional. It should require clear words or a strong implication to give mandatory effect to a given choice of law rule.

The tendency to treat choice of law rules as voluntary is reflected in the authorities. It is apparent, for example, that the mere use of peremptory words will not have the effect of making the introduction of foreign law mandatory. It has been held that a foreign limitation period need not be pleaded merely because the Foreign Limitation Periods Act 1984 provides

---

[37] Cheshire and North, 496 ff; cf. Van Hecke, Belgium, in Rubino-Sammartano and Morse, eds, *Public Policy in Transnational Relationships* (Deventer, 1991), 11–13.
[38] Currie, (1968) 58 *Col L Rev.* 964; Ehrenzweig, (1960), above n. 20; Ehrenzweig and Westen, (1968) 66 *Mich L Rev* 1679, 1685–1690.

that such a law 'shall apply'.[39] Other statutes are more obviously permissive in their application. Part III of the Private International Law (Miscellaneous Provisions) Act 1995 appears to adopt non-mandatory language preserving the principle of voluntary pleading.[40] But not all statutory choice of law rules take this form. It is likely that certain provisions of the 1980 Rome Convention[41] and the 1968 Brussels Convention,[42] read purposively, require the introduction of foreign law in some cases.

Greater doubt may surround the import of certain judge-made rules. This is no doubt because such rules are seldom expressed in a canonical form of words such that it is possible to examine their mandatory status. There is also an argument for saying that a common law rule should never have mandatory effect because only the legislator is entitled to express a view on the policy considerations which justify such status. There is some doubt, for example, whether foreign law must be introduced when this is necessary for the meaningful interpretation of a document.[43] Similarly, the rule of double actionability which governs choice of law in defamation is famously ambiguous.[44] Perhaps this is because it is a rare instance of canonical common law rule whose words have acquired quasi-legislative status. Such examples are not without interest or difficulty. Strictly, however, the very existence of doubt in such cases should indicate that such rules are not mandatory, allowing the voluntary pleading principle to operate freely.

But this is not to deny that a selection of English law, by an omission to plead any other, is different in important ways from any other choice of law. There is no reason why such a choice should be harder than any other. But there are good reasons why it might be easier. Not least, the application of English law in an English court avoids the cost, inconvenience and potential ineffectiveness of applying foreign law in an alien environment. Such considerations ought to be relevant in determining whether a given choice of law rule is indeed mandatory, weighed against the language and purpose of the rule. They should not prevent us from recognizing that an omission to plead foreign law has choice of law implications and should be treated as a choice of law matter. But they add a special dimension to the enquiry whether a given choice of law rule is mandatory. For the question is not merely whether party choice should be permitted, but whether it should be permitted given the fact that the effect is the application of English law.

---

[39] Below, p. 129.
[40] See below, p. 97.
[41] See below, p. 93.
[42] See below, p.128.
[43] See below, pp.135–138.
[44] See below, pp. 99–106.

(d) Conclusion

Litigants are generally free to introduce foreign law (or not to do so) because the content of foreign law is a matter of fact. But there is no reason why English law should not provide that foreign law must be introduced and applied in certain cases. Indeed, whether this is required does not strictly concern the pleading of foreign law at all in the normal, procedural sense. It does not depend, as might be supposed, on the proper scope of the adversarial principle in English law, nor on the extent to which an English judge should be a passive arbiter of proceedings.[45] For English law's traditional stance is simply overriden in a case where the introduction and proof of foreign law is legally required. And whether it is required is squarely a choice of law question, belonging not to the law of civil procedure but to private international law. Indeed, as a choice of law question the issue is a familiar one:[46] how free are litigants to choose the applicable law? The answer to that question, where the mandatory application of foreign law is involved, is this chapter's concern.

3. EXCEPTIONS TO PARTY CHOICE

As we have seen, principle accommodates the possibility that the pleading of foreign law may be mandatory. This depends on the proper construction of the relevant choice of law rule. Several such rules might be thought to have this effect, generally because they are statutory and expressed in peremptory language. Some, in practice, may be more important than others, and few conflicts rules, on inspection, are likely to have mandatory effect. But each, in its own way, challenges the familiar principle of voluntary pleading. And each forces us to engage with an important but neglected issue: when are choice of law rules mandatory; when are litigants free to select the *lex fori* when another law is objectively applicable?

In answering this question the present chapter does not seek to establish categories of case in which reference to foreign law is required. It is tempting to assume, for example, that foreign law must be introduced if the issue goes to jurisdiction, because a court's jurisdiction must be established positively.[47] But this simply begs such questions as whether a given

---

[45] For an account of the respective roles of court and litigant see, Andrews, above n. 4, Ch. 3.
[46] North, above n. 22.
[47] Kahn-Freund, *General Problems of Private International Law*, 2nd edn., (1976), 115; see, below, p. 99 for the problem with regard to choice of law in defamation. In the same way it may not be helpful to adopt the elusive distinction between the application of foreign law as a rule of decision and as a 'datum': Ehrenzweig, *A Treatise on the Conflict of Laws* (1962), 362; Schlesinger, above n. 20, 275.

rule is truly one of jurisdiction, or whether all such rules are mandatory. It is preferable merely to ask what reasons there may be for treating each individual rule in this way. Again, this chapter is narrower in its scope than it might have been. For, if we characterise the freedom of litigants to ignore foreign law as a choice of law issue, the implications are wide-ranging. Any limitation on the parties' freedom to choose the applicable law may potentially restrict their ability to select the *lex fori*, just as it restricts their freedom to choose any other law.

As we have seen, this is not to deny that the selection of the *lex fori* differs in some ways from a choice of foreign law. And, as this suggests, a complete answer to the question whether litigants may always ignore foreign law in favour of English law involves traversing all those occasions on which their freedom to select the *lex causae* is qualified. But limitations of space prohibits such an expansive discussion. The general question of choice in choice of law has also been subjected to searching analysis by Dr North.[48] The present enquiry is thus limited to those situations in which the case law, or the literature, or the terms of a statute, has squarely raised the question whether the parties' usual freedom in pleading foreign law should be confined. In practice, this encompasses most areas in which the parties' freedom to select the applicable law might be abridged.[49] But, in principle at least, the number of potential exceptions to the voluntary pleading of foreign law may be larger than appears.

This chapter continues by examining a number of situations in which the application of foreign law might be mandatory in character. Normally such rules specify how the governing law should be identified, or that a designated law should be to a particular effect. But this chapter concludes by noticing two situations in which a court has a discretion to require the application of foreign law, one concerning the 1859 British Law Ascertainment Act, the other the construction of private documents.

4. CRIMINAL PROCEEDINGS

It is widely accepted that the introduction of foreign law may be required in criminal proceedings.[50] The law of bigamy provides an example. Where a defendant's liability turns on the existence of a prior marriage which is governed by foreign law, the prosecution must establish the validity of the marriage under that law. A failure to do so will lead to dismissal of the

---

[48] Above n. 22. But North treats the non-pleading of foreign law as a procedural matter, albeit one which expresses an indirect choice of law: ibid., 179–181.
[49] See the problems concerning property considered by North, ibid., 191–199.
[50] Dicey and Morris, 238; Hartley, (1976) 45 *ICLQ* 271, 286.

case.[51] Again, statute provides that liability may exist for a large number of offences, even if committed abroad, provided that the relevant acts or events are criminal 'under the law in force where the act, omission or other event was intended to take place'.[52] Presumably, this implies an obligation to establish liability under foreign law in such cases. Again, section 24(1) of the Theft Act 1968 provides that theft may be committed by an act of stealing in a foreign country. In such a case it has been held that the prosecution must positively establish liability under that law.[53]

This position is intuitively attractive given the special nature of criminal liability. Such proceedings implicate considerations of public policy which are often (if not always) lacking in civil litigation, while the requirement of proof beyond reasonable doubt, and the presumption of innocence, suggest that the prosecution must meet the most stringent standards in establishing liability. There is also evidence that courts might approach the interpretation of criminal statutes differently from others. In civil proceedings, as we have seen, they tend to assume that reliance upon foreign law is not required unless the purpose of the statute suggests otherwise. This reflects the presumption that the *lex fori* applies unless the contrary is shown. But no such presumption appears to operate in criminal matters. In interpreting a criminal statute courts are more likely to assume that the application of foreign law is required if this is implied by its terms. Certainly, where the prosecution is obliged to rely upon foreign law by the terms of a statute it may not avoid the proof of that law by relying upon any presumption of similarity between English law and foreign law.[54]

But this does not mean that the treatment of foreign law in criminal matters may be set aside as a special case. Indeed, it may appear to be special only because we are unused to the idea that even civil conflicts rules may be mandatory. Certainly, it would be erroneous to assume that considerations of policy, of the kind which may operate in criminal cases, are entirely absent from civil litigation. It is far from clear, even in an adversarial system, that such litigation involves merely the accommodation of private interests while criminal proceedings serve a more public function.[55] Again, that no presumption of similarity applies in criminal cases may owe less to the special nature of such cases than to the principle, which applies equally in civil proceedings, that foreign law, once relied upon, must be established by evidence. And the fact that the application of foreign law may be required in criminal cases may depend less upon the

---

[51] *R v. Povey* (1852) Dears. C.C. 32; *R v. Savage* (1876) 13 Cox. C.C. 178; *R v. Lindsay* (1902) 66 J.P. 505; *R v. Neguib* [1917] 1 K.B. 359.
[52] Criminal Justice Act 1993, s. 6.   [53] *Noble Julius Ofori* (1994) CR. APP. R. 223 (CA).
[54] Ibid., 227.
[55] Jolowicz, 'On the Nature and Purposes of Civil Procedural Law', Scott, ed., *International Perspectives on Civil Justice, Essays in Honour of Sir Jack Jacob QC*, (London, 1990), 45.

criminal character of the proceedings than upon the terms of the relevant legal rule. It is true that those criminal statutes which implicate foreign law tend to be drafted somewhat differently from those statues which prescribe choice of law rules for particular areas of civil liability. Instead of providing a test for identifying the applicable law, which may or may not be foreign, they specify with precision that a particular foreign law must apply. Typically, this is that of the country where the alleged offence is committed. But, in the end the question which must be asked of such statutes is no different from that which must always be posed: if a statute refers to foreign law, is the application of that law mandatory?

5. MANDATORY PLEADING IN CONTRACT

English courts generally ignore a case's foreign elements unless foreign law is pleaded. This habitual abstentionism may be especially marked in contractual disputes. Not only are judges in such cases likely to respect the parties wishes, in procedural as much as in substantive matters, but the desirability of resolving disputes in as expeditious and commercially viable way as possible—without needlessly introducing conflicts issues and matters of foreign law—is overtly a policy in such cases.[56] But, if English courts are even less likely to favour introducing foreign law in the contractual area than elsewhere, there are grounds for supposing that a foreign *lex causae* must sometimes be applied by an English court. This arresting possibility arises from the terms of the 1980 Rome Convention on the Law Applicable to Contractual Obligations, which entered into force in the United Kingdom on 1 April 1991 for contracts made after that date.[57] The Convention's purpose is to provide, throughout the European Union, a uniform set of rules for ascertaining and applying the applicable law of contracts. In seemingly obligatory terms Article 1 of the Convention provides:

The rules of the Convention shall apply to contractual obligations in any situation involving a choice between the laws of different countries.

Shall apply. *Any* situation. Such peremptory language is echoed in Articles 3 and 4, providing, respectively, that the applicable law shall be that chosen by the parties, or in the absence of choice, shall be that of the country with which it is best connected. Article 3(3) is especially hostile to party autonomy. It stipulates that a contractual choice of law shall not prejudice

---

[56] *Guide to Commercial Court Practice 1995*, 3.
[57] By virtue of the Contracts (Applicable Law) Act 1990; on the Convention generally, see: Dicey and Morris, Ch. 32.

the application of the mandatory rules of any legal system which is, in every other respect, better connected with the situation. To like effect are Articles 5 and 6, whose purpose is to guarantee the protection afforded to consumers and employees by the mandatory rules of their habitual residence or place of employment.[58] Similarly, Article 9(6) apparently requires the application of such mandatory rules as may govern the form of contracts concerning immovables.[59] And Article 12(2) subjects such matters as the assignability of debts to the law of the debt rather than the law applicable to the contract of assignment.[60]

What do these provisions imply? Do litigants no longer have a choice whether to plead foreign law in contract cases, or in some such cases? Must a plaintiff do so in order to establish a claim in contract; must the party in default do so to defend himself? At its strongest, the Rome Convention (presumably) cannot require an English court to adopt a procedure which it otherwise lacks. It would not justify a court in undertaking its own researches into foreign law. And it can scarcely permit (or require) a judge to ascertain a contract's applicable law without hearing argument from the parties as to the choice of law aspects of a case. It is not beyond consideration, however, that the Convention might require a court to dismiss claims which are not properly supported, either by evidence of the applicable law, or argument as to why the law identified as applicable under the Convention should not in fact apply.

Such questions acquire credibility because, although the norm in English law, the voluntary introduction of foreign law is not an immutable principle. It is simply that the relevant choice of law rules seldom, if ever, require the application of the objectively applicable law. Were they to do so, however, it should follow that any relevant foreign law must be introduced and applied. Indeed, herein lies the importance of the Rome Convention. For, although it does not purport to modify English law's rules of pleading, it may require the application of foreign law in so far as it contains mandatory rules of choice of law. Thus posed, the true significance of the present discussion is exposed. Certainly, the problem goes beyond the pleading of foreign law in a strict procedural sense. It is

---

[58] Article 5 preserves, in stated circumstances, the application of the mandatory rules of a consumer's habitual resident notwithstanding the provisions of Article 3 (and 4). Article 6 extends similar protection to employees. In addition, Article 8(2) provides an exception to the application of Articles 3 and 4 to material validity if it would be unreasonable to apply them. It is, however, apparent from its wording—'. . . a party may rely . . .' —that such rules apply at the affected party's motion.

[59] Article 9(6) provides that a contract concerning immovable property 'shall be subject to the mandatory requirements of form of the law of the country where the property is situated', provided such rules themselves apply regardless of the place of contracting or the law which governs the contract.

[60] Matters other than the mutual obligations of the parties are subjected to the 'law governing the right to which the assignment relates'.

concerned with an aspect of the choice of law process—with the extent to which litigants are free to select the *lex fori* as the applicable law.

(a) Preliminary Matters

Before detailing the arguments for and against a change to English law's traditional position, some preliminary matters must be addressed. For, although the answer may be relatively straightforward, the precise nature of the question to be posed is sometimes obscure.

(i) THE POINT OF THE QUESTION

An immediate issue is why it matters to determine the Rome Convention's impact on the pleading of foreign law when, at first sight, the debate may appear to have little practical purpose. Certainly, the logic of the situation presents a difficulty in so far as an English judge may be instinctively reluctant to introduce foreign law *ex officio*. This, and the fact that a court is unlikely to take points of law which the parties have not argued before it, means that the issue of the Rome Convention's impact on the pleading of foreign law will only arise in practice in the event that a party in litigation should raise it. But why would a party do so? Why argue that the rules of pleading are affected by the Convention? One who wishes to plead foreign law in a contract case may still do so, regardless of the Convention. And a party who does not wish foreign law to apply, although the other party does, can simply deny that the law in question is the governing law, a possibility unaltered by the Convention. This being so, how could the ability to plead foreign law become an issue between the parties?

But there is a corrective to this robustly practical position. Whether or not the issue is raised by the parties, whether it is actually raised in proceedings, nothing less is at stake than the correctness of the court's approach to foreign law. Whether or not the point is taken, English courts and litigants may be acting improperly, in defiance of obligations imposed by treaty, if they fail to consider the relevance of foreign law in contractual disputes. And they would be just as much in error (if they are in error) whether or not the parties so allege. In the end, it is nothing to the point to say that English courts may not in practice consider such issues of foreign law of their own motion. The very point at issue is whether in principle they have any choice. Moreover, the position of the English courts on this matter has attracted considerable attention, and gives rise to much disquiet, in other European countries. It is important to be clear as to English law's exact position with regard to party choice and the Rome Convention.

(ii) THE NATURE OF THE QUESTION

A second preliminary matter concerns the nature of the question presently at issue, which must not be misunderstood. In particular, despite superficial appearances, it does not bear on the debate as to whether the parties may choose which rules of private international law shall regulate their contract. This was famously proposed by the late Dr Mann in an effort to ameliorate the ill-effects, as he perceived them, of applying the Rome Convention.[61] He argued that all contracting parties need do to avoid the Convention's application is to provide in their contract that English law's pre-Convention rules should govern instead. This argument has been convincingly opposed, in part on the basis that the uniformity required by the Convention entails that it cannot be regarded as a voluntary regime.[62] To suggest with Dr Mann that contracting parties may oust the Convention altogether is very different, however, from saying that national rules of pleading may lead to the non-application of the law applicable under its choice of law rules. The former argument undermines the Convention where it clearly applies, the latter merely addresses its scope on the assumption that it does apply.

(iii) THE PROBLEM IN PRACTICE

Thirdly, arresting as it is, the question whether the conflicts rules of the Rome Convention are mandatory, such that a foreign *lex contractus* must be applied, may be less far-reaching in practice than might be supposed. Most legal systems permit contracting parties to choose the *lex fori* as their contract's applicable law, even when such a choice would oust the law which would otherwise govern.[63] Moreover, the Convention itself sanctions this result, Article 3(2) providing that the 'parties may at any time agree to subject the contract to a law other than the law which previously governed it'. Admittedly, such a choice of the *lex fori* to the exclusion of foreign law is a choice of law matter, not one of procedure, going to the identity of the *lex causae*. But the effect of selecting the *lex fori* is the same as not pleading foreign law, albeit that the conceptual basis of the *lex fori*'s application is different.[64] If so, English law is far from being unique in allowing litigants to avoid the otherwise applicable *lex causae* in contract cases. Indeed, the Rome Convention itself underwrites this result in all contracting states.

That voluntary pleading and a substantive choice of the *lex fori* are functionally equivalent does not, however, rob the question of the Rome Con-

---

[61] See, (1991) 107 *LQR* 353.   [62] By North, above n. 22, 184–186; Hogan, (1992) 108 *LQR* 12.
[63] See below, p. 268.   [64] North, above n. 22, 42.

vention's mandatory effect of its significance. This is because, by way of exception to the principle of voluntarism, the Convention contains rules which direct which law should apply regardless of the parties' wishes. As we have seen, a generally applicable exception is contained in Article 3(3). Of more limited application, Articles 5 and 6 provide, respectively, that consumers and employees may not lose the protection of certain non-derogable laws notwithstanding the law otherwise applicable to the contract. To similar effect is Article 9, governing form, which operates such that, although the parties may make an initial choice of the law applicable to form, this may not be modified by a subsequent choice of the *lex fori*.[65] Again, the Convention contains certain provisions, notably Articles 9(6) and 12(2) whereby the applicable law is to be identified without reference to the parties' intentions.[66] In some respects, therefore, the Convention mirrors English law's traditional approach by allowing contracting parties to have the *lex fori* applied. But in important ways it designedly may restrict the parties' choice of law, including their ability to select the *lex fori*. May English law ignore such restrictions by insisting on its voluntary rules of pleading? Must an English court stand by and sanction the subversion of Article 5 and 6 and the protective policy which they embrace?

(iv) AN AMBIGUITY

The scope of those of the Convention's rules which limit party choice may not be free from doubt. Indeed, the fourth preliminary matter which must be addressed concerns the strikingly ambiguous language of Article 3(3). We have seen that this preserves the mandatory rules of any legal system with which the contract is in every respect connected, but for the parties' choice of law (and choice of jurisdiction). But it does so only when 'the parties have chosen a foreign law'. Does this mean that Article 3(3) is irrelevant in a case where the parties have chosen the *lex fori* as the governing law? If so, it is necessarily irrelevant where the parties, by omitting to plead foreign law, intend English law to govern. At first sight, the language of Article 3(3) seems inescapably to suggest this conclusion. Nor is it necessarily odd that litigants should be able to avoid the mandatory rules of the best connected law by choosing the *lex fori*, although not otherwise. Certainly, there may be sound reasons for allowing them to do so where their choice of the *lex fori* is effected by an omission to plead any other law. If the purpose of Article 3(3) is to preserve any mandatory rules which might protect weaker contracting parties it is unclear why this is necessary where the

---

[65] Section 3(2) permits variation of the otherwise applicable law, and thus may justify the parties' choice of the *lex fori* by an omission to plead any other law. But such a variation cannot prejudice a contract's formal validity under Article 9.

[66] Above n. 59.

offending choice of law is made in the course of litigation (by the parties' omission to rely upon foreign law). In such a case the weaker party may be assumed to have taken proper advice. And, because at the stage of litigation the real consequences of any choice of law will be clear, there is every reason to suppose that any waiver of protection is informed.

If Article 3(3) is inoperative where the *lex fori* is chosen this confines its reach to cases where the applicable law is that of, say, California, but the contract is better connected either with England or with a third country. The former situation is perhaps more likely to arise in practice. It is entirely comprehensible that Article 3(3) should operate principally when the mandatory rules of the forum are jeopardised by an evasive choice of law. In such a case the forum has a special reason to defend the policies implicit in its mandatory law. It might be objected that this is to duplicate the role of Article 7(2), which expressly permits a forum to displace the law which would otherwise apply under the Convention in favour of its mandatory rules. But such an objection is misplaced. The purpose of Article 7(2) is to preserve the international mandatory rules of the forum, those which 'are mandatory irrespective of the law otherwise applicable to the contract'. The role of Article 3(3), by contrast, is to preserve from evasion any mandatory rule which cannot be derogated from by contract, which encompasses even those rules which are not mandatory in an international sense. As such Article 3(3) has a distinct and legitimate role in enforcing the laws of the forum.

There are, then, sound reasons for limiting Article 3(3) to cases in which the parties have chosen a law other than English, which robs it of any significance where the parties, by not pleading foreign law, have chosen that of England. But it cannot be denied that Article 3(3) is often allowed a wider scope.[67] Indeed, it is generally assumed, and those who drafted the Convention may have intended, that Article 3(3) should operate whenever the chosen law is foreign to the parties or to the situation in which the relevant contract was made. Read in this way the fact that the applicable law is foreign to the forum is immaterial. It is far from clear that such an interpretation, even if true to what was originally intended, is compelled by— or even justified by—the terms of Article 3(3). But, given the ambiguity of Article 3(3), nor is it certain that the opposite view is correct. For that reason the following discussion does not exclude the possibility that it may operate when English law is the applicable law.

(v) A CONFUSION

A final preliminary matter involves a potentially confusing line of argument. It might be suggested that, being an international treaty, the Rome

[67] e.g. Kaye, *International Contracts* (1990), 164–165. Cheshire and North, 480–481.

Convention must immediately be regarded as mandatory, such that it overrides any attempt by the parties to oust any of its provisions. But this is to mistake two different issues. One problem is whether such a convention is to be regarded as a mandatory regime, applying in English law to the exclusion of any other. A quite different issue, which arises even if a convention is exclusive in that sense, is whether it permits litigants to contract out of any of its provisions. The first matter concerns whether a convention is applicable, the second concerns its effect when it does so. With this in mind, it is unlikely that litigants would often be entitled to disapply a treaty altogether, perhaps by agreeing that the law which existed before its implementation should be applied. But a convention might itself permit litigants to disapply any of its provisions.[68]

Confusion sometimes stems from the fact that most international conventions—like the Rome Convention—are implemented by statutes which give them 'the force of law'.[69] It is sometimes suggested that this formula by itself bestows mandatory status on all rules contained in such instruments.[70] On examination, however, this view is not compelled by the cases which are said to support it.[71] A statute may confer the force of law on a convention but that merely exposes the question of what that force should be. That cannot be answered by reference to the convention's having the force of law but depends on its terms.

The idea that mere reference to a convention's having the force of law is irrelevant in assessing the effect of its individual provisions has been judicially endorsed. In *Caltex Singapore Pte. Ltd.* v. *B P Shipping Ltd.*[72] Clarke J saw the effect of the phrase as being to give a convention 'direct' effect in English law, but not mandatory effect.[73] It serves to introduce such a convention into English law. But whether a given rule in such a convention has mandatory effect depends on the terms and purpose of the rule in question.

Another means of giving mandatory effect to international conventions, however, is to emphasise the related goals of harmonization and uniformity. In *The Hollandia*,[74] for example, there is a suggestion that the mere fact that a convention is designed to achieve international uniformity is a

---

[68] Which is not to say that an international convention may not itself make the application of foreign law mandatory: *Singh Batra* v. *Ebrahim* [1982] 2 Lloyd's Rep. 11, 13 (CA); *UCM* v. *Royal Bank of Canada* [1983] AC 168, 189 (HL); Hartley, (1996) 45 *ICLQ* 271, 287–288.

[69] e.g. The Contracts (Applicable Law) Act 1990, s. 2(1).

[70] Dicey and Morris, 24–25; *Corocraft Ltd.* v. *Pan American Airways Inc.* [1969] 1 QB 616; *The Hollandia* [1982] QB 872, 883 (CA); [1983] 1 AC 565 (HL).

[71] In *Corocraft Ltd.* v. *Pan American Airways Inc.*, op. cit., the Warsaw Convention was treated as mandatory because Article 32 was in peremptory terms: *ibid.*, 631. In *The Hollandia*, op. cit., the Hague Visby Rules were given mandatory effect because, as a matter of construction, this was their purpose: *ibid.*, at 572–573 (per Lord Diplock); see further, Mann, (1991) 107 *LQR* 353, 355.

[72] [1996] 1 Lloyd's Rep. 286.   [73] At 297.   [74] Above n. 70.

reason to render its provisions unwaivable.[75] But, again, this is to beg the question. Harmonization is an inevitable goal of international conventions, but the extent to which harmonization requires their rules to be given mandatory effect depends on their wording and purpose.

It is unlikely, therefore, that all rules comprised in international conventions have mandatory force in English law *per se*, or because they have 'the force of law', or because their object is harmonization. Indeed, it could hardly be otherwise, since such devices cannot confer upon the provisions of such conventions a greater effect in English law than they are designed to have. In the present context, therefore, the only question is whether the purpose of the Rome Convention, or of any of its provisions, is indeed to erode the freedom of litigants to ignore the foreign element in proceedings.

(b) Pleading, Proof and the Rome Convention[76]

We may now turn to the arguments for and against giving the Rome Convention, or certain of its rules, mandatory effect such that the application of foreign law may be required. It is helpful to deal first with some false arguments which may cloud the discussion, then to notice some which are merely inconclusive, then, finally, to address the issue of classification which is the core of the problem.

(i) two false arguments

It is necessary to tilt at once at two fallacious arguments against the Convention's having any effect on the previous position in England. The first concerns the extent to which (in particular) the protective role of Articles 5 and 6 requires the application of the relevant mandatory rules of a consumer's or employee's habitual residence. It might be argued that the application of English law in default of pleading can scarcely prejudice such a party, who only has to invoke such foreign rules to obtain their protection. If, say, a consumer has voluntarily submitted to English substantive law why should a judge quarrel with that party's estimation of its best interests?

The point is not without force but encounters an important objection of principle. True, many mandatory rules of law may be waived by those whom they are designed to protect. But many may be of an absolute nature, being unwaivable even in the course of legal proceedings.[77]

---

[75] At 572–573.
[76] Fentiman, (1992) 108 *LQR* 142, 144–145; Hartley, (1996) 45 *ICLQ* 271, 290–291.
[77] Unlike the common law, which articulates no such distinction, civil law jurisdictions commonly differentiate between *lois imperatives*, which are contractually unwaivable but

Whether a rule is of one type or the other is, however, a matter which can only be resolved by reference to the law of the country in question. It is not for an English court to decide that it is permissible for a party to waive the protection of such a rule when the public interest of the country concerned demands its absolute application. In consequence, although a foreign mandatory rule may be derogable, this is something which a court can know only once foreign law has been introduced and proved.

The second false argument is striking, if less practically important. It might be said that a court, so far from being required to apply the law applicable under the Convention, lacks notice of the Convention itself unless its relevance has been argued. This startling—and counter-intuitive—result may come about because the Contracts (Applicable Law) Act 1990, which implements the Rome Convention in the United Kingdom, omits to provide that a court shall have judicial notice of the Convention.[78] In this it differs conspicuously from the Civil Jurisdiction and Judgments Act 1982, which implements the 1968 Brussels Convention on Jurisdiction and the Enforcement of Judgments and expressly provides that a court shall take judicial notice of its provisions.[79] It is extremely unlikely, however, that any significance attaches to this omission.[80] Certainly, section 2 of the 1990 Act expressly gives the Rome Convention 'the force of law',[81] the form of words normally employed to give courts notice of international conventions. Courts readily accept that this gives such conventions the same status as the rules of English domestic law.[82] And common sense resists any other conclusion.

(ii) SOME INCONCLUSIVE ARGUMENTS

Plausible arguments may be deployed on each side of the debate, although most are ultimately inconclusive. Several support a mandatory reading of the Rome Convention, although none by itself is decisive. First, its peremptory language, especially the apparent instruction to consider and to apply foreign law in Article 1(1) may suggest that foreign law must be introduced in any case with a foreign element. Secondly, there is the importance attached to uniformity in the purpose and design of the Convention. This objective, implicit in the very enterprise of legal harmoniza-

---

may be waived at trial, and *lois d'ordre public international* which are unwaivable. The former preserve an affected party's interests, and so are derogable. The latter express a wider public interest and are absolute.

[78] See Contracts (Applicable Law) Act 1990, *Current Law Statutes Annotated 1990*, annotations by C. G. J. Morse, p. 36–6.

[79] Section 2(1) provides merely that the Rome Convention 'shall have the force of law in the United Kingdom'.

[80] Morse, above n. 78, 36–6.   [81] Section 2(1).

[82] e.g. *Caltex Singapore Pte. Ltd.* v. *BP Shipping Ltd.*, above n. 72, 297.

tion, is made explicit in the Giuliano and Lagarde Report.[83] It is also required by a principal purpose of the Convention, to support the 1968 Brussels Convention on Jurisdiction and the Enforcement of Judgments by ensuring that the same governing law is applicable regardless of the EU country's court which assumes jurisdiction in a given case.[84] The need for uniformity is articulated in Article 18, which provides:

In the interpretation and application of the preceding uniform rules, regard shall be had to their international character and to the desirability of achieving uniformity in their interpretation and application.

It is clearly desirable that courts should interpret and apply the Convention uniformly, so as to avoid the Convention's being undermined by receiving different treatment in different countries. Would it not lead, however, to a limping, non-uniform application of the Convention if the English courts were, in effect, to make its operation voluntary by allowing the parties to decide whether or not to plead a contract's applicable law? This argument seems especially hard to circumvent because the predominant (though not invariable) view elsewhere in Europe is that the pleading of foreign law is, indeed, mandatory, at least in cases involving Articles 5 and 6.[85] As such, English law's approach being a minority position, the case for English law having to be amended is superficially compelling.

Finally, and most importantly, if imperative effect is not given to the Convention its provisions concerning foreign mandatory rules might be circumvented. For, as we have seen, the Convention constrains the parties' freedom to choose the applicable law in so far as it contains provisions which give overriding effect to such rules in certain cases.[86] Is it right that the parties should escape such provisions by omitting to plead foreign law? Should their freedom not to plead foreign law be limited in so far as they might thereby avoid its mandatory provisions? Is it not an implicit purpose of the Convention to ensure the enforcement of certain indefeasible rules of law? If so, the only viable means to do so is simply to deprive them of the freedom not to plead.

On examination, however, none of the arguments for a mandatory reading of the Convention is decisive—although nor are those which might be deployed in reply. Take the language of the Convention. Imperative as its wording seems it is clear that this is insufficient by itself to require introduction of the applicable law. The Convention, like all such Community treaties, should be interpreted purposively, not literally. Again, it should not be supposed that Articles 5 and 6 are deprived of all meaning by subjecting them to the principle of voluntary pleading. Both provisions can

---

[83] At 13.
[84] Ibid., 4; North, above n. 22, 186–187.
[85] e.g. in Germany; see, below, p. 269.
[86] Articles 3(3), 5, 6.

meaningfully take effect so as to ensure the application of the designated law once it has been introduced (presumably by the affected consumer or employee).

Nor is it necessarily an obstacle to allowing the parties the freedom to have English law apply in default of pleading foreign law that the Convention sometimes permits or compels the application of the mandatory rules of a country other than the forum. One reason is that (in particular) Articles 3(3), 5 and 6 do not expressly provide that they should be applied by a court on its own motion (although their wording is peremptory). This allows us to say that, although these provisions are designed to preserve the operation of certain mandatory rules, they are not themselves mandatory. Too much should not be made of the point, the interpretation of the Convention being purposive, not merely textual. It is striking, however, that while the Rome Convention does not specify that any of its provisions must be applied by a court *ex officio*, the 1968 Brussels Convention does so in equivalent circumstances.[87] Arguably, the omission of such explicit indications of mandatory force means that Articles 3(3), 5 and 6 of the Rome Convention are subject to the general principle that foreign law must be pleaded.

Similarly, the argument from uniformity may fail for the reason we have noted already. The uniform treatment of the Convention's rules is one thing, the harmonization of national rules of procedure something else. The uniformity undoubtedly required by Article 18, and implicit in the very purpose of the Convention, is simply not an issue in an area where uniformity was never contemplated. Article 18 compels uniformity only in the matters to which the Convention actually applies; it cannot itself define the matters to which the Convention applies.

Again, there is a case for saying that situations in which foreign law has not been pleaded are inevitably beyond the Convention's scope. This argument stems from the fact that Article 1(1) provides that the Convention shall apply only if the situation is one 'involving a choice between the laws of different countries'. Plausibly, this requirement is not satisfied, no such situation and no such choice arising, unless foreign law has been pleaded, for only then does a choice of law issue exist. Logic may thus dictate that the pleading of foreign law is outside the Convention in so far as, in a given case, it is prior to the Convention's operation.

Finally, it is not merely that the text and purpose of the Convention may leave the traditional English position untouched. Policy argues strongly for such a conclusion. Taken to its limits, the effect of requiring the introduction of foreign law is that the parties will have to offer argument as to the identity of the applicable law, and to offer potentially expensive

---

[87] e.g. Articles 20 and 21.

evidence as to its content. This introduces expense and delay into the proceedings, disadvantages which English law's traditionally voluntary approach happily avoids. Not only is this contrary to the policy of ensuring the efficient administration of justice, it conflicts with the objective of respecting commercial efficacy in the handling of contractual disputes.

None of these arguments, however, supplies a conclusive answer to the problem. Indeed, the majority merely beg the question as to what the Convention's true purposes may be. And the last is less consequential than might appear. This is because, if the question concerns at root such mandatory rules as Articles 3, 5 and 6 ordain shall be applied, there may be little difficulty in identifying the laws in question. They are, respectively, those of the legal system which is in all respects (but for any choice of law or jurisdiction) connected with the situation, and those of the law of a consumer's or employee's habitual place of work. In the same way there may be little difficulty in identifying the formalities of the *lex situs* under Article 9 or the law of the debt in Article 12.

Such inconclusive considerations apart, a more important matter is that a mandatory reading of any of the Convention's provisions encounters an apparently decisive reply. Quite simply, even if a court is otherwise compelled to apply a foreign *lex causae*, the Convention might preserve any existing rules concerning the pleading and proof of foreign law. It is uncontroversial that it does not affect the procedural rules of Contracting States. The Giuliano and Lagarde Report says as much.[88] So does Article 1(2)(h) of the Convention, which expressly saves matters of 'evidence and procedure' from the Convention's scope. It might be supposed, therefore, that, even if in some objective sense a foreign country's rules are applicable, the parties are free not to plead and prove its content. This view is unequivocally endorsed by Hartley,[89] and by the editors of Dicey and Morris,[90] although it has not been universally accepted.[91] If this view stands, any suggestion that an English judge must apply a contract's applicable law apparently collapses, given that English law's rules concerning the pleading and proof of foreign law are procedural, and so immune from any alteration by the Convention. On closer inspection, however, the matter is more complex. Indeed, the question whether foreign law must be introduced under the Convention turns ultimately on whether it should, in principle, be regarded as a procedural or a substantive matter. If the former, it is untouched by the Convention. If the latter, then whether such introduction is required depends on the choice of law rules which the Convention supplies. To that critical question of classification we must now turn.

---

[88] Op. cit., 13. [89] Above, n. 76, 290–291. [90] At 229.
[91] Kaye, above n. 67.

(iii) SUBSTANCE, PROCEDURE AND THE ROME CONVENTION

The crux of the present debate is whether the introduction of foreign law is substantive or procedural. But an initial difficulty concerns how a procedural matter is to be classified for the Convention's purposes. Is the definition of what is procedural a matter for the state concerned, or should it bear a community meaning? If the latter, it could be argued that whether or not a foreign applicable law must be applied is not, at root, an issue of procedure, but one of substance, within the Convention's province. Certainly it could be said that the scope of procedural matters must be understood in the light of the commitment to uniformity enshrined in Article 18. It would hardly be conducive to uniformity, however, to allow English law to disapply the Convention by employing its traditional rules of pleading. It is extremely unlikely, however, that a community definition of procedural matters is required by the Convention. To insist upon such a definition would rob the allocation of procedural matters to the forum of any meaning—if the objective is to save a forum's procedural rules how can any law other than that of the forum determine the extent of those rules? Moreover, it is apparent from the Giuliano and Lagarde Report that Member States should retain control over their procedures except in so far as the Convention expressly provides otherwise.[92]

But even if what is procedural is determined by English law, it is unclear whether English law would actually regard the question under review as procedural. Is a requirement to apply the law applicable under the Convention truly a procedural matter under English law? Certainly, the manner in which foreign law is pleaded—its form, specificity and detail—is procedural. But is that true of the question whether the *lex causae*, identified by an English choice of law rule, must be applied or ignored? Are rules which define the identity and scope of the applicable law truly procedural? Is this not a matter belonging to the substantive choice of law rules of the forum concerned? If such issues are truly substantive, as principle suggests, then the English approach to foreign law is scarcely saved by its procedural character. Indeed, if the application of the applicable law is a substantive issue (as it surely is), there seems little doubt that the Rome Convention requires an English court to apply the law designated as applicable by the Convention.

It might be objected, however, that the official report on the Convention supports the view that whether foreign law must be introduced is a matter within a signatory state's procedural rules.[93] This states[94] that, if a choice of law is made in the course of proceedings, the question of 'the

---

[92] Giuliano and Lagarde, Report on the Convention, OJ 1980 No. C282, 36.
[93] Dicey and Morris, 229, n. 37.   [94] Report on the Convention, above n. 92, 18.

limits within which the choice or change can be effective' is 'within the ambit of the national law of procedure, and can be settled only in accordance with that law'. But these remarks should not be taken out of context. They are concerned only with how a parties' subsequent choice of law may be effected in cases to which Article 3(2) applies. They do not affect the restrictions on the scope of Article 3(2) which the Convention itself requires. In particular, they do not affect the limitations which, say, Articles 5, 6 and 9 impose on the parties' freedom to select the *lex fori* as the applicable law. The remarks in the Report are concerned only with the procedural formalities required to evidence such a selection where it is permitted. They do not govern whether it is permitted at all. Is it sufficient, for example, as in English law, to infer a choice of the *lex fori* under Article 3(2) from a mere omission to plead any other law?

It is suggested, therefore, that how foreign law is pleaded is a procedural issue, but whether it should be pleaded is substantive. Such a distinction recognizes that the tacit selection of English law by pleading no other is a choice of law question and, as such, must be governed by the relevant rules for choice of law. In the present context, those rules are contained in the Rome Convention. They indicate that litigants may, indeed, select the *lex fori* as the applicable law in most cases. Such is the effect of Article 3(2). But they expressly provide by, for example, Articles 5 and 6, that party choice may not remove the protection which mandatory rules may afford to consumers and employees. And, subject to the meaning to be given to 'foreign law' in Article 3(3) they preserve the mandatory rules of the best connected legal system. Similarly, Article 3(2) explicitly ensures that any variation in law by litigants—such as (presumably) when they select the *lex fori* by omitting to plead any other—cannot prejudice such rules as to form which may be applicable under Article 9. Again, it is clear that the law applicable by virtue of Articles 9(6) and 12(2) is not to be identified by reference to the parties' intentions but, as a matter of law, by the terms of each article. Under Article 3(2) the parties are only permitted to choose the law applicable to the contract, not the law which regulates those issues to which the *lex contractus* is inapplicable. As the application of the *lex fori* is treated in Article 3(2) as a choice of law matter this suggests that the parties may not alter the law applicable under Articles 9(6) and 12(2) by omitting to plead it, thereby selecting the *lex fori*.

But if, as this suggests, the application of foreign law is sometimes required under the Rome Convention, this begs a further question. What is the status of the English rules concerning the proof of foreign law? Presumably, these must be procedural, as technical rules of evidence generally are. But does that allow a party who might be required to plead foreign law to rob the principle of any point by declining to prove it? Alternatively, is a party who pleads foreign law pursuant to the Convention entitled to escape its obligation by relying on the familiar presumption of similarity between English and foreign law? It is hard to believe that such evasion of the Convention is possible. As we shall see, the presumption of similarity has a somewhat insecure status.[95] But, this aside, if the Rome Convention truly requires the application of foreign law in certain circumstances, that requirement cannot be subverted by classificatory sleight of hand. If foreign law must be applied, it must be both pleaded and proved. The Convention imposes a duty on court and party alike to ensure that foreign law is applied which must override the procedures for pleading and proof.

(iv) A CHANGE IN PRACTICE?

Practical problems emerge if we accept that foreign law must be introduced pursuant to the Convention. What does this actually imply for litigants? In principle, as we have seen, it involves more than merely pleading and proving foreign law. It must also involve argument as to what is the applicable law in a given case. As a matter of logic, foreign law cannot be applied until it has been established that it is actually applicable. And, as a matter of principle, if court and litigant are under a duty to apply any relevant foreign law, this implies a requirement that the conflicts implications of such a case are properly argued and considered. In such cases, it is not merely foreign law, but the relevant choice of law rule, which must be applied.

Take, for example, proceedings concerning a consumer contract. Who bears the burden of pleading and proving the existence (or non-existence) of the protective rules of an affected consumer's habitual residence? Under Article 5 it is presumably for one who relies on the law stipulated in the contract to do so, which inevitably means the supplier. But what exactly must that party demonstrate? In principle, a supplier would need to establish that the applicable law is that which has been agreed by the parties. In order to do so it would need to offer evidence that no mandatory, protective provisions exist under the law of the weaker party's habitual residence. Alternatively, it would have to show that the transaction is not a consumer contract within Article 5. Only if it is such a contract, and if there are such provisions, is the contractually agreed law inapplicable. Only if it is not such a contract, or if there are no such provisions, does it apply. A failure to address the issue raised in Article 5 would, presumably, lead to dismissal of the plaintiff's claim for want of a required ingredient of its case.

Again, the foregoing argument assumes that, in the general case, litigants are free not to plead the otherwise applicable law. But this is only

---

[95] See, below, pp. 146–153, 184–188.

because Article 3(2) allows such a consensual variation of the applicable law. There is no reason in principle why such a choice of the *lex fori* may not be inferred from a simple omission to plead any other. The implications of such an omission are sufficiently obvious that their selection is (presumably) established with the 'reasonable certainty' required under Article 3(1). Moreover, the official report on the Convention suggests that how such a choice is effected is a matter for the procedural law of each signatory state.[96] In English law it is apparent that a choice of the *lex fori* may generally be effected by mere omission.

Inevitably, such reflections on the procedural consequences of the mandatory choice of law rules in the Rome Convention have a somewhat unreal flavour. This does not weaken the argument which supports the existence of such rules. But it reinforces the impression that the true nature of the Convention, and its procedural implications, may not have been appreciated at the time of its implementation. Certainly, it is hard to give effect to the mandatory choice of law rules which it contains in a system such as the English. Only in civil law systems in which courts are generally empowered to establish foreign law *ex officio*, and to exercise a constant supervisory role from the very inception of proceedings is this really possible.[97] An adversarial system of civil procedure does not easily accommodate conflicts rules of a mandatory character.

It must be emphasised, however, that whether or not the Rome Convention marks a change in English law, its practical effect may not be as great as might be supposed. As we have seen, the Convention itself permits a subsequent choice to oust the law otherwise applicable to a contract, which replicates the present position. Again, Article 3(3) applies only if, but for the choice of law and jurisdiction, 'all the other elements relevant to the situation' are connected with another law, which may narrow the cases in which it applies. Greater change may be expected in cases under Articles 5, 6 and 9 in which certain mandatory rules are applicable irrespective of party choice. But even here a requirement that a contract's applicable law should be applied may amount in practice to a somewhat minor incursion into the general principle. As the Giuliano and Lagarde report on the Convention itself admits, mandatory rules as to form of the type contemplated by Article 9(6) are 'probably rather rare'.[98] Nor will courts often need to dismiss claims for want of pleading and proof under Articles 5 and 6. The effect of Articles 5 and 6 having mandatory status may be that employers and suppliers, faced with the need to plead the law of the weaker party's residence, will simply concede that the contractually

---

[96] Report on the Convention, above n. 92, 18. See, however, Lando (1987) 24 *CMLR* 159, 186–188; Cheshire and North, 479–480.

[97] Cf. Andrews, *Principles of Civil Procedure*, (London, 1994), 40.

[98] Report on the Convention, above n. 92, 32.

agreed law is inapplicable whenever the former contains protective rules. As such the effect of the Convention is preventative. Alternatively, protected consumers and employees might plead and prove any mandatory rules for themselves.

Again, it is unlikely that, say, consumers within Article 5, would often wish to invoke the protection of the mandatory rules of foreign law. It is more probable that the mandatory rules in question will be those of the forum. In such a case Article 5, in effect, does not require the introduction of foreign law—indeed it requires the opposite—thus achieving the same result as would follow from an omission to plead foreign law. This comes about because the 1968 Brussels Convention on Jurisdiction and the Enforcement of Judgments allows consumers to proceed in the courts of their domicile. More importantly, it permits litigation against them only in those courts.[99] This mirrors, in practice if not in terminology, the provision in Article 5 which preserves the application of the mandatory rules of a consumer's habitual residence. As such, consumer litigation should generally occur only in the country whose mandatory rules Article 5 of the Rome Convention is designed to protect. The preservation of *foreign* mandatory rules is not really in issue and, in consequence, the situation will seldom arise in which an omission to plead foreign law is a derogation from Article 5.

(c) Conclusion

Any requirement that foreign law be introduced under the Rome Convention may have a restricted impact. But this is not to say that it has no effect. Nor does it undermine the fact that the pleading of foreign law is in principle required under the Convention. Certainly, whatever its practical impact it is important to labour the question of the Convention's status for several reasons. It reveals once again that English law's voluntary approach to pleading foreign law is less secure than might be supposed. It also throws into sharp relief the question to what degree the pleading of foreign law is substantive or procedural. Indeed, by revealing that the introduction of foreign law is a substantive matter of private international law it clarifies a much misunderstood issue. It also emphasises that the application of English law in default of pleading is a central aspect of the choice of law process, not a peripheral question of procedure. Finally, our inspection of the Rome Convention's status reinforces an important general point. It is not invariable that the pleading of foreign law is voluntary in English law. Nor is it inevitable, there being nothing inimical to English law in the idea that it might be mandatory. It simply depends upon

---

[99] Article 14.

whether the relevant choice of law rules forbid or permit the non-introduction of foreign law.

6. MANDATORY PLEADING IN TORT

Proceedings involving foreign torts arise surprisingly seldom in English courts. As a result, despite radical recent changes, English law in this area is relatively undeveloped. The prevailing uncertainty is reflected in English law's approach to the introduction and proof of foreign law in such proceedings. In particular, in choice of law terms, it is unclear whether litigants, by omitting to plead the law of the place of the wrong, may select the law of the forum as applicable to a foreign tort.[100] Indeed, it is unclear whether they may ever choose the law applicable to a tort. Difficulty arises in two situations. One concerns the generality of tort cases within Part III of the Private International Law (Miscellaneous Provisions) Act 1995. The other involves proceedings in defamation which are expressly excluded from the 1995 Act and are subject to the traditional common law rules.[101]

(a) Pleading and the Statutory Regime

Torts in English law are generally governed by the *lex loci delicti*,[102] subject to an exception whereby another law which is substantially more appropriate may be applied.[103] The question arises, however, whether parties in litigation must introduce any foreign law which applies to a given tort by virtue of those rules.[104] Again, it might be supposed, if the application of the applicable law is mandatory, that the court must hear argument as to its identity. Otherwise, there is a risk that a law might be applied other than that which the relevant choice of law rule requires. As we have seen, there is no reason in principle why a choice of law rule should not be mandatory in character, requiring application of a relevant foreign law and overriding the general principle that the introduction of foreign law is voluntary. Differently expressed, such a rule may prohibit the application of the law of the forum in a case to which foreign law properly applies.

It is doubtful that the 1995 Act requires the application of foreign law unless it is introduced by one of the parties. Certainly, the Act contains no

---

[100] North, above n. 22, 187–191. For a general account of the present law see Dicey and Morris, Ch. 35, together with the Third Supplement to the Twelfth Edition (1996), Ch. 35.
[101] Private International Law (Miscellaneous Provisions) Act 1995, s. 13.
[102] Section 11.   [103] Section 12.
[104] Dicey and Morris, Third Supplement to the Twelfth Edition (1996), 23 (amending n. 32 at p. 229), 176.

reference to whether litigants may select the law applicable to a tortious wrong.[105] This suggests that the law applicable under the Act, objectively determined according to its rules, must be applied, and that the parties cannot select the governing law themselves. If an omission to rely upon foreign law amounts to selection of the *lex fori*, such an indirect choice might therefore be illegitimate in tortious proceedings. But it is unclear that an indirect choice of the *lex fori* is on the same footing as the selection of a foreign *lex delicti*. It is certainly arguable that litigants cannot generally select the applicable law in tortious proceedings. But, whatever the position in the general case, the omission of any reference in the 1995 Act to the parties' power of selection may not affect their ability to select English law by omitting to plead any other. In principle, as we have seen, the mandatory application of a foreign applicable law should be regarded as an exception to the general rule that the *lex fori* should be applied. Admittedly, there is a tendency to assume that the opposite is true. This is no doubt because of the survival of the unfortunate fiction that, in the absence of contrary evidence, English law and foreign law are treated as the same. Such a fiction suggests that foreign law 'applies' in some sense in every situation in which a choice of law rule leads to this result, albeit that it has the content of English law. As we shall see, however, the credentials of this often-cited principle are doubtful. It is preferable to say that the law of the forum applies *qua* applicable law unless foreign law is relied upon by one of the parties and proved.[106]

In principle, therefore, it requires clear words to displace the general rule that the parties are free to choose the *lex fori* by not pleading any other. Part III of the 1995 Act contains none. The principal implementing provision of the Act is not peremptory in its terms and does not provide, as might have been expected, that its choice of law rules 'shall' apply.[107] Moreover, so far from displacing the traditional English approach, whereby the introduction of foreign law is optional, the 1995 Act appears to preserve it. Section 14(4) provides that the Act takes effect without prejudice to any rule which modifies, or applies notwithstanding, its provisions. Arguably, this preserves the normal rule that the parties are generally at liberty to apply English law in disputes having a foreign element.[108]

Again, the deliberately limited scope of the reforms brought about by the 1995 Act is confirmed by the terms of section 14(2). This provides that nothing in the Act shall affect any rules of law (including those of private international law) save those which are expressly stated to be abolished.

---

[105] North, above n. 22, 189–190.
[106] See below, p. 184; see further, Ehrenzweig, (1960) 58 *Mich L Rev* 637, 678–679.
[107] Section 9(1).
[108] Or, if preferred, the rule that the *lex fori* governs in the absence of any contrary rule.

The consequence is that only the rule of double actionability and its exceptions are affected. As such, any rule to the effect that the introduction of foreign law is generally at the parties' motion is presumably preserved.

Support for this view might also be derived from section 14(3)(b), which expressly preserves from the scope of the Act 'any rules of evidence, pleading or practice'. Some care must be taken with this argument, because a mere saving of rules of procedure does not by itself meet the argument that the introduction of foreign law is mandatory if that is what an enactment otherwise requires. This is because whether foreign law must be applied—or whether the *lex fori* may be applied instead—is a substantive choice of law question, not a matter of procedure.[109] It is likely, however, that section 14(3)(b) was intended to preserve English law's usual, optional approach to foreign law. Indeed, it is significant that it does not rely on the insecure technique of merely saving rules of procedure from the effects of a choice of law statute. The reference to rules of 'pleading and practice' makes section 14(3)(b) significantly different from, say, Article 1(1)(h) of the 1980 Rome Convention which refers only to saving existing rules of procedure. It means that whether or not the traditional approach to the introduction of foreign law is preserved under the 1995 Act does not turn merely on the controversial question of whether the rules in question are procedural. With this obstacle overcome the reference to 'pleading' in section 14(3)(b) may be understood as an attempt to preserve the usual approach to the introduction of foreign law. It might be taken to include the question whether foreign law must be pleaded. It could also be said legitimately that the usual English 'practice' is that reliance upon the objectively applicable law is not required. Certainly, it is unlikely that the 1995 Act was intended to rob litigants of the freedom not to plead and prove a foreign *lex delicti*.

(b) Pleading at Common Law

It is a truism that litigants never plead foreign law unless they have to. Indeed, more often than not plaintiffs do not initially do so at all. They might prefer to found their claim in English law and wait for the defendant to raise any defence that might be available under foreign law, something the defendant may not choose to do.[110] But there may be an important exception to the principle that the characteristic use of foreign law in England is defensive. Plaintiffs who wish to sue in defamation for

[109] See above, pp. 70–74.
[110] Prominent examples of cases involving foreign torts, in which neither party introduced the *lex loci delicti*, are: *Schneider* v. *Eisovitch* [1960] QB 430; *Winkworth* v. *Hubbard* [1960] 1 WLR 150; *Ichard* v. *Frangoulis* [1977] 1 WLR 1; *McDermid* v. *Nash Dredging and Reclamation Co. Ltd.* [1987] AC 906. Cf. *Camporese* v. *Port Authority of New York and New Jersey*, 415 NYS 2d. 28 (1979).

a libel published abroad might have no choice but to plead and prove foreign law. More accurately, perhaps, whether they are required in law to do so or not, many practitioners assume that reliance on foreign law in such cases is unavoidable. This is not to say that they will necessarily offer evidence concerning that law. Indeed, it is commonly assumed that one who alleges actionability abroad may then rely on the presumption of similarity between English and foreign law, thereby imposing upon the defendant the burden of disproving actionability. But whether this is correct in principle is a matter for the following chapter.[111]

Although English law's choice of law rule has changed for other purposes the familiar, if controversial, rule of double actionability—the rule in *Phillips* v. *Eyre*—remains the basis of the law in defamation proceedings.[112] A claim in defamation is thus unsustainable unless the libel is actionable both in England and in the country where it was published.[113] This is subject to the proviso that non-actionability under either law will be ignored if another country's law has the most significant relationship with the matter.[114] In practice, most disputes are likely to resolve themselves into disputes concerning the ascertainment of the most significantly related law. Indeed, there is a sense in which the applicable law in defamation cases can be viewed simply as that with which the tort is best related. In principle, however, the double-actionability rule is the foundation of the court's response, reference to the most significantly related law being necessary only by way of exception.

In many defamation cases it will be irrelevant to ask whether a plaintiff must plead and prove foreign law. If a claim would fail under English law necessity would compel a plaintiff to proceed under the *lex loci delicti*, or perhaps the law of some third country.[115] But, where a plaintiff hopes to proceed under English law, whether the introduction of foreign law is legally required begs a cluster of questions. Does the basic rule in *Phillips* v. *Eyre* require actionability under the *lex loci delicti* to be pleaded? Does that in turn depend on whether it is a rule of jurisdiction or substance? Whatever the nature of the basic rule, have the exceptions to which it is subject altered its status? The answer to the third question affects our answer to the others. Indeed, it is likely that the transmutation of the tort choice of law into one requiring, in effect, no more than application of the best related law removes any case for according it mandatory status. For, by turning it into, so to speak, a true choice of law rule the reasons for

[111] See below, pp. 143–153.
[112] Private International Law (Miscellaneous Provisions) Act 1995, s. 13.
[113] *Phillips* v. *Eyre* (1870) LR 6 QB 1.
[114] *Boys* v. *Chaplin* [1971] AC 356 (HL); *Red Sea Insurance Co. Ltd.* v. *Bouygues SA* [1994] 3 WLR 926 (PC).
[115] Whether a law other than the *lex loci delicti* or the *lex fori* may apply remains controversial: Cheshire and North, 548.

treating the rule in tort as special, which depend on the structure and language of the double actionability rule, simply fall away. As such the first and second questions are to some extent of academic interest. Certainly, it is hard to see how a plaintiff can be under a duty to plead actionability under the *lex loci delicti* if its case is that English law applies, being that with which the wrong has the most significant relationship.

But the status of *Phillips v. Eyre* is not, even now, entirely irrelevant. Suppose that a claimant resolves not to allege that English law applies by way of exception to the second limb of the traditional test, seeing it perhaps as an impossible task on the facts of the case. Suppose, again, that a plaintiff has done so but has failed to establish that the second limb should not govern. Such situations fall squarely within the double actionability rule in its unadulterated form. In such cases the long-standing debate as to the rule's mandatory status remains alive. Moreover, even allowing that the second limb of the traditional test may be disapplied, because English law is the best connected law, the language and design of the *Phillips v. Eyre* rule may bear on how a claimant should put its case. Assuming that it is obligatory to plead actionability under the *lex loci*, this implies that a party who does not do so must demonstrate why not. This implies that such a party might be obliged to allege that English law is the best connected law because only if it does so is it entitled to ignore the *lex loci delicti*.[116] If so, a plaintiff would not be entitled, as is often supposed, merely to proceed under English domestic law and wait for the defendant to argue non-actionability under the *lex loci delicti*. A plaintiff would be under a duty either to plead actionability under the *lex loci delicti* or to allege that English law is that which is most significantly connected with the issue. Indeed, as ever perhaps, the real importance of saying that the introduction of foreign law is obligatory is not that it forces claimants to rely upon foreign law. It is that it obliges them to argue that the applicable law is English.

In such ways the ambiguous status of the double actionability rule is with us still. But there is a surprising lack of unanimity as to whether actionability under foreign law should be pleaded or not.[117] Inspection suggests that the view that such pleading is required may never have been correct. But, even if it was once correct, the grafting of exceptions onto each of its limbs has altered its status. For the principle that non-actionability under the *lex loci delicti* may be ignored if English law is best connected with the matter does not simply augment the basic rule. It

---

[116] It has been doubted that a claimant must formally plead the exception to the second limb of the double actionability test: Collins, (1977) 26 *ICLQ* 480. But it has been said that an appropriate connection with England must be alleged: *Church of Scientology v. Comr. of Police* (1976) SJ 690 (CA); Dicey and Morris, 1515, n. 51.

[117] The leading account is that of Collins, (1977) 26 *ICLQ* 480.

materially changes its nature by removing any absolute requirement that deference should be shown to the *lex loci delicti*. More importantly, the principle that non-actionability under English law may be ignored if another law is more appropriately applied has dramatic consequences. It destroys the role of the basic rule as a qualifying test for the application of English domestic law. But if its function is no longer simply to guard against the inappropriate application of English law it is hard to see what reason of policy justifies a requirement that the *lex loci delicti* should be pleaded.

The proposition that to plead actionability under the *lex loci delicti* is not required is supported by the editors of Dicey and Morris.[118] It is also taken for granted in a substantial number of decisions.[119] The reasons for supporting this view are compelling. Voluntary pleading in libel allows the parties the freedom to choose whether to introduce matters of foreign law which they enjoy in other types of case. In particular, it removes any distinction between defamation and other torts as regards the pleading of foreign law, there being little doubt that such pleading is voluntary in cases under the general statutory rule.[120] Indeed, the principal reason to permit the voluntary pleading of foreign law in defamation cases is simply that there is, on inspection, no strong reason to treat such cases as special, requiring a departure from the normal rule that the law of the forum applies. Again, as we have seen, voluntary pleading in defamation better reflects the present state of the law, whereby the rule in *Phillips* v. *Eyre* has come to represent a component in a fully-fledged choice of law rule leading to the application of the most significantly related law.[121]

Principle apart, it is perhaps unsurprising that plaintiffs in cases involving foreign torts have sometimes been reluctant to plead foreign law, leaving it to the defendant to do so. One reason is that to introduce a foreign element into proceedings in tort was at one time and, to some extent, still is, to raise particularly intractable issues concerned with the nature of the English choice of law rule in such matters.[122] The temptation to proceed under English law, without reference to a case's conflicts implications is thus considerable. Another reason why plaintiffs might benefit from not

---

[118] Dicey and Morris, 1514–1515. For the treatment of the problem in Australia, see Sykes and Pryles, *Private International Law in Australia*, 3rd edn., (1991), 552–554.

[119] e.g. *Machado* v. *Fontes* [1897] 2 QB 231 (CA); *Carr* v. *Fracis Times & Co.* [1902] AC 176, 184; *Buttes Gas and Oil Co.* v. *Hammer (No. 2)* [1975] QB 557, 575 (CA); *Church of Scientology* v. *Comr. of Police* (1976) SJ 690. Dicey and Morris, 1515, n. 51. This view would appear to be supported in Australia: *Lazarus* v. *Deutsche Lufthansa AG* [1985] 1 NSWLR 188 (see (1986) 60 ALJ 304).

[120] Nothing in the Private International Law (Miscellaneous Provisions) Act 1995 suggests otherwise.

[121] See below, p. 105.

[122] The controversy concerning the scope of the leading decisions is considerable; see Cheshire and North, 547–548.

pleading foreign law in defamation cases in that it allows them to shift the burden of proving foreign law to the defendant, who may find it necessary to allege non-actionability abroad. For, as we shall see, it is by no means clear that they may achieve the same result in a situation in which they were required to plead foreign law but failed to prove it.[123]

But, notwithstanding the intuitive appeal of the contrary view, the idea that actionability under the *lex loci delicti* must be pleaded finds favour in the leading precedent book.[124] Perhaps for this reason it appears to be common practice amongst some practitioners. In reality, however, it is hard to justify this view in terms either of authority or principle. Such authority as there is in support of the practice of pleading the *lex loci delicti* is insubstantial, although it has enjoyed inconclusive support in cases in which it has simply been taken for granted.[125] It has been endorsed directly in one English decision, but the comments were made *obiter* and undue reliance should not be placed on them:

... I think that in a case of this kind it is desirable, and indeed it may be essential, strictly speaking, that the statement of claim should allege that the act complained of—negligence in this case—is a wrongful act by the law of the country where the tort was alleged to have been committed.[126]

There were also cases, under the now superseded rule that all torts were subject to the double actionability rule, in which a plaintiff was required to offer cogent evidence as to the *lex loci delicti* in order to obtain an injunction to restrain passing-off in a foreign country.[127] It is unlikely, however, that much support for mandatory pleading in tort can be derived from such decisions. They are made special by their context, in view of the general principle that interlocutory relief will only issue where that is justified by cogent evidence.[128] Moreover, the leading case is one in which foreign law was relied upon but not proved, as distinct from one in which was not pleaded at all.[129] If so, it is unsurprising that the plaintiffs failed to obtain relief in the absence of proper evidence in support of their pleading.[130]

Finally, there is the Scottish decision in *MacKinnon* v. *Iberia Shipping Co.*[131] which seems at first sight to impose upon a plaintiff the obligation to allege (and to prove) actionability under the *lex loci delicti*. Its authority, however, is insecure. There is some uncertainty as to whether the plaintiff

---

[123] See below, pp. 143–153.
[124] Bullen and Leake and Jacob, *Precedents of Pleading*, 13th edn., (London, 1990), 422–423.
[125] e.g. *University of Glasgow* v. *The Economist* [1997] EMLR 495; below, p. 145.
[126] *Yorke* v. *British & Continental Steamship Co. Ltd.* (1945) 79 Lloyd's Rep. 181, 184 (CA), per Du Parcq LJ; see also, *MacKinnon* v. *Iberia Shipping Co.* 1955 SC 20, 33–35.
[127] *Alfred Dunhill Ltd.* v. *Sunoptic SA* [1979] FSR 337 (CA); *Intercontext* v. *Schmidt* [1988] FSR 575.
[128] *Alfred Dunhill Ltd.* v. *Sunoptic SA*, op. cit.   [129] Ibid.
[130] See below, 152.   [131] 1955 SC 20, 33–35.

had pleaded foreign law but had simply failed to prove it,[132] which makes any obligation to prove foreign law comprehensible. The court also relied on the earlier case of *McElroy* v. *McAllister*,[133] one in which the *lex loci delicti* was pleaded but not proved, which stands for the discrete proposition that foreign law must be supported by evidence where it has been pleaded.

Against such a background of authority, which is at best inconclusive and, at worst, no support for mandatory pleading of the *lex loci delicti*, the issue is one of principle. As such, any requirement that a plaintiff must plead and prove the *lex loci* derives from the logic of the double actionability rule, which appears to operate as a qualifying test the purpose of which is to secure the application of English law as the *lex fori*. As such, actionability under the *lex loci delicti* would appear to be a necessary precondition to the application of English law. Immediate, if superficial, support for this view comes from the formula adopted by Willes J in *Phillips* v. *Eyre*,[134] the source of the double actionability test. The requirement of actionability under English law and the *lex loci delicti* was stated in peremptory terms:

> As a general rule, in order to found a suit in England for a wrong alleged to have been committed abroad, two conditions must be fulfilled. First, the wrong must be actionable if committed in England ... Secondly the act must not have been justifiable by the law of the place where it was done.[135]

The view that actionability under the *lex loci delicti* conditions liability under the *lex fori*, implying that the pleading of the *lex loci* is required, might be expressed in one of two ways. First, it might be said that the rule in *Phillips* v. *Eyre* is a rule of jurisdiction. Secondly, it might be called a choice of law rule leading to the application of the *lex fori*. In either event, actionability under the *lex loci delicti* might be seen as a necessary precondition of liability under English law.

That *Phillips* v. *Eyre* is a rule of jurisdiction is a view endorsed in a number of dicta.[136] It is doubtful, however, that it has survived the decision of the House of Lords in *Boys* v. *Chaplin*,[137] still less that of the Privy Council in *Red Sea Insurance Co.* v. *Bouygues*.[138] Famously, *Boys* v. *Chaplin* concerned a defendant's liability in England for a motor accident which occurred abroad. It is regarded as the source of the modern law concerning foreign torts. Although Lord Hodson appears to have thought that for Willes J the rule was jurisdictional,[139] he apparently assumed that the

---

[132] At 33–35.   [133] 1949 SC 110, 118, 124, 137.   [134] (1870) LR 6 QB 1.
[135] At 28–29.
[136] *Boys* v. *Chaplin*, above n. 114, 383 (Lord Donovan), 381 (Lord Guest), 375 (Lord Hodson); cf. Spence (1949) 27 Can B R 661; Yntema (1949) 27 Can BR 116, 119; Sykes and Pryles, above n. 118, 552–554.
[137] Op. cit.   [138] [1994] 3 WLR 926 (PC).   [139] At 375.

effect of *Boys* v. *Chaplin* was to transform it into a choice of law rule.[140] So too, Lord Wilberforce[141] and Lord Pearson[142] clearly regarded the double actionability rule as one going to choice of law. Lord Wilberforce's position was later endorsed expressly by the Court of Appeal[143] and implicitly in a number of cases, including the *Red Sea* case, which have assumed that Lord Wilberforce's speech represents the true ratio of *Boys* v. *Chaplin*.[144]

The prevailing view, therefore, is that the double actionability rule is not jurisdictional. It may be, however, that the issue is not truly whether *Phillips* v. *Eyre* expresses a rule of jurisdiction. If it were, this might not necessarily make the pleading of the *lex loci* obligatory. More importantly, if it were not, this would not necessarily ensure that such pleading is voluntary. Certainly, there is no reason why Willes J's formula should not be seen as a choice of law rule, albeit one which makes actionability under the *lex loci* a precondition of liability under English law. Indeed, it may be that those who have spoken of Willes J's formula as enunciating a jurisdictional rule have either done so somewhat loosely, or have falsely assumed that any rule which conditions the application of the *lex fori* is necessarily jurisdictional.

The question becomes, therefore, whether *Phillips* v. *Eyre*, if a choice of law rule, requires the mandatory pleading of the *lex loci delicti*. This might be supported by its peremptory terms, or by virtue of the rule's character as a test for the application of the *lex fori*. It might be said that the dynamics of double actionability make the pleading of foreign actionability compulsory, the rule working in such a way as to make English domestic law inapplicable unless the wrong is actionable under the *lex loci delicti*. By this account the practice of pleading claims based on foreign torts under English domestic law, and leaving it to the defendant to assert non-actionability, is illegitimate. To assert a claim under English law alone is to beg the question whether English law may apply; whether it is relevant turns on whether the wrong is actionable abroad.

But, however sound this view of *Phillips* v. *Eyre* might be, it is unlikely to have survived the more recent transmutation of the basic rule. Although a controversial decision, it is clear that the decision of the House of Lords in *Boys* v. *Chaplin*[145] introduced an exception to the second limb of the double actionability test. As such, a plaintiff might legitimately escape pleading the *lex loci delicti* by alleging that English law should be applied even if the wrong is not actionable abroad. Again, the decision in *Red Sea Insurance Co.* v. *Bouygues*,[146] although not without its difficulties,

---

[140] Ibid. [141] At 385–387. [142] At 398.
[143] *Coupland* v. *Arabian Gulf Oil Co.* [1983] 1 WLR 1136, 1154.
[144] *Church of Scientology* v. *Comr. of Police*, above n. 116; *Armagas Ltd.* v. *Mundogas SA* [1976] AC 717, 740–741 (HL); *Red Sea Insurance Co.* v. *Bouygues SA*, above n. 114.
[145] Above n. 114. [146] [1994] 3 WLR 926 (PC).

has radically altered the nature of the traditional test, thereby dissolving the case for the mandatory introduction of the *lex loci delicti*. The Privy Council confirmed that the *lex fori*, not merely the *lex loci delicti*, may be displaced in favour of another law if the latter is more significantly related to the issue. In consequence, English law's choice of law rule in tort is no longer one which guarantees that only the *lex fori* may apply, nor is it one in which the *lex loci delicti* is invariably accorded a decisive role. Indeed, the double actionability rule has become after *Red Sea* but a stepping stone to the application of the most significantly related law. Double actionability is formally still required but non-actionability under either the *lex fori* or the *lex loci delicti* may be ignored if the tort is more significantly related with another country. As such, the rule in tort has come to resemble any other choice of law rule and now (in practice) lacks the features which previously made it special.

It is hard to see, therefore, what justifies treating it differently from other such rules in terms of the pleading of foreign law. Certainly, if we ask why a claimant should have to plead and prove the content of the most significantly related law, it is hard to see why a claimant should do so. The significant connection formula contains nothing to suggest this and there is no other indication that the tort choice of law rule should be mandatory. To acquire mandatory status, the language or purpose of a choice of law rule must compel this result. In the absence of such compelling reasons there is no reason to depart from the general principle that claimants are at liberty to proceed under English law in cases involving foreign torts. Indeed, in the absence of such reasons the view that a plaintiff may proceed under English law, leaving it to the defendant to argue the *lex loci delicti* in defence, is sound in policy. It ensures that the court's time is not wasted on an issue which neither party wishes to address, and that a plaintiff need not address matters which the defendant has not raised.

7. MANDATORY PLEADING AND FOREIGN ILLEGALITY

English courts in purely domestic cases have a duty to notice illegality, whether or not the parties have taken the point.[147] There are also circumstances in which they will deny enforcement to an otherwise valid contract which is illegal under foreign law, at least where the issue of illegality has

---

[147] *Holman* v. *Johnson* (1775) Cowp. 34; *Snell* v. *Unity Finance Ltd.* [1964] 2 QB 203 (CA); the same rule extends to statutory invalidity: *Luckett* v. *Wood* (1908) 24 TLR 617; *Phillips* v. *Copping* [1935] 1 KB 21(CA); Jacob, *Fabric of English Civil Justice*, (London, 1987), 9–10; Furmston, Cheshire, Fifoot and Furmston's *Law of Contract*, 12th edn., (London, 1991), 391–392.

been raised by one of the parties.[148] Can these principles be combined such that a court is required, in effect, to enforce foreign laws which might render a transaction illegal? Is one who seeks the enforcement of an affected contract obliged to demonstrate its legality under the relevant foreign law or face dismissal of its claim?

It will often be unnecessary to provide courts with a power to recognize the illegality of an act or instrument under foreign law. Usually it will be to one party's advantage to allege illegality so the issue will be raised unprompted. But in exceptional cases it may be in both parties' interests to disguise a transaction's illegal nature, as when they have both entered into it with the deliberate intention of evading the rules of a foreign country. Or a defendant might consider it has better grounds on which to rest its case. Moreover, cases have occurred where a defendant has raised the question of foreign illegality only on appeal, not having pleaded it formally in the defence. In such a case the significance of any duty the court may have to enforce foreign law is not that the court may introduce the point *ex officio*. It is that the existence of such a duty ensures that no objection can be taken to the point's being raised belatedly.[149] In all such situations it is understandable why a court might decline to enforce the parties' contract. Certainly, the public interest might justify such intervention.

Any judicial power to ensure the legality of a transaction under foreign law might derive from statute or, less clearly, from common law. As Hartley has observed,[150] a statutory judicial power to introduce foreign law *ex officio* exists under the International Monetary Fund Agreement, originally implemented in the United Kingdom by virtue of the Bretton Woods Agreement Act 1945. Article VIII(2)(b) provides:

Exchange contracts which involve the currency of any member and which are contrary to the exchange control regulations of any member maintained or imposed consistently with this agreement shall be unenforceable in the territories of any member.

This provision has been interpreted as conferring a duty on the courts to introduce the issue of foreign illegality *ex officio*. As Lord Diplock said in *U.C.M.* v. *Royal Bank of Canada*:[151]

If in the course of the hearing of an action the court becomes aware that the contract on which a party is suing is one that this country has accepted an international

---

[148] *De Wutz* v. *Hendricks* (1824) Bing. 314 (contract to further rebellion in Crete); *Foster* v. *Driscoll* [1929] 1 KB 470 (CA) (contract to evade US prohibition laws); *Regazzoni* v. *K. C. Sethia (1944) Ltd.* [1958] AC 301 (HL) (contract to supply jute to South Africa in breach of the law of India).

[149] *Batra* v. *Ebrahim* [1982] 2 Lloyd's Rep. 10 (CA); *Sharab* v. *Salfiti*, *The Times*, 13 February 1997 (CA).

[150] (1996) 45 *ICLQ* 272, 288–289.   [151] [1983] AC 168 (HL).

obligation to treat as unenforceable, the court may take the point itself, even though the defendant has not pleaded it, and must refuse to lend its aid to enforce the contract.[152]

The interpretation of Article VIII(2)(B) has received powerful support elsewhere.[153] It is also consistent with a more general principle that an English court may override the parties' wishes, and will give mandatory effect to an international treaty, where to do so is necessary in order to fulfil its purposes.[154] It must be emphasised, however, that the implications of Lord Diplock's position may be less far-reaching than they seem. There appears to be no other statute or treaty in similar terms or, at least, no such statute or treaty which the courts have construed in like fashion. Again, for Article VIII(2)(b), or any like enactment, to have such mandatory effect it would be necessary for the court to be aware both that is provisions imply such a result—which cannot be taken for granted—and of the fact that there may be a risk of an infringement on the facts of the case in hand. This suggests that Article VIII(2)(b) may offer no more than a largely theoretical incursion, of a specialized nature, into the general principle that foreign law must be expressly pleaded.

A still more speculative question, but one with intriguing implications, is whether a court has a general common law power to prevent the enforcement of a contract which is illegal under foreign law. This admits of no ready answer, largely because it is generally unclear what role illegality under foreign law plays in English law. Doubt surrounds both the scope of the common law rules and the extent, if at all, to which they can be accommodated within the 1980 Rome Convention on the Law Applicable to Contractual Obligations.[155]

According to one line of cases an English court will not enforce a contract when it is illegal under foreign law, and both parties were aware of such illegality.[156] The rule, which is founded on international comity, is familiarly revealed in *Regazzoni* v. *Sethia*,[157] where the parties agreed to export jute from India to South Africa in the knowledge that such contracts were illegal in India. The English court refused to enforce the contract, either by way of specific performance or damages. A different situation is

---

[152] At 189.
[153] See *Batra* v. *Ebrahim*, above n. 149, 13, quoted by the Court of Appeal in the *UCM* case, at 241–242.
[154] Cf. the familiar, if rather different decision in *The Hollandia* [1983] AC 565 (HL), in which an agreement to Dutch jurisdiction was overridden because to permit litigation in the Netherlands would undermine the Hague-Visby rules, which were of English law by virtue of the Carriage of Goods by Sea Act 1971.
[155] Cheshire and North, 518–520.
[156] *De Wutz* v. *Hendricks*, above n. 148; *Foster* v. *Driscoll* [1929] 1 KB 470 (CA) (contract to evade US prohibition laws); above n. 148.
[157] Above n. 148.

one in which a contract which was legal at its inception becomes illegal subsequently under the law of the place of performance. In the controversial case of *Ralli Bros.* v. *Compania Naviera Sota y Aznar*[158] a shipowner failed to recover the amount of freight to which it was contractually entitled in respect of goods delivered in Spain. After the contract was made, but before delivery was due, Spanish law imposed a limit on the amount of freight which a shipowner could charge. Freight above the legal limit was irrecoverable in English proceedings because contracts to charge more had become illegal in the place of performance.

These cases bristle with difficulties. Given that in both the contract's governing law was English, would they have been decided differently had it been that of a country other than England?[159] Is *Ralli Brothers* merely an example of the English domestic law of frustration or, like *Regazzoni*, is it based on international public policy?[160] Where, if at all, may such rules be accommodated within the framework of the 1980 Rome Convention?[161] Such questions are pressing but, whatever the position, we may consider what the consequences may be in principle if, as such cases suggest, foreign illegality is relevant to the enforcement of contracts in English proceedings. It may also be permissible to confine discussion to the principle in *Regazzoni* without addressing the implications of *Ralli Brothers*. The status of the latter decision, and its continuing relevance, are controversial.[162] More importantly, the case for requiring the introduction of foreign law is far weaker under *Ralli Brothers* than under *Regazzoni*. As we shall see, this is partly because it is possible to say that the effect of the rule of *Regazzoni* is that illegality under foreign law renders certain contracts illegal under English law.[163] But it seems clear that illegality under the place of performance in *Ralli Brothers* merely makes the contract unenforceable in English proceedings.[164] As Lord Denning has said of a court's duty to police foreign illegality under the IMF Agreement:

If the word 'unenforceable' were used in the strict sense in which an English lawyer uses that word, the Courts could leave it to the parties to decide whether to raise the point, just as they did in the Statute of Frauds.[165]

---

[158] [1920] 2 KB 287 (CA).
[159] Collier, *Conflict of Laws*, 2nd edn., (1994), 211; Dicey and Morris, 1219–1221; but see Cheshire and North, 519.
[160] Some writers insist on a distinction between these situations: Collier, op. cit., 212; Cheshire and North, (11th ed., 1987) (now superseded), at 485–489; others would consolidate them: Morse, above n. 78, 36–30.
[161] In so far as a rule is one of public policy it is preserved by Article 16 of the Convention; in so far as illegality concerns the manner of a contract's performance it may be accommodated within Article 10(2); in so far as it is itself a mandatory rule it may fall under Article 7(2).
[162] Mann, (1937) 18 *BYIL* 107–113; Reynolds, (1992) 108 *LQR* 553.
[163] See below, p. 111.
[164] Rubino-Sammartano and Morse, eds., *Public Policy in Transnational Relationships* (1991), England, 70.   [165] *Batra* v. *Ebrahim*, above n. 149, 13.

Again, the case for insisting on the introduction of foreign law under *Ralli Brothers* is far from compelling by comparison with the case for doing so under *Regazzoni*. The principle in *Regazzoni* is activated only if the parties entered into the contract knowing of its illegality under foreign law.[166] Their whole enterprise is thus tainted with an unlawful purpose in a way which clearly implicates considerations of public policy. By contrast, the parties are innocent of such intentions in a case of supervening illegality under *Ralli Brothers*. Indeed, even if the principle is regarded as one of public policy rather than merely an aspect of the domestic law of frustration, it is arguably the impossibility of performing the contract, rather than the issue of illegality, which is its essence. As such the public interest is not implicated in the same way and there may be no reason not to leave it to a defendant to argue the point at its option.

But a question remains with regard to *Regazzoni*. Is an English court empowered to introduce the matter of a contract's possible illegality under foreign law, although neither party has pleaded it? More precisely, would a claimant who, prompted by the court, is unable to demonstrate the legality of an affected contract suffer dismissal of the claim? An immediate problem concerns the scope of the *Regazzoni* principle. On a strict reading of the cases it might be said that, whether such a judicial power to introduce foreign law exists or not, it is irrelevant except where English law is the disputed contract's governing law, as it was in *Regazzoni*.[167] The mere fact that the principle is undoubtedly one of public policy does not of itself justify its application in other situations, there being a technical distinction between international and domestic rules of public policy.[168] It is, however, commonly supposed that the principle should apply whether or not the contract's governing law is English.[169] Again, there is the matter of how *Regazzoni* might be accommodated within the framework of the 1980 Rome Convention. Presumably, as an aspect of public policy it is accommodated within Article 16.[170] As such it might be deployed so as to exclude application of any law validating a contract illegal abroad. Alternatively, it has been suggested that the *Regazzoni* rule is mandatory in the sense contemplated by Article 7(2).[171]

---

[166] *Toprak v. Finagrain* [1979] 2 Lloyd's Rep. 98 (CA). [167] Above, text to n. 159.
[168] Cf. *Mackender v. Feldia AG* [1967] 2 QB 590, 601.
[169] See material cited above, n. 159.
[170] Article 16 allows displacement of the applicable law if its application 'is manifestly incompatible with the public policy (*"ordre public"*) of the forum'. Arguably, the purpose of Article 16 is to exclude the application of rules which are objectionable to the forum. If so, it might not accommodate the *Regazzoni* principle, which requires deference to a law other than that of the forum, and which ousts the applicable law although it is not itself objectionable: Hartley, above n. 150, 289. See also, Cheshire and North, 504.
[171] Hartley, op. cit., 289.

Party Choice and Foreign Law

Such matters aside, may the courts intervene to apply *Regazzoni* whatever the parties' wishes? Neither *Regazzoni*, nor cases to the same effect,[172] are of assistance because in such cases the issue of illegality was expressly pleaded.[173] But superficially promising support for judicial intervention may derive from the domestic law concerning illegality. Here there is little doubt that a court has a duty to deny enforcement to an illegal and invalid contract even if neither party takes the point.[174] As Scrutton LJ said of a domestic case concerning statutory invalidity:

It is the duty of the Court when asked to give a judgment which is contrary to statute to take the point, although the litigants may not take it.[175]

As Hartley has suggested,[176] the rule in *Regazzoni* may be seen as a rule to the effect that a contract is illegal under English domestic law if it contemplates acts which are illegal elsewhere (provided that the parties exhibit an unlawful purpose). As such it is governed by the principle that a court may always intervene in the public interest to enforce legality under domestic law. It is certainly the case that foreign illegality has been said to render a contract illegal—and not merely contrary to public policy—in English law.[177] It is also common practice to speak of a contract's being 'illegal' in English law 'on grounds of public policy'.[178] But it is unclear what merit there is in treating a contract which is illegal under foreign law as if it were illegal under English law. A less artificial description might be that such contracts are unenforceable in England by virtue of public policy. It is certainly open to objection whether an English court has the same duty to police foreign law as it has with regard to English law. Should a court act of its own motion to enforce foreign law, given that it may clearly do so in connection with domestic law? Granted, *Regazzoni* is itself a rule of English law, in the sense that it is an aspect of English public policy, but this is not enough to attract the power to police illegal contracts *ex officio* which exists in purely domestic cases. Arguably, such a power exists only in so far as an English judge is obliged to give effect to English law. The duty to do so derives from the mandatory character of the English laws in question. Such laws must be enforced because they impose a duty on a court to enforce them. But an English judge, not being subject to foreign law, is not bound to enforce such laws in the same way, however mandatory their application may be in the country concerned.

The suggestion that the enforcement of foreign rules concerning illegality may be equated with the enforcement of domestic rules also encounters further difficulties. The principle that courts may act of their own

---

[172] e.g. *Foster* v. *Driscoll*, above n. 156.
[173] Ibid at 478.
[174] See cases cited above, n. 147.
[175] *Phillips* v. *Copping*, above n. 147, 21.
[176] Op. cit., 289; see Furmston, above n. 147, 367–368.
[177] *Foster* v. *Driscoll*, above n. 156, 510.
[178] Furmston, above n. 147, 367.

motion to police the legality of domestic contracts assumes that a court has judicial notice of such rules as may affect their legality. This is true of such rules when they are English, but it is not the case when they are foreign. This important distinction between the enforcement of English and foreign illegality is reflected also in a more practical consideration. A court's power of intervention in such cases is only meaningful in so far as a judge knows that the acts in question are illegal. This is a legitimate assumption where the enforcement of domestic law is involved but not where foreign law is in question. Indeed, given that a court may not research foreign law *ex officio*,[179] it would be impossible for a court to know of the risk of illegality unless so informed by one of the parties. As such, it is unlikely that a court's power to police illegal contracts can sensibly extend to cases of foreign illegality.

The special case of the IMF Agreement aside, therefore, it is unlikely that English courts are empowered to ensure deference to foreign law, even in cases such as *Regazzoni*. Indeed the very lack of decisive authority on such an important matter may itself argue against such a proposition or, at least, against its practical importance. Certainly, there is insufficient evidence to rebut the presumption that conflicts rules are generally not mandatory, such that the *lex fori* normally applies.

This conclusion is supported by the decision of the Court of Appeal in *Sharab* v. *Salfiti*.[180] The case concerned an action for remuneration under a contract for services which was governed by English law, but which was to be performed in Libya. No question of Libyan law was raised at trial but on appeal the defendant sought leave to adduce evidence that the contract was illegal *ab initio* under that law. It was argued that comity obliged an English court to 'take notice of the fact . . . that performance of a contract is contrary to a foreign law'.[181] But this view was rejected and leave to amend was denied. Waller LJ, with whom Nourse LJ agreed, recognized that 'there might conceivably be circumstances where the Court of Appeal itself takes for the first time a point on English public policy which might lead to an inquiry as to the position under a foreign law'.[182] But his reasoning leaves a court little room, if any, to exercise such a power. He emphasised that it was difficult to contemplate when a party should be allowed to amend its case by alleging foreign illegality, given the serious implications of such an allegation upon the other party and the fact that such a party might have done so before. But, most significantly, he confirmed that an allegation of foreign illegality 'must be pleaded and proved like any other aspect of the case'.[183] For all practical purposes, it seems, foreign illegality is no different from any other aspect of foreign law.

But, in reality, cases resembling *Sharab* v. *Salfiti* will be rare. Indeed, except

---

[179] See below, p. 189.   [180] Above n. 149.   [181] Ibid.   [182] Ibid.
[183] Ibid. Nourse LJ also found that the plaintiff had, in fact, acted lawfully.

where leave to adduce fresh evidence is sought, it is hard to see how they could arise. Not least, this is because they would have to be cases in which, for some reason, it was in neither party's interest to take the issue of illegality unprompted. It is also improbable that a court would even be aware that it might possess such a power unless one of the parties drew it to its attention. But a party who did so would presumably have pleaded the foreign illegality anyway, in which case the question of the court's *ex officio* power would be irrelevant. Again, it would be relatively easy for the parties to disable any power the court might have simply by framing their submissions with care, such that the court is unaware of the risk of infraction. Most importantly, perhaps, the suggestion that a court might police foreign illegality *ex officio* encounters a logical objection. It assumes that a court will already be aware that the act in question is illegal under foreign law. But how can this be so? It is one thing for a choice of law rule to be mandatory, such that a claimant is obliged to plead and prove the content of foreign law, whatever that may be. But how can the duty to plead and prove foreign law itself be contingent on the fact that foreign law is to a particular effect? Furthermore, it must be recalled that the operation of the *Regazzoni* principle requires not only that the contract in question is illegal, but that the parties should have known of the fact. How is a court to be aware of such a wrongful purpose unless the relevant facts are already before it? In the end, the possibility that an English court might introduce the issue of illegality under foreign law may be of little importance. Statute aside, there is little support for such a power, none of it direct. And, even if such a power exists, under statute or otherwise, it is hard to see how it would operate in practice.

8. MANDATORY PLEADING AND PERSONAL STATUS

Do considerations of policy make the principle of voluntary pleading inappropriate in cases concerning personal status, typically where the validity of marriage is concerned?[184] Even those countries, such as France, which otherwise adopt a voluntary approach to foreign law insist that the principle is inapplicable where the parties purport to waive the law applicable to capacity or status by omitting to introduce foreign law.[185]

---

[184] In *Male* v. *Roberts* (1799) 3 Esp. 163, Lord Eldon held that proof of Scots law was required in a case concerning contractual capacity, dismissing the case for lack of such evidence. As Westlake implies, this may be treated as a case concerning status not contract: *Private International Law* (1858), 383.

[185] Cass. civ. 4 dec. 1990, *Clunet* 1991.371, note Bureau; *Rev. crit. dr. int. pr.* 1991.558, note Niboyet-Hoegy; Lagarde, *Rev. crit. dr. int. pr.* 1994 332, 337; Hartley, (1996) 45 *ICLQ* 271, 279–280.

Indeed, at first sight, it is English law's lack of a clear rule which renders rights in personal status indefeasible which most obviously distinguishes it from many continental approaches to foreign law.[186]

(a) Principle, Policy and Authority

There are compelling reasons for insisting that a case involving matrimonial relief should be determined under any foreign law which, objectively judged, governs the marriage's validity, especially where the interests of children may be implicated. In undefended divorce proceedings it may seem wrong, for example, to allow a petitioner to dissolve a marriage which does not exist. And in nullity proceedings it may be inappropriate for a petitioner to annul a marriage which is invalid in England but valid under its foreign applicable law.[187] Several technical arguments also support the mandatory introduction of foreign law in matters affecting marital status. First, it reflects the principle in purely domestic proceedings that matrimonial relief is predicated upon the existence of a valid marriage which, accordingly, must be proved.[188] Unexceptionally, an English court's power to dissolve a marriage on a petition for divorce assumes the marriage's existence.[189] Secondly, Rule 10.14 of the Family Proceedings Rules 1991 might imply a duty to prove a foreign marriage.[190] This provides that proof of the celebration of a marriage outside England and Wales may be effected, where the marriage's validity is uncontested, simply by the evidence of one of the parties, accompanied by official documentary evidence. Does the fact that the rule applies in uncontested cases mean that a petitioner must always prove a foreign marriage, whether the other party takes exception or not?[191] Thirdly, there are certainly cases in which the court and the parties have assumed that mandatory pleading is required, generally where proof of marriage under foreign law is assumed to be a precondition to matrimonial relief where the marriage is abroad.[192]

---

[186] See below, p. 271.
[187] The true nature of the choice of law rule—or rules—which in English private international law govern marriages with a foreign element is a vexed question: North, [1970] 1 Hague Recueil 9, 59 ff. It is clear, however, that the formal validity of a marriage is governed by the *lex loci celebrationis; Berthiaume* v. *Dastous* [1930] AC 79. It is also clear that divorce petitions are governed by English law, no choice of law questions arising in such cases: *Zanelli* v. *Zanelli* (1948) TLR 556 (CA). Choice of law questions arise in matrimonial proceedings either when, in divorce proceedings, the marriage's existence is in issue, or in nullity proceedings where its validity is in question.
[188] Family Proceedings Rules 1991, rule 2.6(2); *Rayden and Jackson's Law and Practice in Divorce and Family Matters*, 16th edn. (London, 1991), Ch. 20.
[189] Kahn-Freund, *General Problems of Private International Law*, 2nd edn., (1976), 115.
[190] Hartley, above n. 185, 286; Dicey and Morris, 655–661.
[191] Hartley, op. cit., 286.
[192] *Cooper-King* v. *Cooper-King* [1990] P 65; *Wilson* v. *Wilson* [1903] P 157; *Bater* v. *Bater* [1907] P 333; *Westlake* v. *Westlake* [1910] P 167; *Henaff* v. *Henaff* [1966] 1 WLR 598.

Fourthly, English law does not generally allow petitioners for matrimonial relief to rest their case on omissions in the respondent's argument. Grounds for relief must be positively made out.[193]

Such arguments have been strongly supported by some commentators.[194] None, however, is necessarily decisive. By itself the principle that matrimonial relief assumes proof of marriage ordains no such result. This is because, if proof of a foreign marriage is not tendered, there is no reason in principle why a court should not simply assume, in accordance with general principle, that English domestic law applies by default in the absence of another.[195] If so, a foreign marriage would be treated as valid, provided it would be valid under English law. In such a case the marriage would be proved, albeit not under the *lex loci celebrationis*. Again, Rule 10.14 is far from clear in its implications. Certainly, the fact that it is limited to cases where a marriage's validity is undisputed is not decisive. It is nonetheless possible to make sense of the rule even if the mandatory introduction of foreign law is not required. It is entirely comprehensible, for example, that a petitioner in uncontested proceedings might rely on the existence of a marriage which would be invalid under English law but valid under foreign law. If so, there is need for a provision such as Rule 10.14, offering a ready means to prove the marriage under foreign law, since it would be fruitless to rely on a presumption of similarity between foreign law and English law. Nor is it decisive that petitioners have a general duty to establish their case positively. Indeed, the existence of such a duty merely begs the question, for it cannot presumably extend to matters upon which a petitioner is under no obligation to rely.

(b) A Narrow Rule

It is apparent, whatever its scope, that the introduction of foreign law is not a universal rule in status cases. It has generally been required only when the formal validity of marriages celebrated abroad is involved, typically in matrimonial proceedings in which a petitioner has to prove the marriage's existence.[196] It is not clear how much should be read into such cases, however, which may not be truly hostile to the principle of voluntary pleading. Indeed, if a marriage is celebrated in a foreign country it is perhaps inevitable that only that country's law will govern. English law could not apply by default in such circumstances under the usual presumption that it should, the English rules concerning form applying only to marriages celebrated in England.[197] In such circumstances a petitioner

---

[193] Matrimonial Causes Act 1973, s. 1(3).
[194] Fleming, (1951) 25 *ALJ* 406; Kahn, (1970) 87 *SALJ* 145, 148; Leslie, (1990) *JLSS* 475; Hartley, above n. 185, 286–287. But see, Donovan, (1951) 25 *ALJ* 165, 167.
[195] See above, p. 75. [196] See cases cited above, n. 192. [197] Marriage Act 1949, Preamble.

would have to rely on foreign law or face certain defeat. And a court, anxious to ensure the marriage's existence as a prelude to its dissolution has no choice but to require the introduction of foreign law.

Again, in exercising its jurisdiction to grant relief, a court is not concerned with whether a marriage is in all respects valid, but only with whether a marriage prima facie exists. Where it is celebrated abroad this requires evidence of the fact of the ceremony and of its status as a marriage in the country concerned. The effect of the distinction is that a petitioner in divorce proceedings must prove a marriage's prima facie existence, but it is for the respondent to raise issues affecting, say, capacity and consent. It may be necessary, therefore, to establish a marriage's formal validity as a precondition for obtaining matrimonial relief. This does not, however, impose as much of an evidential burden upon petitioners as might appear. Depending on the circumstances, minimal evidence of the marriage's formal validity is acceptable, often amounting to no more than a copy of a certificate and the evidence of one of the parties.[198] Indeed, although technically correct, it may be something of a misnomer to say that foreign law must be pleaded and proved in such a case. In effect, all that occurs in connection with foreign marriages is that a foreign marriage certificate must be produced as evidence that a marriage has taken place. This is very far removed from any requirement that a marriage's validity must be conclusively established.

Nor does the proof of foreign marriage necessarily even require the production of evidence in all cases. There is a rebuttable common law presumption that a marriage is valid if a ceremony has occurred and the parties have cohabited as man and wife.[199] The effect of the presumption is that one who relies on a marriage's existence need not prove the fact under foreign law, the burden being on the other party. This may not absolve the former from having to prove that such a marriage is in principle capable of being a valid marriage under the *lex loci celebrationis*.[200] But, that apart, it renders it unnecessary to prove formal validity under that law.[201]

Cases where a marriage's formal validity must be proved to establish a court's power to grant matrimonial relief should be distinguished from those in which matters of essential validity arise in nullity proceedings. In nullity proceedings involving lack of consent and physical incapacity, it is common practice for English courts to apply English law without demur

---

[198] Family Proceedings Rules 1991, Rule 10.14; below, p. 227.
[199] *Spivack* v. *Spivack* (1930) 46 TLR 243; *Russell* v. *Att.-Gen.* [1949] P 391; *Mahadervan* v. *Mahadervan* [1964] P 233; *Radwan* v. *Radwan* (No. 2) [1973] Fam 35. Where the validity of a foreign marriage is not contested it may be proved under Rule 10.14 of the Family Proceedings Rules. Proof of a foreign marriage need not involve expert evidence: below, p. 226.
[200] *Kalinowska* v. *Kalinowski* (1964) 108 SJ 260.   [201] Cases cited above, n. 199.

where neither party—or the petitioner in uncontested proceedings—has suggested otherwise, even in situations having the clearest foreign elements.[202] True, such cases might support the view that English law as the *lex fori* should govern such aspects of marital invalidity,[203] removing their value as authorities on voluntary pleading. It is difficult, however, to read so much into the reasoning they employed, an omission to plead foreign law rather than a positive choice of English law being at the root of such decisions. Such cases might, alternatively, have been decided *per incuriam*, weakening their status for any proposition.[204] It is hard, however, to avoid the conclusion that they are clear examples of English courts failing to object to the non-introduction of foreign law in cases in which it might have been relevant.

Another well-known case involving the essential validity of marriage which is hostile to mandatory pleading being required is *Szechter* v. *Szechter*,[205] a case involving the existence of consent to marry. Discussing the expert evidence as to Polish law there is no doubt that Sir Jocelyn Simon P assumed that the normal principle applied whereby if 'a party adduces no evidence, or insufficient evidence, of the proper foreign law, the court perforce looks to English law'.[206] The status of these remarks may be weakened in this context by the fact that Polish law and English were to the same effect. But it is apparent that had proof of foreign law failed—or had it not been offered—English law would have applied.

Final evidence that the introduction of foreign law is not required where marital status is in issue derives from a pair of cases concerning the characterization of foreign marriage. In *De Reneville* v. *De Reneville*[207] the question arose as to the court's jurisdiction in defended nullity proceedings, an issue which turned finally on whether the marriage was void or voidable. Although the petitioner's pre-nuptial domicile was French, and the place of celebration and the matrimonial home was in France, French law had not been pleaded or proved. The Court of Appeal itself raised the relevance of foreign law in argument but agreed with counsel that, rather than seek evidence as to foreign law, the case should proceed without it.[208] Although clearly concerned that they were being asked to adjudicate on a basis which they knew to be wrong, the court stopped short of adjourning proceedings or directing that French law should be introduced. They assumed that the presumption of similarity would allow them to decide the case under English law,[209] and that it was, in principle, for the

---

[202] *Easterbrook* v. *Easterbrook* [1944] 1 All ER 90; *Hutter* v. *Hutter* [1944] P 95; *Buckland* v. *Buckland* [1968] P 296; see also, *Prawdziclazarska* v. *Prawdziclazarski* 1954 SC 98, 102.

[203] Cheshire and North, 645, where the authors describe such an interpretation of the cases as 'in truth, an abdication of the problem'.

[204] Ibid.   [205] [1971] P 286.   [206] At 296.   [207] [1948] P 100 (CA).
[208] At 108.   [209] At 108.

petitioner, not for the court, to seek to have the issue of foreign law remitted to the trial judge for determination.[210] Indeed, they implicitly rejected any suggestion that the case should be decided on its proper basis by ruling that the petitioner should not, in the circumstances, have that option.[211] To reopen the case would be inconvenient and potentially unfair to the defendant. It would also be undesirable as, for all its defects, the court had ruled in the parties' dispute and it was better that they should act accordingly, rather than have the case resolved correctly. *Casey v. Casey*,[212] decided by the Court of Appeal shortly afterwards, is to similar effect. Although concerned with jurisdiction in undefended nullity proceedings, no reference had been made to the Canadian law of the husband's domicile. Apparently on his own initiative Bucknill LJ referred to Canadian cases cited in Cheshire's *Private International Law* but in the end applied English law because no point of Canadian law had been taken.[213]

(c) An Indistinct Principle

It appears that the mandatory introduction of foreign law is only required in a somewhat minimal sense as a prerequisite of obtaining matrimonial relief in respect of marriages celebrated abroad. Principle requires that the marriage's prima facie existence be proved in such cases. In so far as this involves confirmation that a valid marriage has occurred in the place of celebration its formal validity under the *lex loci celebrationis* must be established. There is, however, no general obligation to plead foreign law in cases affecting status whenever an issue is governed by foreign law. Nor, given the available means of proving foreign marriage, is the obligation to prove foreign law an especially onerous one, expert evidence being unnecessary save where foreign law is contested.[214] The effect is that a petitioner for matrimonial relief is required to prove the marriage by establishing its formal validity. This does not mean, however, where the marriage has been proved, that a petitioner need rely on foreign law to question the marriage's validity on other grounds. If, for example, in nullity proceedings, a marriage would be invalid under English law but valid under the relevant *lex causae*, as objectively determined, the petitioner may rely on English law. It is for the respondent to contest the proceedings and allege validity under foreign law.

As this suggests, to the extent that English law requires mandatory pleading in status cases, it does not do so because of any desire to protect rights in personal status in the interests of public policy. Nor is it because

---

[210] At 123. [211] At 124.
[212] [1949] P 240. Bucknill and Somervell LJJ sat also in *De Reneville*. [213] At 430–431.
[214] Family Proceedings Rules, Rule 10.14; Dicey and Morris, 655–663.

the *lex loci celebrationis* is objectively the law applicable to a ceremony's validity. Rather it is because proof of even foreign marriages is necessary as a precondition for matrimonial relief. This requires proof of foreign law, however, only because the presumption of similarity cannot assist, English formalities being inapplicable to marriages celebrated abroad.

(d) English Law in Context

It may not be as surprising as initially appears that English law has no general rule requiring foreign law to be pleaded in status cases. One explanation is that the context in which the English law of status operates may not always make it necessary—as in some countries it may be necessary—to require the introduction of foreign law. In contrast with other jurisdictions, English law often applies the *lex fori* to matters concerning marriage and children, notably in connection with divorce, reducing the number of situations in which the matter becomes an issue.[215] Again, English law does not possess the sophisticated taxonomy of legal rules which, in many systems, underwrites the concept of indefeasible rights by distinguishing between those affecting private interests (which may be waived), and those expressing a public interest (which may not be waived).[216] Most importantly, English law lacks the concept of unwaivable 'non-patrimonial' rights on which the mandatory pleading of foreign law in status cases may depend. In several civil law jurisdictions[217] it is this principle—perhaps, only this principle—which requires foreign law to be introduced in cases involving personal status.[218]

To the limited extent that English law requires mandatory pleading in status cases this is sanctioned by general principle. Certainly, an English court lacks jurisdiction to grant matrimonial relief unless the marriage is subsisting.[219] If issues affecting jurisdiction are mandatory it might thus be necessary to establish a marriage's validity under foreign law. More concretely, it is clear that proof of marriage is a pre-requisite for obtaining matrimonial relief, a requirement founded in logic—how can a court, say, in divorce proceedings dissolve what does not exist?[220] Such logic applies as much where the marriage was celebrated abroad. Indeed, were the requirement not to extend to foreign marriages, requiring production of a foreign certificate, the consequence would be dramatic. Because the English rules concerning proof of formal validity cannot, in terms, apply to

---

[215] Morris, 41.   [216] Above n. 77.
[217] The concept of unwaivable personal rights in private international law, embracing rights in status, exists in different forms in several legal systems; see below, p. 272.
[218] See, as to French law, *Cass. civ.* 4 dec. 1990, *Clunet* 1991.371, note Bureau; *Rev. crit. dr. int. pr.* 1991.558, note Niboyet-Hoegy; Lagarde, *Rev. crit. dr. int. pr.* 1994.332, 337.
[219] Kahn-Freund, above n. 189, 115.
[220] See, e.g., *Perrini* v. *Perrini* [1979] Fam 84, 92; *Lawrence* v. *Lawrence* [1985] Fam 106, 140.

foreign marriages an English court would, in principle, be forced to assume that all foreign marriages are formally invalid—unless evidence were tendered of validity under the *lex loci celebrationis*.

English law does not, therefore, possess the conceptual substructure which in other systems requires the introduction of foreign laws in all cases affecting status. Principle might, however, ordain it in the limited circumstances in which it is apparently required in English law. Moreover, absent any principles which invariably compel it, it is unclear whether the mandatory introduction of foreign law is actually necessary in order to protect those whose interests are implicated in cases involving status. Suppose, for example, that a marriage is invalid by English law but valid in the *lex loci celebrationis*. In contested proceedings, it is inconceivable that anyone relying on the marriage would omit to plead foreign law and so face certain defeat. And, in undefended proceedings, a court is unlikely to strive to uphold a marriage it knows to be invalid under English law. By thus abstaining it is merely respecting what is, in truth, an aspect of English public policy.[221] It may be, of course, that a claimant wishes the marriage to be invalid in such a situation, as when annulment is sought. If so, it might seem unacceptable to allow a valid marriage to be destroyed by a trick of pleading. In reality, however, a respondent has a remedy in such a case; he or she can always contest the proceedings and introduce foreign law.

Alternatively, what if a marriage would be valid in England but invalid abroad? Is it possible to turn an otherwise invalid union into a valid one by an omission to plead? One answer (again) is that the other party may prevent this from occurring simply by contesting the proceedings and pleading validity under foreign law. As such, there is no unfairness involved if a respondent fails to take the point because he or she had the opportunity to do so. Another answer is that, although an English court would, in a sense, be countenancing an incorrect result where foreign invalidity is not pleaded, this is at least consistent with the traditional view that a marriage is presumed valid unless the contrary is established.[222]

But, in the end, how we view the voluntary introduction of foreign law in matrimonial proceedings may depend on our perspective. Lawyers experienced in domestic family law will doubtless resist the conclusion that someone's personal status can ever depend on rules of pleading, or on a person's willingness or ability to defend proceedings. They will point to the relatively interventionist approach of the courts in domestic matrimo-

---

[221] Cf. Hartley (1972) 35 *MLR* 571, 577.
[222] *Radwan* v. *Radwan* (No. 2), above n. 192. But contrast *Kalinowska* v. *Kalinowski* (1964) 108 SJ 260. Apart from cases illustrating the formal presumption of marriage, English courts favour treating marriages as valid: *Perrini* v. *Perrini* [1979] Fam 84, 92; *Lawrence* v. *Lawrence* [1985] Fam 106, 140.

nial matters, especially where the position of children is involved. And they will be concerned that, if the introduction of foreign law is optional for petitioners in such cases, the effect is that the respondent must bear the cost of identifying and proving foreign law. But private international lawyers, if no less mindful of these consequences, may accept them more readily. They will recognize how frequently the *lex fori* governs matrimonial matters in English law, which makes the effect of not pleading foreign law seem more natural. They will be keenly aware of the expense and delay involved in proving foreign law and the desirability of giving the parties a choice whether this should be undertaken. They will also be familiar with the marked tendency of English private international law in this area to allow the parties to a marriage to select (if indirectly) the law which should govern it. Some commentators certainly assume that persons should not, in principle, be allowed to affect their status by choice.[223] But English law is less committed than might be supposed to the idea that, say, a marriage, is invariably subject to an objectively determined governing law, the rules of which may never be evaded.[224]

Conflicts lawyers will also know how difficult it is to identify the law applicable to a marriage. Indeed it is singularly difficult even to know by what rules that law is to be identified, for few matters are more controversial in the English conflict of laws than choice of law in marriage.[225] Those familiar with the area will certainly be puzzled by the assumption that, in a given case, there may be a single law which objectively governs but for a petitioner's omission to plead it. It is, in particular, hard to see how a claimant might be accused of 'fraud on the court'[226] by omitting to plead foreign law when, given the uncertainty of the relevant conflicts rules, it may be unclear whether foreign law applies at all. Finally, conflicts lawyers will see how undesirable it would be to require, say, a petitioner in undefended proceedings both to identify the governing law and establish its content. For how can this be done with any guarantee of accuracy unless the other party is present to offer counter arguments and contrary evidence? Again, why should the law favour a respondent by placing the burden of identifying and establishing foreign law upon the petitioner, to the tactical advantage of the former? Certainly, injustice might be done to any petitioner who is prevented from seeking relief by the prohibitive expense of having to argue under foreign law. As these observations suggest, it may be far from ideal that the law should allow the relevance of foreign law to be ignored in cases of personal status. But, however uncomfortable this state of affairs, is any other solution either practical or clearly preferable?

---

[223] See, e.g., Anton, *Private International Law*, 2nd edn., (Edinburgh, 1990), 418–419.
[224] See generally, North, above n. 189, 173–179.
[225] Ibid.   [226] Fleming, above n. 194, 406; Kahn, above n. 187, 148.

(e) Conclusion

Whatever its merits, the position of English law is relatively clear. English law apparently only requires the proof of foreign law where matrimonial relief is sought and a foreign marriage must be proved. It is not, however, necessary to establish the marriage's validity in such a case, merely to offer evidence that it took place. Indeed, for that reason, the requirement that foreign marriages must be proved is a somewhat meagre exception to the principle of voluntary pleading. Beyond cases where a foreign marriage must be proved to ground a petition for matrimonial relief, it is unlikely that the introduction of foreign marriage laws is required. At best, the law is uncertain, such uncertainty itself implying that there is no general rule requiring the proof of foreign law in cases involving personal status.

9. MANDATORY REQUIREMENTS OF JURISDICTION

It is self-evident that a plaintiff who would proceed in the English courts must comply with the legal pre-conditions of jurisdiction. This is not a peculiarity of such rules. Any rule can be mandatory, while rules of jurisdiction need not have this effect. But if any doubt should arise concerning the interpretation or application of the requirements of jurisdiction it is reasonable to suppose that they should be strictly interpreted and enforced, such is the importance of accuracy in such matters. A court which operates beyond its jurisdiction is not merely in error but is acting *ultra vires*. An English court also has an inherent power to preserve its character as a court of justice, which presumably involves ensuring its competence to act.[227] There is also, at least for some purposes within the 1968 Brussels Convention, an affirmative duty upon a court to police its own jurisdiction.[228] Certainly, the Convention assumes that a court has at least a discretionary power to do so.[229] Such considerations suggest that a court's competence cannot always be a matter simply for the parties to determine in framing their submissions. No doubt for such reasons it is sometimes supposed that English law should not be applied by default when a rule which refers to foreign law is characterized as jurisdictional. The requirement in defamation proceedings that publication should be actionable in the place where it occurs has been viewed in this way. It is sometimes assumed that whether a plaintiff must plead and prove action-

---

[227] Jacob, *The Fabric of Civil Justice*, (London, 1987), 60 ff.
[228] Article 20, para. 1.
[229] *Effer* v. *Kantner* [1982] ECR 825.

ability abroad turns on whether the requirement is one of jurisdiction.[230] But, as we shall see, it is unclear why legal rules should acquire mandatory status merely because they are rules of jurisdiction. The true test, as always, is whether, in its terms or by implication, a particular rule requires the application of foreign law. It is not a matter of classification but of construction.

Sometimes it is relatively certain that reference must be made to foreign law in order to confer competence upon a court. Matrimonial relief depends, for example, upon the existence of a valid marriage, which may in turn require evidence of foreign law if the marriage was celebrated abroad.[231] Similarly, a foreign corporation cannot sue or be sued unless its corporate status is established, which may involve the proof of foreign law.[232] Such cases are relatively straightforward because they involve specific rules which directly require the application of foreign law. But not all rules of jurisdiction are so clear in their effect. Particular doubt arises when the process of determining jurisdiction implicates the normal rules for choice of law. Is it appropriate to apply English law by default in a situation where the status of some foreign act or event, on which jurisdiction depends, involves applying foreign law? Suppose that a disputed contract is governed by foreign law. Must a plaintiff affirmatively demonstrate that the contract exists under that law so as to secure jurisdiction under Article 5(1) of the 1968 Brussels Convention, or under RSC Order 11, rules 1(1)(d) and (e)? The former confers jurisdiction upon the courts of the place where a contract is to be performed but only in matters relating to contract. The latter allow service of process over defendants overseas on a number of grounds where the claim is in contract. Similarly, must foreign law be applied in order to establish the validity of a jurisdiction agreement for the purposes of Article 17 of the Convention, or of a tenancy agreement for the purposes of Article 16(1)? Again, is it necessary that a tort be actionable under its applicable law for the purposes of those jurisdictional provisions which relate to claims in tort?[233]

Sometimes the problem in such cases is not whether the application of foreign law is mandatory in the jurisdictional context, but whether the rules for choice of law are even relevant. It is certainly possible that, say, the existence of a contractual agreement might depend in such cases on applying the internal law of the forum or, in the case of the Brussels Convention, some *sui generis*, community requirement of consensus. Which view to take can be controversial. It has been said, for example, that whether an action lies in tort, such that RSC Order 11, rule 1(1)(f) applies,

---

[230] *Walker* v. *W A Pickles Pty. Ltd.* [1980] 2 NSWLR 28; *Lazarus* v. *Deutsche Lufthansa AG* [1985] 1 NSWLR 188; Sykes and Pryles, *Australian Private International Law*, 3rd edn, (1991), 277; above, p. 104.
[231] Above, p. 114.   [232] Below, p. 230.   [233] Article 5(3); RSC Order 11, r. 1(1)(f).

must be referred to the rules for choice of law in tort.[234] Whether the rule is activated depends upon whether such an action lies under the relevant applicable law. Similarly, it is often assumed for the purposes of Article 17 of the Brussels Convention, that the validity of a jurisdiction agreement must be tested by reference to the conflicts rules of the forum.[235] But neither of these propositions is free from doubt. Arguably, RSC Order 11, rule 1(1)(f) is activated merely if a claim can be properly pleaded under English law, no conflicts question arising in such a case.[236] It has also been suggested in connection with Article 17 that whether a jurisdiction agreement is valid is a matter for the internal law of the forum, not for the relevant rules of private international law.[237]

But the relevance of the rules of private international is not always so obscure. It is clear, for example, that the validity of a jurisdiction agreement for the purposes of RSC Order 11 depends upon the law applicable to the contract of which it is part.[238] So does the validity of a contract where this arises in jurisdictional proceedings.[239] It is also apparent that a contract's applicable law must be applied to ascertain the place where a defaulting party's obligation is to be performed for the purposes of Article 5(1) of the Brussels Convention.[240]

In so far as reference must sometimes be made to the rules for choice of law rules in a jurisdictional context, principle suggests two reasons why this might not by itself render the application of foreign law obligatory. First, even if we accept that a court's jurisdiction must be positively established, this does not by itself compel the application of foreign law. A plaintiff's failure to plead and prove foreign law in this context does not mean that a court's jurisdiction has not been determined. It means only that it has been determined under English law rather than foreign law. For that reason is merely begs the question to point, for example, to the principle that the existence of a contract must be established in order to succeed in a claim under RSC Order 11, rule 1(1)(e).[241] Even if that is so, the

---

[234] *Metall und Rohstoff AG* v. *Donaldson Lufkin & Jenerette Inc.* [1990] 1 QB 391(CA). It is unclear how far the court was influenced by the possibility that the rule requiring the 'double actionability' of foreign torts is sometimes supposed to be mandatory; see, above, p. 103.

[235] Hartley, *Collected Courses of the Academy of European Law*, vol. V. Book 1 (1996), 252.

[236] Collier, 'Conflict of Laws', *All England Law Reports Annual Review 1989*, 53–54; Carter, (1989) *BYIL* 489.

[237] Cheshire and North, 316. Cf. the views expressed by Advocate-General Slynn in *Elefanten Schuh* v. *Jacqmain* [1981] ECR 1671, 1697–1699 (ECJ).

[238] *The Iran Vojdan* [1984] 2 Lloyd's Rep. 380; *The Frank Pais* [1986] 1 Lloyd's Rep. 529.

[239] 1980 Rome Convention on the Law Applicable to Contractual Obligations, Article 8(1). Previously the question whether a contract existed for the purposes of determining the effect of a jurisdiction agreement was regarded as a matter of English internal law: *Mackender* v. *Feldia AG* [1967] 2 QB 590, 598–599, 602–603 (CA).

[240] *Tessili* v. *Dunlop* [1976] ECR 1471 (ECJ).

[241] *The Parouth* [1982] 2 Lloyd's Rep. 351 (CA); *Seasconsar Far East Ltd.* v. *Bank Markazi Jomhouri Islami Iran*, [1994] 1 AC 438 (HL).

problem is whether it may be established by default under English law. Secondly, although the requirements of jurisdiction might be compulsory, the rules for choice of law, even if relevant in determining jurisdiction, are substantive in character. They are not themselves rules of jurisdiction.[242] As such, it is unclear why the status of a choice of law rule should be any different in proceedings concerning jurisdiction than it would be in substantive proceedings. Why, if such a rule is otherwise optional, should it acquire mandatory status merely because it arises in the course of determining jurisdiction? Whether a given rule is mandatory should depend upon the nature of the rule, not upon the context in which it is employed.

The latter point may be illustrated by reference to a situation in which choice of law considerations are clearly relevant in establishing jurisdiction. This is required when it is necessary to locate the place of a contract's performance for the purposes of Article 5(1) of the Convention. There is no doubt as a matter of principle that this should be identified by applying the conflicts rules of the forum. As the Court of Justice has ruled, a court

> must determine in accordance with its own rules of conflict of laws what is the law applicable to the legal relationship in question and define in accordance with that law the place of performance.[243]

But it is doubtful that a plaintiff is therefore required to establish foreign law in such a case—or to circumvent such a requirement by demonstrating that the applicable law is English. The relevant conflicts rules in such cases are those of the 1980 Rome Convention. But, as we have seen, this only renders the application of foreign law mandatory in exceptional cases, such as those concerning consumer and employment contracts.[244] It does not impose a general obligation upon a claimant to rely upon foreign law and it is hard to see in practice how it could affect the question of a contract's place of performance. It is entirely consistent with the application of the relevant conflict rules, as the Court of Justice requires, that reliance upon foreign law is merely optional. This conclusion is further supported by reference to cases concerning the validity of jurisdiction agreements under English law's traditional rules. Even where a contract's applicable law is foreign it seems that a plaintiff is under no duty to plead and prove the content of that law. Certainly, there is authority that English law may apply by default in such cases, as it would outside the jurisdictional context.[245]

A different, and more troublesome, problem concerns Article 52 of the Brussels Convention, which appears in identical terms in the 1988 Lugano Convention. This requires particular scrutiny.

---

[242] Cf. *Bank of Baroda* v. *Vysya Bank* [1994] 2 Lloyd's Rep. 87; Morse, (1994) *LMCLQ* 560.
[243] *Tessili* v. *Dunlop*, above n. 240. [244] Above, p. 83.
[245] *The Frank Pais*, above n. 238.

10. DOMICILE AND THE EUROPEAN CONVENTIONS

The United Kingdom is a signatory to the 1968 Brussels Convention on Jurisdiction and the Enforcement of Judgments. This provides, subject to exceptions, that a party domiciled in a Contracting State shall be sued there and, importantly, in no other such state.[246] Where a corporation is domiciled is a matter for the forum's rules of private international law.[247] And whether a natural person is domiciled in the forum is referred (unsurprisingly) to the forum's internal law.[248] Arguably the Convention requires the introduction and application of foreign law in cases involving the domicile of a party who is not domiciled in the United Kingdom. The second paragraph of Article 52 provides:

> If a party is not domiciled in the State whose courts are seised of the matter, then, in order to determine whether the party is domiciled in another Contracting State, *the court shall apply the laws of that State*.[249]

The question, therefore, is whether an English court is bound to apply—and a party who relies on a contention concerning domicile is bound to plead—any foreign rules concerning domicile which Article 52 requires to be applied. The wording of Article 52 is clearly peremptory.[250] But it is unclear whether Article 52 takes effect only once a party has sought to apply such a foreign law by pleading it. By omitting to do so, could such a party secure the application of English law by virtue of the principle that English law applies in default of pleading? Alternatively, does Article 52 imply an obligation on such a party to plead (and prove) foreign law which an English court is required to police by dismissing any defective claim?

Such questions are of more than academic importance. It might be supposed, for example, that it will seldom happen that the application of the statutory test of domicile provided by the Civil Jurisdiction and Judgments Act 1982[251] will yield a different solution from that of any other Contracting State. Indeed, the reason why the 1982 Act contains a test of domicile very different from that normally employed in English law is to achieve a degree of harmonization between the English approach and others.[252] In reality, the differences between national approaches to domicile can be marked, differences which are likely to continue until a single community definition of domicile is introduced.[253]

---

[246] Article 2.   [247] Article 53.   [248] Article 52, first para.   [249] Italics supplied.
[250] Dicey and Morris, 293–294; Cheshire and North, 284, 292; Kaye, *Civil Jurisdiction and Enforcement of Foreign Judgments* (1987), 284–292.
[251] Section 41; see, O'Malley and Layton, 1251.   [252] Cheshire and North, 284–285.
[253] O'Malley and Layton, 833, Chs. 48–55, para. 25; Kaye, above n. 250, 281–284; Droz, *Competence judiciaire et effets des jugements dans le Marché Commun*, (1972), 219.

One solution is to point to the English practice whereby such peremptory words as 'shall apply' are not treated (without more) as affecting the general principle of voluntary pleading.[254] But this is no answer since the interpretation of the Convention should be purposive, not purely semantic. Another approach is to affirm the recognized principle that the Brussels Convention does not affect the general procedural rules of Contracting States.[255] As such, it might be said, it does not touch the English rule to the effect that the pleading of foreign law is voluntary. But, again, the argument is not decisive, since it begs the question whether the introduction of foreign law under Article 52 is truly a procedural matter. Certainly, it ignores the point that, even if the question how foreign law should be pleaded is procedural, the requirement that a particular foreign law should be applied in a given case may be substantive.[256]

On inspection, the weight of argument strongly favours a mandatory reading of Article 52.[257] The first paragraph implies that a state's internal law governs only the question whether a person is domiciled there.[258] It equally suggests that the law of the alleged domicile should determine whether someone is domiciled in the state concerned and, conversely, that it should not apply to determine domicile elsewhere. Moreover, consistent with this view, section 41 of the Civil Jurisdiction and Judgments Act 1982 supplies a test of domicile which is in terms limited to determining whether a person is domiciled in the United Kingdom or a non-Contracting State.[259] Even if foreign law were not pleaded under Article 52 the relevant rules of English law would simply not be available to be applied by default. The presumption of similarity would lead, in effect, to the application of no law at all. The absurdity of that conclusion argues decisively for giving the words of Article 52 their natural effect.

Support for this position is also implicit in the considerations which led to the introduction of Article 52. As the Jenard Report on the Convention makes clear, this was founded on a deliberate policy against allowing the *lex fori* to determine domicile in another Contracting State.[260] In particular,

---

[254] As in connection with the Foreign Limitation Periods Act 1984, see below, p. 129.
[255] See e.g. Case 365/88, *Kongress Agentur Hagen GmbH* v. *Zeehaghe BV* [1990] ECR 1845.
[256] See above, pp. 70–74.
[257] For a general argument in favour of the mandatory application of the Convention's terms, see Kaye, above n. 250, 12. See also, Droz, above n. 253, 51–52; Schlosser, Report on the Convention, 81–82. To say that the Convention is mandatory means only that its rules must be applied, not that every such rule is itself mandatory.
[258] 'In order to determine whether a party is domiciled in the Contracting State whose courts are seised of the matter, the court shall apply its internal law'.
[259] This expressly provides that it applies to determine personal domicile in the United Kingdom, or part of the United Kingdom, or 'in a state other than a Contracting State'. It omits any reference to a domicile in another Contracting State precisely because Article 52, para. 2 provides a rule for such cases: Cheshire and North, 291.
[260] OJ 1979, No. C59/1, 15–17.

it was considered illogical and unfair to allow a situation in which, by applying only the *lex fori*, a party who was in fact domiciled in a given country might not be treated as such. Further support for the obligatory introduction of foreign law lies in the fact that, were Article 52 not taken as requiring that result, the purpose and design of the Convention might be subverted. If a person is domiciled neither in England nor in any other Contracting State the important effect is that, for most purposes, the Convention is altogether inapplicable.[261] As such, an English court is free to apply its traditional, non-Convention rules of jurisdiction.[262] Conversely, if a defendant is domiciled in another such state and not in England, the English court cannot entertain proceedings unless one of the Convention's grounds of 'special jurisdiction' is present.[263] Indeed, whether an English court has jurisdiction on such a ground itself depends on the defendant's being domiciled in another Contracting State. Where a party is domiciled—in England, in another Contracting State, or outside the Convention regime—is therefore critical in determining a number of questions which are central to the Convention's operation. It governs whether the Convention applies, whether an English court has jurisdiction, and according to which rules. To permit a party to ignore the express terms of Article 52 might thus distort the Convention's operation by causing it to be applied—or not applied—in cases where adherence to Article 52 would have achieved a different result.

Apart from such purposive arguments, a mandatory reading of Article 52 conforms to general principles of English law. Indeed, it is apparent that English courts view the application of the Convention's provisions strictly where this is necessary to give effect to its purposes. In one case, for example, proof of foreign law by expert testimony was permitted at the jurisdictional stage of proceedings, in a marked departure from normal practice.[264] This was to ensure that the question whether another Contracting State's court was seised of the same matter was answered correctly. If such strictness is required so as to ensure the correct application of the Convention it follows (presumably) that proof of foreign law should be required under Article 52.

In conclusion, it is hard to resist the argument that Article 52 of the Brussels Convention positively requires a foreign *lex domicili* to be applied. This cannot (presumably) require a judge to establish that a person who is not domiciled in England is not domiciled in any other Contracting State. But it means that one who would rely on a party's domicile—or lack of domicile—in another Convention state should plead and prove the

---

[261] Save, notably, under Article 16.   [262] Article 4.
[263] e.g. under Article 5(3) (party domiciled in one Contracting State sued in courts of another where the tort occurred).
[264] *Grupo Torras SA* v. *Al Sabah* [1995] 1 Lloyd's Rep. 374, affirmed [1995] I L Pr 667 (CA).

relevant foreign law.[265] A failure to do so would lead to dismissal of the defectively-founded claim.

11. FOREIGN LIMITATION PERIODS

Must a party who relies on foreign law plead the relevant foreign limitation period? As a general rule, the law of limitation which governs a substantive claim is that of the governing law.[266] The possibility that this is a mandatory requirement suggests itself because the language of the Foreign Limitation Periods Act 1984 is peremptory,[267] providing that, where relevant, the foreign law of limitation 'shall apply'. At first sight, it is possible that such wording implies a duty upon a claimant relying on foreign law to prove that the claim satisfies the relevant foreign rules as to time. The conventions of pleading, however, appear to be the contrary, leaving it to a defendant to take the point that the claim is time-barred abroad.[268] There is also unequivocal Court of Appeal authority to the effect that the onus is upon a defendant in such cases to take the limitation point and to introduce evidence as to the foreign law of limitation.[269] This reflects the practice in purely domestic cases. As such the relevant provisions of the 1984 Act are thus to be treated as permissive not mandatory.

In reality, it may be of little consequence whether the plaintiff or the defendant should plead a foreign limitation period because a defendant who would gain thereby would presumably introduce the issue of limitation in any event. The burden of proof would differ, however, depending on who was responsible for introducing the issue. In some cases this is unlikely to be significant, since the proof of a foreign limitation period is likely to be straightforward. Indeed, it may often be so straightforward that the proof of a foreign limitation period may seldom be considered by the courts. Either the action is time-barred, in which case proceedings top once a defendant takes the point, or they are not, in which case they continue without the matter being disputed. But greater difficulty may arise when the application of a limitation period is in issue, as when it becomes necessary to ascertain, on the facts, the moment from which time begins to run. Difficulty might also arise when the enforcement of a foreign limitation period is a matter of discretion, in which case an English court is

---

[265] e.g. under RSC Order 11, r. 2, which allows service of process without leave only if, *inter alia*, the defendant is domiciled in a Contracting State.

[266] Foreign Limitation Periods Act 1984, s. 1.

[267] Section 1(1)(a) provides that, where the *lex causae* is foreign 'the law of that other country relating to limitation shall apply . . .'.

[268] Bullen, Leake and Jacobs, above n. 7, provides a precedent for a defendant who wishes to allege that a claim is time-barred under foreign law; ibid., 1171.

[269] *Zapita* v. *Act Group Plc*, unreported, 11 February 1993 (CA).

expressly instructed to exercise such a discretion in the same manner as a foreign judge in the system concerned.[270]

12. MANDATORY PLEADING AND BILLS OF EXCHANGE

Statutory choice of law rules are relatively rare in English law. This partly accounts for the few situations in which it might plausibly be said that the application of foreign law is required, mandatory choice of law rules being most likely to originate in the peremptory words of a statute. But it might be suggested that the Bills of Exchange Act 1882[271] contains such provisions. Section 72 establishes several statutory choice of law rules whereby the rights and duties of the parties to a bill of exchange 'are determined', provided that the case has a foreign element. The necessary foreign element is present if a bill 'drawn in one country is negotiated, accepted, or payable in another'. Most importantly, sub-section (2) provides that

> The interpretation of the drawing, indorsement, acceptance or acceptance supra protest of a bill is determined by the law of the place where such a contract is made.[272]

Again, sub-section (3) provides:

> The duties of the holder with respect to presentment for acceptance or payment and the necessity for or sufficiency of protest or notice of dishonour are determined by the law of the place where the act is done or the bill is dishonoured.

At first sight such provisions are not obviously peremptory,[273] nor is there any clear indication as to their possible status.[274] Nor does the 1980 Rome Convention assist because, by Article 1(2)(c), matters concerning negotiable instruments are excluded from its scope. But the role of section 72 in resolving disputes between commercial parties, where freedom of con-

---

[270] Foreign Limitation Periods Act 1984, s. 4. Arguably, this implies a duty on the parties to lead such evidence as to the exercise of such a discretion as may permit the court to discharge its responsibility.

[271] *Byles on Bills of Exchange*, 26th ed., (London, 1988), Ch. 25; Cheshire and North, Ch. 19. By Article 1(2)(c) the 1980 Rome Convention does not apply to negotiable instruments; see also, *Banco Atlantico SA v. British Bank of the Middle East* [1990] 2 Lloyd's Rep. 504, 507 (CA). Cf. *Bank of Lisbon v. Optichem Kunismus Bpk.*, 1970 (1) SA 447 (W), criticized by Kahn, (1970) 87 SALJ 145.

[272] 'Interpretation' in this context has been held to extend to matters of essential validity: *Alcock v. Smith* [1892] 1 Ch. 238, 256.

[273] Although they are rendered in apparently imperative terms in Dicey and Morris, Rule 194.

[274] As the editors of Dicey and Morris observe: 'There is nothing in the Bills of Exchange Act 1882 which expressly prevents the parties from choosing the law to govern an instrument, but there is nothing which permits it either': ibid., 194.

tract and party autonomy might be regarded as important, argues that they should not be mandatory. It is also apparent that the 1882 Act was not intended to represent an exclusive code for handling the conflicts aspects of negotiable instruments, implying that the issue of party choice might properly be subjected to general principles. Such significant matters as essential validity and capacity, for example, are not treated within section 72.[275] At its weakest, therefore, neither principle nor the terms of the 1882 Act suggests that section 72 should be mandatory or exclusive. As such, general principle suggests that it must be presumed not to have that effect. Certainly, the editors of Dicey and Morris, in a departure from their previous position, suggest that the parties' ability to select the governing law might be unfettered, a freedom which presumably extends as much to their choice of the *lex fori* as of any other law.[276]

The position is thus unclear, although the weight of argument might favour allowing the parties the freedom to choose the applicable law, including the *lex fori*. Two leading commentaries suggest, however, that the parties should not be entitled to select the governing law in substitution for that which section 72 would apply.[277] It has also been suggested that any such choice should be restricted to the *lex loci contractus* or the *lex loci solutionis*.[278] True, selection of the *lex fori* through an omission to plead foreign law might be permitted even on such a view, provided we accept that such an omission is a matter of procedure, and thus outside the Act's scope. But, as we have seen, it is not sufficient merely to classify the issue as procedural; what is important is the status, mandatory or otherwise, of the Act's provisions. It is significant, therefore, that in at least one case both the parties and the court may have assumed that section 72 has mandatory effect, although the point was not apparently addressed. In *Österreichische Länderbank* v. *S'Elite Ltd.*[279] the drawers negotiated a bill to the plaintiff bank which was aware of the drawer's insolvency. Both parties were Austrian but the bill was payable in London, potentially attracting section 72. The bill was subsequently dishonoured and the bank sued the acceptors, an English company, for its value. The defendants eventually failed in their attempt to defeat the bank's title to the bill on grounds of fraud. But the case is of interest in the present context because the defendant's position was that Austrian law governed although they supplied no evidence of Austrian law and sought to rely on the presumption that, in the absence of such evidence, foreign law and English law are presumed to be the same.[280]

[275] Ibid., 1424–1425.   [276] Ibid.
[277] *Chalmers and Guest on Bills of Exchange, Cheques and Promissory Notes*, 14th edn., (London, 1991), 566; Cheshire and North, 523.
[278] Dicey and Morris, 1425–1426.
[279] [1981] 1 QB 565 (CA); see also, *Banca Populare di Novara* v. *John Livanos & Sons Ltd.*[1965] 2 Lloyd's Rep. 149. Oddly, s. 72 was not expressly mentioned in *S'Elite*.   [280] At 569.

It is intriguing to speculate why the defendants took such a course, given that they were effectively relying on English law. Why did they not merely argue the case under English law without referring to Austrian law? Perhaps they anticipated that the bank would argue that Austrian law governed, and that under that law there was no question of fraud. But they might simply have assumed that section 72 required the application of Austrian law.[281] Although, as we have seen, this may not have been strictly necessary, it is not hard to see why they might have done so. While the conflicts rules contained in section 72 may not be mandatory when they are read alone, it may be important that the defendants had relied on other, substantive provisions of the 1882 Act, principally sections 29(2) and 30(2). They may thus have felt unable to rely on those sections without also complying with section 72. In any event, one further feature of the *Österreichische Länderbank* case deserves mention. True, Austrian law may have been relied on because it was assumed to be mandatory in its application. But, if the purpose of the 1882 Act is that the stipulated laws should govern, why did the court not simply refuse to apply the presumption of similarity on that ground?[282] For, if section 72 is truly mandatory any claim or defence which relies on it should simply fail where the applicable law is not established. In that sense, if in no other, the decision does not argue for, but argues against, a mandatory reading of the Act's choice of law provisions. That its implications are so ambiguous may, however, simply confirm that the status of section 72 is profoundly uncertain.

13. WILLS AND TRUSTS

Brief mention must be made of two English statutes, the mandatory status of whose conflicts rules remains unclear. Neither has apparently occasioned litigation on the point, and it is uncertain how far the question is of practical importance. But both reveal how mandatory choice of law rules may be more common than is often supposed. They also illustrate the ambiguity which so often surrounds the mandatory status of English statutory rules. The first statute is the Wills Act 1963 which governs the formal validity of testamentary dispositions. A will is treated as validly executed if it is valid according to the law of the place of execution, or that of the testator's nationality, domicile or habitual residence.[283] In many

---

[281] There is also an indication that the relevance of Austrian law had been pressed on the defendants by the trial judge; ibid., at 569.

[282] That question is all the more intriguing because Roskill LJ did express doubts about the presumption, although for the very different reason that it was inappropriate to invoke it where the relevant English rules are statutory: ibid.

[283] Section 1. See further, Cheshire and North, 840–841.

cases at least one of these laws will coincide with that of the forum, which immediately reduces the likelihood of a conflict between the application of English law and one of those specified in the Act. But what if it is claimed that a will is valid under English law, although it would be invalid under each of those specified? It might be argued that nothing in the statute purports to override the general rule of voluntary pleading. But this might be countered by arguing that the Act makes no attempt to save the general rules of pleading, procedure or practice.[284] Other things being equal, this might suggest that the rules of the Act cannot be waived, being an exclusive regime in such cases. Perhaps the answer lies in the fact that the Act originated in the 1961 Hague Convention on the Conflicts of Law Relating to the Form of Testamentary Dispositions, and that as such its terms must be strictly enforced so as to preserve the uniformity of approach which is its purpose.

The second example concerns the Recognition of Trusts Act 1987, the proper interpretation of which is equally opaque in this context. This provides that the law applicable to the validity, construction, effect and administration of a trust shall be that chosen by the settlor,[285] failing which the law with which is has the closest connection shall apply.[286] Provision is also made for the application of the mandatory rules of a country whose law would, but for the choice of law rules prescribed by the Act, govern entitlement to trust assets.[287] The proprietary interests of, for example, creditors, minors, secured creditors and forced heirs are protected in this way. But what would be the effect of these provisions were foreign law not introduced? The language of the Act is at first sight inconclusive. That of the primary choice of law rules in Articles 6 and 7 is, as is normal, peremptory; the specified law 'shall apply'. The protective provision in Article 15 is phrased differently, but it is unlikely that anything is intended to turn on this. Again, no express saving is made for matters of procedure which might suggest that voluntary pleading is not permitted. But nor is it expressly excluded. On inspection, however, it is unlikely that the Act's provisions may be undermined by an omission to rely upon foreign law. Certainly, the Act does not apparently contemplate that a direct choice of law can be made other than by the settlor, apparently at the creation of the trust. Provision is made for a subsequent alteration to the applicable law where this is itself permitted by the applicable law.[288] But it is unclear that this should extend to a change made in the context of litigation. Certainly, if English law were the applicable law such an alteration would only be permitted if effected in accordance with a power expressly conferred by the trust instrument, or if in accordance with statute.[289] Again, the

---

[284] See above, p. 99. [285] Schedule, Article 6. [286] Schedule, Article 7.
[287] Schedule, Article 15. [288] Schedule, Article 10.
[289] Under the Variation of Trusts Act 1958.

mandatory nature of the Act's choice of law rules is suggested by its origins in the 1984 Hague Convention on the Law Applicable to Trusts and their Recognition. Would the uniformity intended by the Convention be achieved by allowing litigants to select English law as the applicable law to the exclusion of that which would govern under the Convention?

14. THE BRITISH LAW ASCERTAINMENT ACT

We have so far considered the potential effect of certain mandatory choice of law rules which define precisely when foreign law is applicable. But the introduction of foreign law might also be required simply because a court considers this a proper course in particular circumstances. English courts have a statutory power to introduce foreign law *ex officio* in certain cases, not because of the nature of the relevant choice of law rule, but because of a general discretion to do so. The British Law Ascertainment Act 1859[290] provides a procedure for obtaining proof of the laws of British colonies and many Commonwealth countries. Although also available on a party's application, a court may itself direct proof to be obtained under the Act. Arguably, the court's power is properly limited to invoking the Act's evidential procedures where foreign law has been pleaded. But the Act may be read more broadly, implying that such procedures might be used even when foreign law has not been introduced, and it has sometimes been understood in this way by the courts.[291] Whenever it is 'necessary or expedient for the proper disposal of the action' the court may remit a case for the purpose of obtaining a binding opinion from the courts of any of 'Her Majesty's dominions'.[292] The effect is that the application of foreign law is required and, in effect, to render any given choice of law rule mandatory for the purposes of the case in hand.

Courts once displayed some readiness to use this procedure.[293] But it would be unwise to read much into such decisions. The reluctance of English courts to expose litigants to greater cost and delay is a powerful disincentive to their using the Act's machinery and it is unlikely to be

---

[290] See below, p. 238.
[291] *Topham* v. *Duke of Portland* (1863) 1 DJ & S 517. The Preamble to the Act refers to its applying when foreign law has been pleaded, although the Preamble was repealed by the Statute Law Revision Act 1892. But the Act was employed in *Topham*, which was decided in 1863, apparently in the absence of such pleading. Perhaps *Topham* should be read as a case where foreign law was pleaded at the court's instigation in order that the Act might apply. Alternatively, it may be taken as an example of the rule that a preamble should not be referred to where to do so would disturb the clear meaning of statutory words: Bell and Engle, *Cross: Statutory Interpretation*, 2nd edn., (1987), 122–127.
[292] Section 1.
[293] *Topham* v. *Duke of Portland*, above n. 291; *Eglington* v. *Lamb* (1867) 15 LT 657.

invoked. It is revealing that in one of the very few cases in which it appears to have been used the judge explicitly employed the Act so as to save the parties time and money.[294] He clearly thought that if foreign law were ascertained it might reveal no difference between it and English law, thereby saving the parties the expense of litigating any question of choice of law. Moreover, perhaps it should be 'expedient' for a court to invoke the procedure only if the relevant choice of law rule is, in its nature, mandatory. This is especially so if the rule is statutory; why should a court (in effect) give mandatory status to a conflicts rule which was intended to be optional?

Certainly, there appears to be no recent case in which the 1859 Act has been invoked. But, although described as a 'not very important' exception to the principle of voluntary pleading,[295] the court's ability to intervene is significant in three senses. Its use, or non-use, suggests that the courts are highly sensitive to the expense of introducing and proving foreign law.[296] The Act's somewhat barren history also illustrates that, even if an English court is empowered to introduce foreign law *ex officio* it is very unlikely to do so. Finally, and crucially, the existence of this limited power is further evidence that there is nothing in principle inherently surprising or wrong with English courts' having such a power. The fact that English lawyers are used to seeing things differently, and the fact that the procedure is never used, is not so much a matter of principle or doctrine as of practicality. Courts demur from introducing foreign law in this way, not because they cannot do so, but because it might be undesirable. Certainly, it is striking that the courts' statutory power to introduce foreign law *ex officio* fell into disuse merely because of the difficulty of proving foreign law under the statutory procedure. No objection of principle has ever been voiced to the exception it offers to the principle of voluntary pleading.

15. FOREIGN LAW AND DOCUMENTARY CONSTRUCTION

An important, if somewhat ambiguous, line of cases suggests that foreign law must be introduced when this is essential for the proper construction of a private legal document. This occurs when, say, a contract or a deed employs terminology which can only be understood by reference to foreign law.[297] Such a rule has potentially far-reaching importance, although

---

[294] *Eglington* v. *Lamb* (1867) 15 LT 657; see also, *Lord* v. *Colvin* (1860) 1 Dr & Sm 24; *MacDougall* v. *Chittinaris*, 1937 SC 390, 407–408.
[295] Morris, *The Conflict of Laws*, 4th edn., (London, 1993), 36.
[296] *Eglington* v. *Lamb*, above n. 293.
[297] Dicey and Morris, 1222–1223; see below, pp. 251–257.

in most cases it may be unnecessary to invoke it. It only applies when a document incorporates or alludes to foreign law. And, even when it does so, its meaning may be discernible by the court, making evidence of foreign law unnecessary. Moreover, in a system such as the English, in which principle is generally led by practice rather than the converse, it may be that the rule has so seldom been invoked that its existence is simply not recognized. Indeed, the possibility that such an exception exists may have been undermined by the widespread conviction that strict adherence to the fact doctrine is always required. Taken literally the fact doctrine implies that the introduction of foreign law is invariably voluntary, obscuring any contrary indications in the case law.

The possibility that evidence of foreign law may be required in the construction of documents is suggested by *Di Sora* v. *Phillipps*,[298] a case which turned directly on the necessity of proving foreign law in order to construe a marriage settlement. As Vice-Chancellor Woods said, it was 'absolutely necessary'[299] to hear expert evidence on the meaning of foreign terms of art. Moreover, it was not 'open to the Court, otherwise than upon testimony, to form an opinion upon the translation of the language, or the translation of peculiar terms, or the application of peculiar principles of foreign law . . .'.[300] This might imply no more than a requirement that, if introduced, no proof of foreign law is acceptable other than that of experts. But, if so, it is unclear why the court went to such lengths to emphasise so unexceptional a proposition. It is also clear that the question in issue did not concern how foreign law was to be proved, but whether it was relevant at all. If so *Di Sora* stands for a broader proposition: in the absence of proof of foreign law a court should not construe a foreign document by itself where doing so depends on rules of foreign law. This view was apparently endorsed by the House of Lords on appeal. As Lord Cranworth said, suggesting that the introduction of foreign law is mandatory, the 'Judge or Court must obtain' evidence as to foreign principles of construction.[301] The same principle is revealed in *Earl of Eglington* v. *Lamb*,[302] a case, like *Di Sora*, concerning the interpretation of a marriage settlement. The Vice Chancellor regarded the introduction of Scottish law as essential because the document was only comprehensible under that law. He directed the introduction and proof of that law by invoking the British Law Ascertainment Act 1859, whereby a case would be stated for the opinion of the courts of Scotland. As the report says:

The language of Scotch law which was here used was foreign to the language of this court, and the meaning of the terms of Scotch law must be determined for the court.[303]

[298] (1863) 33 LJ Ch. 129. [299] At 130. [300] At 131. [301] At 131.
[302] (1867) 15 LT 657. [303] At 658.

But there are more recent examples.[304] One is *Stafford Allen & Sons Ltd.* v. *Pacific Steam Navigation Company*.[305] This concerned a dispute arising from the shipment of goods out of Cristobal in the Panama Canal Zone. The bill of lading provided that US maritime law would apply to shipments made 'from a port in the United States'. For Sellers J whether Cristobal was such a port turned on the scope of the US Carriage of Goods by Sea Act 1936. He was adamant that proof of foreign law was involved, insisting that better evidence should be supplied as to Cristobal's status under American law.[306] One reason was the danger that his answer to that 'momentous' question might differ from that of the US government.[307] Another was the difficulty of discerning the parties' presumed intentions on the matter. He clearly felt unable to arrive at any meaningful view as to what a US port was without some authoritative guidance.[308]

It should be noticed that the *Di Sora* principle is not confined to cases in which a document's governing law is foreign.[309] Although this was so in *Di Sora* itself, the bill of lading in *Pacific Steam* was governed by English law. It is necessary only that a document employs terms or makes assumptions which are only comprehensible under foreign law. This may become an issue either when a contract is governed by English law, but implicates issues of foreign law, or when it is governed by a foreign law which the parties have not pleaded. In either event it may be impossible to interpret it in accordance with English assumptions. Nor is the principle undermined by the presumption that, in the absence of evidence of foreign law, English law applies.[310] For the question is not whether a court should construe a document under foreign or English law. It is whether it can do so at all without evidence of foreign law.

At first sight *Di Sora* and its successors have radical implications. But the principle tends to be invoked only in exceptional circumstances. As *Pacific Steam* illustrates, it might be employed where the meaning attached to a phrase has diplomatic implications, or when the parties could have had no real intentions as to its meaning. Evidence of foreign law might also be required if illegality under foreign law is in question.[311] But it will not be invoked if a court is able to give a sensible meaning to the phrase, either because the parties must have had a view as to its meaning, or because the foreign term is contained in an international convention which applies also in English law, and which may thus be interpreted under that law.[312] The *Di Sora* principle is also self-limiting. For, if a will or contract is

---

[304] *The Glenbank* [1961] 1 Lloyd's Rep. 231 (HL); *The Merak* [1964] 2 Lloyd's Rep. 527; *The Stolt Sydness* [1997] 1 Lloyd's Rep. 273.
[305] [1956] 1 Lloyd's Rep. 105.   [306] At 114.   [307] At 114.   [308] At 120.
[309] See below, p. 252.
[310] *Re Parana Plantations Ltd.* [1946] 2 All ER 214 (CA); cf. *Hartmann* v. *Konig* (1933) 50 TLR 114, 117 (HL).
[311] *The Glenbank*, above n. 304.   [312] *The Stolt Sydness*, below p. 304.

effectively uninterpretable except under foreign law the parties will plead and prove foreign law without any prompting. Conversely, if the parties consider it unnecessary to plead foreign law in order to construe a document, a judge is very likely to agree with them, if only to save the delay and expense that would result were foreign law introduced. *Eglington* v. *Lamb*,[313] seemingly clear authority for the principle, is instructive in this respect. The Vice Chancellor apparently hoped to save the parties time and money by seeking proof of Scottish law. He hoped that by doing so a protracted choice of law dispute might become unnecessary.[314] But in the majority of cases, as we have seen, the effect of introducing foreign law is likely to be the opposite.

In theory the *Di Sora* principle may be an important incursion into the doctrine of voluntary pleading as traditionally conceived. Once again it reveals the courts in control of the evidential process, willing to ensure that they have before them adequate information on which to decide. And it reinforces the important doctrinal point that there is nothing inimical to the common law tradition in the mandatory introduction of foreign law.

16. CONCLUSION

It is a commonplace that the pleading of foreign law is voluntary. But this familiar principle is not quite what it seems. Certainly, it describes the simple fact that, generally, litigants need make no reference to foreign law in a case with a foreign element. But this is not always so. Reliance upon foreign law is usually unnecessary because, save in exceptional cases, the substantive rules of English private international law do not demand it. But in principle there is no reason why a given choice of law rule should not be mandatory in character. Nor is it unthinkable that a court may have a discretionary power to require evidence of foreign law in particular cases. In either event, one whose case depends upon foreign law must in principle plead and prove its content or, alternatively, demonstrate that English law is applicable under normal choice of law principles. To express the point differently, the familiar presumption that English law and foreign law are similar is to this extent qualified. Certainly, invocation of that presumption should not spare a claimant from the obligation to establish foreign law.

But, however expressed, it is clear that the mandatory introduction of foreign law is exceptional in English law. In default of a contrary rule, the matter is governed by the basic principle that, being facts, foreign laws must be expressly pleaded and proved. Moreover, as the foregoing dis-

[313] Above n. 302.   [314] At 658.

cussion has indicated, there may be little enthusiasm amongst practitioners and the courts for ascribing mandatory effect to choice of law rules. Most strikingly, the court's general power to introduce foreign law *ex officio* under the British Law Ascertainment Act 1859 has become largely redundant in practice. And even the use of peremptory words in a statute, as under the Foreign Limitation Periods Act 1984, is treated with scepticism—even if foreign law 'shall apply', it shall apply only when pleaded. Nor does the public interest greatly influence the courts' response. Neither in connection with foreign illegality nor, more arrestingly, in cases involving personal status is the introduction of foreign law required. True, proof is needed that a foreign marriage has taken place. But this falls far short of requiring the introduction of foreign rules concerning substantial validity.

But there is nothing odd in this. English law's essentially voluntarist position has considerable merit, as we shall see in Chapter X. It shows proper respect for party autonomy in choice of law matters. And it reflects the distinctive advantages in having English law applied in an English court. Not least, to require the introduction of foreign law in English proceedings does not necessarily involve the straightforward application of a readily identifiable law. It may require lengthy argument as to the nature of the relevant choice of law rule and as to its application. For the effect of ascribing mandatory status to a given conflicts rule is to require litigants to argue, and the court to determine, which law actually applies by virtue of that rule. Indeed, that the application of a foreign governing law is required in a given case does not necessarily mean that the party concerned will establish foreign law. They are as likely to argue that the applicable law is, upon examination, English. The effect is to make not simply the application of the governing law mandatory, but the choice of law process as well. Together with the practical difficulty of proving foreign law this may considerably extend the duration and expense of proceedings.

But there are other reasons why the introduction of foreign law is seldom required in English law. We have already noticed the persistence of the idea that whether foreign law must be introduced in a given case is a procedural matter. There is also the surprising durability of the presumption that English law and foreign law are similar, a matter with which the following chapter is concerned. But the roots of the English position lie also in the law's conceptual structure. It may be significant, for example, that English law does not possess an established taxonomy of mandatory rules. When and why particular legal rules are unwaivable by the choice of the parties are not questions to which English law offers any systematic answer. Certainly, given the difficulty which English lawyers encounter in identifying mandatory rules of domestic law, it is unsurprising that they may not discern such rules in private international law.

Another explanation for the English position is that English law has not traditionally employed statutory choice of law rules.[315] This has a double effect in the present context. First, it contributes to the relative uncertainty which surrounds many rules for choice of law. It is not always apparent how such rules should be formulated and, in consequence, it is not always clear whether foreign law is even applicable in particular cases. It is difficult, however, to speak sensibly of a choice of law rule having a mandatory character when it is unclear how the rule should be expressed. How can litigants have a duty to introduce foreign law, and how can a court police that duty, unless it is clear that foreign law is actually applicable? Secondly, it is normally meaningful to think of choice of law rules as being mandatory only when they are enshrined in statutory formulae. Except in some canonical formulation how can the meaning and import of such a rule be discerned? Only then is it possible to ask whether it is in peremptory form and whether the legislation in question expresses some identifiable purpose. Civil lawyers may find this suggestion odd, for they are more used to the idea that it is general considerations of public policy, or the nature of the legal rights in question, which confer imperative status upon rules of law.[316] For them the task of determining the mandatory status of a rule is one of classification. But English lawyers do not normally think in terms of a given rule belonging to a pre-ordained category. For them the character of a given rule—is it mandatory or optional?—is a function of its particular purpose and, more importantly, of its language.

But, as the examples considered in this chapter have shown, the conflict of laws in England is increasingly subject to statutory regulation. It is therefore troubling that so little attention is paid in drafting such statutes to the mandatory status of the choice of law rules which they contain. So far from addressing the problem of mandatoriness, for example, the Private International Law (Miscellaneous Provisions) Act 1995 makes no reference to whether litigants may ever choose the *lex delicti*.[317] This partly echoes English law's somewhat *ad hoc* approach to mandatory rules generally. But it also reflects a reluctance to address the wider question of the scope of party autonomy in matters of choice of law. Indeed, it may also reflect the distinctive pragmatism of the English approach to the subject in which consideration of its theoretical basis is rare.

But, if it is explicable, English law's approach is not inevitable. Indeed, it is striking how close English law came to adopting a position radically different from its present stance. For some years English law recognized the possibility of courts having a general power, not merely to dismiss claims for want of proof of foreign law, but to introduce and determine foreign law of their own motion, irrespective of the parties' wishes. The

---

[315] See the classic remarks of Dr Cheshire, in Cheshire and North, vii.
[316] See below, p. 271.   [317] North, above n. 22, 189–191.

Foreign Law Ascertainment Act 1861 conferred on English courts the power to state a case for the opinion of a foreign court in any action in which to do so was 'necessary or expedient'. Similar in terms to the British Law Ascertainment Act 1859, but not confined to 'Her Majesty's Dominions', it was designed to apply in respect of any country with which a reciprocal convention existed. No such convention was made and the 1861 Act was finally repealed, a dead letter, in 1973. But it stands as an arresting reminder that English law's characteristic position, whereby the pleading of foreign law is voluntary, is far from being inevitable. Certainly, it suggests that English law's reluctance to require the application of foreign law is not based on doctrinal considerations but on pragmatism. It is not so much theory, but the preference of bench and bar for a voluntarist approach which explains English law's position.

IV
Party Choice and Proof

Courts are reluctant to intervene in how conflicts cases are presented. But, as we have seen, the introduction of foreign law is exceptionally mandatory. And, as the present chapter shows, courts may sometimes regulate whether, how, and by whom foreign law is proved. This is not to say that a court will make directions to this effect, still less that it will seek to determine foreign law on its own. But a party who is duty-bound to plead foreign law and does not do so, or who offers insufficient proof, faces a powerful and persuasive sanction. The penalty for insufficiently proving foreign law is the failure of the defence or claim, either because the court will prefer the other party's evidence, or will apply English law by default. Where foreign law is relied upon but no evidence is tendered, the effect may be still more severe. Arguably, the defective case should simply be dismissed.

How courts assess evidence of foreign law, and what the consequences are if such evidence is found to be inadequate, are matters for Chapter VI. We are now concerned with a prior question, with the degree to which litigants are free to establish foreign law as they wish, and (conversely) with the extent to which the courts may control that process. Courts might police the proof of foreign law, and the parties' freedom is thus cabined, in several ways. First, it is possible that a court should dismiss a claim or defence when foreign law has been relied upon but no evidence introduced as to its content. More precisely, it may regard as defective any statement of reliance on foreign law in the pleadings, unaccompanied by a proper pleading of its content.[1] This curious situation may arise because of the presumption that foreign law, once invoked, is deemed to be the same as English law unless the contrary is established. Where claimants (rightly or wrongly) regard themselves as bound to argue that the applicable law is foreign they might seek nonetheless to enjoy the advantages of a more favourable English rule, or may simply wish to avoid the cost of proving foreign law, by relying on the presumption of similarity. They might also see a tactical advantage in not proving foreign law, leaving it to a defendant to bear the burden of rebutting the presumption. Secondly, a court might intervene, where foreign law is pleaded and proved, but proved inadequately, to ensure that further, better proof should be sup-

---

[1] On a preliminary application by the other party.

plied.[2] Courts might be prevented in principle,[3] or might be inhibited in practice, from making a formal direction to this effect, although they may not always be as reticent as principle demands.[4] But a judge can always warn a party that its case is likely to fail in the absence of the necessary evidence. And a litigant, so warned, is likely to respond by obtaining better proof.[5] In practice, however, the almost invariable practice of offering expert evidence of foreign law makes the power largely a matter of academic interest. Certainly, those cases in which it has been exercised are old and somewhat exceptional. Most are cases in which proof was attempted other than by employing expert evidence. Thirdly, a court might regulate the process of proof when the parties, far from having proved foreign law inadequately, have done so to excess. Typically this occurs when expensive expert evidence is deployed to prove straightforward points of law, or when the parties insist on contesting issues on which they might easily have agreed. Finally, we should address, if briefly, the possibility that a court might appoint an independent expert or assessor in cases involving foreign law, irrespective of the parties' wishes.

1. FOREIGN LAW WITHOUT EVIDENCE

A party might rely upon foreign law without pleading its content or proving it. The statement of claim or defence might state that a given contract is void (or valid), or legal (or illegal), or that a tort is actionable under the *lex loci delicti*. But it might provide no particulars in the pleadings of the foreign rule which supports such a proposition, nor might the party introduce evidence at trial to justify it. It will strike most observers as odd that a litigant might wish to rely upon foreign law without also proving it. Why bother to argue for the application of foreign law when the effect of not doing so is, in effect, to cause English law to apply by default? If the objective is that English law should be applied, why not simply argue the case under English law? It is understandable that a cost-conscious claimant might plead foreign law but offer something short of formal proof by expert testimony as evidence of its content. In such a case the claimant wishes foreign law to apply but hopes to avoid the cost of proving it. But that is not the same as invoking it without pleading its content and proving it at all. The practice of relying upon foreign law without proving it sometimes exists where the introduction of foreign law is—or is perceived to be—mandatory. This has occurred in at least one case

---

[2] See below, p. 153.   [3] *Tay Bok Choon* v. *Tahansan Bank* [1987] 1 WLR 413, 418 (PC).
[4] See e.g. *Stafford Allen & Sons Ltd.* v. *Pacific Steam Navigation Co.* [1956] Lloyd's Rep. 104; above, p. 137.
[5] *Tay Bok Choon* v. *Tahansan Bank*, above n. 3, 418.

concerning a bill of exchange.[6] But it is most visible in cases involving defamatory publications abroad in which, as we have seen, the requirement of double actionability is often supposed to oblige claimants to allege that a foreign wrong is actionable where it occurred.[7] Although probably unnecessary, especially in the light of recent changes to the common law rules,[8] many practitioners assume that such an obligation exists. Claimants in such proceedings, apparently considering themselves bound to allege actionability under the *lex loci delicti*, sometimes avoid the burden of proving foreign law by declining to particularise foreign law in the pleadings or to offer evidence at trial.[9] They rely instead on the presumption that, in the absence of proof, foreign law is deemed to have the content of English law. They do so although there is a more direct means of avoiding the proof of foreign law by seeking the application of English law on the basis that it is that with which the wrong has the most significant relationship.[10]

But there is another reason why foreign law may be invoked in defamation cases although its content is neither pleaded nor proved. By doing so, and by relying on the presumption of similarity between English and foreign law, a plaintiff may transfer the burden of proving foreign law to the defendant, with the attendant inconvenience and expense. The effectiveness of this controversial practice is well-recognized. As has been said:

> ... the plaintiff can use this right as a daunting tactical ploy against the defendants by simply asserting, so it seems, that the foreign law is presumed to be the same as English law and leaving it to the defendants to incur the considerable cost of showing the contrary.[11]

In some cases this tactical advantage may be exploited to the full. A plaintiff may magnify the burden on a defendant by alleging, say, defamatory publication in numerous jurisdictions without offering proof as to actionability in any of them. A plaintiff may even, apparently, claim actionability throughout the world, requiring a defendant to disprove it in every known jurisdiction.[12]

In the light of such tactics, the practice whereby claimants, especially in defamation proceedings, may rely upon foreign law without particularising and proving its content has been strongly criticised and reform has been suggested.[13] Some writers have also condemned the practice in prin-

---

[6] *Österreichische Länderbank* v. *S'Elite Ltd.* [1981] QB 565, 569; above, p. 131.

[7] See above, p. 103.

[8] See above, p. 105. The rule now only applies in defamation proceedings: Private International Law (Miscellaneous Provisions) Act 1995, s. 13.

[9] *University of Glasgow* v. *The Economist* [1997] EMLR 495. Carter-Ruck, *Libel and Slander*, 5th edn., (London, 1997), 295; Gatley, *Libel and Slander*, 8th ed., (London, 1981), 249.

[10] Sir Brian Neill, *Report of the Supreme Court Procedure Committee on Practice and Procedure in Defamation* (1991), 47.

[11] Ibid., 48.   [12] Ibid.   [13] Sir Brian Neill, above n. 10, 50.

ciple. They would allow a plaintiff to claim on a foreign tort under English law, or (more precisely) to rely upon the fact that the tort was committed abroad without making any allegation as to the *lex loci delicti*.[14] In such a case English law would be applied unless the defendant argued that the wrong was not actionable where it was done. Such writers would not, however, allow a party who founds its case on foreign law—by alleging actionability abroad—to escape the obligation to particularize and prove that law.[15] By contrast, the opposite view has attracted influential support. The editors of Dicey and Morris would apparently not require one who relies upon a tort's actionability under foreign law to plead and prove that law.[16] Such a party is entitled to rely upon the presumption of similarity. The latter view was endorsed by Popplewell J in *University of Glasgow* v. *The Economist*, a rare case exemplifying the practice in defamation cases. He took the view that

> the plaintiff need only set out that it [the tort] is actionable by the law of the foreign country and then say there is the presumption. If he chooses to do that, it is then for the defendant to raise the issue that the foreign law is different from English law.[17]

The case concerned an alleged libel published by *The Economist* magazine. The plaintiffs sought to amend their original statement of claim, which alleged only publication in England, by adding publication in a large number of foreign jurisdictions. The defendants objected to the form of the amendment, to the extent that it simply asserted that the publication was actionable in each of the additional countries. They argued that it was for the plaintiffs, having relied upon foreign law, to particularise in the pleadings the foreign rules on which their claim depended and to prove their assertions at trial. The contested pleading stated:

> The publication of said words and symbols in the countries set out in the schedule hereto is and was actionable by the law of those countries.[18]

Popplewell J held that if the plaintiffs had in their pleadings affirmatively set out the law of each of the countries whereby each publication was actionable they would, indeed, have been required to give details of the foreign rules on which they relied and to bear the burden of proof. Not having done so, however, it was for the defendant to show that each such law differed from English law. The case may therefore have turned on a somewhat technical distinction between merely signalling reliance upon a proposition of foreign law in a statement of claim or defence, and formally

---

[14] Anton, *Private International Law*, 3rd edn., (Edinburgh, 1990), 411.
[15] Ibid., citing *McElroy* v. *McAllister* 1949 SC 100, 118, 124, 137.
[16] Dicey and Morris, 1514.   [17] *University of Glasgow* v. *The Economist*, above n.9.
[18] At 497.

pleading the content of foreign law. The former may entail no obligation to prove that law, while the latter does so. Perhaps this expresses the proper distinction between merely invoking a foreign applicable law, which is a matter of law, and issues of pleading and proof which concern how facts are established. But such a distinction collapses if the invocation of foreign law is coupled with a statement that it is to a particular effect. And, at root, it is hard to regard the plaintiff's position in *University of Glasgow* as anything other than an attempt to rely upon foreign law without also proving it. Certainly, whatever the correct technical analysis, there is little doubt that Popplewell J simply applied the traditional presumption of similarity. The consequence is as clear as it is arresting. A claimant may rely upon a proposition of foreign law, but expect the other party to establish its incorrectness. Differently expressed, it is possible to invoke foreign law yet simultaneously invite a court to apply (in effect) English law.

This conclusion is troubling because it threatens the mandatory application of foreign law. Although we saw in Chapter III that an obligation to introduce foreign law entails a duty to plead its content *University of Glasgow* suggests otherwise—at least if reliance upon the *lex loci delicti* was there required. But such an approach also affords procedural benefits to those who freely invoke foreign law, and in cases very different from *University of Glasgow*. In *Royal Boskalis NV* v. *Mountain*[19] a dispute between an insured and its insurer turned on whether French arbitrators, applying French law, would accept that the former had waived its contractual rights against a third party. The Court of Appeal allowed the insurer to take the point for the first time at trial although it had pleaded its case exclusively under English law. The insured could not object that it had been given no warning of the relevance of foreign law because the presumption of similarity permits a claimant to allege foreign law without pleading its content. Any reliance upon foreign law at trial was consistent with having argued the case under English law, given that English law and foreign law are deemed to be the same.[20] As *Boskalis*, like *University of Glasgow*, suggests the presumption of similarity, far from being an innocuous evidential tool, is a tactical weapon of some potency. As such it warrants close scrutiny.

The presumption of similarity between English law and foreign law is common currency amongst English lawyers and is regularly endorsed in the cases. Indeed, the Court of Appeal has re-affirmed the principle, going so far as to hold that even foreign conceptions of public policy are presumed to be similar to those of English law.[21] But the argument for

---

[19] [1997] 2 All ER 929(CA).   [20] At 976–977.
[21] *Royal Boskalis NV* v. *Mountain*, 976–977 (CA). See also *Dynamit AG* v. *Rio Tinto Co.* [1918] AC 260, 295; *The Parchim* [1918] AC 157, 161 (PC); *The Colorado* [1923] P 102, 111 (CA);

relying upon such an unlikely fiction has always been insecure. To speak of such a presumption at all, rather than admitting that English law applies as the *lex causae* where no other is proved, may rest on a conceptual mistake.[22] And the inappropriateness of deeming English and foreign law to be the same in all situations has long been recognized. Certainly there are cases in which the courts have declined to do so where this would strain credibility. Courts have in the past refused to apply it where the rules of the *lex fori* are statute-based,[23] or where the foreign law is not that of a common law system,[24] or where the relevant concept in English law is perceived to be of a unique character.[25] Nor has the presumption been applied in circumstances where the relevant English rule is territorially limited to claims arising within the jurisdiction of the English courts. It cannot be assumed, for example, that the law of copyright of a foreign country is the same as that of England because the relevant English legislation applies only to infringements in England.[26] The role of the presumption has also been doubted where fairness requires a claimant to establish its case positively, as where an allegation of fraud has been made.[27] Nor may the presumption be relied upon in applications for summary judgment where fairness requires full consideration of any issues of foreign law at trial.[28] Again, it may happen in prosecutions for bigamy that the validity of an accused's previous marriage may depend on foreign law. If so, the prosecution is required to prove its validity under that law. Should the prosecution fail to do so, or fail to offer evidence as to foreign law, the court will not apply English law by default but will direct an acquittal.[29]

It is unclear therefore that it is ever appropriate to speak of a presumption of similarity between English and foreign law. And even if we do so it is apparent that it has never been treated by the courts as a universal rule. This is not to say that the existence of such a presumption, although dubious in principle, is always harmful. It may cause little practical

---

Casey v. *Casey* [1949] P 420, 430 (CA); *Bumper Development Corp.* v. *Comr. of Police* [1991] 1 WLR 1362, 1369 (CA). Dicey and Morris, 238; Fentiman, (1992) 108 *LQR* 142, 147–148. See also, Currie, (1954) 58 *Col L Rev* 964 (1954); Nussbaum, (1941) 50 *Yale LJ* 1018 (1941); Sass, (1981) 29 *Am Jl Comp L* 96, 102–107.

[22] See above, p. 75.
[23] *Purdom* v. *Pavey* (1896) 26 SCR 412, 417; *Schnaider* v. *Jaffe* (1916) 7 CPD 696.
[24] *Guepratte* v. *Young* (1851) 4 De G & Sm 217.
[25] Westlake gives the example of English procedures in bankruptcy: *Private International Law*, (7th edn., 1925), by Bentwich.
[26] *Österreichische Länderbank* v. *S'Elite Ltd.* [1981] 1 QB 565, 569 (CA); *Mother Bertha Music Ltd.* v. *Bourne Music Ltd.*, 31 July 1977 (unreported).
[27] *Österreichische Länderbank* v. *S'Elite Ltd.*, above n. 26. Cf. *France* v. *Hutchinson* (1891) 17 VLR 471 (allegation of illegality).
[28] *Western National Bank of New York* v. *Perez, Triana & Co.* (1890) 6 TLR 366; *National Shipping Corpn.* v. *Arab* [1971] 2 Lloyd's Rep. 363.
[29] Dicey and Morris, 228.

difficulty where it merely explains why English law applies where foreign law is not introduced at all, or where it has been pleaded and proved but the evidence is inadequate. But this cannot be said where foreign law is relied upon but not proved. One danger in applying the presumption in such a case is that the mandatory introduction of foreign law might thus be subverted. A party who is required to introduce foreign law by a mandatory choice of law rule may attempt to employ the presumption to defeat that rule's obligatory character. Another risk is that a plaintiff who relies upon foreign law even when no such duty exists might oppress a defendant by requiring the latter to disprove the presumption. Certainly, there is something potentially unfair not to say irrational, about requiring one party to disprove what the other has not sought to prove.

If, however, the presumption of similarity rests on insecure foundations, it is important to notice that more is in question than the plausibility of equating English and foreign law. Nor is the problem merely whether we should adopt the language of presumption and rebuttal, or speak instead of applying English law where no other is proved. However the matter is expressed, two more fundamental issues are involved. One is whether English law should in principle be applied when one who has relied upon foreign law has deliberately failed to establish its content. The other is whether, in consequence, the other party should be obliged to establish the content of foreign law. In that light, several considerations suggest that one who relies upon foreign law should not escape the obligation to establish its content by proper evidence. First, there are cases, which strictly belong in the category of those in which foreign law was not relied upon at all, which are intriguingly close to those in which it has been relied upon but not supported by evidence. There are, for example, those in which courts have declined to treat a matter of foreign law as if it were one of contractual construction.[30] Strictly speaking, the parties do not rely upon foreign law in such cases, the issue having been characterized as one of construction not foreign law. In a sense, however, such claimants have relied on the fact that foreign law is to a certain effect, although they have offered no proof in support of their contention. As such they have, effectively, introduced foreign law without proving it as such. If so, those cases in which courts have suggested that formal proof of foreign law is needed, construction being an inadequate means to establish what amounts to a point of foreign law, support the court's power to require the proof of foreign law.

Secondly, there are several cases in which the courts have intervened to require better proof of foreign law where the tendered evidence is inade-

---

[30] *Stafford Allen & Sons Ltd.* v. *Pacific Steam Navigation Company* [1956] Lloyd's Rep. 104; *Di Sora* v. *Phillipps* (1864) 10 HLC 624.

quate.³¹ If they are thus prepared to ensure the proper proof of foreign law it is hard to see why they should not take the short step towards requiring foreign law to be proved where it has been relied upon. Indeed, many decisions in which courts have intervened to require better proof of foreign law concern, in truth, situations in which the proof of foreign law which was originally offered was so meagre as barely to amount to evidence at all.³² Such cases, in which the distinction between poor proof of foreign law and no proof at all reduces to vanishing point, reinforce the idea that a court may intervene to seek the proof of foreign law where it has been introduced but not proved.

Most importantly, whatever role it may have in other situations, there is scant support in the cases for the principle that English law should govern by default in a case where a proposition of foreign law is relied upon by a party who declines to prove it. Admittedly, the presumption of similarity has been endorsed when foreign law has not been invoked.³³ It is also mentioned in cases where the proof of foreign law, although supported by evidence, has failed.³⁴ But, on closer investigation, it is unclear that the presumption of similarity properly applies where foreign law has been relied upon but no evidence has been tendered. It is especially important to notice that *Dynamit AG* v. *Rio Tinto Co.*,³⁵ which is often taken to support the presumption in such cases (as it was in *University of Glasgow*), may not have this effect. The case turned on whether an English party's contract with a German company was rendered void by the onset of war. Under English law but not (it seems) German law the contract was illegal. While the court clearly presumed that English law and German law were the same,³⁶ the effect of its doing so was not what might be supposed. This is because, perhaps unusually, the party which had relied upon foreign law without proving it had sought to establish not that English and German law were the same, but that they were different. It was argued, without evidence, that the contract was legal in German law, notwithstanding that it was illegal by the law of England. Typically, however, the party who relies upon foreign law without proving it intends that both laws should be treated as the same, as in *University of Glasgow*. By applying the presumption of similarity the court in *Dynamit* thus penalised that party for not supplying evidence to support its claim under German law.

---

³¹ See below, p. 153.   ³² See below, p. 154.
³³ *Lloyd* v. *Guibert* (1865) LR 1 QB 115, 129; *Hartmann* v. *Konig* (1933) 50 TLR 114, 117 (HL); *Re Tank of Oslo (A/S)* [1940] 1 All ER 40, 42.
³⁴ *The Nouvelle Banque de l'Union* v. *Ayton* (1891) 7 TLR 377; *The Colorado* [1923] P 102, 111 (CA); *Re Parana Plantations* [1946] 2 All ER 214, 217–218; *Szechter* v. *Szechter* [1971] P 287, 295–296. See also, *Casey* v. *Casey* [1949] P 420, 429–431 (foreign law not evidenced in the strict sense but court referred to Canadian cases cited in Cheshire's Private International Law and found them inconclusive as to Canadian law).
³⁵ [1918] AC 260.   ³⁶ At 295.

In doing so, it protected the other party from having to establish foreign law, with all the inconvenience and expense that might have involved.

As such, the message to be derived from *Dynamit* is that one who relies upon a proposition of foreign law must prove the allegation or see it fail. The true role of the presumption of similarity is to sanction those who rely upon foreign law but decline to prove it, not to reward them. The same point is expressed with particular clarity in the Australian case of *BP Exploration Co. (Libya) Ltd. v. Hunt*.[37] The question was whether positive evidence of foreign law was required where service of process was sought in a foreign country, conformity with foreign law being a precondition for such service. Hunt J, denying that the plaintiff could rely upon any presumption of similarity, held that it was. As he said:

> The application of the presumption is intended to operate against, not in favour of, the party whose obligation it is to prove the foreign law, so that he is deprived of the benefit of a right or exemption given by that foreign law, but not by New South Wales law, if he does not establish that foreign law in the proper way.[38]

To similar effect is the Scottish case of *McElroy v. McAllister*.[39] There the plaintiff's husband had died in a motor accident in England. She sued in Scotland but her claim failed because, although she had relied on the actionability of her claim under English law she had not made specific averments as to the points of English law on which she relied. Far from endorsing the view that English law should be regarded as the same as that of Scotland (whereby the claims were indeed actionable), the Court of Session found against the plaintiff. The decision is not without difficulty, not least because the court may have realized that English law and Scots law were different on the point in issue.[40] As such it might be read not so much as a case in which the role of the presumption of similarity was ignored, as one in which it could not sensibly operate on the facts. With that caveat, however, the principle articulated by the court was more widely drawn. As Lord President Cooper put it:

> A pursuer who sues not in the *forum delicti* but in another forum, and there seeks a remedy founded on foreign law, must make a sufficiently specific and relevant case as to her rights by that foreign law . . .[41]

Such a view does not require a party to rely upon foreign law when claiming in tort.[42] But it means that one who does so must support any contentions as to foreign law.

On occasion the courts, while adopting the presumption of similarity in such cases, have employed inventive means to avoid using it. It may be, for example, that English law should not be applied if it has no interest in,

---

[37] [1980] 1 NSWLR 496.   [38] At 503.   [39] 1949 SC 100.
[40] At 136–137.   [41] At 137; see also, 118, 124.   [42] Anton, above n. 14, 411.

or connection with, the issue in dispute. This might involve merely excluding the default rule in, say, cases involving English statutes which are expressly limited in their scope to events or persons within the jurisdiction.[43] Or it may imply a form of interest analysis, involving a consideration of the nature and purpose of the relevant English rule. Alternatively it may be viewed as an application of the general principle that an English statute which is silent as to its scope is presumed not to be applicable extraterritorially.[44] Such an approach, however expressed, may be the true rationalization of the Court of Appeal's approach in *Österreichische Länderbank* v. *S'Elite Ltd*.[45] There the plaintiff, an Austrian bank, sued the defendants on a dishonoured bill of exchange which had been drawn by an Austrian company. The appeal turned on whether the bank's title to the bill was vitiated by fraud as defined in sections 29(2) and 30(2) of the Bills of Exchange Act 1882. The defendants apparently assumed that the question was governed by Austrian law.[46] But they argued that fraud was established under English law and, in the absence of evidence of Austrian law, that English and Austrian law should be treated as similar. The argument failed on the ground that no fraud was disclosed under English law. But Roskill LJ also doubted the applicability of the presumption—'if that be the right word'[47]—that, in the absence of contrary evidence, English law and foreign law are deemed to be the same:

In proper cases, of course, that presumption may be applied but I question whether it has any place in a matter of this kind where an assertion is made of fraud, based upon a provision of an English statute *which does not have any direct application, at any rate at first sight, to the law of the country of the incorporation of the company whose conduct is complained of—or indeed, of the bank, whose conduct is complained of*.[48]

Another original means of requiring the pleading and proof of foreign law where it has been relied upon is to dismiss claims which are insufficiently pleaded for purely tactical reasons. In such cases the focus is upon the motives of the claimant in omitting to offer evidence of foreign law. For example, in *Mother Bertha Music Ltd.* v. *Bourne Music Ltd*.[49] it was held that to rely upon foreign law without seeking to establish its content might amount to an abuse of process. The plaintiffs had argued that their

---

[43] *Mother Bertha Music Ltd.* v. *Bourne Music Ltd.*, 31st July 1977 (unreported).
[44] *R* v. *West Yorkshire Coroner, ex parte Smith* [1983] QB 335, 358 (CA); *Clark (Inspector of Taxes)* v. *Oceanic Contractors Inc.* [1983] 2 AC 130, 152 (CA); Mann, (1972–1973) BYIL 117, 127 ff.; Dutson, (1997) 60 MLR 668, 674–676.
[45] [1981] 1 QB 565 (CA).
[46] Perhaps because Austria was the locus of any fraud, or because they took the terms of Section 72(2) of the Bills of Exchange Act 1881 to be mandatory, requiring Austrian law to be applied as the law of the place where the contract was made.
[47] At 569.　　[48] Ibid. (italics supplied).　　[49] 31 July 1977 (unreported).

copyright in a musical work had been infringed in several countries although they had not pleaded the content of the relevant laws. Ferris J dismissed the claims in question as being insufficiently pleaded, describing them as an abuse of process, or something resembling an abuse of process. The plaintiffs could not seriously have supposed, as their reliance upon the presumption of similarity implied, that the copyright laws of so many different countries were similar to English law. Nor could they seriously have expected the case to have proceeded under English law, given especially that English copyright law applies only to infringements in England. Assuming that they must have known that the dispute would ultimately turn on questions of foreign law it was for them to make out their case accordingly. Moreover, the absence of any particulars of foreign law in the pleadings was unfair to the defendants in so far as they could not know precisely what aspects of the laws in question they were to address in their defence.

Although the judgment in *Bourne* was not expressed in such terms, it seems that a failure to plead foreign law fully will be treated as purely tactical, designed merely to place the plaintiff at an advantage, whenever it is likely that English and foreign law are different. Only a claimant who has good reason to believe that nothing would be served by seeking to establish foreign law is thus entitled to rely upon it without doing so. The argument that English law applies unless foreign law is established cannot be employed to shift to the defendant the burden of disproving what, in truth, the plaintiff must prove.

It is apparent, therefore, that authoritative support for the presumption of similarity, at least where foreign law is relied upon but no evidence is tendered, is at best, questionable and, at worst, entirely lacking. It is also unsatisfactory in principle for a number of reasons. It is intuitively unacceptable for a party to seek the application of foreign law and at the same time, with luminous inconsistency, to invite the court to apply English law by declining to offer evidence of any other. It is also potentially unfair that one party should (in effect) be made to prove (or disprove) a matter which another has introduced. No doubt the ethics of argumentation would prevent counsel from relying upon a proposition of foreign law which is plainly untrue. But the idea that an unproved foreign law is presumed to be the same as English law may allow a plaintiff to allege a fact which is arguable but which may have scant foundation—typically that a tort is actionable in the *lex loci* when in truth it is not.

It may also be inconsistent with general principle that a plaintiff should shelter behind the presumption of similarity so as to avoid establishing the truth of any assertion as to foreign law. But for that presumption the usual rule would presumably apply whereby any assertion of fact must be established by evidence, which imposes the burden of proof on one who makes such an assertion.[50] It might be objected that the general principle should indeed apply to one who gives particulars of the content of foreign law in the pleadings but offers no evidence, although not to one who merely states that foreign law is to a certain effect without particularising that assertion in the pleadings. This is implied by Popplewell J's reasoning in *University of Glasgow*. But it is hard to find merit in a distinction between, on the one hand, pleading the content of foreign law (which requires proof), and merely relying upon an unsubstantiated proposition of foreign law in the statement of claim or defence (which does not).

Such arguments suggest that a party who relies upon foreign law must normally offer evidence as to its content or face dismissal of its claim or defence. It must be emphasised, however, that this does not depend upon whether or not the introduction of foreign law is, by the relevant choice of law rule, mandatory. The requirement is a matter of fairness and consistency and applies even if a claimant voluntarily relies upon foreign law. But a further, obvious consideration supports the proof of foreign law in cases where the introduction of foreign law is obligatory. In such a case it would undermine the very purpose of having a mandatory choice of law rule if its application could be avoided merely by omitting to lead evidence as to foreign law. The point is made with stark clarity in the *BP Exploration* case, in which Hunt J clearly regarded the relevant provisions of the Rules of the Supreme Court of New South Wales as mandatory:

> It would, in my opinion, be an absurd interpretation of the requirements of Pt 10, r. 5 (that non-personal service be in accordance with the law of the country in which service is to be effected) which enabled a judgment creditor, by mere non-disclosure of the *ex parte* application for registration, to obtain the benefit of a more advantageous New South Wales provision as to service, which is in fact not available in the foreign jurisdiction in which service is to be effected. Such an interpretation would render the requirement in r. 5 otiose.[51]

2. FOREIGN LAW INADEQUATELY PROVED

A court may select from a range of responses when it becomes apparent that foreign law is unlikely to be adequately proved.[52] It might leave the evidence undisturbed, only to treat the claim under foreign law as having failed, applying English law by default.[53] Or it might try its best to determine foreign law on the material available.[54] Or it might suggest to the

---

[50] Sir Brian Neill, above n. 10, 50.   [51] [1980] 1 NSWLR 496, 503.
[52] We are now concerned with what steps a court may take to ensure that it has proper evidence of foreign law; see below, p. 182 for its options where, on the basis of such evidence, it cannot sufficiently determine foreign law.
[53] See cases cited above n. 34.   [54] See below, p. 194.

parties what steps might be taken to improve the tendered evidence.[55] Our present concern is with this latter course. If such a suggestion is made the court could not penalise a party for failing to comply. Its power is only to influence, not direct, the provision of evidence, the sanction of contempt of court being unavailable.[56] But a party who fails to heed a warning as to the insufficiency of its evidence faces the real threat that the court will rule that its claim under foreign law has failed and apply English law instead.

The courts' power of intervention is illustrated by a short but revealing series of decisions concerning the Evidence (Colonial Statutes) Act 1907. The 1907 Act was designed to facilitate the proof of colonial and Commonwealth statutes.[57] All that need be demonstrated for this purpose is that the foreign statute emanated from the appropriate Government printer. In several cases, however, the courts declined to treat the test provided by the Act as conclusive and have insisted that further proof should be offered in addition to the text of the foreign law.[58] They did so because, although the Act might prove the authenticity of a foreign statute, it contains no mechanism for proving whether it is still in force, a point on which expert evidence is required. A more general example of the court's power is *Beatty* v. *Beatty*,[59] concerning the effectiveness of a New York judgment. This was assumed by the parties to be a matter for the law of New York, but no evidence of that law was introduced at trial, and the judge assumed it to be the same as English law. On appeal, one party put in evidence a United States Supreme Court decision but, again, offered no expert evidence to support it, apparently expecting the court to take it at face value. Rather than do so, however, the Court of Appeal adjourned the proceedings so that expert evidence could be sought.[60] Neither party obtained such evidence and both asked the court to rule on its own, an invitation which the court accepted.

Re State of Norway's Application[61] exemplifies in a different way how a court might influence the quality of evidence supplied to prove foreign law. The principal issue was whether a request for assistance from a Norwegian court under the Hague Evidence Convention was a 'civil or commercial' matter when its proceedings concerned a matter of revenue law. But was this to be answered by applying English law, Norwegian law, or both? The question arose in two sets of proceedings, *Re State of*

---

[55] See below, Chapter VII.

[56] *Edmeades* v. *Thames Board Mills Ltd.* [1969] 2 QB 67, 72–73 (HL). Nor may RSC Order 38, r. 37 be used to compel a party to produce an expert report if they do not propose to lead expert evidence at all: *Derby & Co. Ltd.* v. *Weldon (No. 9)*, unreported, 18 October 1990 (CA), cited in *Prudential Assurance Co.* v. *Page Ltd.* [1991] 1 WLR 756, 768–769.

[57] See below, p. 224.

[58] *Brown* v. *Brown* (1917) 116 LT 702; *R* v. *Governor of Brixton Prison, ex parte Shuter* [1960] 2 QB 89; *Jasiewicz* v. *Jasciewicz* [1962] 1 WLR 1426.

[59] [1924] 1 KB 807.   [60] At 811.   [61] [1989] 1 All ER 661.

Norway's Application (No. 1)[62] and *Re State of Norway's Application (No. 2)*.[63] Preferring the third, mixed approach the Court of Appeal in *Norway (No. 1)* expressed dissatisfaction with the paucity of the Norwegian law evidence. As Kerr LJ said: '. . . if a similar issue should arise in the future, I hope that our courts will be provided with more satisfactory evidence in the light of the considerations to which I have referred'.[64] In consequence,[65] the parties provided extensive evidence of Norwegian law in *Norway (No. 2)*.

Finally, a court might require the proof of foreign law in those rare situations in which the parties seek to treat a point of foreign law as one of construction.[66] The parties' purpose in doing so is to ensure that the court does not treat the case as one involving foreign law at all in any formal sense, with attendant savings in time and costs. A court may be reluctant to treat such issues as going merely to construction, requiring foreign law's pleading and proof, but it is apparent that they will permit it where both parties agree on this course.[67]

There is, then, some indication that courts may seek the introduction of improved proof of pleaded foreign law. But it remains unlikely that they will often do so. First, it will normally be unnecessary, given that each party will normally introduce full expert evidence without any prompting.[68] Secondly, in those relatively unusual cases where non-standard modes of proof are adopted it is generally because the parties have agreed to this course. As such, a court may be reluctant to disturb their agreement, especially where to do so would increase the cost and duration of proceedings. This is especially so if, as is likely, the parties have sought to dispense with expert evidence in relatively straightforward cases, such as those concerning the interpretation of judicial decisions,[69] legislation[70] or legal documents.[71] Thirdly, from a procedural point of view, steps might be taken at an earlier stage to ensure that adequate evidence is available. The development of the Summons for Directions procedure may tend to ensure that such control as the court may wish to exercise over the proof of foreign law should be exercised so far as possible before trial.[72] This is not to deny, however, that the inadequacy of the evidence may only become fully clear once the testimony of the parties' experts has been heard. Indeed, the Summons procedure is designed more to address the nature of the evidence supplied than its quality. Fourthly, if the courts' relative willingness to seek better proof of foreign law is a feature of their

---

[62] Ibid.   [63] Ibid.   [64] At 681 (per Kerr LJ).   [65] At 757–758.
[66] *Stafford Allen & Co. Ltd.* v. *Pacific Steam Navigation Co.*, above n. 30.
[67] Ibid.
[68] If anything, the need is for the courts to limit the introduction of expert evidence: see below, p. 156.
[69] *Beatty* v. *Beatty* [1924] 1 KB 807.   [70] See below, p. 257.
[71] See below, p. 251.   [72] RSC Order 38, r. 3.

desire to save the proof of foreign law from failure, it must be set beside other mechanisms for doing so. In particular, the courts are willing to resort to such original materials concerning foreign law as may be in evidence so as to cure any inadequacy in expert testimony. Typically, this occurs in situations in which the defective proof of foreign law lies in the expert witnesses, in which case, rather than seek better proof, a court may simply turn to such written evidence as may be before it and determine foreign law alone.[73] In such situations, courts are often able to resolve matters of foreign law, notwithstanding deficiencies in the evidence, by making do with such evidence as is available. In truth, however, given that expert evidence is already before the court it is hard to see how better evidence might be sought. Finally, those cases in which a court has sought better proof of foreign law must be set against their probable reluctance to adjourn proceedings at trial (and *a fortiori* perhaps, on appeal). Given the expense and delay occasioned by the late submission of evidence, and that it is incumbent on the parties to prepare their case fully, it is perhaps doubtful that this is how a court would respond in the majority of cases. It is certainly unlikely that a court would permit one party to introduce improved evidence where to do so would prejudice the other party.[74]

3. FOREIGN LAW EXCESSIVELY PROVED

A persistent problem in English civil procedure is the tendency of litigants, by their lawyers, to deploy excessive means to establish relatively simple propositions. Tactical considerations and straightforward conscientiousness tend to disincline the parties to show moderation. The problem is a general one and detailed consideration of current initiatives to solve it are beyond the scope of the present discussion.[75] It is clear, however, that the problem of excess may be as problematic in connection with questions of foreign law as elsewhere. In one case the trial judge expressed regret that the parties' counsel had underestimated the time required to cross-examine foreign law experts, ten days eventually being expended on such cross-examination in a case which involved a preliminary issue of jurisdiction.[76] More strikingly, another judge took the unusual course of adding an epilogue to his judgment in which he castigated the parties for their procedural intemperance, not least with regard to foreign law.[77] A

---

[73] See below, pp. 194–199.   [74] *De Reneville* v. *De Reneville* [1948] P 100, 124 (CA).
[75] See further, Lord Woolf, *Access to Justice, Interim Report to the Lord Chancellor on the Civil Justice System in England and Wales*, (London, HMSO, 1996), esp. Chs. 3 and 4.
[76] *Grupo Torras SA* v. *Al Sabah* [1995] 1 Lloyd's Rep. 374, 379, affd. [1996] 1 Lloyd's Rep. 7 (CA).
[77] *Macmillan Inc.* v. *Bishopsgate Investment Trust plc (No. 3)* [1995] 1 WLR 978, 1013–1016.

failure to clarify the issues of foreign law in dispute, one party's insistence on taking a 'wholly untenable'[78] point which depended on foreign law, and the lengthy examination of numerous foreign law experts all added to the delay and expense of proceedings. More critically, they tended to obscure the issues for determination, hindering the court. The difficulty revealed in such cases is not, of course, special to the proof of foreign law. And, at the time of writing, significant changes to the framework of civil procedure are imminent. But it is instructive to see how the problem may be handled, even within an adversarial framework, traditionally conceived.

The tendency for issues to be argued, and evidence introduced, in an over-elaborate fashion is a feature of any party-led system of adjudication. But it might be entirely justified, in the sense that complex cases are likely to have—and should have—proportionately sophisticated treatment.[79] The question is whether the courts have adequate tools to prevent the misguided or purely tactical elaboration of relatively simple matters.[80] English law's approach to case-management, although increasingly interventionist, has not traditionally been coercive. But, although the court's instinct may be to police the parties' control of litigation rather than take control themselves,[81] a more regulated framework is compatible with an adversarial model. English judges are not insensitive to the cost of litigation and to the need to encourage cost-effective procedures.[82] And, even short of complete case-management it is possible to employ a variety of mechanisms to encourage a greater narrowing and specification of the issues between the parties, whether of foreign law or otherwise. Such practices as holding pre-trial meetings of experts[83] and directing the exchange of expert reports[84] are means to this end. Again, various devices may be employed to streamline the presentation of foreign law evidence. It is questionable whether such possibilities as directing the appointment of a court expert, or invoking some other alternative means of proof would be appropriate or advantageous.[85] But, even in a system in which expert evidence may not be excluded altogether it is possible to limit the number of experts called[86] and to encourage counsel to set time-limits for cross

---

[78] At 1013.   [79] See below, p. 174.

[80] Despite his comments concerning cross-examination, Mance J recognized the particular difficulty of the points of foreign law at stake in *Grupo Torras SA* v. *Al Sabah*, above, n. 76, 379.

[81] As Lord Woolf has commented: 'I do not propose that we should abolish our adversarial oral tradition in England and Wales in favour of an inquisitorial system. The approach I am advocating is to preserve the best features of the adversarial system while giving a more interventionist management role to the courts': *The Times*, 16th June 1995.

[82] See e.g. the remarks of Mance J in *Grupo Torras SA* v. *Al Sabah*, above n. 76, 379, and of Millet J in *Macmillan Inc.* v. *Bishopsgate Investment Trust plc (No. 3)*, above n. 77, 1013–1016; Practice Note [1995] 1 All ER 385.

[83] RSC Order 38, r. 38.   [84] RSC Order 38, r. 37.   [85] See below, Chapter VII.

[86] *Grupo Torras SA* v. *Al Sabah*, above n. 76, 379; cf. RSC Order 38, r. 4.

examination.[87] Such familiar techniques as making wasted costs orders may also be used to penalise procedural profligacy.[88]

4. COURT-APPOINTED ADVISERS

Brief mention should be made of the possibility that a court might appoint an independent expert or assessor on its own motion, irrespective of the parties' wishes, either instead of the parties' own experts or in addition. It has always been possible for a court to appoint an assessor on its own motion.[89] Nor is there any reason of principle why the judicial appointment of court experts should not be expressly provided for and, indeed, encouraged, irrespective of the parties' wishes.[90] But it is instructive to ask why no use has traditionally been made of this possibility, and whether there are particular reasons for or against doing so in the future. It is true that RSC Order 40, for some time the primary source of the courts' power to appoint such experts, refers only to such an appointment at the motion of one of the parties.[91] But there have always been strong grounds for supposing that a residual power of appointment survived the creation of the Order 40 procedure,[92] albeit that it was never used.

Is a court likely in principle to employ any power it might have to appoint a court adviser in cases concerning foreign law? If a residual power of appointment indeed survived the introduction of the Order 40 procedure, it is telling that so little use has been made of it, just as assessors have never been employed in such cases. But if it did not, it is equally striking that so few judges and practitioners have seen the need for change. The courts' reluctance to employ their *ex officio* power to seek judicial assistance under the British Law Ascertainment Act 1859 also suggests that such appointments are unlikely.[93] More importantly, it is far from clear that the appointment of a court expert is, in principle, an appropriate mechanism for establishing foreign law.[94]

---

[87] Practice Note [1995] 1 All ER 385, para. 2.
[88] Ibid., para. 1.
[89] RSC Order 33, r. 6; *Waddle* v. *Wallsend Shipping Co Ltd.* [1952] Lloyd's Rep. 105, 131.
[90] Lord Woolf, above n. 67, Ch. 13; Draft Civil Proceedings Rules, Rule 32.5.
[91] RSC Order 40, r. 1.
[92] As the annotation to RSC Order 40, and the cases there cited, imply. See also, Basten, [1970] 40 *MLR* 174, 175–178; Howard, Crane and Hochberg, *Phipson on Evidence*, 14th edn., (London, 1990), 823–824; Hodgkinson, 65–68.
[93] See below, p. 238.
[94] See below, pp. 213–218, 235–238.

V
Exercising Party Choice

We have seen that litigants generally have a choice whether or not to plead and prove foreign law, a choice reflecting the voluntarism of the English approach to civil procedure and choice of law. Indeed, the principle of party choice, whatever its merits, whatever its scope, powerfully shapes the process of international litigation. It raises an important strategic issue for litigants which is lacking where the introduction of foreign law is invariably required. And it accounts for the large, unassessable, number of English cases with a foreign element in which foreign law goes unpleaded. It also begs an arresting question: why should litigants choose to introduce foreign law in some cases but not in others? More strikingly, why should they not do so where they might have an advantage under foreign law which is lacking in English law? In the nature of things, cases in which foreign law has not been relied upon, although it might have been, are hard to detect. Parading as purely domestic decisions, assuming they are reported at all, their foreign elements necessarily pass unmentioned, revealed only by traces in the facts. That one or both parties are not English signals a foreign dimension, for example, as would the fact that a contract was performed, or a tort committed, abroad, or that a contract is expressly subject to foreign law.

A prominent example of a concealed conflicts case is *Aluminium Industrie Vaassen BV* v. *Romalpa Aluminium Ltd.*[1] Famous as the source of the English domestic law of retention of title, decided without demur as a purely domestic case, *Romalpa* has conspicuous foreign elements. The plaintiff was foreign, a Dutch company which had sold aluminium foil to an English buyer, which thereafter became insolvent, subject to the disputed reservation of title on which the case turned. Again, as the foil was located in the Netherlands at the time of contracting, English law would have regarded the law of the Netherlands as applicable to the proprietary

---

[1] [1976] 1 WLR 676. See also an important series of Scottish decisions. In neither *Emerald Stainless Steel Ltd.* v. *South Side Distribution Ltd.*, 1983 SLT 162, nor in *Deutz Engines Ltd.* v. *Terex Ltd.*, 1984 SLT 273, was the relevance of foreign law referred to. In *Armour* v. *Thyssen Edelstahlwerke AG* [1991] 2 AC 339 (HL) German law was relied upon but not adequately pleaded or proved (see 1989 SLT 183; SLT 94). See further, Anton, *Private International Law*, 3rd edn. (Edinburgh, 1990), 618–620. On the reasons for not pleading foreign law see, Fentiman, [1992] 108 *LQR* 142, 149–152.

effects of the sale.[2] Most strikingly, the contract was expressed to be governed by Dutch law,[3] indicating that Dutch law should govern the contractual implications of the transaction and, just possibly, its proprietary aspects as well.[4] Surprisingly, given this cluster of Dutch connections, Dutch law was never apparently alluded to by either party in the proceedings, although one judge on appeal expressed passing interest in knowing what Dutch law might have been on the point in dispute.[5] The absence of any reference to Dutch law in *Romalpa*, notable enough given the case's foreign elements, is all the more intriguing given that Dutch law might, perhaps, have provided a very different answer to that eventually arrived at under English law. The specific issue in the case was whether the terms of the seller's reservation of title gave them a proprietary interest, in preference to other creditors, in the proceeds of sub-sales by the buyers of unpaid-for foil. The Court of Appeal, applying English law, held that it did. Under Dutch law, however, it is possible that the sellers would have enjoyed no such interest, denying them any priority over the buyer's other creditors.[6] Why the buyers, on that assumption, might not have invoked Dutch law is a matter to which we will return.

Other examples of similar abstentionism, some of them prominent domestic cases, are numerous. They are drawn from all departments of law. Some, like *Romalpa*, concern title to goods.[7] Others concern actions for breach of contract,[8] others proceedings in tort.[9] Surprisingly, perhaps, foreign law has not been pleaded even in cases where it might have been expected that a court, for policy reasons, would have insisted upon it. It has been omitted even where a contract contains an express choice of foreign law,[10] and in cases involving nullity of marriage.[11] Apart from such

[2] *Cammell* v. *Sewell* (1860) 5 H & N 728; Benjamin, *Sale of Goods*, 5th edn., (London, 1997), para. 25–098, 25–105 ff.

[3] Benjamin, op. cit., para. 25–003; cf. *Emerald Stainless Steel Ltd.* v. *South Side Distribution Ltd.*, above n. 1.

[4] Although not in conformity with general principle, there may be reasons to subject even the proprietary aspects of a transfer to the contract's applicable law: Benjamin, op. cit., para. 25–114. But see North, (1990) *Recueil des Cours*, vol. 220, 267–268.   [5] At 684, 688.

[6] Goode, *Commercial Law*, (London, 1982), 992, n. 43 (discussion of the point is not included in the 2nd edn., 1995): 'Under Dutch law the plaintiff sellers would not have acquired real rights to the proceeds successfully claimed in that action'.

[7] See cases cited above, n. 1.

[8] e.g. *Stafford Allen & Sons Ltd.* v. *Pacific Steam Navigation Co.* [1956] Lloyd's Rep. 104, below, p. 166; *Suisse Atlantique Societe d'Armement SA* v. *NV Rotterdamsche Kolen Centrale* [1967] 1 AC 21 (contract for carriage of goods between America and countries other than England); *C. Czarnikow Ltd.* v. *Koufos* [1969] 1 AC 350 (goods shipped from Constanza to Basra); *R. Pagnan & Fratelli* v. *Corbisa Industrial Agropacuaria Limitada* [1971] 1 All ER 165 (contract between Italian buyers and Brazilian sellers).

[9] e.g. *Winkworth* v. *Hubbard* [1960] 1 Lloyd's Rep. 150 (tort committed in Monte Carlo); *Schneider* v. *Eisovitch* [1960] 2 QB 430 (tort committed in France).

[10] *Aluminium Industrie* v. *Romalpa Aluminium*, and other cases cited above, n. 1.

[11] *Easterbrook* v. *Easterbrook* [1944] 1 All ER 90; *Hutter* v. *Hutter* [1944] P 95; *Buckland* v. *Buckland* [1968] P 296; Cheshire and North, 643, 645.

individual examples, the tendency to ignore a foreign element is visible also in entire lines of cases. In these, the application of English law by default has become habitual, even conventional. Take, for instance, those involving contracts of sale governed by English law in which the goods in question are located abroad at the time of contracting. Under normal principles, whatever role English law might have in determining the contractual aspects of such a transaction, its proprietary effect, principally whether property has passed, is a matter for the law of the place where the goods are located at the time of sale.[12] There are cases, however, in which the question whether title has passed in goods located abroad at the time of sale has been referred, unquestioningly, to the contract's English applicable law, not to the foreign *lex situs*.[13] Again, there are those situations, supposedly 'too numerous to mention',[14] involving the sale of goods by an English seller to an English buyer, in which the goods are shipped to or from another country, or between foreign countries. In such cases foreign law is rarely, if ever, pleaded, presumably because English parties would never suppose that any law but English law should apply. Another situation in which, almost by convention, foreign law is not relied upon concerns the nullity of marriage. In a striking but typical case English law governed the validity of a marriage which had no connection with England apart from the fact that the petitioner had, since the marriage, acquired a domicile there.[15] At first sight it is strange that such important matters affecting status, implicating the public interest, are thus subject to the normal rules of pleading. An obvious explanation is that such cases concern uncontested petitions for nullity in which it may not be in the claimant's interest to have foreign law applied, although this does not account for the leniency of the courts in permitting this course.

But such arresting examples of cases in which foreign law is not relied upon must be placed firmly in perspective. We should not suppose, for example, that every such case somehow strikes at the choice of law process. Indeed, in many cases the relevant choice of law rule may require the application of English law, especially because English private international law endorses the application of the *lex fori* relatively frequently. As such there are, perhaps, an unusual number of situations with palpable foreign elements in which it is simply irrelevant to plead foreign law. English law, for example, applies the *lex fori* to many important aspects of the law of personal status. Petitions for divorce and legal separation are

---

[12] *Cammell* v. *Sewell*, above, n. 2; *Re Anziani* [1930] 1 Ch. 407, 420; Benjamin, op. cit., 107 et seq.
[13] *Badische Anilin und Soda Fabrik* v. *Basle Chemical Works* [1898] AC 200, 204; *Kursell* v. *Timber Operators and Contractors Ltd.* [1927] 1 KB 299, 312.
[14] Sassoon, *Cif and Fob Contracts*, 4th edn., (London, 1995), para. 404, n. 74.
[15] See cases cited above, n. 11; Cheshire and North, 643, 645.

invariably governed by English law,[16] so too proceedings for the financial maintenance of spouses and children.[17] Many matters concerning guardianship, adoption and the custody of children are similarly treated.[18] Again, until recently it was effectively impossible to bring claims in England for torts committed abroad when the wrong would not also be actionable under English law.[19] More accurately, perhaps, the difficulty of demonstrating the contrary would itself have been a deterrent to litigation. A significant consequence of this rule is that proceedings in England for the infringement abroad of foreign intellectual property rights were generally regarded as inconceivable, only local infringements being actionable in English law.[20]

Nor should it be assumed that it is never to a claimant's advantage to plead foreign law. Sometimes it will be essential, as (obviously) where no action lies under English law.[21] It may also be tactically advantageous to do so, perhaps in the hope that the other party will be forced to settle rather than bear the potential cost and delay of disproving the claimant's case under foreign law. This is notoriously true of defamation claims in which a plaintiff might impose an onerous evidential burden on a defendant by alleging defamation in several jurisdictions and relying on the presumption that England law and foreign law are the same.[22]

Moreover, where foreign law is not pleaded, leading to the application of English law, such abstinence need occasion no surprise, still less anxiety. Consider those cases involving the sale of goods where the parties assume that English law should govern questions of title. Where a contract's applicable law is English it is natural, if not strictly accurate, that the parties should expect English law to govern even its proprietary aspects, however distinct to a lawyer issues of contract and property may be. So too, where both parties to a contract are English they are likely to imagine that English law will govern their commercial dealings, whatever their contract's foreign dimension, whether it is to be performed partly or wholly abroad. Indeed, the obviousness of this result, in layman's terms, explains why express applicable law clauses are often omitted in contracts between English parties. English law, they might suppose, self-evidently will govern. Even where only one, or neither, litigant in English proceedings is English, a not uncommon occurrence, both may have their own reasons to wish English law to apply. The very fact that they are going to trial

---

[16] Cheshire and North, 639–642.   [17] Cheshire and North, 714.
[18] Cheshire and North, 730.
[19] Because of the requirement that the wrong should be actionable under both the *lex loci delicti* and in English law; see now, *Red Sea Insurance Co. Ltd.* v. *Bouygues SA* [1944] AC (PC); Private International Law (Miscellaneous Provisions) Act 1995, Part III.
[20] *Def Lepp Music* v. *Stuart Brown* [1986] RPC 273.
[21] e.g. *Red Sea Insurance Co. Ltd.* v. *Bouygues SA*, above n. 19.
[22] *University of Glasgow* v. *The Economist* [1997] EMLR 495; see above, p. 145.

in England might imply a readiness to submit to English domestic law, notwithstanding the important, if technical, distinction between issues of choice of law and of jurisdiction. In one sense this produces circularity, because it is likely that England will be the forum precisely because the governing law, typically a contractually agreed governing law, is English. But whatever reasons the parties—or the stronger of them—may have for selecting English jurisdiction, it is rational to wish for congruence between the *lex fori* and the *lex causae*. Certainly, if a contract contains an English jurisdiction or arbitration agreement, even if—perhaps, especially if— there is no accompanying choice of governing law, the parties may want and expect English substantive law to be applied. The same applies if, as often occurs, a contract litigated in England is in a form which reflects both English law and the practices of a London market, such as that in finance, insurance, or shipping.

But the most important reason why such examples of voluntary pleading need not be surprising is that most legal systems obtain similar results, albeit by different means, and not in all cases. In contractual disputes, for example, many systems endorse the principle of party choice and allow contracting parties to alter the governing law for the purposes of trial.[23] Notably, Article 3(2) of the 1980 Rome Convention on the Law Applicable to Contractual Obligations provides that the parties may at any time agree to subject the contract to a law other than that which previously governed it. Such respect for party choice is also revealed even in other areas. The position in English law is unclear[24]—although the principle of voluntary pleading would lead to it by other means—but many legal systems permit litigants to choose the law which should govern liability in tort. Normally, this will involve a choice of the *lex fori* in preference to a foreign *lex loci delicti*.[25] Indeed, sometimes such displacement of the otherwise applicable law is possible only when the *lex fori* is applied instead.[26] In whatever form, however, the effect of allowing litigants to choose the *lex causae* is to replicate, at the choice of law level, the result which English would secure through its rules of pleading.

There are, then, numerous examples of abstinence in matters of foreign law encouraged by English law's distinctively voluntarist attitude to foreign law. But the consequences are often unexceptional, and often consistent with the results which other legal systems would achieve by different means. Certainly, in approaching the reasons litigants might have for abjuring foreign law it is as well to counterbalance the conflicts lawyers' instinct, which is to find the non-pleading of foreign law surprising, with

[23] Below, Ch. IX.
[24] North, *Essays in Private International Law* (Oxford, 1993), 187–191.
[25] Ibid. 188, n. 87.
[26] As under the 1987 Swiss Law on Private International Law, Art. 132.

a quite different perspective. To non-lawyers, and to many practitioners, it must seem entirely natural. There are, however, many cases in which the decision not to rely upon foreign law is not so easily explained. Whether or not to plead foreign law in a given case is a complex question. So much is it coloured and informed by the diverse circumstances of particular disputes that any attempt to rationalize the process of choice is at once a generalisation and a distortion. Practitioners, moreover, are apt to view the decision whether to plead or not in robust terms. They will introduce foreign law only if absolutely necessary to their case or, alternatively, if their opponent does so first, making a defence on the point essential. Either way, strict necessity, not some abstract desire for completeness, is the benchmark of decision. Lawyers, then, are unlikely to undertake anything resembling a complete survey of all the implications of pleading foreign law or not. But it is worthwhile marshalling some reasons which might, depending upon the case, influence the decision whether or not to plead foreign law.

The first reason for ignoring foreign law is special to cases where the governing law has been contractually agreed. It might seem unlikely that litigants would fail to rely on an express governing law clause. But there can be sound reasons to do so, assuming such a course is permitted. One party, or both, may never really have wanted the chosen law to govern. Certainly, if the contract were in a standard form it is possible that neither party conscientiously paid attention to the question of a governing law at the time of contracting. Even if both parties meaningfully agreed to a given choice of law, one party may regret doing so once a dispute arises. Contracting parties cannot visualise all the implications of such an agreement in advance and foresee how the applicable law might bear on every issue that might arise. Again, a litigant might have a particular reason to walk away from a previously agreed choice of foreign law: it might have changed since their agreement. The English rule is that a choice of applicable law is a choice of that law as it is from time to time in force.[27] It is not a choice of that law as it was at the time of agreement. A change in the foreign law, making it less preferable than it was, is no justification for ignoring the usual choice of law rule that the chosen law should govern. But it might explain why a party might wish to ignore a previous selection of foreign law. Finally, merely because the parties in dispute are parties to a contract containing a foreign governing law clause does not mean that the chosen law need apply to every issue between them. This is because, correctly classified, an issue may not be contractual at all, in which case it is simply beyond the scope of the agreed governing law.

---

[27] *Re Helbert Wagg's Claim* [1956] Ch. 323.

A more common reason for ignoring foreign law is that definite information concerning its content may be hard to acquire. At the time when strategic decisions are taken as to how a claim or defence should be argued it may be unclear whether it would be advantageous to do so or not. The absence of hard evidence, more than any conclusion that a point is a weak one under foreign law, may incline practitioners to rely on English law instead. Sometimes the problem lies in the uncertainty of foreign law itself. The answer to the point in question may be unclear, perhaps because it has never been decided. Or the nature of legal reasoning in the system in question may not readily yield practical, usable answers, as where great reliance is placed on the writings of commentators and the *doctrine* is divided. Nor is it always easy to identify suitably qualified experts, or those whose opinion in sufficiently favourable or unequivocal, or those who are likely to withstand the rigours of oral cross-examination. Yet without reliable expert evidence it is a perilous course to embark on the introduction of foreign law.

A more obvious, even self-evident, reason for ignoring foreign law is that it might have no relevance to the proceedings. Sometimes, as we have seen, English law must apply, despite a case's foreign dimension. Alternatively, English law and foreign law may be the same,[28] or, more likely, similar enough in effect that nothing would be served by proceeding under the latter. Or English and foreign law might be alike enough in their consequences that the gain in pleading foreign law would be eroded by the cost of doing so. Certainly, it is a truism of comparative law that the world's legal systems, at least in commercial matters, are more alike than not and conceptual differences and matters of outlook and idiom often obscure close similarities in practice. Moreover, several international conventions, common to many countries, govern, in particular, important aspects of international trade, ensuring a degree of harmonization of the world's laws, a trend which seems likely to continue.[29] It should be emphasized, however, that it is one thing to ignore foreign law because it is thought to be the same, or similar, to English law. It is another thing to be correct in that assumption. It is impossible to speculate as to how many cases have been affected because incorrect or misleading evidence was obtained at an early stage concerning foreign law.

Sometimes litigants and their advisers may, from the start, visualise a case in such a way that its foreign elements take on a particular shape, or are obscured altogether. Such informal classification of the issues may amount to little more than an assumption, perhaps unconscious, that English law, not foreign law, will govern. It may arise from an insufficient grasp of the conflicts issues involved, private international law being

[28] As in *Pfeiffer Weinkellerai-Weineinkauf GmbH* v. *Arbuthnot Factors Ltd.* [1988] 1 WLR 150.
[29] Cheshire and North, 10.

regarded as something of a mystery by many practitioners. Or it may derive from a legitimate, common sense, expectation that English law should apply, as in the cases involving the sale of goods and marital validity described above. It is certainly unusual to find in the cases novel or speculative arguments founded upon private international law. Unless a case falls within, or comes close to, an established principle, or reflects a view supported by one of the leading textbooks, it is more likely that the conflicts aspects of a case will not be exploited. In any event, the omission to plead foreign law may stem from a conscious decision not to do so, or from straightforward ignorance that a conflicts issue arises, or from a more or less reflective classification of the issues such that foreign law becomes irrelevant.

Two illustrations reinforce the point that self-classification by the parties may render foreign law irrelevant. In the *Pacific Steam*[30] case, for example, neither party thought that US law was relevant to the question whether a port in the Panama Canal Zone was a 'US port'. The phrase occurred in bills of lading governed by English law and the parties clearly treated the issue as one of the construction of the contract, something to be resolved using English principles without reference to foreign law. Had the trial judge not intervened, insisting unusually on the proof of US law, the case would have proceeded, presumably, on that basis. No doubt the parties' intuitive assumption was that English law governed every aspect of the contract's construction, given that its applicable law was English. But it is equally apparent that they wished to avoid the delay and expense of introducing expert evidence of foreign law by classifying the case in such a way that it became irrelevant.

Again, we have seen that Dutch law might have been applied in *Romalpa*.[31] The omission of any reference to Dutch law has long puzzled conflicts scholars, and the case is often treated as a classic example of the English approach to foreign law. But, on inspection the omission is less surprising. It is certainly possible to depict the issue in dispute as one to which only English law could have applied. The core of the dispute, it should be recalled, was whether the seller had an interest, by virtue of its reservation of title, in the proceeds of various sub-sales effected by the buyer with third parties. There are thus grounds for supposing that the Dutch governing law clause was irrelevant, in so far as the dispute turned on the seller's proprietary interest in the proceeds of sale, which was not a contractual issue and so beyond the control of the *lex contractus*. Moreover, although the Netherlands was the location of the aluminium at the time of sale, it is unclear that Dutch law would have applied on that ground.[32] That it was the *lex situs* might not have been relevant, for example, had the

---

[30] See above, p. 137.   [31] See above, p. 159.
[32] See generally, Benjamin, op. cit., para. 25–122.

issue been seen as remedial, concerning whether the seller was entitled to the remedy of tracing, in so far as the availability of a remedy is normally for the *lex fori* to determine. Nor would Dutch law have been applicable had the issue been seen, as it might have been seen, as turning on the creation of a constructive trust affecting the proceeds of the English sub-sales, those proceeds being the product of English transactions. Nor, again, would Dutch law have been relevant on the basis that the proprietary aspects of dealings in property are governed by the *lex situs* at the time of the dealing. True, it might have governed proprietary rights under the original transaction, and in particular the seller's interest in the foil itself. But the foil at the time of the sub-sales, of which the disputed monies were the product, was located in England, making English law the relevant *lex situs*.[33] Moreover, the mere fact that the goods in *Romalpa* had been delivered to the buyer in England might be thought to change the character of the case. It certainly begs the question whether the parties' respective rights to property in England (and the proceeds of its sale) should be governed by English law.[34] Finally, even if Dutch law had governed according to the relevant English choice of law rule, would the appropriate Dutch rules have been applicable according to Dutch law? Certainly, the parties might reasonably have doubted that Dutch law would have applied to determine a seller's right to monies located in England.

Viewed in any of these ways the governing law in *Romalpa* would probably have been English. But a case might still have been made for the application of Dutch law.[35] Plausibly, the obligation to account to a seller for the proceeds of sub-sales which are subject to a reservation of title is a matter for the law applicable to the contract of sale, in so far as it represents the source of the parties' relationship. This might be so whether the obligation is expressed in terms of a fiduciary relationship between seller and buyer, or as a restitutionary obligation to restore benefits conferred on the buyer through the sub-sales. It is also doubtful that the availability of the right to trace is purely remedial if, for example, it is only by applying the law of the obligation to account that a seller's rights thereunder could be preserved. In each of the ways, Dutch law might have governed in *Romalpa*, a solution which would no doubt have reflected the parties' expectations at the time of sale. But in the end it is profoundly unclear whether the obligation to account in such a case truly concerns any

---

[33] Cf. *Kruppstahl AG v. Quittmann Products Ltd.* [1982] IRLM 551; *Zahnrad Fabrik Passau GmbH v. Terex Ltd.* 1986 SLT 845; *Armour v. Tyssen Edelstahlwerke AG*, above n. 1.

[34] *Armour v. Tyssen Edelstahlwerke AG*, above n. 1; North, above n. 24, 269–271.

[35] For a full treatment of the possibilities see, Benjamin, op. cit., 25–122, 25–123; North, above n. 4, 265–271. Which law might govern a trust affecting the proceeds of sale is now a matter for the Recognition of Trusts Act 1987. It is now more likely than at the time of *Romalpa* that such cases might be analysed in terms of an independent restitutionary obligation: Dicey and Morris, Rule 203(1).

pre-existing relationship between the parties, or independent rights and duties affecting the proceeds of the sub-sales. It is also unclear whether the right to trace should be regarded as procedural or substantive for conflicts purposes and, if the latter, which law should govern. In one sense such uncertainty might present opportunities to a party wishing to have Dutch law applied. But, more realistically, the very existence of such intractable questions of classification might be a powerful disincentive to raising them, given the cost and unpredictability involved. Certainly, the mere fact that an issue cannot easily be classified may be a sound reason for avoiding the foreign elements in a case. *Romalpa*, therefore, is not so much a case in which foreign law was clearly not relevant, as one in which it was not sufficiently clear whether it was relevant or not.

It is also important for other reasons to emphasize how difficult it can be to classify a particular dispute in conflicts terms. In a practical sense, the very difficulty of doing so, and the likelihood of an open-ended dispute concerning classification with an unpredictable outcome, may incline litigants to prefer the relative stability of English law. More theoretically, such difficulty is a reminder that we should not suppose that some cases obviously concern choice of law while others do not. Certainly, English courts are effectively powerless to impose a given characterization on the parties if this is at odds with how the case was argued. The consequence is that there are many cases of which it cannot be said that they are conflicts cases in which foreign law has not been introduced. In some, the very issue is whether they are conflicts cases. In others, the parties have ensured that they are not conflicts cases, not so much by omitting to plead foreign law, but by imagining their dispute in such a way that no choice of law issues arise.

Another reason for ignoring the foreign element in a case concerns the unpredictability of introducing foreign law. It is hard to generalize about the effect of unpredictability on the decision-making of litigants. A well-financed party may be less concerned with its effects than one more impecunious. Indeed, unpredictability may favour the stronger party, adding to the pressure on the weaker party to capitulate or compromise. Nor need unpredictability always deter litigants from taking controversial points. If they have a chance of success, they might argue a point whatever the odds, especially if few other arguments are open to them. Other things being equal, however, a sensibly risk-averse lawyer is likely to prefer to fight a case on a relatively predictable basis. In many cases, at least if other arguments are available, there is little purpose in arguing (expensively) for the application of foreign law if, in the end, there is a tolerable degree of certainty that it will be applied in the manner intended—or, indeed, at all.

To rely upon foreign law in English proceedings invites unpredictability in two ways: in the doubt that must exist in any contested case as to what the court will find foreign law to be; and in the uncertainties of the choice of law process. As to the first, the process of proving foreign law is notoriously uncertain. Where party experts are employed, much depends on such elusive elements as the competence and clarity of a party's expert, or on counsel's skill in handling the evidence. Indeed, the challenge involved in examining and cross-examining foreign law experts puts a premium on a lawyer's skills, requiring not so much proficiency in advocacy as in comparative law.[36] Again, a court has considerable discretion in assessing evidence of foreign law. It has a range of responses at its disposal although it is often hard to predict which might be employed in any given case.[37] One party's evidence might be adopted without reservation; or the court might accept parts of each expert's position; or it might reject the opinions of both experts entirely. There is also the elusive question of what weight a court will place on each expert's evidence, or on any part of it, a difficulty enhanced by the fact that foreign law experts are sometimes hard to locate, which means that less than ideal evidence is sometimes introduced. This is not to say that the proof of foreign law is any less predictable than that of other facts, nor to deny that the legal process is always uncertain. But, weighed against the costs, measured against the fact that settlement or not pleading foreign law are alternative options, the unpredictability of proving foreign law may persuade litigants not to proceed under foreign law, or not to proceed at all.

Another source of unpredictability concerns the nature of the choice of law process. For to rely upon foreign law invites argument as the true identity of the law applicable in any given case. This is particularly problematic because so many choice of law rules are uncertain in their formulation. One example concerns the vexed question of choice of law in marriage.[38] Another is the notorious ambiguity which until recently affected choice of law in tort, and which may have deterred many potential litigants from relying on the foreign aspects of their case.[39] Uncertainty may also surround the interpretation of statutory choice of law rules, especially those which govern proceedings in contract[40] and in tort.[41] It may also affect how any given issue should be classified, a central feature of the choice of law process.[42] More fundamentally, perhaps, there are several areas of English private international law in which the relevant choice of law rule is not so much uncertain as entirely lacking. What law governs consent to marry is, as we have seen, an entirely open question. So too, no

---

[36] Sykes and Pryles, *Australian Private International Law*, 2nd edn. (1991), 268.
[37] See below, pp. 188–201. [38] Cheshire and North, 586–603.
[39] Ibid., Ch. 20; Dicey and Morris, Ch. 35.
[40] By the Contracts (Applicable Law) Act 1990.
[41] By the Private International Law (Miscellaneous Provisions) Act 1995, Part III.
[42] Dicey and Morris, Ch. 2.

authority governs the status of retention of title clauses, a consideration which may further explain why the parties in *Romalpa* may have been reluctant to see their dispute as one involving the conflict of laws. Not only would the lack of authority have considerably increased the risk of an appeal had foreign law been involved, it is hard to know how the case would have been argued. It is hard to found a claim on law which does not exist.

A further reason for not introducing foreign law is that litigants may simply wish English law to govern, a result achieved (in most cases) by omitting to plead any other. This is partly a matter of convenience, given that it is normally simpler and less expensive for an English court to apply its own law than that of another country. But it may also amount to a positive choice of English law as the governing law. Indeed, we have seen how important it is to regard the omission to rely upon foreign law as, in effect, a choice of law issue. One reason for selecting English law, at least in commercial cases, is the general commercial orientation of English contract law, bred of the courts' habitual desire to reflect the needs of the business community. Another reason is the sophistication of English law in certain areas of international commerce, especially in matters affecting insurance, banking and maritime law. A third reason is the role in international commerce of English standard form contracts which assume the application of English law and English principles of construction and practice, making it almost inevitable that they should be governed by English law. In such cases it is not simply natural that English law should govern, reflecting the expectations of those involved. It may also be correct in choice of law terms, English law being the applicable law in such cases, objectively judged. The fact that both parties to a contract are English, or that it contains an English jurisdiction or arbitration clause, are certainly potent factors in determining a contract's applicable law in the absence of an express agreement to that effect.[43] Indeed, a strength of the English system of voluntary pleading, at least in cases where English law obviously applies as the governing law, is that it may so often reflect the fact that the substantive applicable law is English. Moreover, it compels this result without occupying the court's time with a choice of law issue the resolution of which may be a foregone conclusion. A reluctance to plead foreign law before the English courts should be viewed, therefore, as much as a choice of law matter, as one concerning procedure. There may be good reasons, in the type of case which is litigated in England, why English law should be applied. And voluntary pleading may offer a 'fast track' to this result without the need for a court to address the issue.

But the most decisive reason for not pleading foreign law, at least where foreign law might otherwise be advantageous, concerns the cost of doing

---

[43] By Articles 3(1) or 4 of the 1980 Rome Convention.

so. Litigation, commercial litigation at least, is seldom, or is seldom perceived by the parties' to be, a search for justice, an enquiry after truth. It is an investment, a calculated attempt to obtain commercial advantage, normally in the form of monetary compensation for an alleged wrong. As with any other investment, whether to embark upon litigation requires a balancing of the likely benefits against the probable costs of securing them. One prominent factor in such a cost-benefit analysis is the predictability of the outcome. Another is the expense of achieving it. To plead foreign law, however, is to introduce an element into litigation which is at once notoriously unpredictable and potentially costly. Other things being equal, such unpredictability and such expense, taken together, supply good reasons, either to avoid pleading foreign law, or even to abandon proceedings altogether. Conversely, such difficulties may incline one (better-funded) party to introduce it in the hope of precipitating settlement or surrender by the other.

The cost of introducing foreign law may also be direct. Certainly, where points of foreign law are contested the financial stakes are raised. Generally, foreign law cannot be proved without expert evidence, normally provided orally at trial. Although an expert's report might be introduced, cross-examination is normal. This increases the duration of proceedings with all the cost implications which this entails in terms of lawyers' and experts' fees. Admittedly, foreign law may be established less formally (a matter to which we will return in a later chapter). But this is not widely recognized, nor will it be appropriate in many cases. In one recent case nine of the nineteen days of trial were devoted solely to the examination of foreign law experts.[44] The introduction of foreign law may also increase the expense of proceedings indirectly, not least because it invites consideration of the choice of law aspects of a case. Often the true nature of the relevant choice of law rule will be unclear and, if it is not, its application may be.

There may, then, be good reasons not to rely upon foreign law in English proceedings. Self-evidently, a party will not do so to found a claim or defence where English law is hostile or of no assistance, although it may not always be clear that this is so. But where English law supplies an alternative way of proceeding, a more subtle assessment is required. Much depends on the circumstances and on the relative difficulty of the questions of foreign law and English law which are involved. Much also turns on the relative financial strength of the parties. But even if the prospects of succeeding under English law are less—or are less predictable—than under foreign law, the nature of the conflicts process, and the inconvenience of proving foreign law may tip the balance against relying upon

---

[44] *Dubai Bank Ltd. v. Galadari, The Times*, 20 June 1990.

foreign law. A party who has a chance of success under English law may refrain from relying upon foreign law even if their chance of success is greater under that law. Some would say that the neglect of foreign law is less deliberate, owing more to the fact that not all practitioners are as schooled in conflicts principles as scholars might suppose. Certainly, the actual behaviour of litigants and their advisers maybe less tidy, less rational, than the foregoing discussion implies. But whether practitioners approach the problem of introducing foreign law reflectively or intuitively, the experienced, cost-conscious litigator is likely to pay close attention to the implications of activating the foreign elements in a case.

VI
Proof by Experts

Foreign laws are facts in English doctrine, albeit that their legal character makes them different from other facts.[1] Being facts, they remain unknown to a court unless pleaded and proved. And, being facts, courts generally lack judicial notice of their content, which they consequently cannot establish by independent research.[2] Exceptionally, courts take judicial notice of foreign law, and sometimes the determination of foreign law requires no special expertise but falls within a court's inherent knowledge or competence.[3] Standardly, however, the proof of foreign law belongs to the category of matters which must be established by expert evidence.[4] Save in exceptional cases, in which written evidence alone may suffice,[5] or in which the examination of a foreign expert abroad may be sanctioned,[6] this requires, to some degree, the examination of expert witnesses in open court. True, such examination is normally as to the contents of reports already prepared by the experts and exchanged between the parties. And other means of establishing foreign law exist, described in Chapter VII, which dispense with party experts altogether. No method is so commonly used, however, as the examination of party-led experts.

This chapter is concerned, in general, with the proof of foreign law by expert evidence and, in particular, with the normal case in which foreign

---

[1] 'The way of knowing foreign laws is by admitting them to be proved as facts . . .': *Mostyn v. Fabrigas* (1776) 1 Cowp. 161, 174 (per Lord Mansfield); *Fremoult v. Dedire* (1718) 1 P. Wms. 429; *Nelson v. Bridport* (1845) 8 Beav. 527; *Guaranty Trust Co. of New York v. Hannay & Co.* [1918] 2 KB 623, 667 (CA); *Bankers and Shippers Insurance Co. of New York v. Liverpool Marine and General Insurance Co. Ltd.* (1926) 24 Ll L R 85, 93 (HL); *Ottoman Bank of Nicosia v. Chakarian* [1938] AC 260, 279 (PC); *A/S Tallina Laevauhisus v. Estonian State Steamship Line* (1947) 80 Ll LR 99, 107, 113 (CA); *Parkasho v. Singh* [1968] P 233, 250; *Dalmia Dairy Industries Ltd. v. National Bank of Pakistan* [1978] 2 Lloyd's Rep. 223, 286 (CA); *Bumper Development Corpn. Ltd. v. Comr. of Police* [1991] 1 WLR 1362, 1369 (CA).

[2] '. . . the Judge has not organs to know and to deal with the text of foreign law, and therefore requires the assistance of a lawyer who knows how to interpret it': *The Sussex Peerage Case* (1844) 11 Cl. & Fin. 85, 115 (per Lord Brougham); *Nelson v. Bridport* (1845) 8 Beav. 527; *Di Sora v. Phillipps* (1863) 10 HLC 624, 640; *Lloyd v. Guibert* (1865) LR 1 QB 115, 129. For the court's traditional passivity in connection with facts see, Pollock, *Expansion of the Common Law* (1904), 33–34.

[3] *Nelson v. Bridport*, above n. 1.

[4] *The Sussex Peerage Case*, above, n. 2; *Baron de Bode's Case* (1845) 8 QB 208, 246–267; *Nelson v. Bridport*, above, n. 3; *The Earldom of Perth* (1846) 2 HLC 865, 873; *Castrique v. Imrie* (1870) LR 4 HL 414, 430.

[5] See below, pp. 203–207.

[6] See below, p. 210.

law is proved by the examination of the parties' own witnesses. Chapter VII supplements the discussion by surveying the several mechanisms whereby the process of proof by party experts might be expedited or improved—by relying on written evidence, or by appointing an independent expert to assess the parties' evidence. Chapter VIII completes our investigation by examining those situations in which foreign law might be established without employing party experts at all, as when a court appoints its own expert instead.

In one sense the present chapter's focus is narrower than might appear. The proof of foreign law is intimately connected with the proof of technical facts generally, but full consideration of the procedural background to expert proof is beyond its scope.[7] Not least, this limitation is justified because the general law of expert evidence is rapidly evolving, making any account of the topic provisional.[8] Inevitably therefore, the present discussion confines itself to those aspects of the problem which relate particularly to the proof of foreign law. In another sense, however, the discussion is more far-reaching. For, although its primary concern is the proof of foreign law by party experts, many aspects of this process are as relevant to establishing foreign law in other ways. The problem of assessing evidence of foreign law arises by whatever means it is provided, whether by oral examination, written reports, judicial assistance, or a court-appointed expert. So does consideration of the consequences of a failure in proof, and the grounds for appealing a point of foreign law. Moreover, who qualifies as an expert is as much an issue whether the expert is examined orally or not, and whether the expert is appointed by a party or the court.

But in so far as our concern is with expert witnesses, deployed by the parties in the traditional fashion, some explanation is required. English procedural law now presents a very different picture from that which would have been visible even recently. The adversarial process, although intact, is subject to an increasing degree of judicial intervention, prompted by concerns over the system's protractedness and cost.[9] But against the background of a changing legal framework, the orientation of English civil procedure remains adversarial and party-based, especially in connection with complex litigation.[10] It is also apparent that expert evidence, led by the parties, may be the most appropriate means of canvassing and assess-

---

[7] For a detailed account see, Hodgkinson, *Expert Evidence: Law and Practice* (London, 1990).

[8] Lord Woolf, *Access to Justice, Interim Report to the Lord Chancellor on the Civil Justice System in England and Wales*, (London, HMSO, 1995), Ch. 23; *Final Report*, (1996), Ch. 13; Draft Civil Proceedings Rules, Rule 32.

[9] Practice Direction, Civil Litigation: Case Management [1995] 1 All ER 385; *Thermawear Ltd. v. Linton* (unreported), 17 October 1995; Lord Woolf, *Interim Report*, Ch. 23.

[10] Lord Woolf, *Final Report*, above n. 8, 138–139.

ing rival opinions in contested cases. Indeed, this is implicit in Lord Woolf''s *Final Report* which, in principle, strongly favours a controlled approach to expert evidence:

> There are in all areas some large, complex and strongly contested cases where the full adversarial system, including oral cross-examination of opposing experts on particular issues, is the best way of producing a just result. That will apply particularly to issues on which there are several tenable schools of thought, or where the boundaries of knowledge are being extended.[11]

Even in a more controlled legal climate, therefore, it is unclear to what extent, if at all, the proof of foreign law should be affected. The growing perception that the law should aspire to proportionality between process and purpose, between the complexity of the case and the cost of the procedure, is certainly significant.[12] This may encourage fuller consideration of alternative mechanisms for establishing foreign law, such as those described in Chapter VIII. As the litigation process increasingly focuses upon settlement, and upon encouraging the parties to limit the issues which divide them, this may also decrease the number of foreign law issues which are contested.[13] But how foreign law is established is less likely to change than might be expected. Most foreign law disputes are likely to involve contests between equally plausible opinions the strength of which can best be tested by examination. Moreover, the traditional technique has much to commend it, at least in cases involving foreign law. Certainly, English law recognizes the existence of a variety of means of establishing foreign law other than by reference to party experts.[14] But the fact that the proof of foreign law by this means should be so invariable in English practice, notwithstanding the existence of alternatives, says much about the effectiveness of the traditional approach.

It is instructive in this context to notice how party experts are viewed in the United States, in the context of a system in which considerable flexibility is permitted in proving foreign law.[15] As one commentator has said, recognizing the benefits of such a relatively complex process:

> The most expensive but probably the most effective method of presenting information about foreign law is through live examination....[16]

Again, as another has said, viewing the possibility of proof by affidavit alone from a litigant's perspective:

---

[11] Ibid., 141.   [12] Lord Woolf, *Interim Report*, Ch. 1., *Final Report*, Ch. 1.
[13] Lord Woolf, *Interim Report*, Ch. 24, *Final Report*, Ch. 11.   [14] See below, Chapter VIII.
[15] Federal Rules of Civil Procedure, Rule 44.1 provides that a court 'in determining foreign law, may consider any relevant material or source, including testimony, whether or not submitted by a party or admissible under the Federal Rules of Evidence'; *Restatement, Second, Conflict of Laws*, para. 136; Schmertz, (1978) 18 *Virginia Jl. of Intl. L.* 696, 703 ff; Sass, (1981) 29 *Am Jl Comp L* 96, 107–110.
[16] Schmertz, op. cit., 707–708.

From a tactical point of view, a party may still find it advisable to present his view of the foreign law through an expert witness testifying in open court; and this remains the prevailing practice in big and important actions.[17]

However much the legal framework of litigation may change in future, therefore, it is doubtful that the current practice in connection with foreign law need change significantly. On this assumption, this chapter continues by examining the role of party experts in foreign law, the consequences of a failure in proof, the assessment of such evidence, and the possibility of appeal.

1. THE EXPERT

Both the form of expert evidence and the essential role and responsibility of the expert are the same whenever such evidence is employed.[18] But it is necessary to define the expert's role in relation to foreign law, and to describe what qualifications an expert must possess.[19]

(A) THE FOREIGN LAW EXPERT'S ROLE

Several considerations define a foreign law expert's role, and to some extent distinguish it from that of other technical experts. First, such an expert, like any other, should not assume the role of counsel, the provision of expertise, not advocacy, being an expert's task.[20] But this is not to say that partiality is as great a problem as might be supposed. Bias seriously weakens an expert's testimony and lawyers go to great lengths to ensure that their expert's report is objective. This might mean substituting an unfavourable report with one which is more advantageous. But this itself ensures that such evidence as is finally submitted is a genuine expression of opinion. The fundamental requirement of impartiality encounters difficulties, however, in its application to foreign law. Courts have sometimes shown considerable leniency in accepting evidence which is tainted by partiality at least where it is uncontradicted.[21] Unable to research foreign law themselves, they have felt constrained to follow even partial evidence. There is also an important sense in which an opinion as to foreign law

---

[17] Schlesinger, Baade, Damaska and Herzog, *Comparative Law*, 5th. edn., (Mineola, 1988), 128.

[18] For a classic statement see, *The Ikarian Reefer* [1995] 1 Lloyd's Rep. 455 (CA).

[19] See further, Falconbridge, *Essays on the Conflict of Laws*, 2nd edn., (1954), 833–838; Dicey and Morris, 230–232; Cheshire and North, 109–111; Hodgkinson, 298–302; Howard, Crane and Hochberg, *Phipson on Evidence*, 14th edn., (London, 1990), 837–839.

[20] *Whitehouse* v. *Jordan* [1981] 1 WLR 246, 256–257, 268 (HL); *Hinds* v. *LTE* [1979] RTR 103 (CA).

[21] e.g. *Rossano* v. *Manufacturers Life Insurance Co. Ltd.* [1963] 2 QB 352, 381.

must, like any expression of legal opinion, take the form of an argument. As such it becomes difficult to ignore testimony merely because it argues a party's case when this is, in a sense, inevitable.[22] Indeed, it could be said of foreign legal opinions—although the courts generally have not—that the test of acceptability is not so much whether an expert argues a party's case, as whether it complies with the normal standards of open advocacy and intellectual honesty. An opinion, however, which, by reason of partiality, becomes incoherent, or fails to reflect the import of such documentary material as in evidence, may be rejected on those grounds.[23]

Secondly, the nature of any legal opinion confers upon courts a subtle but important power to measure the strength of expert legal evidence. It is a feature of legal argument generally that the strength of a proposition does not depend so much on the knowledge of one who relies on it. It turns as much (or more) on the logic and coherence of the argument which supports it and its conformity with the available evidence. Indeed, unlike, say, an experimental science, legal reasoning is a matter of persuasion not demonstration. As such, simply because a judge is a lawyer, skilled in legal reasoning, he or she may have an insight into the force and effectiveness of a legal expert's evidence which is less likely in cases involving, say, scientific evidence. This is especially evident with regard to its conformity with the written material which normally accompanies it.[24] Typically, where foreign law is concerned, this is in the form of legislation, decided cases, and authoritative works. Because English courts are unable to conduct their own researches into foreign law they have sometimes been reluctant to challenge such evidence, whatever its inadequacy.[25] In principle, however, a statement of opinion which is unsupported by, say, the text of a foreign statute, may be disregarded by the court, even if uncontradicted.[26] Some commentators would argue against this liberal view of the court's role.[27] But, in principle, it is justified because courts in such cases are not assuming a knowledge of foreign law. They are exercising common sense honed by their experience in the law. And, in practice, there is little doubt that the legal character of foreign law enables courts to test foreign legal evidence simply by deploying elementary standards of reasoning and coherence. As has been said:

The witness, however expert in the foreign law, cannot prevent the Court using its common sense; and the Court can reject his evidence if he says something patently absurd, or something inconsistent with the rest of his evidence.[28]

---

[22] As it will not be inevitable where other types of expert evidence are involved: *Hinds* v. *LTE*, above n. 20.
[23] See below, p. 195.   [24] Cf. *R.* v. *Turner* [1975] 1 QB 834, 840.
[25] e.g. *Rossano* v. *Manufacturer Life Insurance Co. Ltd.*, above n. 21, 381.
[26] *Buerger* v. *New York* (1927) 96 LJKB 930, 941 (CA).
[27] Hodgkinson, 306–309.
[28] *A/S Tallinna Laevauhisus* v. *Estonian State Steamship Line* (1947) 80 Ll L R 99, 108 (CA).

Thirdly, an expert's role in the construction of documents requires special mention. Sometimes the construction of private instruments, such as contracts or deeds, is involved.[29] Alternatively, the meaning of foreign legal materials, such as statutes or law reports, may be in issue.[30] Despite obvious similarities the role of expert evidence differs depending on whether a private document or a foreign legal text is involved. The meaning of the former is always for the court to ascertain, albeit on the basis of evidence of any special rules of construction under foreign law.[31] The meaning of foreign legal materials, by contrast, is in principle for the expert alone to determine.[32] But, despite this technical distinction, the practical difference between these situations should not be exaggerated. In either the parties might introduce evidence as to construction under foreign law. But in both a court might rely on its own ability to interpret such documents, in which case no such evidence is required. In such a case the construction of the document concerned, whatever its character, is within the court's province.[33] Again, although it is an expert's task to determine a statute's meaning, this is subject to an important qualification. A court may always reject an expert's evidence as to construction if it is at odds with the commonsense meaning of the words in question.[34] Any disparity between the expert's construction and the court's is justified only if it is a foreign term of art, or governed by a distinctive rule of construction. Moreover, if an expert supplies no evidence concerning how a statute is interpreted under foreign law, the court will inevitably apply English canons of interpretation.[35]

(B) An Expert's Qualifications

It is usual for evidence at trial to begin with a statement of an expert's qualifications. And a court will assess the true nature of an expert's competence as the trial proceeds. It may be rare, however, for a foreign law expert to be disqualified altogether for lacking adequate credentials. This may be for the obvious reason that the basic qualifications required of such experts are well known and it is unlikely that a party's lawyers would employ a wholly unqualified person. It may happen, however, that a person is found to lack appropriate expertise as to the particular points in issue, or at least as to some of them.[36] But even then it is more likely that a judge would simply give less weight to such evidence than ignore it alto-

[29] See below, p. 251.
[30] See below, p. 257.
[31] *Trotter v. Trotter* (1828) 4 Bli. (NS) 502; *King of Spain v. Machado* (1827) 4 Russ. 225, 239–240; *Rouyer Guillet & Cie. v. Rouyer Guillet & Co. Ltd.* [1949] 1 All ER 244 (CA).
[32] Dicey and Morris, 234–235.
[33] See below, p. 245.
[34] *A/S Tallina Laevahisus v. Estonian State Steamship Line*, above n. 28, 108.
[35] *F & K Jabbour v. Custodian of Israeli Absentee Property* [1954] 1 WLR 139, 148.
[36] Ibid.

gether, although this is possible in exceptional cases.[37] Again, merely because a person qualifies as an expert on the laws of a given legal system does not make that person qualified to express an opinion as to any or all of the issues arising in a particular case. A court may disregard an expert's opinion where he or she lacks expertise as to the specific point in issue.[38]

Whether an expert is qualified to give evidence as to a particular matter must depend on the facts of a given case. But the general principles are clear. The starting point is section 4(1) of the Civil Evidence Act 1972 which establishes, although it may never have been in doubt,[39] that a foreign law expert need not be a current legal practitioner in the country concerned. Section 4(1) provides:

. . . in civil proceedings a person who is suitably qualified to do so on account of his knowledge or experience is competent to give expert evidence as to the law of any country or territory outside the United Kingdom . . . irrespective of whether he has acted or is entitled to act as a legal practitioner there.[40]

Although the wording of section 4(1) suggests that its principal function is to allow non-practitioners to act as experts, this is misleading. As the examples examined below suggest, it was always possible to employ non-legal experts where their practical experience was relevant as, typically, is the case with experienced commercial men or government officials. The most significant impact of section 4(1) may be to remove any doubt that scholars—whose expertise is embraced by 'knowledge'—may qualify as experts. Even here it is unlikely that the previous law really excluded scholars from giving evidence. The idea that it might do so appears to have been based on extrapolation from those cases which decided that mere undergraduate study of a foreign legal system is insufficient to establish competence.[41] A further important effect of section 4(1) is to remove the possibility that a non-legal expert, such as a trader or official, might be treated as less qualified than a legal practitioner to give evidence. It had been suggested that a non-practitioner's evidence, although admissible, might *per se* be accorded less weight than a practitioner's.[42] Section 4(1) makes it clear that legal practice is not by itself a factor going to the weighing of evidence.

Although much of the case law pre-dates section 4(1), it suggests, in general terms, that experts may have knowledge or experience for many

---

[37] *Vander Donckt* v. *Thelluson* (1849) 8 CB 812.
[38] *Ajami* v. *Comptroller of Customs* [1954] 1 WLR 1405, 1408 (PC).
[39] Further research beyond mere study was treated as sufficient in *Brailey* v. *Rhodesia Consolidated Ltd.* [1910] 2 Ch D 95.
[40] See also, Practice Direction (Foreign Law Affidavit) [1972] 1 WLR 1433; Non-Contentious Probate Rules 1987, r. 19.
[41] *Bristow* v. *Sequeville* (1850) 5 Exch. 275; *Re the Goods of Bonelli* (1875) 1 PD 69; Cheshire and North, 110–111.
[42] *Lazard Bros. & Co.* v. *Midland Bank Ltd.* [1933] AC 289, 299 (HL).

reasons. Most obviously, as section 4(1) implies, an expert may be a legal practitioner in the country concerned. But if 'knowledge or experience' is made out any person may be qualified. As this suggests, a foreign legal expert may belong to one of three categories. First, the expert may be a jurist from the system concerned, such as a practitioner,[43] a judge (who need never have practised law),[44] a former practitioner,[45] or an academic, even one who is not professionally qualified.[46] But merely having studied the law of the system in question is insufficient unless some further expertise can be demonstrated.[47]

Secondly, a jurist from a system other than that whose law is in issue may be acceptable. This might include an expert from a related system, although not simply because it is related.[48] All that is required is relevant knowledge or experience.[49] This would presumably include a person from one country whose law was, in the relevant respect, the same as that of the country concerned. Alternatively, the category might include a person from a legal system which is quite unrelated. This would include English scholars or practitioners with experience of a non-common law system.[50] Indeed, the relative ease and low cost of employing a local English expert, rather than one abroad, may incline an English court to admit such evidence where otherwise it might not do so.[51]

Thirdly, non-jurist experts may be called. These need not be lawyers of any description but persons having legal knowledge gained by other means. In extreme cases, mere residence in a country, coupled with relevant knowledge may suffice.[52] More usually, to have engaged in a partic-

---

[43] *Bristow* v. *Sequeville*, above n. 41; *Hansen* v. *Dixon* (1906) 96 LT 32. A person may be qualified in a country but unable to practice: *Burford* v. *Burford* [1918] P 140.

[44] Dicey and Morris, 230.

[45] *Re Duke of Wellington* [1947] Ch. 506, 514–515; *Rossano* v. *Manufacturers Life Insurance Co.*, above n. 21, 373.

[46] This follows *a fortiori* from the fact that an English academic expert in foreign law is thus qualified: *Brailey* v. *Rhodesia Consolidated Ltd.*, above n. 39.

[47] *Bristow* v. *Sequeville*, above n. 41.

[48] *Re Mosovitch* 138 LT 183; *Cartwright* v. *Cartwright and Anderson* (1878) 26 WR 694, 685.

[49] *Reinblatt* v. *Gold* (1928) QR 45 KB 136.

[50] *Brailey* v. *Rhodesia Consolidated Ltd.*, above n. 39 (Reader in Roman Dutch law to the Council of Legal Education gave evidence as to Rhodesian law); *Wilson* v. *Wilson* [1903] P 157 (English barrister had relevant experience of Maltese marriage law); *Re Whitelegg's Goods* [1889] P 267 (English solicitor had experience of Chilean law); *McCabe* v. *McCabe*, the *Independent*, 3 September 1993 (English scholar gave evidence as to African customary law).

[51] *Cooper-King* v. *Cooper-King* [1900] P. 65 (cost of obtaining evidence from a qualified lawyer; affidavit evidence from former colonial administrator admitted); *Wilson* v. *Wilson*, op. cit. (difficulty in qualified Maltese experts appearing; English lawyer admitted as expert).

[52] *Abbott* v. *Abbott* (1860) 29 LJPM & A 57 (English merchant trading in Chile gave evidence as to local marriage law); but see *The Sussex Peerage Case*, above n. 2, (mere residence not itself sufficient); *R* v. *Naguib* [1917] 1 KB 359 (CCA) (Egyptian resident in Egypt not as such expert in local law); *R* v. *Brampton* (1808) 10 East 282, 287 (Scots tradesman not expert in Scots marriage law).

ular form of commerce in a country may provide the necessary expertise.[53] Relevant governmental experience may also do so.[54] But the mere fact that a witness holds high government office does not entitle his opinion to particular respect,[55] party experts being different in nature from officials whose certification of a point of foreign law is sought.[56] As a general rule, the narrower the issue of foreign law the more likely it is that a non-jurist may be allowed to give evidence.[57] In some cases, especially where the point at issue is restricted, the evidence of a suitably qualified non-jurist may be preferred even to that of a foreign practitioner.[58]

In reality, the requirement that a foreign law expert must be suitably qualified is self-policing, in the sense that a party's legal advisers are likely to seek the best qualified expert available, rather than run the risk of their evidence being given reduced weight or ignored. In reality, such an expert will generally be a foreign academic or practitioner.[59] Ideally, they should be fluent in English, generally familiar with English law and practice, commercially minded (in commercial cases) and likely to be persuasive on examination. Indeed, in most cases the difficulty lies not in locating someone who is technically qualified, but someone who has the additional qualities required of a witness. It may be difficult to find a suitable person, at least without incurring considerable expense.[60] Alternatively, the acknowledged expert in the field may have been retained by the other party, leaving few practical alternatives and putting the other expert at an immediate disadvantage. The courts in such cases may show latitude in assessing the expertise of such persons. Both the cost[61] and logistical difficulty[62] of employing a truly competent expert have in the past weighed

---

[53] *Vander Donckt v. Thelluson*, above n. 37 (Belgian former merchant expert in Belgian banking law); *Ajami v. Comptroller of Customs*, above n. 38 (Nigerian banker an expert on legality of Nigerian negotiable instruments); but see *Direct Winters Transport v. Duplate Canada* (1962) 32 DLR (2d.) 278.

[54] *The Sussex Peerage Case*, above n. 2, 124 (Roman Catholic bishop an expert on the canon law of marriage); *Lacon v. Higgins* 3 Stark 178 (French consul in England an expert as to French commercial law); *In the Goods of Dost Aly Khan* (1880) 6 PD 6 (Peruvian diplomat expert as to Peruvian law); *Gossage v. Gossage and Heaton* 78 SJ 551; *Associated Shipping Services Ltd. v. Department of Private Affairs of the Ruler of Abu Dhabi*, The Independent, 14 August 1990 (legal adviser to defendant an expert as to defendant's legal status).

[55] *Trendtex Trading Corpn. v. Central Bank* [1976] 3 All ER 437, 441; [1977] QB 529, 560, 563 (CA); Phipson, 838–839.

[56] See below, p. 221.

[57] *Abbot v. Abbot and Godoy* 4 SW & TR 254 (Englishman who observed Chilean marriage expert as to Chilean marriage formalities); *The Sussex Peerage Case*, above n. 2; *Ajami v. Comptroller of Customs*, above n. 38.

[58] *De Beeche v. South American Stores* [1935] AC 148 (evidence of English banker preferred to Chilean practitioner in relation to Chilean bill of exchange).

[59] e.g. *X AG v. A Bank* [1983] 2 All ER 464 (one party employing a New York practitioner, the other a distinguished academic author).

[60] Memorandum from Norton Rose, *Private International Law (Miscellaneous Provisions) Bill, Proceedings of the Special Public Bill Committee*, (London, HMSO, 1995), 46, 48.

[61] *Cooper-King v. Cooper-King* [1900] P. 65.   [62] *Wilson v. Wilson* [1903] P. 157.

with the courts in admitting expert evidence which they might otherwise have rejected. But in practice, whether admitted or not, the evidence of an under-qualified expert may be unsatisfactory and may be given reduced weight. And even a qualified person may be an inappropriate witness. For such reasons, litigants may be forced to settle, or concede the point of foreign law, for want of a suitable expert.

3. FAILURE IN PROOF

The burden of proving foreign law, whether in support of a positive claim or a defence, falls, unsurprisingly, on the party relying upon it.[63] In practice, at least in complex cases, a party's evidence will contain several allegations as to different points of foreign law. For this reason it is rare that a party's case under foreign law will fail entirely. More likely, a party will succeed in discharging the burden of proving some allegations of foreign law, if not all. The consequence is that a judge may sometimes accept parts of each party's evidence, applying an amalgam of points drawn from the successful evidence of both.[64] This imports a risk that the version of foreign law eventually applied by the court will lack the coherence of each party's individual evidence. But this is inherent in the idea that it is not the judge's task to determine objectively what foreign law is, so much as to weigh whether, and to what extent, each party has discharged the burden of proving foreign law.

If one party fails to prove a point of foreign law, but the other succeeds, the latter's evidence will, of course, be preferred. Indeed, one party's failure in proof normally leads to the success of the other, not to the application of English law by default. But it is theoretically possible that neither party will succeed in establishing its contentions as to foreign law, in the sense that the evidence of the rival experts is equally convincing or unconvincing. The competing opinions may be equally scant, badly reasoned, or partial.[65] Even in cases in which one party's evidence is uncontradicted, such evidence may be so unsatisfactory that its proof will fail. English law will be applied by default in such cases.[66] But this time-honoured rule

---

[63] *Brown v. Gracey* (1821) Dow & Ry NP 41n; *Dynamit AG v. Rio Tinto Co.* [1918] AC 261, 295 (HL); *Guaranty Trust Co. of New York v. Hannay* [1918] 2 KB 623, 655 (CA); *Schapiro v. Schapiro* [1904] TS 673; *Ascherberg, Hopwood and Crew Ltd. v. Casa Musicale Sonzogno* [1971] 1 WLR 173; 1128 (CA).

[64] *Dubai Bank Ltd. v. Galadari, The Times*, June 26, 1990.

[65] *Macmillan Inc. v. Bishopsgate Investment Trust plc* [1995] 1 WLR 978, 1009.

[66] *Ward v. Dey* (1849) 1 Rob Ecc 759; *Lloyd v. Guibert* (1865) LR 1 QB 115, 129; *Nouvelle Banque de l'Union v. Ayton* (1891) 7 TLR 377; *Hartmann v. Konig* (1933) 50 TLR 114, 117 (HL); *Re Tank of Oslo* [1940] 1 All ER 40, 43 (CA); *Re Parana Plantations Ltd.* [1946] 2 All ER 214, 217, 218.

must be carefully glossed if it is not to mislead. Contrary to what is commonly supposed, it may be mistaken to see the application of English law by default as the consequence of a presumption that English and foreign law are the same unless otherwise proven. Nor should it be assumed that an English court is often likely to find itself in the position of having to apply English law by default, the proof of foreign law having somehow failed. Nor should it be forgotten that there may be situations in which foreign law must be affirmatively established, such that a failure in proof will lead not to the application of English law but to dismissal of the claim.

Like most legal systems, English law has committed itself to the general rule that one who fails adequately to prove foreign law should not generally be penalised by dismissal of its case.[67] English law will be applied instead. In practice it will make little difference whether the result is outright dismissal or the application of English law. In either event, the claimant's preferred law will not be applied and, presumably, foreign law would not have been relied upon at all unless it offered an advantage lacking under English law. But if English law certainly applies in such cases, how is this to be explained? As we have seen, it is often said that foreign law is deemed to be the same as English law unless the contrary is proved.[68] Indeed, the principle has acquired the ring of truth simply by repetition and familiarity. It is readily apparent that such a presumption is especially inapt to explain the application of English law when foreign law has not been relied upon at all.[69] How can foreign law be deemed to apply in such a case, albeit endowed with the content of English law, when it has not been suggested that it should? Such a view is meaningful only if we assume that foreign law is always prima facie applicable in a case with a foreign element. But that may not be the basis on which English law proceeds.[70] Again, we have seen how unlikely it is that any presumption of similarity permits a party to allege foreign law without also proving it, not least because it allows a party the rare privilege of relying on a fact

[67] See below, p. 281.
[68] The cases are numerous. Examples include: *Dynamit AG v. Rio Tinto Co.* [1918] AC 261, 295; *The Parchim* [1918] AC 157, 161 (PC); *The Colorado* [1923] P. 102, 111 (CA); *Casey v. Casey* [1949] P. 420, 430 (CA). *Jabbour v. Custodian of Israeli Absentee Property* [1954] 1 WLR 139, 148; *National Shipping Corpn. v. Arab* [1971] 2 Lloyd's Rep. 363, 366 (CA); *Österreichische Länderbank v. S'Elite Ltd.* [1981] 1 QB 565, 569 (CA). *Bumper Development Corp. v. Comr. of Police* [1991] 1 WLR 1362, 1369 (CA); *Royal Boskalis NV v. Mountain* [1997] 2 All ER 929, 943, 948, 964–976–977 (CA).
[69] See above, p. 62. Westlake, who first analysed the topic, thought only that there was 'in effect' a presumption, and only apparently in cases where foreign law was alleged but unproved: *Private International Law* (1858), 393. Otherwise 'judgment will pass according to the law of England': ibid.
[70] Currie, (1958) 58 *Col L Rev* 964; Ehrenzweig, (1960) 58 *Mich L Rev* 637, 678–679; Ehrenzweig & Westen, (1968) 66 *Mich L Rev* 1679, 1685–1690. This is not to say that a court should give preference to its own law in the choice of law process, as Ehrenzweig suggests: *A Treatise on the Conflict of Laws* (1962), 311; Schmitthof, *International Trade Law and Private International Law*, 549.

without establishing it by evidence.[71] But what of the rather different case where foreign law is pleaded and proved but its proof has failed for want of satisfactory evidence?

Here also the presumption of similarity has little to commend it. It has the look of an improbable fiction and is highly suspect in a case where a claimant may have introduced (if unsuccessfully) substantial evidence suggesting that foreign law is different. Principle certainly argues against the traditional presumption where the proof of foreign law has failed. True, it meets the difficulty that evidence of foreign law will be relevant only in a case which a court has decided is governed by foreign law. It thus makes sense of the fact that a court may find itself applying English law *de facto* to a case in which foreign law applies *de jure*. But it is simpler, and less misleading, to take the view that foreign law applies only when its content has been affirmatively established. As such, if the proof of foreign law has failed, a precondition for its application has not been complied with and English law governs. If any justification were needed for the application of English law by default in this way, the structure of the English conflicts process supplies it. The logic of the situation is that English law always governs in English courts unless the conflicts process (including the proof of foreign law) establishes otherwise.[72] This does not happen if the proof of foreign law has failed, such that English law continues to apply. Certainly, it is more realistic to jettison any presumption of similarity and to accept, for sound reasons of practicality and principle, that a court directly applies English law where proof of foreign law has failed.[73]

But the presumption of similarity, underwritten by long usage, has proved to be improbably resistant to reform. Although, for example, the trial judge in one recent case doubted whether it could legitimately apply to the proof of foreign public policy the Court of Appeal held that it did.[74] It might have been expected that the uniqueness of national conceptions of public policy, or the importance of establishing positively a matter of such importance to a foreign country, would have suggested the opposite conclusion. It is also surprising that the role of the presumption should have been accepted without any real consideration of its merits or its implications. True, the case, *Royal Boskalis NV* v. *Mountain*, was one in which foreign law had been relied upon although not pleaded and proved, not one in which its proof had failed, our present concern. But it might have been expected that the tactical benefits to be derived from the presumption in such cases should make the courts more, not less, vigilant to police its use.

---

[71] See above, p. 143.
[72] Currie, above n. 70; Ehrenzweig, above n. 70; Ehrenzweig & Westen, above n. 70.
[73] Dicey and Morris, 238, supporting the view expressed in Fentiman, (1992) 108 *LQR* 142, 147–148.
[74] *Royal Boskalis Westminster NV* v. *Mountain* [1997] 2 All ER 930, 976–977 (CA).

For this very reason, however, *Boskalis* may serve as a reminder that the presumption of similarity remains firmly, if unreflectively, part of the idiom of English private international law.

But there have always been cases in which the suspect nature of the presumption of similarity has been recognized by the courts. As we saw in Chapter IV there is some evidence that the presumption might not operate where it is implausible to suppose that English and foreign law are the same. It was once doubted for example that foreign law should be presumed to be the same as English law unless the foreign law is that of a common law system.[75] And some courts have declined to presume that foreign law is the same as local statute law.[76] Even Westlake's treatise, which otherwise favours such a presumption, assumed that it could not apply where some 'special institution' of English law was involved.[77] The possibility of such exceptions is not, however, so much a cure for the inappropriateness of the presumption of similarity as a confirmation of its damaging effects. For as long as such a presumption is treated as a general rule it cries out for exceptions in cases where it is simply implausible. But in a case to which such an exception applies the effect, presumably, is that the claim or defence in question will be dismissed. That might be acceptable if foreign law is relied upon but no attempt is made to prove it. But is it the appropriate outcome where a party has attempted to prove foreign law conscientiously, if ultimately without success? The only way to avoid such a draconian result is to dispense with the presumption altogether and accept that English law applies directly when foreign law has not been established to the court's satisfaction. Again, the unfortunate effect of the presumption is that it focuses attention on the wrong question. For the issue is not whether English and foreign law are similar. It is whether English law should be applied by default if the proof of foreign law has failed.

Whether or not we employ the presumption of similarity there will always be cases in which the application of English law by default is inappropriate. For example the abbreviated nature of the proceedings might make it inappropriate to determine foreign law at all, whether positively or by way of the presumption. The default rule has not been applied where summary judgment was sought,[78] the proper course in such cases being to allow a defendant to contest the point at trial. Nor is the presumption favoured in proceedings under the doctrine of *forum non conveniens*.[79] In such a case foreign law is normally established on the basis of affidavit evidence without examination. As such it may be especially inappropriate to penalise a party who had not the evidential means to establish foreign law.

---

[75] *Guepratte* v. *Young* (1851) 4 De G & Sm 217.
[76] *Purdom* v. *Pavey* (1896) 26 SCR 412, 417; *Schneider* v. *Jaffe* (1916) 7 CPD 696.
[77] Westlake, above n. 69, 423.   [78] *National Shipping Corpn.* v. *Arab*, above n. 68.
[79] *The Polessk* [1996] 2 Lloyd's Rep. 40.

It may be preferable to form the best view possible on the available evidence. Indeed, it may be in such cases that the objective is not to establish foreign law, but to identify what it might be.[80] Conversely, the default rule might be inapplicable where it might be unfair to allow a party to do anything less than establish foreign law affirmatively. Where this is so a claim or defence founded upon foreign law will simply fail. In criminal prosecutions for bigamy, for example, the existence of a marriage under foreign law must be positively made out.[81] Nor has the presumption of similarity been applied where fraud was alleged,[82] the seriousness of such an accusation suggesting that it should be affirmatively established. Logic also suggests that this should be the case where the application of foreign law is required because the relevant choice of law rule is mandatory, or where English law cannot apply because territorially limited in scope.[83]

It is doubtful, therefore, that anything is achieved by speaking of a presumption of similarity between English and foreign law. Even if the terminology is to survive it may not be applicable in every case. And even if it is jettisoned there may be cases in which English law should not be applied in default of the adequate proof of foreign law. But in practice it may seldom happen that a court will decide that the proof of foreign law has altogether failed. This may of course occur. But it is misleading to assume that a court will often find itself in the position of having to apply English law where the burden of proving a pleaded foreign law has not been discharged.[84] This is normally because, in contested cases, the opinion of the other expert will be preferred. But where neither party has supplied adequate evidence a court may adopt one of two strategies for ensuring that foreign law is successfully proved. It will either suggest that the parties provide better evidence of foreign law, courts occasionally going as far as specifying what form such improved evidence might take. Alternatively, a court might remove responsibility for proof from the parties and their experts, usually by considering afresh such documentary evidence as they have tendered and forming an independent view as to its meaning and import.

As to the first such strategy, we have seen the extent to which courts have the power to regulate the proper proof of foreign law.[85] If the evi-

---

[80] *The Adhiguna Meranti* [1988] 1 Lloyd's Rep. 384 (HK).   [81] Dicey and Morris, 238.
[82] *Österreichische Länderbank* v. *S'Elite Ltd.*, above n. 68.   [83] See above, pp. 147; 153.
[84] Similarly, a survey of the relevant US case law between 1966 and 1981 revealed only two cases in which foreign law was relied upon but not proved to the court's satisfaction: Sass, (1981) 29 *Am Jl Comp L* 97, 111; see also, Morentin, 5 *Ariz J Intl & Comp L* 228. It is revealing that in *Szechter* v. *Szechter* [1971] P 286, 296, where this occurred, the one expert had fallen ill, and the court may have been inclined to apply English law in order to validate a subsequent marriage.
[85] See above, pp. 153–156.

dence as to foreign law is insufficient to allow a proper determination of the matter, proceedings might be adjourned to allow the parties to improve it. To do so is highly unusual. But it virtually guarantees the successful proof of foreign law because, in the nature of such cases, a court is unlikely to find foreign law unproved once improved evidence as to its content has been presented. Typically this occurs when a court insists on the submission of expert evidence, the parties having attempted, perhaps, to rely on foreign legal materials alone.[86] As to the second strategy, where expert evidence is provided, it is unlikely that a judge will often be completely unable to form any opinion as to the content of foreign law. As we shall see in the following section, English courts are much inclined to save the process of proof, and ensure the application of foreign law, typically by returning to any documentary evidence before the court as to foreign law and reviewing its implications. In one such case it was held that, when the evidence as to foreign law is deficient and conflicting, a court is at liberty to look afresh at the materials adduced by expert witnesses and determine their proper meaning.[87] Another court went further, deciding that a judge may do the same where expert testimony is obviously at odds with the plain words of a supporting document, notwithstanding that the evidence is uncontradicted.[88]

If the proof of foreign law will seldom fail in an English court this does not mean that foreign law will be correctly proved, especially if the court is obliged to determine a difficult and novel issue of foreign law merely on documentary evidence. But it ensures that the courts will seldom be in the position of having to apply English law by default by reason of its being inadequately proved, such is their willingness to overcome the difficulties of unsatisfactory or conflicting evidence. It might be objected that the willingness of English courts to facilitate the successful proof of foreign law by reviewing documentary evidence is undesirable.[89] It tends to subvert the principle that foreign laws are facts to allow a court, in effect, to rescue the proof of an unproved fact. It involves English courts in the difficult, even invidious task, of trying to resolve questions of foreign law without the assistance of qualified experts. It also, for that reason, encourages, perhaps, the misapplication of foreign law. Indeed, it might be thought preferable for an English court to reconcile itself to the failure of the parties' proof of foreign law, leading to the application of English law instead, on the assumption that it is better in such a case for a judge to apply English law well than foreign law badly. Against such criticisms, however, should be placed the important consideration that foreign laws are not

---

[86] *Brown* v. *Brown* (1917) 116 LT 702; *Beatty* v. *Beatty* [1924] 1 KB 807 (CA).
[87] *Concha* v. *Murietta* (1889) 40 Ch D 543 (CA).
[88] *Buerger* v. *New York Life Assurance Co.* (1927) 96 LJKB 930 (CA).
[89] Hodgkinson, 306–307.

facts in the usual sense, nor is a failure in the proof of foreign law, and the application of English by default, to be equated with the multitude of other situations in which other facts are unsuccessfully proved. The effect of allowing proof of foreign law to fail, requiring English law's application, is to undermine both the conflicts process and whichever choice of law rule, in a given case, justifies reference to foreign law in the first place. It leads to the result that English law, not the applicable foreign law, becomes the *lex causae* by default. Whatever its faults, the tendency for English courts to bring the proof of foreign law to a successful conclusion, amounts to an attempt to prosecute the choice of law process.

4. THE ASSESSMENT OF EXPERT EVIDENCE

How should a court behave once evidence of foreign law is before it? At a superficial level, the court's role is simply stated. It is empowered and required to form its own view in the light of the tendered evidence. In doing so it weighs the evidence as it would any expert testimony, giving due weight to the coherence and plausibility of the opinion, its consistency with any supporting documents and the clarity and demeanour of the witness.[90] But in relation to foreign law the nature of a court's powers and duties in the face of the tendered evidence gives rise to a number of distinctive issues. It is especially necessary to notice that courts are limited to considering such evidence as the parties themselves have introduced, an inhibition outweighed by the several respects in which its powers are more extensive than might be supposed. It is also important to notice how foreign law is assessed on appeal. How foreign law is treated in interlocutory proceedings is best addressed in Chapter VII.

(a) A Limitation: Adherence to Documents Produced

A significant limitation is that a court is not permitted to assess any documentary evidence of foreign law save that which is introduced in support of expert opinion. When an expert witness refers to documentary evidence in support of his or her testimony a court is entitled to consider its import. In consequence, when an expert witness as to foreign law refers to foreign commentaries, statutes, or law reports a court may read and evaluate them as part of the expert's evidence.[91] By doing so the court may test the cred-

---

[90] *Concha* v. *Murietta*, above n. 87; *Russian Commercial and Industrial Bank* v. *Comptoir d'Escompete de Mulhouse* [1923] 2 KB 630 (CA); *Bumper Development Corpn.* v. *Comr. of Police* [1991] 1 WLR 1362, 1368 (CA); *Grupo Torras* v. *Al Sabah* [1996] 1 Lloyd's Rep. 7, 18–19.

[91] *Nelson* v. *Bridport* (1845) 8 Beav. 527, at 541; *Concha* v. *Murietta*, above n. 87; *Lazard Bros.* v. *Midland Bank Ltd.* [1933] AC 289, 298 (HL).

ibility of the expert's testimony, and may resolve any conflicts between the testimony of rival experts. But it follows from the principle that courts may not conduct their own researches into foreign law,[92] that a court is circumscribed in the extent to which it may refer to foreign documentary materials. It may not refer to such materials save in so far as they have been cited expressly in the expert's testimony. If an expert refers expressly to particular passages in a foreign commentary the court may not have regard to other parts of that work.[93] Conversely, an appeal based on the claim that a judge has conducted independent research into foreign law will not succeed if it transpires that the sources referred to formed part of an expert's testimony.[94] Similarly, it may be assumed that, if an expert adduces selected parts of a foreign law report or statute, other portions of such texts are inadmissible.[95] Although this self-denying ordinance stems from the prohibition on independent judicial research into foreign law it also has a more pragmatic basis: if a judge strays beyond material directly put in evidence there is a risk that such extraneous material may be outdated or inaccurate (for which reasons the expert may not have cited it).

(b) The Court's Extensive Powers

Generally speaking, a court's role in relation to foreign-law evidence is relatively passive, at least in the sense that it is required to adjudicate on the evidence as presented by the parties. Certainly, a court's room to act independently in such cases is circumscribed by its lack of judicial notice of foreign law, ensuring that a court may not normally trespass beyond the evidence the parties have led. In several senses, however, a judge's domain is more extensive than might commonly be supposed. First, a court's role is not confined to applying settled propositions of foreign law. It may be required—indeed will almost invariably be required—to determine points which no foreign court has yet adjudicated upon. Secondly, a court is free to accord such weight to the evidence before it as it may consider appropriate, a powerful instrument in controlling the process of proof. Thirdly, if controversially, a court may sometimes draw upon its own knowledge or competence in the process of proof. This allows a court to disregard expert testimony in favour of its own reading of any textual evidence, at least where such testimony is at odds with any sensible construction of such evidence.

---

[92] *Di Sora* v. *Phillipps* (1863) 10 HLC 624, 640; *Bumper Development Corpn.* v. *Comr. of Police*, above n. 90, 1368
[93] *Nelson* v. *Bridport*, above n. 91, 542; *Waung* v. *Subbotovsky* [1968] 3 NSWR 261, 499.
[94] *Bumper Developments Corp. Ltd.* v. *Comr. of Police*, above n. 90, 1371.
[95] Dicey and Morris, 232.

(i) NOVEL POINTS OF FOREIGN LAW

A court's handling of foreign law is not inhibited by the novelty of the point in question. English courts may find themselves in the position of having to resolve questions of foreign law to which the relevant foreign system itself supplies no answer. They may find themselves having to determine an issue of foreign law in circumstances in which the expert witnesses, in the absence of clear guidance as to foreign law rule, can do no more than express their own opinion as to the answer without pointing to decisive authority.[96] The fact that a court may be required to establish novel points of foreign law need occasion no surprise. Indeed, such a situation is entirely commonplace and is almost bound to arise whenever a point of foreign law is disputed, for were foreign law clear it would give rise to no dispute. It could be argued that the relevant foreign court, rather than an English judge, is best placed to resolve a hard case under foreign law. Unlike the English judge the foreign court may call upon its experience of the foreign system to assist in resolving the question, a fact which may influence an English court in deciding at the jurisdictional stage that it is not the *forum conveniens*.[97] But English judges can display considerable robustness in the face of such difficulties, as they must in cases in which the doctrine of *forum non conveniens* is unavailable.[98] They do not necessarily see any objection to resolving a novel question of foreign law without any deeper understanding of the system concerned, equipped only with the unsupported opinions of the expert witnesses. In doing so, the cogency, conviction, and plausibility of the evidence are of paramount importance. As a distinguished judge expressed it, in a case involving difficult issues of German law:

> The fact that the plaintiff's expert was not able to do more than assert, in this novel situation, his own view on how the German court would react when faced with a similar problem does not disqualify his evidence from being relied on. There are many fields of law in which the books provide no direct answer, and where the skill of the lawyer lies precisely in predicting what answer should be given. If the judge concludes that the expert's prediction is reliable, he is fully entitled to give effect to it.[99]

---

[96] *G & B Montage GmbH v. Irvani* [1990] 1 WLR 667, 684, 691 (CA).

[97] See especially, *The Nile Rhapsody* [1992] 2 Lloyd's Rep. 399, 410–411. Egypt was the *forum conveniens* in a case in which both parties' experts were in almost total disagreement, in which they cited little authority for their opinions, and in which the English court would be applying unfamiliar principles, the Egyptian legal system being a civil law system.

[98] i.e. when the Brussels or Lugano Conventions apply and the alternative forum is also a Contracting State.

[99] *G & B Montage GmbH v. Irvani*, above n. 96. The difficulty may be greater at the interlocutory stage if only affidavit evidence is available: *The Adhiguna Meranti* [1988] 1 Lloyd's Rep. 384, 390–391 (HK).

Proof by Experts

Novel points of foreign law may arise in several ways. The point may not have been subjected to authoritative determination by a foreign court, perhaps because no relevant cases have arisen, or because different lines of authority are in conflict.[100] Or the foreign system may lack any developed law in a particular area.[101] If so, the court might conclude that foreign law not been proved (because it cannot be proved), or that, being non-existent, it can scarcely be applied, such that English law must govern. Special problems may also arise with regard to disputes involving those civil law countries in which a court is prohibited from enunciating rules of law at all and in which decided cases are not regarded as a source of law.[102] In such cases it is inevitable that a disputed issue will not have been subject to judicial determination in the common law sense. In such instances the question is not whether a particular point has been judicially resolved, but whether or not the relevant doctrine, the academic conventional wisdom, favours one position or another.

Almost inevitably, the test for resolving a novel point of foreign law is to ask what the foreign court would probably decide.[103] One method of doing so is to select what is on its face the most convincing expert testimony.[104] Another, which might be available in some cases, is to assume that the foreign court would act in accordance with the principle of international comity,[105] or that it would seek to comply with general principles of public international law.[106] Whatever the method, however, English courts resolve novel points of foreign law with arresting alacrity.

(ii) THE DIFFERENTIAL WEIGHTING OF EVIDENCE

Although generally confined to the evidence as presented by the parties, a court may exercise considerable influence over the process of proof by according different weight to different items of evidence. As the authorities disclose, not all items of evidence of foreign law attract the same weight and require the same treatment. Sometimes, expert evidence as to foreign law may be regarded as defective, and accorded reduced weight (or none at all). This might happen for any one of three principal reasons. The witness may be unqualified, at least as to specific portions of evidence, or (especially if a practitioner) may have acted too much as an

---

[100] *Breen* v. *Breen* [1964] P. 144, 151–152; *Re Duke of Wellington* [1947] Ch. 506, 515.
[101] Cf. *Amin Rasheed Corpn.* v. *Kuwait Ince. Co.* [1984] AC 51, 63–64 (HL); *Vesta* v. *Butcher* [1986] 2 All ER 488, 497.
[102] See e.g. Article 5 of the French Civil Code.
[103] *Re Duke of Wellington*, above n. 100; *Vesta* v. *Butcher*, above n. 101, 497.
[104] *G & B Montage GmbH* v. *Irvani*, above n. 99, 684.
[105] *Breen* v. *Breen*, above n. 100, 151–152.
[106] *A-G for New Zealand* v. *Ortiz* [1984] AC 1, 19 (CA); affd. without reference to the point, [1984] 1 AC 41 (HL).

advocate, or (especially if an academic) may have offered too speculative an opinion.

The proof of foreign law is especially exposed to the risk of defective evidence. Perhaps more than in most areas in which proof is effected by expert testimony, there is the possibility that evidence may be offered by a relatively unqualified witness. This reflects the difficulty of finding suitably qualified experts in many areas of foreign law. It also reflects the desire of the courts to accede to the parties' wishes as to how foreign law should be proved and a reluctance to declare a witness so unqualified as to make his or her testimony totally inadmissible. More simply, perhaps, the phenomenon of the unqualified expert may reflect the fact that it is only once experts have been orally examined that their real competence, as opposed the admissibility of their testimony, becomes clear. There is also a particular risk in connection with the proof of foreign law that a witness will cross the line which separates evidence from advocacy. The argumentative nature of legal reasoning suggests as much and the risk is all the greater if an expert is a practising foreign lawyer used to taking his or her client's part. Finally, where academic experts are employed, there is the rather different danger that their evidence will be too speculative.

In the light of such inherent potential flaws, courts sometimes give reduced weight to at least part of the evidence of particular witnesses. This may be attributable to the expert's relative lack of expertise in a given area,[107] or to the fact that the expert has acted so much as an advocate as to taint the testimony.[108] Although it is commonplace for foreign academics to act as witnesses, the courts may also react adversely when too academic an approach has been adopted. In one case there is a suggestion that the mere fact that an expert has academic rather than practical expertise should be reflected in the weight accorded to his or her testimony, although it is likely that a court would now adopt a more respectful attitude towards academic expertise than this implies.[109] In another case the speculative nature of an academic expert's opinion led the court to ignore it.[110]

By contrast, evidence of foreign law may be given special weight when it takes the form of a previous judicial decision. Certainly, English courts accord particular respect to foreign court decisions in determining points of foreign law.[111] Worthy of respect as such decisions are, however, they

[107] *Ajami v. Comptroller of Customs* [1954] 1405, 1408 (PC); *Gulf Consolidated Co. v. Credit Suisse First Boston Ltd.* [1992] 2 Lloyd's Rep. 301, 310, 311.
[108] *Rossano v. Manufacturers Life Insurance Co.* [1963] 2 QB 352, 381; *Macmillan Inc. v. Bishopsgate Trust plc (No. 3)* [1995] 1 WLR 978, 1009.
[109] *Lazard Bros. v. Midland Bank,* above n. 91, 298.
[110] *Adams v. Cape Industries plc* [1990] 2 WLR 657, 683 (CA).
[111] *Walpole v. Ewer* (1789) Ridg temp H 276n.; *Bremer v. Freeman* (1857) 10 Moo PC 306; *Beatty v. Beatty,* above n. 86; *Re Annesley* [1926] Ch. 692, 707–708; *Bankers and Shippers Co. of New York v. Liverpool Marine and General Insurance Co. Ltd.* (1926) 24 Ll L R 85; *In the Estate of Fuld (No. 3)* [1968] P. 675, 701–702.

are not to be treated as decisive and do not absolve the judge from determining foreign law in the light of all the evidence.[112] In some cases it has been recognized that court decisions may not have the same binding status in civil law countries as in common law jurisdictions.[113] A court is permitted, by the principle that regard should be had to the totality of the evidence, to ignore a foreign decision if the balance of the evidence suggests that it does not correctly state the law. In one prominent case the Court of Appeal preferred the agreed evidence of both parties' experts to the exposition of foreign law provided by a superior foreign court.[114]

The insistence of English courts on proving foreign law by expert testimony may restrict the reliance parties might wish to place on foreign decisions. Merely putting the judgment of a foreign court in evidence, even when exhibited to an explanatory affidavit, will not usually be regarded as adequate proof of foreign law.[115] This may result in the court requiring further and better evidence on the point from the parties[116] or, more likely, in the court admitting the evidence but according it minimal or diminished weight. Reliance on a foreign decision, at least where it is exhibited to an explanatory affidavit,[117] may exceptionally be permitted where the judgment's import is uncontradicted, or where such a method of proof has been agreed by the parties.[118]

Sometimes the previous decision of an English court on a question of foreign law may be relied upon, although it is unclear how often identical points of foreign law actually recur. Statute requires that special weight should normally be attached to previous decisions of English courts on points of foreign law.[119] By virtue of section 4(2) of the Civil Evidence Act 1972 such decisions are presumed to be correct although the presumption may be rebutted in the light of contrary evidence,[120] presumably that of an expert in the normal fashion. Previous English decisions are devoid of special weight, however, in proceedings in which the House of Lords has judicial notice of the law in question.[121] An English High Court decision on a point of Scots law would carry no weight, therefore, in proceedings before the House of Lords. Previous English decisions are also deprived of their presumptive correctness in the event that another English decision offers a conflicting statement of the foreign law in question.[122]

---

[112] *Guaranty Trust of New York* v. *Hannay* [1918] 2 KB 623, 638; 667 (CA); *Callwood* v. *Callwood* [1960] AC 659 (PC).
[113] *Fothergill* v. *Monarch Airlines* [1981] AC 251 (HL); *The Nile Rhapsody*, above n. 97.
[114] *Bumper Development Corp. Ltd.* v. *Comr. of Police*, above n. 90, 1368–1369.
[115] *Callwood* v. *Callwood*, above n. 112.
[116] *Beatty* v. *Beatty*, above n. 86.
[117] *Callwood* v. *Callwood*, above n. 112.
[118] *Beatty* v. *Beatty*, above n. 86, 808; 811.
[119] See below, p. 223.
[120] Section 4(2)(b).
[121] Ibid.
[122] Ibid.

(c) Supplementing Expert Evidence

The need to supplement expert testimony as to foreign law arises either when the evidence is unsatisfactory, or when it is satisfactory but the evidence of parties' experts is conflicting. In such cases a court might find that foreign law has not been proved, causing English law to apply by default. But this is unsatisfactory because it defeats the principal purpose of proving foreign law, which is that it should be accurately applied. Indeed, it subverts the choice of law process by preventing application of the governing law altogether. Particular problems arise where one party has introduced unsatisfactory evidence which the other has not contradicted. Here a court might accept the uncontradicted evidence on the basis that the parties have effectively agreed it. But, again, this is to undermine the application of foreign law. Given the consequences of allowing the application of foreign law to fail, there are grounds for thinking that a court will only adopt such default measures once it is clear that foreign law cannot be accurately applied. In particular, the court might be prepared to supplement the evidence it has heard by forming an independent view of such written material as may have been tendered. The justification is that a court cannot be expected to apply foreign law in a manner which it knows to be incorrect, and that the proof of foreign law should not fail if means exist to save it. The accurate application of foreign law is thus encouraged.

If the doctrine that foreign laws are facts were strictly enforced a court should not attempt to supplement the expert testimony in this way. For, taken to its limits, the doctrine deprives the court of any independent expertise or knowledge in matters concerning foreign law. But, as we have seen, the principle is honoured as much in the breach as in its application.[123] Certainly, as Chapter VIII suggests, there is greater flexibility in the proof of foreign law than is sometimes supposed. And as Lord Langdale MR said of the court's power to supplement expert testimony:

> In this, as in so many other instances, there is room for the exercise of a sound and cautious discretion, by the employment of which, Courts are enabled to bring some cases, otherwise interminable, to a good and even satisfactory conclusion.[124]

The court's capacity to supplement expert testimony derives not from any pretended expertise in foreign law, but from the judge's intelligence and powers of reasoning. As has been said:

> The witness, however expert in the foreign law, cannot prevent the Court using its common sense; and the Court can reject his evidence if he says something patently absurd, or something inconsistent with the rest of his evidence.[125]

---

[123] See above, p. 187; *Parkasho v. Singh* [1968] P 233, 250; *Dalmia Dairy Industries Ltd. v. National Bank of Pakistan* [1978] 2 Lloyd's Rep. 223, 286; O'Malley and Layton, 230.

[124] *Nelson v. Bridport*, above n. 91, 541.

[125] *A/S Tallina Laevauhisus v. Estonian State Steamship Line* (1947) 80 Ll L R 99, 108 (CA).

In theory, any situation in which a court has inherent knowledge or competence is one in which it may supplement expert testimony. Arguably, certain familiar rules of foreign law may be notorious.[126] And in rare cases a court might perhaps rely on its own awareness of general principles of law.[127] The effect is that proof of such matters becomes unnecessary and, if evidence is tendered, a court should be able to reject it in so far as it does not conform to its appreciation of the matter. In practice, there are certainly cases in which a court might resort to its own expertise to dispense with strict proof of foreign law.[128] There is also at least one case in which, in the absence of any evidence at all, a court has declined to apply English law by default, preferring to rely on the commonplace nature of the foreign rule.[129] But there seem to be none in which a court has relied on such independent knowledge to reject expert testimony where it has been offered. In other ways, however, the possibility that a court might supplement expert testimony by reference to its independent knowledge or competence assumes greater practical importance. These are those in which a court employs its power to construe according to its own lights, in common sense fashion, any documentary legal material which has been put in evidence before it. In such cases, unless the court has evidence as to how such material is to be construed under the relevant foreign law, it is entitled to interpret it on English principles.[130] An important consequence is that a court may rely on its own competence in construing legal material to justify disregarding an interpretation placed upon such material by an expert.

(i) UNSATISFACTORY EVIDENCE

An expert's testimony might be unsatisfactory in so far as it is irrelevant, incoherent or might conflict with the documentary material which is offered in its support. Normally, its unsatisfactory nature will be addressed by the other party. If so, and if the other party's evidence is sound, the problem of inadequacy is resolved by preferring the better evidence in the usual way. But both parties' evidence might be equally unsatisfactory. In that event the choice for the court is between applying English law by default or attempting to resolve the question by reference to the documentary evidence. A more difficult problem arises where the unsatisfactory evidence of one party's expert is uncontradicted or agreed. In

---

[126] See below, p. 248.   [127] See below, pp. 247–248.   [128] See below, p. 245.
[129] *Saxby* v. *Fulton* [1909] 2 KB 208.
[130] *Prowse* v. *European and American Shipping Co.* (1860) 13 Moo PC 484; *Papadopoulos* v. *Papadopoulos* [1930] P 55; *The Torni* [1932] P 78 (CA); *F. & K. Jabbour* v. *Custodian of Israeli Absentee Property* [1954] 1 WLR 139, at 147–148; *Jasiewicz* v. *Jasiewicz* [1962] 1 WLR 1426; *Mahadervan* v. *Mahadervan* [1964] P 233.

such a case the court must choose between, on the one hand, allowing the case to proceed on evidence which is probably flawed and, on the other, correcting the defect for itself. This choice conceals a difficult issue of principle. To ignore the fault is to adhere strictly to the view that only an expert may speak to foreign law. It is also to respect the parties' wishes. But to do so is also to tolerate an error of which the court is aware, and which it has the means at hand to correct. More technically, to supplement evidence where it is uncontradicted may be to undermine the principle that a point of foreign law on which one party relies, like any fact, may be admitted by the other.[131] How can a court undo what amounts to an agreement between the parties?

The argument that courts should never under any circumstances supplement expert evidence is not without support.[132] Some judges have doubted their competence to decide questions of foreign law unaided by expert testimony, a position which would disable the court from rejecting such evidence. In *Nelson* v. *Bridport*[133] it was doubted even that a judge should read materials put in evidence in support of foreign law testimony:

. . . if he reads them, they may appear to him to accord with the testimony or to differ from it. If, in his view, they accord with it, nothing is gained. If, in his view, they differ from it, he, being ignorant of the foreign law, cannot weigh his opinion against the clear and uncontradicted opinion of the witness.[134]

Other judges, apparently accepting that a court may have to resort to an independent assessment of textual material where the expert evidence is conflicting, have doubted their power to displace such evidence when it is uncontradicted.[135] By contrast, another group of cases endorse a court's power to reject such evidence. A number of decisions accept that a court may construe such written evidence as is before it, although they confirm that a judge should be reluctant to do so.[136] And several authorities in other common law jurisdictions further endorse the possibility of displacing defective expert testimony.[137]

---

[131] *Prowse* v. *European and American Shipping Co.*, op. cit.; *Moulis* v. *Owen* [1907] 1 KB 746; *The Torni*, op. cit.; RSC Order 18, r. 13.
[132] Hodgkinson, 306–309.
[133] Above n. 91, at 541; see also *Re Banque des Marchands de Moscou* [1958] Ch. 182, 202.
[134] Ibid., 381; but these remarks must be read in the light of those at 537.
[135] *Lazard* v. *Midland Bank Ltd.*, above n. 91, at 298.
[136] *Buerger* v. *New York Life Assurance Co.* (1927) 96 LJKB 930, 940–941 (CA); *Koechlin & Cie.* v. *Kestenbaum* [1927] 1 KB 616, 622; *A/S Tallina Laevauhisus* v. *Estonian State Steamship Line*, above n. 125, 108 (CA); *Re Banque des Marchands de Moscou*, above n. 133; *Rossano* v. *Manufacturers Life Insurance Co.* [1963] 2 QB 352; *Sharif* v. *Azad* [1967] 1 QB 605, 616 (CA); *Bumper Developments Corp. Ltd.* v. *Comr. of Police*, above n. 130; *Associated Shipping Services Ltd.* v. *Department of Personal Affairs of H. H. Sheikh Zayed Bin Sultan Al-Nahayan*, The Financial Times, 31 July 1990, (CA).
[137] *Allen* v. *Hay* (1922) 69 DLR 193, at 195–196; *O'Callaghan* v. *O'Sullivan* [1925] 1 IR 90, at 119; *Macnamara* v. *Hatteras* [1933] IR 675, at 695; 699; *Etler* v. *Kertesz* (1960) 26 DLR (2nd) 209.

The existence of such conflicting lines of authority is partly explained by the continuing confusion which surrounds the juridical status of foreign law in English courts. To insist that foreign law can only be established by expert evidence is to cleave strictly to the doctrine that foreign laws are facts. But to allow the courts to supplement defective expert evidence—to adopt a 'constructionist', rather than a 'factual' approach[138]—is to allow that foreign laws are also laws. It is to recognize the reality that English law treats such laws as laws as much as it classifies them as facts.[139] It also avoids the unfortunate consequences if the accuracy of the proof of foreign law is put in doubt. Such inaccuracy undermines the purpose of the choice of law process and is unjust to litigants whose rights fall to be regulated under foreign law. It is also a matter of concern that any legal system might allow a court to endorse an error of which it is aware and has the means to correct.

To treat foreign laws strictly as facts also ignores the important sense in which an English court's general legal expertise may to some extent qualify it to determine foreign law unaided. Certainly, the standards of relevance, coherence, and linguistic accuracy which lie at the root of legal reasoning may be brought to bear on the determination of foreign law as much as on domestic law. In doing so a court is not assuming expertise in foreign law, but deploying its basic legal skills. Indeed, it has been said that such general principles of legal reasoning are universal, within the legitimate province of the court.[140] As such, even uncontradicted expert evidence may be rejected if it involves 'a misunderstanding of conceptions familiar to lawyers of all countries'.[141]

The ambiguous case law may also be explained because, in reality, two distinct issues are involved, each attracting a different judicial response. One question is whether a court may ignore expert evidence simply because it suspects—or even knows—that it is wrong as a matter of foreign law. The other is whether they may do so when it conflicts with common sense, or with written material which is in evidence before the court. English courts are unsurprisingly reluctant to intervene in the former case.[142] Indeed, given their inability to research foreign law independently, how would they know that the evidence is flawed, and on what basis could they substitute their own opinion? But they are relatively confident about disagreeing with an expert's testimony when it defies common sense or is unsupported by the written evidence. Most obviously,

---

[138] Hodgkinson, 306–309.   [139] See above, p. 66.
[140] *Di Sora* v.*Phillipps* (1863) 10 HLC 624.
[141] *Buerger* v. *New York Life Assurance Co.*, above n. 136, 940.
[142] *Nelson* v. *Bridport*, above n. 91, 541; *Re Banque des Marchands de Moscou*, above n. 133; [1958] Ch. 192 194; *Rossano* v. *Manufacturers Life Insurance Co.*, above n. 140, 381.

they will do so if the defect lies in the interpretation of the words of a foreign statute or document. As Scrutton LJ expressed it:

> I can see no reason why a court is bound to accept the evidence of an expert witness as to fact, when he supports it by a document the plain words of which render his opinion impossible.[143]

But expert evidence may be defective not only when it depends on a misreading of the relevant material. As we have seen, an expert may misapply universal legal principles. Or, arguments which support the expert's reading of foreign law may be entirely lacking.[144] Again, judges have been understandably willing to disregard an expert's opinion where the expert simply failed to address the real point at issue.[145] An expert's opinion may also be rejected because 'extravagant',[146] or 'patently absurd'.[147] What unites such examples is that in such cases the evidence is falsified in so far as it is incoherent or irrational. It is not that the court claims an expertise in foreign law which it plainly lacks. Indeed, however comfortable courts may be in disturbing, say, an expert's reading of a foreign text, they are unlikely to reject an opinion on foreign law directly. Certainly, it is insufficient to justify disturbing expert testimony that a judge finds it unreasonable, unlikely or counter-intuitive, unless the defect appears from the face of the tendered evidence. To take but a prominent example, McNair J once declined to depart from an expert's opinion, although he clearly found it wanting and was concerned that the expert had crossed the line which divides the dispassionate expert from the advocate: 'there being no evidence to the contrary I feel constrained to accept this as the true view, however unreasonable it may be'.[148] As such deference implies, it is not enough that a court should find such an opinion unacceptable. If the court's decision to substitute its view for the expert's is justified it is only because the latter defies common sense, or is wrong when judged according to the textual evidence.[149] Nor will a court intervene if the expert is correctly applying a rule of construction which is recognized under the foreign law,[150] or if the words in question bear a technical meaning,[151] however odd such a meaning may appear.

---

[143] *Buerger v. New York Life Assurance Co.*, above n. 136, 937. To the same effect see *A/S Tallina Laevauhisus v. Estonian State Steamship Line*, above n. 125, 108.
[144] *Associated Shipping Services Ltd. v. Department of Personal Affairs of HH Sheikh Zayed Bin Sultan Al-Nahayan*, above n. 136.
[145] *Re Valentine's Settlement* [1965] Ch 831, 855 (per Salmon LJ, dissenting).
[146] *Buerger v. New York Life Assurance Co.*, above n. 136, 941.
[147] *A/S Tallinna Laevauhisus v. Estonian State Steamship Line*, above n. 125, 108.
[148] *Rossano v. Manufacturers Life Insurance Co.*, above n. 136, 381.
[149] *Buerger v. New York Life Assurance Co.*, above n. 136, 937.
[150] *A/S Tallinna Laevauhisus v. Estonian State Steamship Line*, above n. 125, 108.
[151] *Camille and Henry Dreyfus Foundation Inc. v. IRC* [1954] Ch 672, 692.

The degree to which judicial activism is acceptable, and the extent to which it is not, is neatly illustrated by Roxburgh J's approach in *Re Banque des Marchands de Moscou*,[152] in which he felt constrained to accept uncontradicted evidence concerning Russian law. Some of the evidence was surprising. But an English court does not know foreign law and the expert, so far from committing palpable errors, showed 'remarkable understanding, resourcefulness and consistency'.[153] Moreover the evidence depended on Russian rules of construction which had themselves been satisfactorily proved, leaving the court no room to construe Russian law in its own way.[154] The court's power to depart from uncontradicted expert evidence has once more been confirmed in *Bumper Development Corporation Ltd. v. Comr. of Police*,[155] concerning the standing of various claimants under Hindu law to assert title to certain works of religious art, then in London. Both experts agreed that one such claimant lacked the necessary status. Ian Kennedy J, notwithstanding such agreement, rejected the expert evidence on the ground that it conflicted with two Indian decisions. The Court of Appeal overruled the judge's rejection of the agreed testimony partly because they accepted that a court cannot research foreign law for itself. But they accepted that a court may depart even from agreed evidence, provided that the supporting material justifies such a departure.

Only rarely, no doubt, will it be necessary for a court to supplement the testimony of an expert whose opinion is plainly defective. Not least, this is because the problem tends to arise in practice only when the evidence is uncontradicted. As such, a court will only rarely be aware of its deficiencies because often no evidence will be before the court in such cases. Nor is it in every case that such intervention will be possible. It is one thing to form an independent view of texts in English emanating from a common law system. But it is another to hazard an independent view, without expert assistance, of texts in translation which represent a quite different legal tradition.[156] In principle, however, it seems that an English court is empowered to depart even from uncontradicted expert evidence, at least where its misgivings depend on its inherent knowledge or competence. Those cases which reveal a reluctance to review expert testimony tend to be explicable as ones in which the court is counselling caution more than disputing the power. Or they are those in which the court is not declining to review the testimony in the light of common sense or the construction of written materials but is refusing, quite properly, to present itself as an expert on foreign law.

---

[152] [1958] Ch 182.   [153] At 194, 201–202.   [154] At 199.
[155] *Bumper Developments Corp. Ltd. v. Comr. of Police*, above n. 136.
[156] *Buerger v. New York Life Assurance Co.*, above n. 136, 940.

(ii) CONFLICTING EVIDENCE

The opinions on foreign law may be satisfactory but conflicting, such that neither clearly prevails. Unless it can remove the conflict by giving more weight to one than to the other,[157] it will be necessary for the court to resolve it by other means. One approach to such an impasse is to apply the familiar rule that one who alleges a point of foreign law bears the burden of proving it.[158] Arguably, where the evidence is conflicting, foreign law has not been shown to be different from English law, so that the latter should apply by default. Such an option is unattractive, however, in so far as it too readily permits the proof of foreign law to fail when the means may be at hand, in the shape of materials before the court, for preventing such a failure. Moreover, as we have seen, a failure to prove foreign law is something which English courts are reluctant to encourage.[159] It must also be noticed that a case involving conflicting testimony is actually very different from one where it is unsatisfactory. In the latter, a court is substituting an independent reading of the evidence from that contended for by the parties. But in the former, it is relying upon its own estimation of the matter to decide between such evidence as the experts have tendered.

It is unsurprising, therefore, that a considerable weight of authority supports the view that a court faced with balanced testimony should determine the matter for itself.[160] Indeed, the courts have perhaps taken the power to its limits by exercising it even where the point at issue concerns the *vires* of foreign legislation.[161] Even those cases which are essentially hostile to the possibility of a court's construing foreign law independently would seem to favour such a solution to the problem of tied testimony.[162] There is some suggestion in the case law that this power to resort to independent construction should be limited to situations in which the conflicting evidence is also unsatisfactory[163] but it hard to see any merit in such a view. Such resort to the textual evidence will not, however, always pro-

---

[157] See above, p. 191.
[158] *O'Callaghan* v. *O'Sullivan*, above n., 137, 119.
[159] See above, p. 186.
[160] *Dalrymple* v. *Dalrymple* (1811) 2 Hagg.Con. 54; *Trimbey* v. *Vignier* (1834) 1 Bing NC 151; *Devaux* v. *Steele* (1840) 6 Bing NC 360; *Nelson* v. *Bridport*, above n. 91, 537; *Bremer* v. *Freeman* (1857) 10 Moo PC 306; *Concha* v. *Murietta* (1889) 40 Ch D 543 (CA); *Guaranty Trust Corp. of New York* v. *Hannay* [1918] 2 KB 623 (CA); *Russian Commercial and Industrial Bank* v. *Comptoir d'Escompte de Mulhouse* [1923] 2 KB 630; *Princess Paley Olga* v. *Weisz* [1929] 1 KB 718 (CA); *Re Duke of Wellington* [1947] Ch 506; *In the Estate of Fuld (No. 3)* [1968] P 675, at 703–703; *Dubai Bank Ltd.* v. *Galadari (No. 5), The Times,* 26 June 1990; *Bumper Development Corp. Ltd.* v. *Comr. of Police*, above n. 136, 1269–1370.
[161] *King of the Hellenes* v. *Brostrom* (1923) Ll L R 167, 190, 192; *Re Amand* [1941] 2 KB 239; *Re Amand (No. 2)* [1942] 1 KB 445; *A/S Tallina Laevauhisus* v. *Estonian State Steamship Line*, above n. 125, 114; *Dubai Bank Ltd.* v. *Galadari (No. 5)*, above n. 160.
[162] *Lazard* v. *Midland Bank Ltd.* above n. 91, 298.
[163] *Concha* v. *Murietta*, above n. 160, 550.

vide a solution to the problem of conflicting testimony. It may be relatively difficult unless the foreign system approximates to English law and any foreign text is in English. It may be also that the written evidence is itself opaque or incoherent, or that the court considers that its proper construction requires a technical grasp of foreign law which it lacks. In any such case the court will have no alternative but to resolve conflicts of evidence by weighing the competing evidence and, in hard cases, to rule that foreign law has not been proved, English law being applied by default.

5. EXPERT EVIDENCE ON APPEAL

It is a recurring theme in this work that, although characterized as facts, foreign laws are not invariably treated as such in English practice. One of the more important respects in which the determination of foreign law belies its factual status is that appeals are readily entertained from findings on foreign law.[164] This may lead to a thorough re-examination of the evidence, including transcripts of the oral examination of the parties' experts at trial.[165] Certainly, appellate courts are willing to engage in such review, no doubt because it affects the legal rights and obligations of the parties. This willingness may be at its most pronounced in cases involving the construction of the statutes of other Commonwealth countries, in which such review may involve little more than reading the legislation in question.[166] Certainly, the more an issue of foreign law depends on matters of expert testimony rather than construction, the effectiveness of appellate review diminishes. The Court of Appeal may, it seems, refer to the transcripts of the experts' examination in the court below. But as has been said of cases involving oral expert testimony:

> An Appellate Court must not by uncritical acceptance of a trial judge's conclusions of fact shirk its function of considering the evidence afresh and forming its own view of the cogency of the rival contentions, whilst of course always remembering that the trial judge had the undoubted initial advantage of having seen and heard the witnesses.[167]

Foreign law may be handled differently depending on which appellate court is hearing the appeal. If, for example, an issue of Scots law arises in

---

[164] *Parkasho* v. *Singh* [1968] P 233, 250; *Dalmia Dairy Industries Ltd.* v. *National Bank of Pakistan* [1978] 2 Lloyd's Rep. 223, 286 (CA); *A-G of New Zealand* v. *Ortiz* [1984] AC 1; *The Saudi Prince* [1988] 1 Lloyd's Rep. 1, 3 (CA); *Bumper Development Corp. Ltd.* v. *Comr. of Police* [1991] 1 WLR 1362 (CA), 1370; *Grupo Torras SA* v. *Al Sabah* [1996] 1 Lloyd's Rep. 7, 18 (CA). See also, *G & H Montage GmbH* v. *Irvani* [1990] 1 WLR 667, 691 (CA).
[165] *The Saudi Prince*, op. cit., 6.   [166] Hartley, (1996) 45 ICLQ 271, 284–285.
[167] *Dalmia Dairy Industries Ltd.* v. *National Bank of Pakistan*, above n. 164, at 286 (per Megaw LJ), approving the remarks of Cairns J in *Parkasho* v. *Singh*, above n. 164.

the course of an appeal from an English court, the House of Lords, unlike the courts below, may take judicial notice of Scots law.[168] This is because it is the highest court in Scotland as much as in England and is thus aware of its laws. Similarly, the Privy Council presumably has notice of the laws of all states over which it has jurisdiction.[169] Although the jurisdiction of the House of Lords and of the Privy Council is formally distinct, the reality is that the membership of both bodies is effectively co-extensive. This may lead the former to assume a knowledge of the laws of a Commonwealth country from which appeals lie to the latter,[170] although strictly this is incorrect.

Theoretically, the readiness of English courts to review a trial court's findings as to foreign law underscores how foreign laws, although formally facts, are nonetheless laws, and are treated as such. The possibility of appellate review may also offer comfort to those who might doubt the effectiveness and fairness of leaving questions of foreign law to be determined by reference to a trial judge's assessment of competing evidence. It should be noticed, however, that the Court of Appeal will confine itself to the task of assessing the evidence as it was presented to the court below. Its task is to police errors by the trial judge, not to determine the question of foreign law *de novo*. Indeed, it can hardly do otherwise since English courts may not conduct their own researches into foreign law, or depart from the evidence presented by the parties' experts.[171]

---

[168] *De Thoren* v. *Att-Gen* (1896) 1 App Cas 686; *Elliot* v. *Joicey* [1935] AC 209, 236; *MacShannon* v. *Rockware Glass Ltd.* [1978] AC 795, 815, 821. The converse is also true: *Cooper* v. *Cooper* (1888) 13 App Cas 88.

[169] Dicey and Morris, 228.   [170] *A-G of New Zealand* v. *Ortiz*, above n. 164.

[171] In US Federal Practice, whereby courts may undertake independent research in foreign law, it is possible for an appeal court to determine points of foreign law on fresh evidence: *Esso Standard Oil* v. *S. S. Gasbras Sul*, 387 F2d 573 (1968); Sass, (1981) 29 Am Jl Comp L 97, 113–115.

VII
Improving Expert Proof

Evidence of foreign law is normally provided by the parties' experts, orally examined. But, given the delay, difficulty and expense of this process, how might cost-conscious litigants establish foreign law more easily? How might the court's task be made easier and the determination of foreign law made more efficient and effective? In certain circumstances, as Chapter VIII will show, resort to party experts may be dispensed with altogether, offering litigants the opportunity to avoid completely the delay and expense which such proof entails. But, short of this, there are several means whereby the use of expert opinion might be improved and the disadvantages of such evidence minimised. Some avoid the normal practice of examining experts orally. Foreign law might be proved in writing, perhaps by sworn affidavit. Or an expert might be examined abroad and not, as usual, at trial. But even the handling of expert testimony which is presented in the normal way might be improved. Independent assessors or experts may be appointed, for example, to resolve conflicts of opinion or to assist the court's appreciation of the evidence. It is important to define with precision the scope of such exceptions, each of which promises litigants savings in terms of cost and time, and to assess their desirability when compared with expert proof by standard means.

1. WRITTEN EVIDENCE OF FOREIGN LAW

We have seen that expert reports are normally used in support of oral expert testimony as to foreign law. But such evidence may be provided in writing without the need for oral examination. Typically, evidence of foreign law is supplied in this form where such evidence has been agreed by the parties.[1] Written statements of opinion, such as those in expert reports, might also be admitted in this way in contested cases as hearsay evidence.[2] But this is very exceptional, and is permitted only when it can be shown

---

[1] *Memec plc* v. *Inland Revenue Commissioners* [1996] STC 1336.
[2] Civil Evidence Act 1995, s. 2(1); RSC Order 38, r. 41; *Markes* v. *Markes* (1955) 106 LJ 75; Hodgkinson, 54–55; Cross and Tapper, *Evidence*, 8th edn., (London, 1995), 781; O'Malley and Layton, 234. It is apparent that access to the hearsay provisions of the 1995 Act is possible only if an application has been made under RSC Order 38, r. 36: *Rover International Ltd.* v. *Cannon Film Sales Ltd.* [1987] 1 WLR 1597.

that the expert cannot or should not be called in person.[3] It is unlikely that a court would make such a direction in practice were another expert available. And, notwithstanding the familiar difficulty of identifying suitably qualified experts, it will be rare that a person's expertise in foreign law would be so particular that no substitute could be found. The courts' habitual reluctance to allow foreign law to be established other than by expert examination also weighs against proof by informal means. But the decisive argument against introducing written hearsay evidence is tactical. It may be unwise for a party to rely on such means, given the reduced weight which it must carry by contrast with affidavit evidence or oral testimony.[4]

More commonly, expert evidence may be offered by sworn affidavit alone, without the need for oral examination in open court. This occurs in interlocutory proceedings, especially in disputes concerning jurisdiction and the staying of actions, but also in any proceedings of an abbreviated nature.[5] The general rules concerning affidavit expert evidence apply as much in this context as nature. At any time before trial, typically on the hearing of the summons for directions, a court may order that the affidavit of a witness may be admitted at trial 'if in the circumstances of the case it thinks it reasonable so to order'.[6] Subject to any contrary order the court might make, such a witness need not attend at trial, nor shall such a witness be subject to cross-examination.[7]

Given that the primary method of testing expert opinion is by oral examination, the alternative of employing affidavit evidence is exceptional. Interlocutory proceedings apart, the procedure exists mainly to facilitate proof where the expert is abroad, or where the evidence is uncontested. The courts have consistently refused to accept affidavit evidence as an acceptable foundation for establishing controversial facts. As one judge unequivocally put it: 'the court cannot resolve disputed questions of fact on affidavit evidence'.[8] But why do courts consistently deprecate reliance on affidavit evidence as a method of proving foreign law?[9] One reason

---

[3] RSC Order 38, r. 41.   [4] Hodgkinson, 55.
[5] *Calgar* v. *Billingham* [1996] STC (SCD) 150 (hearing before Inland Revenue Commissioners); *Re Arton* [1896] 1 QB 509 (application for writ of habeas corpus); *National Shipping Corpn.* v. *Arab* [1971] 2 Lloyd's Rep. 363 (CA) (application for summary judgment).
[6] RSC Order 38, r. 36(2)(a).   [7] RSC Order 38, r. 36(2)(b).
[8] *Seasconsar Far East Ltd.* v. *Bank Markazi* [1994] 1 AC 438, 452 (per Lord Goff) (HL).
[9] *Callwood* v. *Callwood* [1960] AC 659; *Re Valentine's Settlement* [1965] Ch 83; *National Shipping Corpn.* v. *Arab* [1971] 2 Lloyd's Rep. 363. The position is starkly different under the US Federal Rules of Civil Procedure, Rule 44.1 which permits great flexibility in the mode of proof adopted. There the use of affidavit evidence without examination is commonplace. It is often considered both adequate and desirable: Nussbaum, (1941) 50 *Yale LJ* 1018, 1029; Schmertz, (1978) 18 *Virginia Jl Int L* 697, 708, 711; Sass, (1981) 29 *Am Jl Comp L* 97, 108; Miner, (1995) 43 *Am Jl Comp L* 581, 588. But practitioners may regard it as tactically unwise to rely upon affidavit evidence alone: Schlesinger, Baade, Damaska and Herzog, *Comparative Law: Cases, Text, Materials*, 5th edn., (Mineola, 1988), 128.

may be the risk, absent the clarification offered by oral testimony, that foreign law will be misapplied. Another is that such evidence cannot easily be tested and probed without examination. Courts also, to an extent, decide issues of foreign law according to the logic and forcefulness of the competing expert opinions. To deprive the court of the opportunity to hear oral testimony is to rob them of an important element in the decision-making process.

No clear guidance is offered in the case law as to when the concession of allowing affidavit evidence will be granted in cases involving foreign law.[10] Of the four most prominent cases in which the question has arisen, none is of real assistance. One is best regarded, not as a case on affidavit evidence but as one concerning, in effect, certification;[11] another exemplifies the use of affidavits in abbreviated or urgent proceedings, in which they may be particularly appropriate;[12] a third case is easily disposed of as one in which the evidence as to foreign law was uncontested;[13] and the fourth never actually required the court to decide what weight to attach to the affidavit evidence as to foreign law, the substance of the evidence being irrelevant on the facts.[14]

Principle suggests that relevant factors in deciding whether to admit affidavit evidence might include the complexity of the relevant point of foreign law, the scope of the affidavit, and whether the demands of speed and economy outweigh the desire to apply foreign law correctly. Ultimately, the question for the judge is the same as that which arises when the issue is whether to dispense with expert evidence altogether and decide on the basis of foreign legal materials alone:[15] can foreign law be adequately determined by such means? In practice there may be very few cases in which the parties will regard proof by affidavit alone as a satisfactory mechanism for proving foreign law, which accounts for the dearth of cases more than the misgivings of the courts. But a special rule applies to the proof of foreign law in non-contentious probate matters. Where an issue of foreign law arises on any application for a grant of probate a registrar may accept an affidavit from anyone whom he regards as suitably qualified to give expert evidence as to the law in question.[16] Proof by affidavit may also be relied upon where one party simply admits the evidence offered by the other, in which event the latter's affidavit evidence represents the basis upon which the court will proceed.[17] Surprisingly,

---

[10] No explanation was given for doing so in *Westlake* v. *Westlake* [1910] P. 167.
[11] Ibid. (proof of Jersey marriage by affidavit of Solicitor General).
[12] *Re Arton*, above n. 5.
[13] *Re Valentine's Settlement* [1965] 1 Ch 831.
[14] *Callwood* v. *Callwood* [1960] AC 659 (PC).   [15] See above, p. 194.
[16] Non-Contentious Probate Rules 1987, r. 19(a).
[17] *Re Valentine's Settlement*, above n. 13.

however, even this concession to written procedure may have to be viewed as exceptional.[18]

But, given the need for economy and expedition, it is unsurprising that reliance is placed on affidavit evidence alone in abbreviated proceedings, such as jurisdictional disputes and summary proceedings, where a trial of the merits is not involved. Because it is generally inappropriate to determine foreign law finally in such cases the introduction of expert evidence by affidavit is commonplace.[19] But it is not invariable and a court has the power to admit oral testimony as to foreign law, even in interlocutory proceedings, where an affidavit alone would be inadequate, at least if the parties so wish.[20] That proof of foreign law may be effected by affidavit alone in such proceedings does not mean that oral testimony as to the same issue can be dispensed with at trial.[21]

Although affidavits as to foreign law are generally employed in interlocutory proceedings courts are mindful of the limitations of such truncated evidence. They may be willing to allow the oral examination of experts where the issues would otherwise be especially hard to resolve,[22] or where the proper implementation of, for example, the 1968 Brussels Convention imposes a special burden on the court to find foreign law correctly in jurisdictional proceedings.[23] Similarly, in summary proceedings they may decline to employ the presumption of similarity between English law and foreign law where proof of the latter is by affidavit alone.[24] Where issues of foreign law arise in summary proceedings the court's proper course is to allow the matter to go to trial where more complete evidence may be supplied.

Of particular importance, and special difficulty, are jurisdictional disputes involving the doctrine of *forum non conveniens*. In such proceedings the very difficulty of proving foreign law may be an issue. But we are now concerned with those cases, which commonly arise, in which it is necessary to determine foreign law so as to locate the most appropriate forum.[25] The question in such cases is often whether it would be unjust, by staying English proceedings, to force a plaintiff to sue abroad in the light of the

---

[18] *Re Valentine's Settlement*, above n. 13, 845.
[19] *The Forum Craftsman* [1985] 1 Lloyd's Rep. 291; *The Adhiguna Meranti* [1988] 1 Lloyd's Rep. 384; RSC Order 41, r. 5(2); O'Malley and Layton, 234.
[20] *Grupo Torras SA v. Al Sabah* [1995] 1 Lloyd's Rep. 374, 378–379.
[21] *Perkins v. Slater* (1876) 1 Ch D 83; *Blackburn Union v. Brooks* (1878) 7 Ch D 68.
[22] *Western National Bank of New York v. Perez, Triana & Co.* (1890) 6 TLR 366; *Grupo Torras SA v. Al Sabah* [1995] 1 Lloyd's Rep. 374, 378–379.
[23] *Grupo Torras SA v. Al Sabah*, above n. 22.
[24] *National Shipping Corpn. v. Arab*, above n. 5. Although the court deprecated what they regarded as the scant nature of the evidence, the parties may have intended the case to turn, in effect, on English law by virtue of the presumption of similarity; hence their focus on the facts which would determine liability under English law.
[25] See above, p. 51.

foreign law that would be applied there.[26] In proving the law of the alternative forum, especially where it is unclear, the absence of oral testimony may cause difficulty, depriving the court of the guidance and amplification which this normally provides. This is accentuated by the importance attached to such jurisdictional disputes by litigants, for whom the outcome may be decisive in prompting compromise or capitulation. As such a court is effectively required to determine issues of foreign law on provisional evidence, although the consequences are, for all practical purposes, final. This is not to say that matters of foreign law can never be resolved satisfactorily by affidavit evidence alone in the majority of cases.[27] But where the foreign law is controversial or highly complex the courts have been compelled to devise a number of procedural strategies to ease the difficulty.

One method is to recognize the inherent inadequacy of written evidence in determining the *forum conveniens*. *The Adhiguna Meranti*,[28] for example, turned on conflicting evidence concerning the limitation of a shipowner's liability under Indonesian law. The Hong Kong Court of Appeal was unable to conclude what that amount was and regarded any final determination of the matter as inappropriate. As Hunter JA said:

We think that a court should approach such evidence with hesitation and within the limits of the possible. It cannot purport to resolve such disputes on affidavit evidence. It can make firm findings only when the evidence is clear. Where it is in conflict it can do no more than reach such tentative conclusions as are necessary for the exercise of this discretionary jurisdiction, upon the balance of probabilities, making full allowance for the risk that an Indonesian Court on very different and much more extensive material might take another view.[29]

Subject to those constraints, the court made such findings as the evidence permitted and determined the *forum conveniens* accordingly. It was possible to establish the upper and lower limits of recovery which each party had contended for, and it was also clear on the evidence that the position in Indonesian law was uncertain. On that basis, the court refused a stay. Set against the amount which was clearly recoverable under the law of Hong Kong the recovery permitted in Indonesia, given the conflicting evidence, was 'at best uncertain, and at worst derisory'.[30]

An alternative response is to recognize the importance of determining foreign law in jurisdictional proceedings and to permit the examination of experts. As we have seen, this may be justified in cases under the 1968

---

[26] e.g. *The Magnum* [1989] 1 Lloyd's Rep. 47 (CA); *Banco Atlantico SA v. British Bank of the Middle East* [1990] 2 Lloyd's Rep. 504 (CA).
[27] e.g *The Forum Craftsman* [1985] 1 Lloyd's Rep. 291; *Sarrio SA v. Kuwait Investment Authority* [1996] 1 Lloyd's Rep. 650, 659.
[28] [1988] 1 Lloyd's Rep. 384 (HKCt.).   [29] Ibid., at 390–391.
[30] Ibid., at 392.

Brussels Convention.[31] In such cases, the objectives of the Convention would be ill-served if decisive questions of foreign law were answered incorrectly. But in cases involving *forum non conveniens* it is less likely that a court would take this course.[32] It would no doubt be wrong to exclude the possibility, especially if both parties agree to it. It may also be unrealistic to maintain the illusion that jurisdictional disputes are simply interlocutory, without dispositive consequences, requiring submissions measured merely in hours not days.[33] But nonetheless a court may consider it inappropriate to transform interlocutory applications into substantive proceedings by allowing the examination of experts.[34]

A further possibility is to contain the difficulty of establishing foreign law by securing appropriate undertakings from the parties. Suppose that a plaintiff argues that it would be unjust to stay an English action, given the disadvantages it would suffer under foreign law in the alternative forum. The court, however, is unable to establish on the evidence whether that would be the case. Assuming there is no dispute about English law, it might avoid the impasse by ordering a stay subject to the defendant's agreeing that principles similar to those applicable in England should be applied in the foreign proceedings. This novel course was adopted in *The Polessk*[35] as an alternative to permitting the oral examination of experts. The case concerned an action by various cargo owners against the owners of a Russian vessel which had sunk. The question was whether the Admiralty Court in London or the City Arbitration Court in St. Petersburg was the *forum conveniens*. Clarke J stayed the English proceedings subject to an undertaking by the defendants that the Russian court should determine the case, as would an English court, under the Hague Rules.

This creative approach is limited to cases where the foreign tribunal will countenance such a course and where it would regard the defendant's rights under local law as waivable. This may be more likely where the foreign proceedings are more in the nature of an arbitration, and may depend ultimately on the conflicts rules in force in the country concerned. It also assumes that the foreign court is the appropriate forum but for the matter of foreign law. Most importantly, perhaps, it depends on agreement between the parties as to what law an English court would apply. In principle, however, the technique resolves the problem of assessing foreign legal evidence, at the same time preserving the interlocutory character of the proceedings. It also confirms that a court is unlikely to allow either party to exploit the difficulty of establishing foreign law to its own advantage. In particular, it reveals once again how reluctant English courts may be to resolve important matters of foreign law simply by employing the

---

[31] *Grupo Torras SA* v. *Al Sabah*, above n. 22, 378.
[32] *The Polessk* [1996] 2 Lloyd's Rep. 40, 43–44.   [33] Ibid., 44.   [34] Ibid.
[35] Ibid., at 43–45, 52.

fictitious presumption of similarity, at least where the evidence, in the nature of the proceedings, is incomplete.[36] Certainly, Clarke J in *The Polessk* was not prepared to accept the defendant's argument that, as Russian law had not been clearly established, it must be taken to be the same as English law.[37] Nor did he favour the plaintiff's ingenious suggestion that, if Russian law was not clearly made out, that meant that there was at least a fifty per cent chance that they would lose in Russian proceedings, a consideration which, it was argued, justified denying a stay.[38]

Too few cases exist to establish a practice for handling interlocutory evidence of foreign law. But, in principle, it may be appropriate in the first instance to follow the approach in *The Adhiguna Meranti*. This would involve refusing a stay where the evidence suggests that a plaintiff would be prejudiced in the alternative forum, albeit that the precise nature of that prejudice is unclear. But, just as Clarke J rejected the suggestion in *The Polessk*, so generally it should not be enough that a plaintiff faces no more than a risk of such prejudice. Instead, where the evidence is conflicting it may be preferable to require an undertaking of the type employed in *The Polessk*, provided that is feasible. Where it is not, it is hard to see an alternative to applying the burden of proof strictly. But it would be wrong to employ the presumption that English law and foreign law are similar where, in the nature of things, the evidence is bound to be incomplete. And if the matter is determined by applying the burden of proof, the standard of proof should be less than that which might be expected at trial. Rather than requiring foreign law to be established it should be necessary merely for a plaintiff to show a substantial risk that it would suffer prejudice under foreign law in the foreign forum. This should require positive proof and it should be enough to rely merely on the inference that if foreign law is not finally established there is at least a risk of such prejudice.

The final possibility is that the parties might agree to the oral examination of experts. The court should be mindful of the need to minimise cost and delay in considering an application to admit oral evidence. And, given the interlocutory nature of such proceedings, and the risk that one party might be prejudiced by the additional delay and expense, this should not be contemplated except where both parties wish it. Certainly, where examination occurs by consent, the parties should so far as possible seek to limit the issues in dispute and the length of the proceedings.[39]

As the previous discussion confirms, the proof of foreign law in preliminary proceedings causes special difficulty. In part this reflects the tension inherent in English practice, in which substantive matters often have to be resolved without a full trial. But it also reveals the inherent weakness of establishing foreign law on written evidence alone, at least as it is

---

[36] Cf. *National Shipping Corpn.* v. *Arab*, above n. 5, 365, 366 (CA) (summary proceedings).
[37] Ibid., at 43.   [38] Ibid., at 43.   [39] *Grupo Torras SA* v. *Al Sabah*, above n. 22, 378.

perceived by English courts and practitioners. Indeed, it helps to explain the almost invariable practice whereby foreign law is proved at trial, often at considerable expense, by the oral examination of experts. But, in the end, the difficulty of determining foreign law in jurisdictional proceedings must be put in perspective, and the lessons to be learned from it qualified. Certainly, there are cases in which the courts have skilfully resolved questions of foreign law on affidavit evidence alone.[40] Indeed, it is unclear whether the problems to which such evidence gives rise are inherent in that method of proof. However limited affidavit evidence may be in establishing foreign law at trial, it is especially unclear whether such evidence is necessarily inadequate for the more restricted purpose of doing so in jurisdictional proceedings. The perceived difficulties may be as much a function of the inadequacy of particular affidavits in certain cases. Or they may owe more to the willingness of counsel to treat the limitations of such evidence as ammunition in the battle to determine the *forum conveniens*.

2. EXPERT EXAMINATION ABROAD

It is well recognized that witnesses in civil proceedings who are abroad may give evidence by means of examination abroad rather than at trial in England. The familiar rules which regulate this practice apply as much to the proof of foreign law as to obtaining other types of evidence.[41] As with other types of evidence the practice is exceptional. Witnesses outside the jurisdiction may not be compelled to attend before an English court, by subpoena or otherwise. But evidence from witnesses abroad may be obtained pursuant to an order of an English court appointing a special examiner to take such evidence abroad, normally a British consular official in the country concerned.[42] Alternatively, especially if the law of the country concerned so requires, an English court may issue a letter of request to the relevant foreign authorities to arrange for such an examination to be conducted according to local procedures.[43] There is a marked tendency for English practitioners to favour the appointment of a special examiner to issuing a letter of request, should a choice exist, because the former procedure is subject to the parties' control in a way which submission to the procedures of a foreign authority is not. Whichever option is utilized, however, the purpose of the process is to obtain a written deposition, recording the witnesses' evidence, for presentation at trial in England.

---

[40] *Sarrio* v. *Kuwait Investment Authority*, above n. 27, 659.
[41] RSC Order 39, r. 2. The general principles affecting video-conferencing as a means of examining witnesses who are abroad would also presumably apply: RSC Order 38, r. 3.
[42] RSC Order 39, r. 2(1)(b).   [43] RSC Order 39, r. 2(1)(a).

It is certainly open to an English court to order the examination abroad of a foreign law expert.[44] It will do so, however, only if it is impossible to obtain the attendance of a competent witness in English proceedings,[45] and if the applicant has exhausted all other reasonable means of obtaining such evidence, perhaps by obtaining an appropriate affidavit.[46] Presumably, if a court felt itself able to rule on a question of foreign law by reference to foreign legal materials alone, or by some other means not requiring an expert at all, it would not order a foreign examination.[47] In practice, it is doubtful whether the examination abroad of foreign law experts will often occur. Useful as the procedure might be in very exceptional cases, it is hard to envisage many situations in which a competent witness would be unavailable for oral examination at trial, harder still to contemplate cases in which an affidavit could not be obtained instead. It is also unclear how advantageous it would be for litigants to employ foreign examination. In relatively simple cases, affidavit evidence will be adequate, and far more easily and cheaply obtained than by invoking the foreign examination procedure. In harder cases, by contrast, there are considerable advantages in the examination of witnesses in open court, in terms of the ability of the parties, by their counsel, to control the presentation of the evidence.

3. INDEPENDENT ADVISERS

A number of techniques exist whereby a court may seek assistance, other than from the parties, in matters concerning complex evidence of foreign law. Such assistance may possibly be obtained through official channels from abroad, a matter to which we shall return.[48] Alternatively, the usual process of proof by oral testimony might be augmented by seeking the appointment of advisers to the court. Full discussion of the role of court advisers belongs to Chapter VIII, in so far as they might be employed *instead* of party-appointed experts. But, in so far as their task is sometimes to *supplement* the role of the parties' own experts, their role is relevant here. There appears to be no case involving foreign law in which such an appointment has been made. But whether it is generally appropriate to appoint court advisers in this fashion is controversial in English law, for to do so challenges the very basis of an adversarial approach to

---

[44] *Armour* v. *Walker* (1883) 25 Ch D 678 (CA); *Lawson* v. *Vacuum Brake Co.* (1876) 1 PD 107 (CA).
[45] *Armour* v. *Walker*, above n. 44.
[46] *Lawson* v. *Vacuum Brake Co.*, above n. 44, 115.   [47] See below, Chapter VIII.
[48] See below, p. 238. A further issue is whether a court is entitled to appoint a court adviser on its own motion: see above, p. 158.

evidence-gathering.[49] It is instructive to consider the role of court advisers in establishing foreign law as a contribution to that wider debate. More practically, it is illuminating to see why they are never employed. And, given the trend towards a more court-centred approach to litigation, it is necessary to know whether and in what circumstances a court, given the choice, should regard such an appointment as desirable.

Court advisers may be designated in some cases as experts,[50] in others as assessors,[51] each title implying a subtle difference in function. An expert's role is to offer an impartial view of the particular issues in dispute—a third opinion, so to say—by reference to which the court may better decide as between the testimony of the parties' experts (or dispense with such testimony altogether). The function of an assessor, by contrast, is to act as guide and companion to the judge in matters of specialist evidence. Effectively the judge's technical assistant at the trial, an assessor will be present during proceedings, although not a member of the court. The difference between assessors and court experts is emphasised by the fact that, traditionally viewed, the former should not sit in cases where expert evidence is also supplied, normally making their appointment inappropriate as a means of expediting expert proof.[52] Court experts, however, are commonly seen as valuable in resolving conflicts of expert testimony.[53]

This suggests that an objection to the use of assessors in this context is that it may not be possible to appoint them where expert evidence is also introduced. Although the general rule is that they should not be employed together this is subject to an exception of somewhat uncertain scope.[54] The rule is explained because the assessor is perceived as a source of information and expertise, albeit that their formal status is different from experts. As such the exception would seem to permit experts to be called where the particular point in issue is outside the assessor's direct knowledge. It may be, for example, that the assessor has expertise in Utopian law, but not as regards particular recent developments or a particular specialist area. If so, it would be appropriate to combine expert evidence with resort to an

---

[49] Lord Woolf, *Access to Justice, Final Report to the Lord Chancellor*, (London, HMSO, 1996), Ch 13. For criticism of greater use of court experts see, Jack (1994) 144 *NLJ* 1099; Lee, (1995) *NLJ* 128; Goldrein, (1995) *NLJ* 381. See further, *Abbey National Mortgages plc v. Key Surveyors Nationwide Ltd.* [1996] 3 All ER 97 (CA).

[50] RSC Order 40; cf. Lord Woolf, *Access to Justice, Draft Civil Proceedings Rules*, (London, HMSO, 1996), rule 32.5.

[51] RSC Order 33, r. 6; Supreme Court Act 1981, s. 70. cf. Lord Woolf, ibid., rule 32.13.

[52] *The Ann and Mary* (1843) 2 Wm. Rob. 189; *The Assyrian* (1890) 63 LT 91; *The Kirby Hall* (1883) 8 PD 71, 76; Dickey, (1970) 33 *MLR* 494, 501–505.

[53] RSC Order 40, annotation; Lord Woolf, above n. 49, 140–142; Miner, (1995) 43 *Am Jl Comp L* 581, 588.

[54] *Neptun v. Humber Conservancy Board* (1937) 59 Ll L R 107, 109; *The Chad* [1965] 2 Lloyd's Rep. 1; Dickey, (1970) 33 *MLR* 494, 501–505.

assessor. But this has a curious consequence. It means that an assessor could only be used in those situations in which his or her assistance might be irrelevant or pointless.

It may be equally inappropriate to appoint a court expert in addition to those of the parties, at least in the eyes of the parties and their advisers. Whenever expert evidence is contested it is unlikely that litigants will wish to dispense with their own experts, nor with any opportunity to cross-examine the court's appointee.[55] If so, such an appointment, far from expediting the proof of foreign law, may complicate the evidential process and increase its expense. Certainly, if the parties, or the losing party, will bear the cost it is unlikely that litigants would embrace such a procedure—unless they saw it as a means of reducing the overall expense of establishing foreign law. Nor are litigants likely to favour surrendering such an important matter, however indirectly, to the influence of a third party. For, even if the court retains the role of determining the final outcome, there may be concern that it would give disproportionate weight to the independent expert's opinion. The possibility of cross-examining the court expert offers litigants a degree of control over the process but, weighed against the additional cost and delay, they are unlikely to find it advantageous. Certainly, there may be a justified perception that an experienced judge is as good at resolving an issue of foreign law without a court expert as with one. Moreover, the only case in which an independent expert could deal with a matter straightforwardly is a straightforward case. But if it is straightforward it is hard to see why an independent expert would be necessary. Indeed, should the parties favour some swift and expeditious alternative to the usual process of proof by expert testimony, there are faster, cheaper options available than employing an independent expert, such as relying upon foreign legal materials.[56]

But this is to adopt the parties' perspective. It might be objected that an independent expert's appointment would lessen the court's burden in reconciling conflicting opinions and encourage the more accurate application of foreign law. But this is unclear, perhaps doubtful. A court's task would, indeed, be easier were it to treat the independent expert's opinion as conclusive. But this would be inappropriate, and possibly unjust, where each party has relied upon its own evidence. It would be to replace a system of evidence by one of expert determination. And it would rob the court of its responsibility to assess the evidence before it. If, by contrast, the independent expert's role is to supply a third view—or even a range of views—this may further obscure, rather than illuminate, the points in dispute. Moreover, easing a judge's task is not by itself an argument for such an

---

[55] *Re Saxton* [1962] 1 WLR 968, 972; *Abbey National Mortgages plc* v. *Key Surveyors Nationwide Ltd.*, above n. 49, 186–187.
[56] See below, p. 257

appointment if there is no saving of costs to the parties, and no improvement in the determination of foreign law.

The value of independent experts in establishing foreign law may thus be reduced, in so far as their role is to offer a further opinion. But perhaps the role of such experts might be viewed more widely, although English law has not traditionally done so.[57] There is no reason, for example, why they should not take instructions from the parties, although their responsibility would be to the court. Nor need court experts merely offer a further opinion in the sense of advocating a particular solution. They might do so, but might also summarise, explain and assess the parties' experts' views. Indeed, an expert might be appointed to enter into discussions with the parties' experts, maybe at a pre-trial conference, with a view to submitting a report which would review, assess and supplement the parties' experts' opinions. A more formal approach would be to appoint an expert to determine disputed issues of foreign law.[58] This need involve no surrender of the court's adjudicatory role since the court might be entitled to reject the expert's opinion, perhaps in favour of seeking another. Nor need litigants be deprived of the right to make representations to the court expert, perhaps through their own experts.

But whether independent advisers are cast as assessors or experts, and however their current roles are re-imagined, there are powerful objections to introducing additional personnel into the process of establishing foreign law. This is not to deny the immediate appeal of the idea that a court might be assisted by a qualified person in considering difficult issues of foreign law, whether an expert or an assessor. The process augments, but need not threaten, the principle that it is for the parties to establish matters of fact. The assistance of a qualified person may also seem exactly what is required to improve a judge's grasp of the principles, assumptions and standards of reasoning employed in a foreign system. As such, it might be a response to those cases which courts find especially hard and in which, if possible, they might otherwise stay the action. But the utility of appointing court advisers, whether experts or assessors, is questionable. An important virtue in any procedural institution, for example, is that it enjoys the confidence of litigants. But procedures which, as we have seen, may add to the cost of proceedings, and which may diminish the role of the judge, are unlikely to meet this criterion. Again, if foreign law is contested at all it is likely that the questions involved will be highly controversial, attracting a range of plausible opinions. Whatever an independent adviser's formal role there is a risk that he or she might compound the difficulty more than dispel it. Alternatively, if the case is highly complex it is

---

[57] Lord Woolf, above n. 49, 140–141.
[58] Cf. the little-used practice whereby masters or official referees may resolve selected issues of fact: RSC Order 38, rr. 8 and 11.

unclear how another expert might make matters more comprehensible. At a practical level it may also be hard to identify an appropriate expert or assessor. It is notoriously difficult for litigants to locate suitable experts of their own in matters involving foreign law. Why should it be easier to find a suitable court adviser? Precisely because the parties will already have employed their own experts the field of likely candidates may be reduced, a particular problem with regard to foreign law where the pool of available experts is often small. Certainly, it may be difficult to identify someone with as great—or greater—expertise than that of the parties' own experts.[59] Indeed, the opposite may be the case. This implies that the process may be less effective, or may be no more effective, than proof without the intervention of a third party. And it may further diminish the parties' confidence in the procedure.

It may also be unnecessary to appoint an independent adviser. Courts certainly have alternative means at their disposal for resolving difficult cases concerning foreign law. Exceptionally, they might find foreign law to be unproved and apply English law instead. More typically, they might dispense with the parties' experts' testimony and rely directly on such written material as is in evidence.[60] This technique may not, of course, lead to the correct application of foreign law. But it may be preferable to the possible delay, uncertainty, and expense of appointing an adviser.

Again, those cases in which the normal process of expert proof is likely to be inadequate may be those which are properly determined in the courts of the foreign system concerned. Certainly, if even the examination of experts, the most intensive of evidential techniques, is insufficient to achieve a tolerable result the case must be one of quite exceptional difficulty. But English law has a mechanism for handling such cases. A court may stay its proceedings in favour of proceedings in the relevant foreign court.[61] The technique is an imperfect one. But it prompts the suggestion that perhaps the proper response where expert proof is inadequate is not to augment the evidential process but to exclude the case altogether.

Moreover, whether the quality of adjudication would be improved by appointing an independent adviser is uncertain. This is an important consideration because, given the disadvantages in terms of cost and efficiency already identified, the success of the procedure must lie in its capacity to establish foreign law more effectively. If, say, a court expert were appointed both the parties' experts and their counsel would doubtless bear less of the burden of explaining foreign law to the court. But this is simply to transfer that responsibility from the parties to the independent expert without otherwise changing the situation. Again, when the parties

---

[59] Ormrod, [1968] *Crim L R* 240, 245.   [60] See above, p. 194.
[61] See above, pp. 44–50.

offer competing solutions to a question of foreign law this is not simply a process of explanation. It is a matter of argument. Ultimately a court must weigh the arguments contained in the competing testimony and form its own conclusion. Given the unique experience of courts in such matters it is uncertain that an independent expert would improve that process.

Finally, there is an important sense in which cases involving foreign law are different from others in which the use of court advisers might be contemplated. The proof of foreign law is important in such cases because it establishes the rights and liabilities of the parties. It is, in this sense, more than a matter of evidence and might properly deserve the full attention of the court, almost as if it were a matter of domestic law. Anything less might amount to a surrender by the court of its adjudicatory role. Indeed, this suggests a decisive reason against employing court advisers in cases involving foreign law. For, at root, the appropriateness of using court advisers in the present context turns on how we view the nature of foreign law. If foreign laws are merely facts they should be established just like other facts. This implies a minimal role for the court and encourages resort to party experts. At its strongest, it suggests that a court has no interest in how, or how successfully, foreign law is established, apart from umpiring the contest between the parties. But if we recognize the legal character of foreign law, and the importance of determining the legal position of the parties thereunder, the implications are different. At first sight, it becomes clearer why the court might have an independent interest in ensuring the success of the evidential process. And it no longer seems so natural to submit the proof of foreign law to the normal processes for establishing other types of fact. Certainly, before English law committed itself to treating foreign laws as facts,[62] and the legal quality of foreign law was more pronounced, it was common for courts to refer questions of foreign law to independent experts.[63] But this may be to draw the wrong inference from the legal character of foreign law. To view foreign laws as laws supports another, more compelling conclusion. It suggests that the judge, the arbiter of legal matters, should retain maximum control of the determination of foreign law, without reference to a third party. And, importantly, it implies that litigants should have every opportunity to put their case under foreign law. As such it argues against resort to independent experts and in favour of relying on those called by the parties.

The uncertain value of court advisers in cases concerning foreign law might be contrasted with those specialised situations in which they are of recognized (if limited) utility. Nautical assessors are regularly employed,

[62] Probably in *Mostyn* v. *Fabrigas* (1774) 1 Cowp 161, 174.
[63] Anon. (1610) 2 Bro. & Goulds 16, 17, cited by Baker (1979) 28 *MLR* 141, 146. Resort to court experts survived the introduction of the fact doctrine by some years: Baker, op. cit., 147.

for example, in Admiralty proceedings.[64] But their role is different from that which might be useful in connection with foreign law. They provide the court both with information and advice and are generally employed instead of party experts. Again, court experts and scientific advisers are sometimes appointed in patent litigation involving complex technical matters.[65] But the practice is not as common as might be supposed. It is generally adopted only when the issues in dispute are themselves unclear,[66] which may be unlikely in cases involving foreign law where the battle lines tend to be clearly drawn.

As the use of court advisers in other areas suggests, they are likely to be of value only where party experts are not also used, or where the court lacks even a basic grasp of how contested issues of a technical nature should be resolved. But it is unlikely that a court is truly in such a position of total ignorance in matters of foreign law. For, unaware of foreign law as they are, courts will always bring to bear on such issues a basic understanding of the requirements of sound argument and justification. Indeed, as lawyers, if not foreign lawyers, the basic grammar of legal discourse is something with which they are familiar. This may not always be enough to establish foreign law correctly. But the appointment of court advisers will not be required to make the determination of foreign law possible.

As this implies, the value of court advisers in establishing foreign law is unclear, although the arguments against their use heavily outweigh those in favour. True, discussion is hampered by the fact that English law has traditionally allowed little scope to such advisers, and no practice has developed against which to measure their value. But the nature of the foreign law problem suggests, whatever their potential elsewhere, that court advisers may have only a minimal role in such cases. The legal character of foreign law implies that courts should retain the fullest control of the process, and that the adversarial nature of proof by party experts is both necessary and appropriate by allowing litigants to put their case with maximum force. It also suggests that courts will seldom find cases involving foreign law altogether impossible to resolve, in so far as they can draw on their basic legal competence to do so. Traditionally, however, it is only in cases where progress would otherwise be impossible that English courts have (exceptionally) turned to court advisers. This is not to say that the development of novel or expanded evidential techniques should not be encouraged, nor that the appointment of court advisers should not be available in the present context, for in variety lies efficiency. But it is clear, once again, how misleading it is to equate foreign laws with facts, for how

---

[64] Dickey, above n. 52. [65] Hodgkinson, Ch 21.
[66] Ibid., 374–375.

foreign law should be established must allow for its legal character. Certainly, whatever the merit in using party advisers in connection with scientific and technical facts, it is singularly apt to establish foreign law by the judicial assessment of party-led expert evidence. This is not, however, because foreign laws are merely facts, but because they are also laws.

VIII

Replacing Party Experts

In the previous chapter we examined such techniques as may augment the process of proving foreign law by party experts. Our present concern is with those techniques which allow such evidence to be dispensed with altogether. Foreign law is normally determined by obtaining expert opinions. But this is not the only method available. Unexceptionally, other methods may be employed in uncontested cases. Points of foreign law will be taken as settled, for example, and need not be proved, where they are admitted.[1] Previous rulings on foreign law by English courts are binding in the absence of contrary evidence.[2] And expert evidence is not required in uncontested cases to prove the occurrence of foreign formal acts, such as marriages abroad.[3] More controversially, it may be possible to dispense with the evidence of the parties' experts even where the content of foreign law is disputed. It is conceivable, although unlikely, that a point of foreign law may be certified by a foreign official.[4] Alternatively, assistance might be sought abroad through official channels.[5] Or a single expert might be appointed by the court instead of those of the parties.[6] Most importantly, perhaps, foreign law might be determined without evidence where the issue is within the court's inherent knowledge or competence.[7] This occurs when the court has specific notice of the point of law in question, or when it is notorious or represents a general principle of law. Significantly, it also occurs when a court is required to do no more than construe a foreign document.

But courts and commentators are sometimes reluctant to recognize the existence of such alternatives to proof by party experts. Indeed, it is sometimes supposed that foreign law must be established, as a matter of principle, by expert evidence.[8] Perhaps proof by party experts is assumed to be the only method because it is the most common. Or maybe the explanation lies in the important distinction between proving and merely determining foreign law.[9] For even if foreign law can only be *proved* by experts, it might be established without strict proof. To put the point differently, the only admissible *evidence* of the content of foreign might be expert testimony.

---

[1] *Moulis* v. *Owen* [1907] 1 KB 746 (CA). [2] See below, p. 223.
[3] See below, pp. 226–230. [4] See below, pp. 221–223. [5] See below, pp. 238–244.
[6] See below, pp. 232–238. [7] See below, pp. 244–262.
[8] Hodgkinson, 294. [9] Dicey and Morris, 227–229.

But that is not to say that foreign law cannot be established without evidence. By insisting upon this distinction we may assert with accuracy that foreign law may only be proved by party experts. But this can be misleading if not handled with care, if it is taken to mean that foreign law can only be established by formal proof to the exclusion of other methods. The idea that foreign law can only be established formally is itself a reflection of the tendency to adhere with unwavering strictness to the notion that foreign laws are simply facts. It appears, to take but one example, in Millett J's recent ruling that foreign laws cannot be notorious but must be proved by expert evidence.[10] That conclusion was arrived at without reference to previous decisions on the question, and without discussion of the issues involved. Applying the fact doctrine strictly the judge assumed that foreign laws cannot be treated at notorious facts because foreign laws must be proved by expert evidence. No consideration was given, however, to the possibility that, if a foreign rule is indeed notorious, proof ought not to be required at all.

Little is served by insisting that foreign law may be ascertained only by reference to party-led expert evidence.[11] It obscures the important reality that foreign laws, although certainly facts, are not invariably treated as such in English practice. Truly, they are facts 'of a peculiar kind'.[12] It makes it hard to account for the considerable body of case law in which English courts have determined foreign law without expert evidence.[13] It also ignores the lesson taught by US Federal Practice, which has comprehensively rejected strict adherence to the fact doctrine in favour of a more flexible approach.[14] Most importantly, such fundamentalism limits the options available to those who would establish foreign law. The proof of foreign law by party experts is notoriously expensive and time-consuming. The want of an alternative may deter those with legitimate claims from proceeding in England at all, or compel them to proceed under English law which may be less favourable. It may distort the process of determining jurisdiction by convincing English courts that they are not the *forum conveniens*.[15] And it may diminish confidence in the choice of law process by making the application of foreign law inherently unattrac-

---

[10] *El Ajou* v. *Dollar Land Holdings plc* [1993] 3 All ER 717, 736.

[11] Wolff was forthright in his criticism: 'The whole system of treating foreign law as if it were an extra-legal fact, in particular of not admitting judicial knowledge, would seem inconsistent with the court's frequent practice when dealing with purely English law, of citing parallels from foreign laws, quoting American decisions, and basing its own decision on the facts expounded there. The English (and American) method of ascertaining foreign law is, to borrow an expression from an American judge, 'an anachronism which comes down from the time when statutes of other states were not readily accessible': *Private International Law*, 2nd edn., (Oxford, 1950), 220.

[12] *Parkasho* v. *Singh* [1968] P 233, 250 (per Sir Jocelyn Simon P).

[13] See especially below, pp. 257–262. [14] Miller, (1967) 65 *Mich L Rev* 615.

[15] See above, pp. 44–50.

tive.[16] Above all, perhaps, it is now widely accepted that rules of procedure should aim at proportionality between the complexity of the issue and the sophistication of the procedure employed.[17] The proof of foreign law by party experts may be appropriate in difficult cases. But is it necessary, by strict adherence to the fact doctrine, that it should be required in all cases?

On inspection, there exist a number of techniques available to litigants whereby disputed questions of foreign law might be resolved more quickly, more cheaply, perhaps more predictably, than is usually possible using traditional means. The flexibility of the English approach was well expressed in a previous edition of a leading commentary:

> How far can judges examine foreign law themselves? On this point it is impossible to lay down any absolute rule, the courts wisely having avoided any pronouncement which might unduly fetter their discretion. They recognize as obvious the impossibility in normal cases of judges forming any useful opinion on foreign law except on the basis of expert evidence, but by prudent exercise of commonsense they have shown themselves willing to waive proof by experts where such is manifestly unnecessary . . .[18]

As this suggests, proof by party experts may be the most effective means of establishing foreign law in complex cases. Indeed, it may be in the nature of things that disputes as to foreign law are generally complex, requiring such evidence. But if this is the case, the conclusion to be drawn from the authorities is more interesting and more important than might be supposed. They reveal not that foreign law must be established in the traditional way because there is no choice. They show how, given a range of options, litigants and the courts regard proof by expert evidence as the most effective method. It remains to identify those options, and to assess their value.

1. CERTIFICATION

The process of certification, whereby foreign law might be established by obtaining a definitive statement from a single, authoritative source, is hard to distinguish from proof by an officially qualified expert, at least where the evidence of the latter is uncontradicted. But an expert's opinion, however authoritative, is non-binding while certification is dispositive. And the status of a certificate does not depend on the skill, knowledge or expertise of one who gives it, but derives from their official standing.

[16] See above, p. 15.   [17] See below, p. 306.
[18] Dicey, *Conflict of Laws*, 6th edn., (London, 1949), 868. Although cited with approval in *Re Cohn* [1945] Ch. 5, and in *F & K Jabbour* v. *Custodian of Israeli Absentee Property* [1954] 1 WLR 139, 147–148, the passage is omitted from the present edition.

On inspection, there is scant support for the view that foreign law may be established by an official certificate. This is not to deny that such evidence is admissible, at least where neither party objects, but it does not appear to be conclusive. It may be that such evidence was decisive in a number of nineteenth century probate cases in which proof was required as to the formalities necessary for a valid will.[19] But more recent authorities are rare and the scope of certification has become obscure.[20] It is apparent that an ambassador's certificate will now be treated simply as ordinary expert evidence, as such not conclusive.[21] This is consistent with the trend towards treating expert opinion as the only evidence of foreign law. It has been suggested that such a certificate, even as expert evidence, should carry special weight.[22] But, being merely in essence expert evidence, it is doubtful whether it has 'some special persuasive power',[23] at least where it concerns the private law of the country concerned.[24] Officials other than ambassadors have sometimes given opinions as to foreign law. In one case the Solicitor General for Jersey gave evidence as to the validity of a marriage there, although apparently as an expert and not by virtue of his office.[25] In another case, an official of the US State Department gave an opinion as to whether a port in the Panama Canal Zone was a US port for the purposes of the American Carriage of Goods by Sea Act. But, again, this was treated simply as expert evidence.[26]

It is unlikely, therefore, that foreign law may be established by certification. But, even if the technique is available, it is unlikely to be employed. In contested cases of any sort the parties would, presumably, prefer to offer their own evidence in the usual way. In uncontested cases it may be simpler, more efficient and no less effective simply to rely, as is normal, on affidavit evidence. Certainly, litigants may regard official certificates as persuasive evidence of foreign law, although whether *per se* they should be given special weight is open to question. But they may see in certification, strictly so called, all the difficulties inherent in submitting questions of foreign law to a single source for determination.

---

[19] *Re Dormoy* (1832) 3 Hagg. Ecc. 767; *In the Goods of Oldenburg* (1884) 9 PD 234.

[20] *In the Goods of Klingemann*, 32 LJP 16; *In the Goods of Oldenburg*, op. cit.

[21] *Krajina v. Tass Agency* [1949] 2 All ER 274, 281 (CA); *Trendtex Trading Corp. v. Central Bank of Nigeria* [1976] 3 All ER 437, 441 (Donaldson J), revsd. on other grounds, [1977] QB 529, 560, 563 (CA).

[22] *Krajina v. Tass Agency*, op. cit., 281; *Trendtex Trading Corp. v. Central Bank of Nigeria*, op. cit., 560, 563.

[23] *Trendtex Trading Corp. v. Central Bank of Nigeria*, 441.

[24] Howard, Crane, and Hochberg, *Phipson on Evidence*, 14th edn., (London, 1990), 838–839.

[25] *Westlake v. Westlake* [1910] P 167.

[26] *Stafford Allen & Sons Ltd. v. Pacific Steam Navigation Co.*, [1956] 1 Lloyd's Rep. 105, 119; see below, p. 254.

2. PROOF BY REFERENCE TO ENGLISH DECISIONS

By virtue of statute foreign law may be established without expert testimony when an English court has previously ruled on the same point.[27] In a sense this is a means by which English courts are permitted to take judicial notice of matters of foreign law, by allowing them to treat findings of foreign law as if they were, in effect, findings of English law. There was powerful authority at common law that this could not be done.[28] But some courts adhered less strictly to the fact doctrine, taking the more flexible view that previous decisions were conclusive as to foreign law,[29] at least in proceedings before the same judge.[30] Under the Civil Evidence Act 1972 the previous decision may be one of the Crown Court, High Court, or one on appeal from such courts[31] and must be in an appropriate citable form.[32] The presumption that such a decision is correct, which may be invoked only by the party concerned giving notice to the other,[33] may be rebutted by contrary evidence[34] and does not operate when the decision conflicts with that of another court adduced in the same proceedings.[35] Although cases where this procedure has been invoked are rare, no reported decision apparently existing, there were occasions before the 1972 Act in which the courts refused to rely on previous decisions, requiring the parties to provide expert evidence in the usual fashion.[36]

In practice it is unlikely that the content of foreign law will often be decided by reference to previous decisions. If the point of foreign law is not in dispute between the parties, it may simply be pleaded by one party and admitted by the other in the normal way, making the 1972 Act irrelevant. If, however, one party sought to rely on a previous English decision, but the other party wished to contest the point, the latter would inevitably introduce expert evidence in support of its position. If that occurred, however, it is unlikely that the first party would simply rely on the previous English authority. It would, more probably, introduce its own expert evidence, in which case the dispute would resolve itself into a familiar contest between competing expert opinion.

---

[27] Civil Evidence Act 1972, s. 4(2).
[28] *Lazard Bros.* v. *Midland Bank Ltd.* [1933] AC 289, 297–298 (HL).
[29] *Re Sebba* [1959] Ch. 166, noted, Furmston [1959] 22 *MLR* 317.
[30] *Jasiewicz* v. *Jasiewicz* [1962] 1 WLR 1426, 1428.   [31] Section 4(4).
[32] Section 4(5).   [33] Section 4(3).   [34] Section 4(2)(b).
[35] Section 4(2).   [36] *Lazard Bros.* v. *Midland Bank Ltd.*, above n. 28.

3. PROOF OF FOREIGN FORMAL ACTS

The proof of foreign law does not always involve contested matters of opinion. Sometimes all that is required is proof that an official act has taken place and has the desired legal significance in the country concerned. Proof that a foreign statute is authentic is one example. Another is proof of the occurrence of an official legal act, such as the filing of a document in a foreign court or an entry in a foreign official register. A third example, overlapping with the second, is proof that a foreign marriage has been celebrated, a matter of surprising complexity in English law. Finally, special issues may arise concerning the legal status of foreign corporations. Generally, the evidential devices employed in such cases, most of them statutory, are permissive not mandatory, designed for use in situations where the relevant questions of foreign law are not contested. Where such questions are contested they will be subject to proof in the normal way, generally by employing party experts. If a party needlessly calls expert evidence in a case where such a statutory mechanism is available it is likely that the costs of doing so will be disallowed.[37]

(a) Proof of Foreign Statutes

Under the Evidence (Colonial Statutes) Act 1907 the authenticity and content of the statutes of many Commonwealth countries—not necessarily colonies—may be proved without expert evidence.[38] In particular, if such a statute purports to have been printed by the government printer of such a country there is no need for independent proof of this fact.[39] Although it has sometimes been used[40] the effectiveness of this provision is somewhat reduced in so far as a court may require expert evidence that such a statute, however authentic, is still in force.[41] Moreover, there are many cases in which the 1907 Act might have been employed but the court has been content to admit the foreign statute on the simple agreement of the

---

[37] *Kent v. Kent and Aysseh* (1962) 106 SJ 16 (proof of foreign marriage).

[38] The Act extends to 'any part of [Her] Majesty's dominions exclusive of the United Kingdom': section 1(3). This includes all countries in which the monarch is head of state, as well as the Channel Islands and the Isle of Man. See further, 6 Halsbury's Laws (4th.edn.), para. 803; 7 Halsbury's Statutes (4th.edn.), para. 4. In so far as the statutes of a colony are concerned section 6 of the Colonial Laws Validity Act 1865 may apply. Isle of Man laws may be proved under section 12 of the Isle of Man Act 1979. Cf. Colonial Laws Validity Act 1865, s. 6; *R v. Brixton*, 21 Cox 387.

[39] Section 1(1).

[40] *Taylor v. Taylor* [1923] WN 65; *Waterfield v. Waterfield* (1929) 73 SJ 300; *Papadopoulos v. Papadopoulos* [1930] P 55.

[41] *Brown v. Brown* (1917) 116 LT 702; *R v. Governor of Brixton Prison, Ex parte Shuter* [1960] 2 QB 89; *Jasiewicz v. Jasiewicz* [1962] 1 WLR 1426.

parties.[42] Indeed, the utility of the 1907 Act, like that of many devices intended to ease the proof of foreign law, is, in practical terms, not always clear. If a statute's authenticity is contested—perhaps an unlikely event— both parties will introduce expert evidence in the usual fashion. But if it is not contested, the parties' agreement as to its authenticity effectively removes the need to prove foreign law. The rationale behind the 1907 Act, and the similar statutory devices considered in this section, may be that a court is obliged to satisfy itself as to the authenticity of foreign law, whether or not the parties are content to treat it as such. In practice, however, such matters appear to be as much subject to the parties' control as other aspects of foreign law.

(b) Proof of Foreign Registers and Court Documents

Entries in foreign registers may be admitted in English proceedings and treated as authentic in situations governed by the Evidence (Foreign, Dominion and Colonial Documents) Act 1933, as amended by the Oaths and Evidence (Overseas Authorities and Countries) Act 1963. Where an Order in Council is made in respect of a particular country, entries on that country's public registers, when treated as authentic by the local courts and properly kept, may be admitted without further proof.[43] Without prejudice to these provisions, an overseas adoption may be proved under the relevant statutory instruments by reference to a certified copy of an appropriate foreign register, or to a certificate signed by a suitable foreign official.[44]

Proof of foreign executive acts, such as treaties, proclamations and other acts of state may be effected under the Evidence Act 1851. This provides for proof of such acts by the production of copies of the relevant documents, which must be either examined or officially authenticated. An examined copy is one which a witness swears is a true copy of the original with which it has been compared.[45] An authenticated copy is, in general terms, one which bears an official seal or signature.[46] Proof of documents emanating from a court or having formal status in foreign proceedings, such as judgments, orders, affidavits and pleadings, is effected in the same

---

[42] *Roe* v. *Roe* (1916) 115 LT 792; *L* v. *L.* (1919) 36 TLR 148; *Bonhote* v. *Bonhote* [1920] WN 142.
[43] Evidence (Foreign, Dominion and Colonial Documents) Act 1933, s. 1(2); Oaths and Evidence (Overseas Authorities and Countries) Act 1963, s. 5(1).
[44] The Adoption (Designation of Overseas Adoptions) Order 1973, SI 1973 No. 19, para. 4; The Convention Adoption (Miscellaneous Provisions) Order 1978, SI 1978 No. 1432, para. 4.
[45] *Reid* v. *Margison*, 1 Camp. 469.
[46] Section 7. The provisions of the Act are not, however, exclusive. Proof may exceptionally be made by other means appropriate to the case: *Finske Anfartygs A/B* v. *Baring* (1937) 54 TLR 147, 1031.

way. Special rules govern the proof of foreign judgments by the production of authenticated or certified copies where their registration and enforcement depends on statute.[47] Again, the Evidence Act 1851 is also suitable for the proof of foreign grants of probate, although even without it an officially certified or attested copy of the original is admissible.[48] The Act does not, however, regulate the proof of foreign wills, not being official documents, which may be proved by the production of certified or examined copies.[49]

(c) Proof of Foreign Marriage

A court cannot dissolve a non-existent marriage, so its existence must be proved before a matrimonial decree is granted.[50] This is as much a problem in domestic law as in the conflict of laws, although only in the latter is proof of foreign law involved.[51] Where a marriage occurs in England involving foreign parties proof of the marriage's celebration is straightforwardly a matter for English domestic law.[52] But if a marriage is celebrated abroad, proof of the existence of the marriage under foreign law is required.[53] One of a number of different rules may govern its proof depending on the precise circumstances.

It is important to draw an initial distinction between those cases in which a foreign marriage's validity is contested and those where it is not. In the former, the parties will doubtless introduce evidence of foreign law in the usual way. Indeed, they will be bound to do so since the proof of marriage in a contested case must be effected in the usual way, typically by expert evidence.[54] In such contested cases the more specific rules for the proof of marriage considered below will be of little account, save in one important respect. This is that the specific rules for proving foreign marriage, although only sufficient to prove such a marriage in uncontested cases, also represent prima facie evidence of a marriage's validity or existence. As such, whether the matter is contested or not, they have the effect of shifting the burden of proof onto the party who would deny validity. Where a marriage's validity is not disputed the rules considered below provide sufficient proof of marriage, such that it is unnecessary to intro-

---

[47] Section 11 of the Civil Jurisdiction and Judgments Act 1982 regulates the proof of foreign judgments and related documents for the purposes of the 1968 Brussels and 1988 Lugano Conventions on Jurisdiction and the Enforcement of Judgments.
[48] *Re Cliff* [1892] 2 Ch. 229; *Re Fraser* [1891] P 285; for colonial probates see the Colonial Probates Act 1892, ss. 2 and 3.
[49] *Halket* v. *Dudley* [1907] 1 Ch 590.
[50] Family Proceedings Rules, rule 2.6(2); *Viswalingham* v. *Viswalingham* [1979] 1 FLR 15 (CA).
[51] See generally, Rayden and Jackson, *Law and Practice in Divorce and Family Matters* (16th ed.), Ch. 20.
[52] Ibid.   [53] See above, p. 114.   [54] Rayden and Jackson, above n. 51, 401.

duce expert evidence on the point. Indeed, to supply such evidence where such a rule applies may be expensive, as it is unlikely that the costs of such a needless procedure would be allowed.[55]

Of the mechanisms for proving a foreign marriage without expert evidence the most important, which applies whenever a marriage's validity is undisputed, is that contained in Rule 10.14 of the Family Proceedings Rules 1991. This provides that:

The celebration of a marriage outside England and Wales and its validity under the law of the country where it was celebrated may, in any family proceedings in which the existence and validity of the marriage is not disputed, be proved by the evidence of one of the parties to the marriage and the production of a document purporting to be-
(a) a marriage certificate or similar document issued under the law in force in that country; or
(b) a certified copy of an entry in a register of marriages kept under the law in force in that country.

Although Rule 10.14 must be regarded as the primary means of proving foreign marriage in uncontested cases, a number of older mechanisms remain in force, their practical value since Rule 10.14's enactment being unclear. Strictly, these traditional techniques are unnecessary when a marriage's validity is not disputed, Rule 10.14 applying in all such cases. But they are also irrelevant in contested cases in which a marriage's validity will depend on the conflict of expert evidence. Their role in such cases is that, being prima facie indicators of a marriage's subsistence, they impose the burden of proof on one who would disprove the marriage. The continued existence of other means of proof is expressly preserved by Rule 10.14 which 'shall not be construed as precluding the proof of marriage in accordance with the Evidence (Foreign, Dominion and Colonial Documents) Act 1933 or in any other manner authorised apart from this rule'.

Rule 10.14 aside, a foreign marriage may be proved in one of two ways: first, by reference to a certificate accompanied by evidence from a party or witness; secondly, by reference to the common law presumption of marriage. The general rule, reflected in Rule 10.14, is that a marriage may be proved by production of a certificate, accompanied by the evidence of a party or witness. This is possible by a variety of means, each depending on the precise circumstances. Although any organization of this intricate material is ungainly, four types of marriage must be distinguished, although proof by certificate is permitted in each. First, a marriage celebrated abroad, one party to which is a United Kingdom national, may be

---

[55] *Kent* v. *Kent and Aysseh*, above n. 37.

proved by the certificate of a British consul.[56] Secondly, marriages in Scotland or Northern Ireland may be proved pursuant to statute by production of a certificate and identification of the parties.[57] Thirdly, marriages in the Channel Islands according to the rites of the Church of England may be proved by certificate and identification without further formality on the basis that the Channel Islands are within the Diocese of Winchester.[58] It is possible that marriages in any other form might be proved under the Civil Evidence Act 1968.[59] If not, expert evidence of validity must be supplied.[60] Fourthly, marriages in British colonies and Commonwealth countries may be proved in several ways.[61] Many cases will fall within the provisions, considered above, of the Evidence (Foreign, Dominion and Colonial) Documents Act 1963, and the Oaths and Evidence (Overseas Authorities and Countries) Act 1933. These provide for the admissibility in evidence of entries in official public registers where an Order in Council has extended them to the country concerned.

Proof may also be possible pursuant to the Evidence (Colonial Statutes) Act 1907. This requires production of a certificate in local form accompanied by a copy of the relevant local statute in accordance with which the marriage was celebrated. In principle, the 1907 Act is wide in its scope, extending to former colonies to which United Kingdom laws are regarded as continuing to apply after independence.[62] Although intended to dispense with the need for expert evidence as to a statute's authenticity, the courts have sometimes undermined the 1907 Act's effectiveness by requiring such evidence as to a statute's continuation in force.[63] Proof is also possible under the common law doctrine that a marriage in a British colony in Church of England form will be treated as valid on production of a certificate and identification of the parties.[64] Although the precise relationship

---

[56] Foreign Marriage Act 1892, s. 1 (marriages celebrated under the *lex loci celebrationis* at which a consul is present); s. 18(2) (added by Foreign Marriage Act 1947, s. 6) (marriages celebrated under the *lex loci celebrationis* at which a consul is not present). See further Foreign Marriage Order, SI 1970 No. 1539; SI 1990 No. 598.

[57] Registration of Births, Deaths and Marriages (Scotland) Act 1965.

[58] *Pritchard* v. *Pritchard* (1920) 37 TLR 104.

[59] Sections 2 and 4; *Henaff* v. *Henaff* [1966] 1 WLR 598 (certificate of marriage in Guernsey register office admitted as evidence under Civil Evidence Act 1938): Dicey and Morris, 656–657.

[60] *Westlake* v. *Westlake* [1910] P. 167.

[61] Present and former colonies, as well as the Channel Islands and Isle of Man, are alike comprised within the statutory defintion of '[Her] Majesty's dominions': see, *Halsbury's Laws* (4th ed), para. 803. In the case of the Isle of Man the 1907 Act would appear to supersede the previous common law methods of proof: *Rohmann* v. *Rohmann* (1908) 25 TLR 78; *Roberts* v. *Brennan* [1902] P 143; see, Isle of Man Act 1979, s. 12.

[62] See O'Malley and Layton, 238 n. 79.

[63] *Brown* v. *Brown* (1917) 116 LT 702; *R* v. *Governor of Brixton Prison, Ex parte Shuter* [1960] 2 QB 89; *Jasiewicz* v. *Jasiewicz* [1962] 1 WLR 1426.

[64] *Ward* v. *Dey* (1849) 1 Rob. Ecc. 759. The most recent instance appears to be *Winmill* v. *Winmill* (1934) 78 SJ 536.

between these different methods of proving colonial and Commonwealth marriages is uncertain it is likely that the 1933 and 1963 Acts should be employed where applicable.[65] It has been doubted that the 1907 Act truly operates at all in the fashion which practice commonly endorses.[66] It is also unclear what is the present status of the common law rule regarding colonial marriages in the light of more recent statutory enactments. Rule 10.14 of the Family Proceedings Rules 1991 applies to all cases within the scope of the 1907, 1933 and 1963 Acts, although its operation is without prejudice to proof under the 1933 Act or in any other manner.[67]

Although the normal practice requires production of a certificate accompanied by the evidence of a party or witness, either requirement may be dispensed with in appropriate cases. On the basis that a certificate is simply prima facie evidence of marriage a court may dispense with its production if otherwise satisfied of the fact that the marriage was celebrated or, *a fortiori*, of evidence that it was valid. Conversely, if the evidence of a party or a witness to the ceremony is unavailable, a court may rely on the certificate, together with appropriate evidence of identification.

The validity of a marriage may also be established by resort to presumptions. Two presumptions exist whereby both foreign and domestic marriages may be validated. Marriage may be presumed either from cohabitation such that a couple acquire the reputation of being married, although there is no evidence of any ceremony,[68] or from the celebration of a marriage followed by cohabitation.[69] In practice the importance of these presumptions in the present context is not that they might obviate the need for evidence as to foreign law. It is that they control the court's assessment of such evidence as may be introduced. Indeed, such presumptions are more concerned with proof of marriage than with the necessary evidence whereby a marriage may be proved. In one case, for example, a judge gave effect to the presumption from reputation despite accepting that the marriage lacked formal validity under the *lex loci celebrationis*.[70] The only explanation is that exceptionally cogent rebuttal evidence of foreign law is required in such cases.[71] It is not enough to prove foreign law according to the normal standard, such proof must be strong enough to outweigh what is traditionally regarded as a particularly adamantine presumption. Again, in another case,[72] the court resolved a conflict of expert evidence by applying the presumption from celebration and cohabitation, rather than by applying the different presumption that,

---

[65] Rayden and Jackson, above n. 51, 309.   [66] Ibid.   [67] Rule 10.14(3).
[68] *Re Shephard* [1904] 1 Ch. 456.
[69] *Piers v. Piers* (1849) 2 HL Cas. 331; *Tweney v. Tweney* [1946] P 180.
[70] *Re Shepherd* [1904] 1 Ch. 456, 462. Kekewich J implies that, however clear the evidence as to foreign law, it would be insufficient to rebut the presumption of validity.
[71] Cf. *Williamson v. Auckland Electric Tramways Co.* (1912) 31 NZLR 161.
[72] *Radwan v. Radwan* [1973] Fam. 35, 45.

if foreign law is not adequately proved, its content is deemed to be that of English law.[73] By doing so it signalled that the usual rules for the proof of foreign law are subordinate to the presumption of marriage.

(d) Foreign Corporate Status

Recurring problems surround the status of foreign legal entities, in particular whether they have the capacity to sue or be sued, and whether they are government agencies attracting sovereign immunity.[74] It is clear that whether a corporation exists, and what its capacity is, are matters to be governed by the place of incorporation.[75] But problems sometimes arise concerning the extent to which foreign official acts—or the lack of them—are conclusive as to an entity's nature. To what extent may this be established by reference merely to an official certificate, a statute which creates the entity, or a certificate of incorporation? How far, alternatively, is expert evidence required to establish corporate status?

A striking case is *Krajina v. Tass Agency*,[76] which concerned whether the defendant was an entity separate from the Soviet government. Little evidence was supplied and reliance was placed on a certificate from the Soviet ambassador and a translation of the statute creating the agency. The Court of Appeal found that the agency had the status of a government department, although without hearing expert evidence, and with some reluctance. Clearly, however, the court regarded the certificate as limited and inconclusive, and would have preferred expert testimony as to the statute's meaning. Similarly, in *Associated Shipping Services Ltd. v. Department of Private Affairs of H. H. Sheikh Zayed Bin Sultan Al-Nahayan*[77] the question was whether the defendant department existed as a separate entity under the law of Abu Dhabi. This turned partly on the effect of a letter from the Minister of Justice of the United Arab Emirates certifying that no official decree had been issued and that consequently the Department had no legal status. It also turned on the effect of affidavit evidence provided by the legal adviser to the Department who was not, however, qualified in the law of Abu Dhabi.

In one sense the court's handling of the evidence in the *Associated Shipping* case is revealing in its flexibility. Despite the lack of expertise the legal adviser was treated as a qualified expert, partly because of his special position with regard to the Department, partly because of the

---

[73] At 45.
[74] *Associated Shipping Services Ltd. v. Department of Private Affairs of HH Sheikh Zayed Bin Sultan Al-Nahayan*, The Times, 31 July 1990; *Dubai Bank Ltd. v. Galadari*, The Times, 26 June 1990; *Bumper Development Corp. Ltd. v. Commissioner of Police* [1991] 1 WLR 1362 (CA).
[75] Dicey and Morris, Rule 155. For a case concerning the capacity to sue of an unincorporated entity see *Bumper Development Corp. Ltd. v. Comr. of Police*, op. cit.
[76] [1949] 2 All ER 274 (CA).   [77] Above, n. 74.

straightforwardness of the question whether it was the will of the Ruler of Abu Dhabi that the Department should be a legal entity. In two important ways, however, the court affirmed that proof of such cases cannot easily be effected without expert testimony. First, they refused to accept that the legal adviser's evidence, if not admitted as expert evidence, could be treated simply as evidence of primary fact, the fact in question being whether incorporation had occurred. Secondly, the Minister of Justice's certificate was to be disregarded. Being in form an opinion as to the law of the United Arab Emirates it could not be evidence as to the law of Abu Dhabi. And, like the legal adviser's evidence, it could not take effect as evidence as to primary fact.

Another case which turned on attempts to dispense with expert evidence as to an entity's status is *Dubai Bank Ltd. v. Galadari*.[78] The question was whether the plaintiff bank had the legal status to sue. This was eventually answered by reference to expert evidence led by both parties but only after the plaintiff had tried unsuccessfully to argue that various official acts were conclusive without the need for expert testimony. It was argued, first, that a certificate given by a Minister of the United Arab Emirates was conclusive as being a foreign act of state; secondly, that compliance with the Dubai Law of Evidence 1971 was sufficient to establish the bank's corporate status; and, thirdly, that various official certificates as to incorporation were admissible under the Civil Evidence Act 1968[79] and established such status.

Each of these attempts to prove incorporation without further evidence was rejected. The Act of State doctrine was irrelevant because the acts in question were those of an official purporting to act for a sovereign, not those of the sovereign itself, in circumstances where the validity or constitutionality of foreign law was not in issue.[80] Similarly, mere compliance with the law of Dubai was irrelevant because the evidential requirements for establishing the status of a foreign corporation were a matter for English law, the matter being procedural in character. Equally unsuccessful was the attempt to bring various foreign documents concerning the state of Abu Dhabi law within the Civil Evidence Act 1968. Although several had been issued by government officials there was no evidence that they were qualified to give an opinion as to foreign law as required by section 4(1) of the Civil Evidence Act 1972.[81] Again, by effectively regarding

[78] Above, n. 74.
[79] As amended by the Civil Evidence Act 1972, this provides in section 2 that: 'In any civil proceedings a statement made . . . in a document . . . shall . . . be admissible as evidence of any fact stated therein of which direct oral evidence by him would be admissible'.
[80] *Buttes Gas* v. *Hammer* [1982] AC 888 (HL).
[81] Dicey and Morris suggest that a more lenient approach to a foreign official's qualifications might be appropriate in cases concerning the proof of foreign marriage: op. cit., 656. But it is unclear how this view can be reconciled with that expressed in the *Dubai Bank* case, above n. 74.

such officials as experts, to admit their evidence would contravene the already existing order which limited the number of foreign law experts to one per party. Moreover, even had such evidence been admissible under the Civil Evidence Act 1968 a question would presumably have remained as to the conclusiveness of such evidence, a matter which could only have been referred to the law of Dubai.

It is apparent, therefore, as might be expected, that proof of a foreign corporation's legal status may be successfully effected only on the basis of expert evidence. It is, however, a recurring feature of such cases that this is often not forthcoming, or that reliance is placed on official acts in preference to expert testimony.

4. COURT ADVISERS

We have considered already whether assessors or court experts might assist in handling such expert evidence as the parties may themselves introduce.[82] We are now concerned with the closely connected question whether foreign law might be established by such advisers alone without resort to the parties' experts. Although foreign law is apparently never proved in this way the question is not without importance. It reflects renewed interest in a non-adversarial approach to fact-finding generally.[83] It is also striking in a comparative context. The practice is commonly adopted in civil law jurisdictions[84] and has been much discussed in the United States.[85] Indeed, it has been said in connection with American practice that the 'use of a court-appointed expert is a highly desirable tool for ascertaining the governing foreign law . . .'.[86]

We have seen that court experts must be distinguished from assessors. An assessor's role is to assist the court with a trial's technical aspects. A court expert's function, by contrast, is to provide an opinion on specific issues. Being essentially a variety of expert witness a court expert may be cross-examined by the parties;[87] but not being such a witness an assessor may not.[88] The essential difference between court experts and assessors emerges from the different rationales for appointing each type of adviser. An assessor's function is to enable a judge to take judicial notice of facts

---

[82] See above, pp. 211–218.
[83] Lord Woolf, *Access to Justice, Final Report to the Lord Chancellor*, (London, HMSO, 1996), Ch. 13.
[84] At least in those which follow the German model, see below, p. 277.
[85] Schmertz, (1978) 18 *Virginia Jl Intl L* 697, 712–713; Miner, (1995) 43 *Am Jl Comp L* 581, 588–589.
[86] Miner, op. cit., 589. [87] As under RSC Order 40, r. 4.
[88] *The Queen Mary* (1947) 80 Lloyd's Rep. 609, 612.

which are not within the judge's knowledge.[89] It is as if the court has extended its knowledge by incorporating that of the assessor. But the court expert's role is principally to obviate the need for party-led expert testimony, in substitution for the process of expert proof. It is to

> enable the parties to save costs and expenses in engaging separate experts in respect of a technical or scientific question which can be resolved fully, quickly and comparatively cheaply by an independent expert appointed by the Court . . .[90]

In a sense, the court assessor procedure modifies the process of adjudication; the court expert procedure modifies the process of proof.

It is hard to imagine that the appointment of an assessor might assist the proof of foreign law unless expert evidence is also available. There is some controversy as to whether an assessor, in the strict sense, may be employed at all where such evidence has been introduced[91] but it is now commonly accepted that assessors have a wider role in resolving conflicts of evidence.[92] The principle that the use of assessors excludes resort to expert evidence derives from admiralty practice. In nautical cases, however, the assessor's function is largely to guide the court in understanding the evidence of factual witnesses, for example as to navigation and seamanship. It is to assist the court's comprehension of matters before the court not to introduce evidence which is not already available. As such, given that foreign law will be entirely unfamiliar to both the court and counsel, it would be particularly inapt to employ an assessor unless evidence of foreign law, presumably supplied by the parties' experts, were already available. Whatever role assessors might have in assessing evidence of foreign law they are unsuited to supplying it.

By contrast, giving an authoritative opinion on a point of foreign law would seem at first sight to be a natural task for an independent expert. There are few English cases where such experts have been employed,[93] none, it appears, concerning foreign law. But there is historical support, somewhat antique but intriguing, for the use of independent experts

---

[89] *Baldwin and Francis v. Patents Appeal Tribunal* [1959] AC 663, 691.
[90] RSC Order 40, para. 40/1–6/1; Lord Woolf, above n. 83.
[91] *The Ann and Mary* (1843) 2 Wm. Rob. 189, 197; *The Assyrian* (1890) 63 LT 91; *The Kirby Hall* (1883) 8 PD 71, 76; *The Chad* [1965] 2 Lloyd's Rep. 1, 4 (CA); Sir Jocelyn Simon P expressed similar views at first instance: [1965] 1 Lloyd's Rep. 107, 109; *The Victory*, 2 July 1996 (unreported).
[92] *Neptun (Owners) v. Humber Conservancy Board* (1937) 59 Lloyd's Rep. 158, 167; *Richardson v. Redpath, Brown & Co. Ltd.* [1944] AC 62, 70; Lord Woolf, above n. 83, 151.
[93] *Kennard v. Aslam* (1894) 10 TLR 213; *Henson v. Ashby* [1896] 2 Ch. 1, 26; *Coles v. Home and Colonial Stores Ltd.* [1904] AC 179, 192; *Badische Anilin v. Lewisham* (1883) 24 Ch.D. 156; *Partington and Son v. Tameside Metropolitan Borough Council* (1985) 32 BLR 150, 164; *Abbey National Mortgages plc v. Key Surveyors Nationwide Ltd.* [1996] 3 All ER 97–192 (CA); *Re K (A Minor), The Times*, 6 April 1995; cf. *Re Saxton* [1962] 1 WLR 968, 972 (CA).

(without the parties calling their own) in matters of foreign law.[94] Many early cases show the courts using a variety of specialists as *amici curiae*, charged with providing unsworn written opinions on technical questions of foreign law. In *Lindo* v. *Belisario*,[95] a prominent example, the Court of Arches referred a question concerning a Jewish marriage settlement, treated expressly as an issue of foreign law, to the Bethdin in London. In another, older case the Court of Chancery obtained written opinions from French lawyers in London as to the construction of a French will.[96] The court cited the analagous custom of enquiring of merchants as to the meaning of mercantile terms, and of the brethren of Trinity House as to marine matters: 'so in like manner grammarians, critiks, chymists, and artificers have been in the Court of King's Bench consulted ... upon words belonging to, and used in their respective professions'.[97] As the court said in a still earlier decision, encapsulating its power to seek independent advice on foreign law:

> ... if at common law [a] matter comes in question upon a conveyance, or other instrument, made beyond the sea according to the course of the Civil Law, or other law of the nations where it was made, the judges ought to consult with the Civilians or others which are expert in the same law; and according to their information give judgment.[98]

The distinction between what we would now recognize as the role of assessors and experts, and of official certification, is sometimes indistinct in the early cases. But the essence of the approach they endorse is clear. Information as to foreign law was generally derived from the unsworn, written, typically non-binding opinions of qualified experts appointed by the court.

But what of current practice? Such English cases as there are concern RSC Order 40, introduced in 1934, which may effectively have replaced the court's traditional powers in this area. Detailed examination of the general procedure for appointing an independent expert is beyond the scope of this discussion, not least because the law is evolving.[99] But there is recent evidence that English courts have become more ready than they might have been to consider the appointment of a court expert, albeit not in matters concerning foreign law.[100] This parallels growing official encouragement to do so, based upon the assumption that the use of such

---

[94] See generally, Baker, [1979] 28 *ICLQ* 141; Hand, (1901) 15 *HLR* 40; Rosenthal, (1935) 2 *Law & Contemp. Prob.* 403.
[95] (1795) 1 Hagg. Con. 216.   [96] *Foubert* v. *Cresseron* (1698) Show.P.C. 194.
[97] Ibid. at 197.
[98] Anon., 2 Bro. & Goulds. 16, at 17 (repunctuated by Baker, above n. 94).
[99] See further, Hodgkinson, Ch. 3; Dickey, (1970) 33 *MLR* 494; Basten, (1977) 40 *MLR* 174; Lord Woolf, above n. 83, Ch. 13; Draft Civil Proceedings Rules, Rule 32.5.
[100] *Abbey National Mortgages plc* v. *Key Surveyors Nationwide Ltd.*; *Re K (A Minor)*, above n. 93.

experts might be more efficient than relying upon those of the parties.[101] It is therefore important in principle, and may become increasingly important in practice, to assess whether such a procedure might assist the proof of foreign law. In doing so it is important to consider not only the efficiency and cost of the process, but also its fairness and its effectiveness as a means of establishing foreign law.

We have already identified several general objections to the use of court experts in establishing foreign law.[102] Not least, there may be difficulty in identifying a suitably qualified person, and it is unclear whether litigants would have confidence in any procedure which refers essentially legal questions to someone other than a judge. But there is a particular obstacle to the use of court experts in place of those of the parties. It is doubtful that foreign law could be established either fairly or effectively by an independent expert unless the parties also called their own experts.[103] True, party-led experts might be unnecessary in straightforward cases, but in such cases expert evidence may not be required at all. If the parties are in real dispute over a point of foreign law they will want to retain complete control over the presentation of their case. This can best be achieved, however, by the usual process of examining and cross-examining each other's experts. Again, even if an opinion is obtained under the court expert procedure, one party (possibly both) will surely challenge it by calling their own testimony. The other will doubtless reply by calling its own expert, thus transforming the case into a familiar dispute between party experts.[104] But, if so, the determination of foreign law becomes more cumbersome, not less. Indeed, in this respect the court expert procedure signally fails in its avowed purpose of enabling the parties to save costs. The dynamics of litigation also make it unreal to suppose that litigants would seek the appointment of a court expert as an alternative to their own. In any case involving foreign law each party will have sought the advice of experts from an early stage. Having already incurred the expense which that entails, having constructed their case, and having decided to proceed, around their expert's opinion, they are likely to rely on that opinion at trial by offering their expert as a witness.

Admittedly, such difficulties might in principle be avoided by forbidding the parties from calling their own experts. But this may be neither fair nor efficacious. Indeed, the court expert procedure may be unsuited in

---

[101] Lord Woolf, above n. 83, 140–142.   [102] See above, pp. 212–218.

[103] Suggestions that greater use should be made of court experts have attracted hostility: Lord Woolf, above n. 83, 140–142; Jack, (1994) 144 *NLJ* 1099; Lee, (1995) 145 *NLJ* 128; Goldrein, (1995) 145 *NLJ* 381. Judicial response to attempts to make greater use of the existing procedures has been guarded: *Abbey National Mortgages plc* v. *Key Surveyors Nationwide Ltd.*, above n. 93, 192.

[104] Lord Denning saw this as the reason for the near redundancy of the procedure under RSC Order 40: *Re Saxton* [1962] 1 WLR 968, 972.

principle to resolving contested questions of foreign law—unless party experts are also employed. Solutions to such questions are reached by weighing competing arguments, not by a process of discovery.[105] As such, the normal process whereby a court hears rival testimony as to foreign law, although theoretically an enquiry into fact, in reality captures the essentially dialectical character of legal reasoning. Indeed, to suppose that a single expert might provide the answer in such cases, without room for doubt or further argument, may be to endorse the dubious fallacy that there can be right answers to questions of law.[106] Certainly, to establish foreign law on the basis of the parties' experts' evidence reflects the reality that legal adjudication is as much (or more) a matter of establishing the relative soundness of the competing arguments as their correctness. Admittedly, a court expert might develop his or her opinion by a dialectical process of reasoning, taking account of conflicting points of view. But if too scrupulous in canvassing rival views it may be impossible for an independent expert to reach a conclusion at all, making the report but a catalogue of possibilities from which the judge must choose. If, on the other hand, the expert does hazard a definite conclusion, it is unclear that he or she is better placed to do so than an experienced judge properly assisted by counsel and expert witnesses. Indeed, given that responding to questions of law, albeit foreign law, is a matter of judgment, it might be thought that a judge is better suited to the task. More importantly, perhaps, such a process of personal deliberation by an independent adviser is unlikely to be as comprehensive, or as respectful of different views, as when rival opinions are forcefully expressed by interested parties.[107]

There is therefore a serious danger that a court, deprived of the opinions of the parties' experts, will be less able to resolve questions of foreign law effectively. There is a risk that the range of information and opinion before it will be less. And it may be denied the benefit of the mutual exploration and testing of opinion which is the essence of an adversarial approach to evidence. But it might be objected that a court expert should not be viewed merely as supplying one opinion for the court's consideration. Provision might be made for such an expert to take instructions from each of the parties, or to hear representations from them, thus removing many of the supposed difficulties with the procedure.[108] But such a broadening of the independent expert's role has an important consequence. It means, in effect, that independent experts will be able to function only where the parties have themselves supplied expert evidence, for litigants could hardly make representations concerning foreign law except with expert

[105] See further, Perelman, *Justice, Law and Argument* (Deventer, 1980); Perelman and Olbrechts-Tyteca, *The New Rhetoric* (Notre Dame, 1969).
[106] Woozley, 'No Right Answer', *The Philosophical Quarterly* 29 (1979), 25.
[107] *Jones* v. *NCB* [1957] 2 QB 55 (CA).   [108] Lord Woolf, above n. 83, 140–141.

assistance. But this at once implies that they have no role as an alternative to the use of party-led experts. More fundamentally, given that an independent expert is an expert like any other, it would be difficult to devise a system which did not give the parties a right to examine such an expert.[109] Indeed, once that is conceded it becomes difficult to exclude the calling of party experts, since such cross-examination may be inadequate without the support of expert evidence.[110] To deny the parties such opportunities to state their position might be unjust given the reality that views may legitimately differ on points of law. Indeed, it would be arbitrary, in so far as this would mean preferring the court expert's view to any other. It is one thing to save time and costs by adopting streamlined procedures, or reducing the issues in dispute. But it is hardly just to prevent litigants from contesting what is reasonably contestable.

The Court of Appeal has explicitly recognized the potential injustice in appointing a court expert without also allowing the parties to call their own evidence in the usual way. In a rare case concerning the procedure provided by RSC Order 40 the Master of the Rolls recognized the efficiency of appointing a single expert. But he emphasised the danger of denying litigants the right to call their own experts:

To expedite the just despatch of cases is one thing; merely to expedite the despatch of cases is another. The right of both parties to a fair trial of the issues between them cannot be compromised.[111]

But if, as justice requires, the right to cross-examine and to lead expert evidence must be retained, the effectiveness of the court expert procedure is immediately reduced. It almost guarantees that court experts will be used in addition to those of the parties, which increases the cost and delay involved.[112] If so, it might be as ineffective as it might be unfair to deny a role to the parties' experts in establishing foreign law. And if so, such a procedure will never—or will never entirely—replace the traditional approach to the proof of foreign law. Court experts will generally only ever have a role in assessing the opinions of the parties' own experts. But, as we have seen in Chapter VII, it is unclear what role an independent expert may have even when such party-led evidence has been supplied.

Finally, it is necessary to guard against superficial comparisons between English practice and that in systems where court experts are commonly used to determine foreign law.[113] True, it is normally possible in such systems for the parties to make submissions as to foreign law, to question the

---

[109] As under RSC Order 40; r. 4; Lord Woolf, above n. 83, 140–141.
[110] Compare the German practice whereby an expert may be required to explain the opinion: section 411 ZPO; Thomas and Putzo, *Zivilpozessordnung*, 17th edn. (1991) para. 411 No. 3.
[111] *Abbey National Mortgages plc* v. *Key Surveyors Nationwide Ltd.*, above n. 93, 192.
[112] *Re Saxton*, above n. 104.   [113] See below, p. 277.

court expert and even to introduce their own evidence. The practice in such countries is thus more familiar than English lawyers might suppose. But the conceptual starting point in such systems is entirely different. On the one hand, no other possibility often exists. Court experts are not employed because, in principle or in particular cases, the procedure is perceived as being better than reliance upon the parties' experts. They are employed because there is no possibility that the parties might establish foreign law by themselves. Indeed, given that the responsibility for determining foreign law is the court's alone it is natural—perhaps inevitable—that a court should appoint its own expert. Certainly, in assessing whether an English court might choose to appoint an independent expert it is of little help to refer to legal systems where no such choice exists.

5. FOREIGN OFFICIAL ASSISTANCE

There are two mechanisms whereby English courts may seek assistance from foreign legal authorities to establish the content of foreign law.[114] Neither, however, is apparently employed in practice. Each, as their names imply, have somewhat different functions. One, provided by the British Law Ascertainment Act 1859, allows a foreign court to determine matters of foreign law conclusively. The other, contained in the 1968 European Convention on Information on Foreign Law, offers a means whereby a non-binding opinion as to foreign law may be obtained through official channels.

(a) THE BRITISH LAW ASCERTAINMENT ACT

The British Law Ascertainment Act 1859 offers a procedure for establishing the laws of British colonies and some Commonwealth countries.[115] Potentially the Act's scope reaches beyond the British Isles, although it covers the Channel Islands and the Isle of Man, and it may extend to independent Commonwealth countries which are no longer British possessions, provided that by local law the Act remains effective. The Act provides that an English court may refer specified questions of foreign law to a superior court in the foreign country concerned.[116] It may do so on its own motion or, if it approves, upon application by a party. The court

---

[114] Resort to such assistance might be regarded as a means of improving proof by party experts, although it is more likely to be seen as an alternative to such proof. It is more convenient to consider the possibility in the present context.

[115] It applies, by section 1(3), to 'Her Majesty's Dominions', as to which see, 6 Halsbury's Laws, 4th edn., para. 803.

[116] Section 1.

enjoys complete discretion in such matters. It has the power to activate the procedure even if foreign law has not been pleaded, and may refuse to do so even if it has.[117] The parties may settle by agreement the questions to be posed, failing which the court will do so. The opinion of the foreign court, once received, binds all courts but the House of Lords and is therefore beyond challenge by the parties, except on appeal before the House of Lords.[118] The parties may, however, petition the foreign court in question, requesting an appearance to make representations on the point at issue.[119]

It is intuitively attractive that a question of foreign law might be determined by the foreign court concerned, although if the issue is of decisive importance the most appropriate way of achieving this may be to litigate in the court concerned. But the inherent flaws in the 1859 Act's procedure will be apparent. Indeed, there are several cases in which its provisions have been ignored deliberately in favour of quicker, cheaper modes of proof.[120] It is expensive and time-consuming, more so than proof by expert testimony, because the only means available to the parties to make representations concerning the evidence is by appointing local counsel and appearing in the foreign court. Yet the fact that the foreign court's opinion is binding on an English trial judge, with an appeal to the House of Lords as the only means of questioning it, would effectively compel any party using the procedure to petition the foreign court. Indeed, the reliance on the foreign court and the prospect of, effectively, a mini-trial abroad would, in the eyes of the parties, introduce an unacceptable degree of risk, unpredictability and delay into the process. Moreover, the courts, which possess the power to seek proof under the Act *ex officio*, have been no more ready than litigants to use its procedure, no doubt being sensitive to the expense and delay involved. Overall, the 1859 Act has fallen into disuse, an object lesson perhaps in how not to design a mechanism for obtaining proof of foreign law, an indicator of the pragmatism and cost-consciousness of litigants and their advisers.

(b) THE EUROPEAN FOREIGN LAW CONVENTION

The United Kingdom is a party to the 1968 European Convention on Information on Foreign Law,[121] the purpose of which is to facilitate the

---

[117] *Lord* v. *Colvin* (1860) 1 Dr. & Sm. 24; *Topham* v. *Duke of Portland* (1863) 1 De GJ & S 517; *Eglington* v. *Lamb* (1867) 15 LT 657.

[118] Section 3. It was originally intended that the foreign court's opinion might, at the court's discretion, be put to the jury, possibly as non-conclusive evidence, but a jury now has no role in determining foreign law: Supreme Court Act 1981, section 69(5).

[119] Section 1.

[120] *MacDougall* v. *Chitinavis*, 1937, SC 390, 407–408. It was employed in *Topham* v. *Duke of Portland*; *Eglington* v. *Lamb*, above n. 117.

[121] Cmnd. 4229, TS No. 117 (1969). The treaty came into force on 17 December 1969. See generally, O'Malley and Layton, 239–240; Rodger and van Doorn, (1997) 46 *ICLQ* 151;

task of the courts in signatory states in obtaining information on foreign law. There is no evidence that the Convention has been employed to seek information from abroad, although the Foreign and Commonwealth Office has been designated as the appropriate liaison body, and some incoming requests from other countries have been received.[122]

The Convention operates by the courts of one signatory state, through governmental channels, transmitting a request for information to the relevant receiving agency in the state whose law is in issue.[123] Such a request must be approved by the court and will take the form of a question or questions which specify precisely the information on foreign law which is requested, the nature of the case and such facts as may be necessary to permit an accurate reply.[124] Where necessary, documents may be appended to clarify the issue.[125] A request for information must emanate from a court.[126] The language of the request and of the reply is that of the foreign country concerned, except where the signatory states concerned have otherwise agreed.[127] The court in the receiving state need not respond itself to the request. It may pass it to a private body, such as a research institute, or to a qualified lawyer.[128] Whoever replies, the reply must provide the necessary information in 'an objective and impartial manner'.[129] Explanatory material, commentaries, legal texts, judicial decisions, and scholarly works, may be appended if necessary.[130] Once the reply is received the requesting court may treat it as it wishes. It is not bound by the information it contains.[131]

In principle, the costs of this procedure fall on the states concerned, not the parties.[132] Generally, the cost of the reply will fall on the authorities in the receiving state. One exception is where the requesting and receiving states have their own arrangements regarding expenses. Another is where, by sending the request to a private body or a lawyer, the receiving authority has incurred additional costs. In such cases the authorities in the requesting state shall in the first instance bear the cost, provided they have consented to it in advance.[133] In the English context, however, this cost will presumably be met by the parties, or by the losing party.

Although the Convention has been ratified by the United Kingdom it has not been expressly implemented by statute. But its provisions may nonetheless be accessible to litigants in English proceedings, although this is a matter of speculation. As O'Malley and Layton suggest this might be justified by analogy with the court's existing powers to obtain documen-

---

Bülow-Böcksteigel, *Internationaler Rechtsverkehr in Zivil- und Handelssachen*, (Munich, 1990), section 380.

[122] Rodger and van Doorn, op. cit., 172. [123] Articles 2 and 5.
[124] Article 4. [125] Article 4(2). [126] Article 3(1). [127] Article 14.
[128] Article 6(2). [129] Article 7. [130] Ibid. [131] Article 8.
[132] Article 15. [133] Ibid.

tary evidence located abroad.[134] Certainly, these procedures, or similar procedures, may apparently be employed when seeking judicial assistance under the British Law Ascertainment Act 1859, which is similar in its terms and objectives to the Convention.[135] But a more direct, if no more certain, gateway to the Convention may be afforded by invoking the court's inherent power in evidential matters.[136] The case of *Panayiotou* v. *Sony Music Entertainment (UK) Ltd.*[137] is here instructive. This concerned the singer George Michael, who applied to the English courts for a letter of request, seeking *inter alia* the production of documents held by a third party abroad which was associated with Sony. Sony's defence was that RSC Order 39, implementing the Hague Evidence Convention, contemplated no more than the production of documents held by witnesses who were orally examined. This, they argued, did not extend to the production of documents held by a corporation which, not being a real person, could not be examined orally under English law. Only the Supreme Court Rules Committee, it was argued, could cure that omission by amending Order 39 but, under the rules as they stood, the plaintiff should fail. Sir Donald Nicholls V-C rejected that restrictive view and directed the issue of the plaintiff's letter of request. He did so by appealing to the courts' inherent power in such cases:

> The jurisdiction of the High Court to make a request to the court of another country for assistance in obtaining evidence does not derive from statute, or even from the Rules of the Supreme Court. In my view the court's power to issue a letter of request stems from the jurisdiction inherent in the court. Inherent in the court is the power to do those acts which the court needs must have to maintain its character as a court of justice.[138]

This was but an aspect of the court's wider supervisory jurisdiction over matters of evidence: '. . . the subject matter on which assistance is sought, the obtaining of evidence, is one over which the court has long exercised close control. This is a subject peculiarly within the court's own control'.[139] The lack of specific statutory authority was, moreover, no obstacle to the exercise of this power: 'It cannot be right that, in the absence of legislation or a rule, the English court is unable to take advantage of this situation when necessary'.[140]

Given the width of these remarks, and of the power claimed by the Vice-Chancellor, an application for a request under the Information

---

[134] At 239.   [135] RSC Order 39, para. 39/2–3/10.
[136] Suggested by O'Malley and Layton, 239.
[137] [1994] Ch. 142, noted, Andrews, [1994] CLJ 247. See further, *Edmeades* v. *Thames Board Mills* [1969] 2 QB 67; *Abu Dhabi National Tanker Co.* v. *Product Star Shipping Ltd.* [1991] 2 Lloyd's Rep. 508.
[138] At 149.   [139] At 150.
[140] At 150.

Convention seems indistinguishable in principle from the request contemplated in *Sony*. Both situations involve employing an existing framework of legal co-operation, in a way not provided for expressly in legislation, in furtherance of the court's inherent power to seek evidence from abroad. Certainly, there are limits to the court's power in such cases, as the Vice-Chancellor recognized.[141] A procedural framework for co-operation must be in place, the foreign court must be in a position to accede to the request, and the evidence sought should be identified with specificity. It may also be necessary that, in making the request, the court is doing no more than asking the foreign courts to do what an English court could do in a purely domestic case. But each of these requirements would be satisfied in cases under the Convention. The Convention provides an appropriate procedure, to which the foreign agency concerned might be expected to reply, and the Convention itself requires precision in formulating the request. It is also apparent, in a purely domestic case, that a court could appoint an independent expert as to foreign law, which is effectively the consequence of applying the Convention in a transnational context.

But even if the Convention is accessible to litigants in English proceedings, are they likely to avail themselves of its provisions? The procedure has clear disadvantages, judged from the perspective of an adversarial system of procedure. The opinions given in reply are not binding, nor are the parties prevented from introducing their own expert evidence. Indeed, it is difficult to see how the question to be referred abroad could be formulated without the assistance of such experts. Nor is it clear that an opinion received under the Convention should be given greater weight than those of the parties' experts. If the opinion is obtained from a private practitioner or academic commentator its weight is no greater than that of any other expert. And, even if it is supplied by a foreign government agency the fact that it is not binding underlines that it does not amount to a certificate as to the point in question.

But if, as this suggests, and its title implies, the Convention offers but one source of information concerning foreign law, in addition to that supplied by the parties' experts, it is unclear what value the procedure may have. If it is almost bound to be used in conjunction with such experts, and is not itself binding, the procedure may complicate rather than illuminate the situation, and can only increase the cost and delay of proceedings. Moreover, even if the Convention were employed to the exclusion of expert evidence it could not stand alone as a fair or effective mechanism for establishing foreign law. It would suffer from those same disadvantages which, as we have seen, would afflict the exclusive use of indepen-

[141] Ibid.

dent experts. Resort to the Convention may also be pointless. One reason is that it does not obviate the need for expert evidence which, in the English context, is very likely to be introduced. Another reason is that, if the purpose of the Convention is to facilitate the proof of foreign law in those relatively simple cases in which expert testimony will not be required, there are other simpler, less expensive means of resolving cases of a straightforward nature. Another difficulty is that the giving of the opinion is inevitably detached from the circumstances of the dispute. This might introduce an element of objectivity into the process but it also imports a degree of unreality, in so far as questions of law are always answered, to a greater or lesser extent, against the background of actual litigation. Indeed, it might be supposed, at the risk of overstating the case, that an English judge assisted by expert evidence may be in a better position to replicate the reasoning of a foreign judge than a foreign expert who is addressing a purely abstract question. Certainly, there is a danger that a foreign agency or its nominee will not appreciate all the circumstances of the case in making its reply. Although it expressly provides that the parties should supply all the information, in terms of documents and factual background, necessary to obtain 'an exact and precise reply', the Convention's procedure is divorced inevitably from the context of the dispute.

Finally, there may be a danger, or a danger perceived by the parties, that the parties will lose control of the issue were a matter of foreign law referred to a foreign court. One aspect of this is the foreign receiving agency's power under the Convention to assign the question to 'another State or official body', or to a 'private body or to a qualified lawyer', apparently without consulting the parties.[142] Not only would they have no control over the foreign court's choice of expert, they might be concerned as to the expert's likely identity. English lawyers are unlikely to relish the prospect of a pivotal issue in a dispute being resolved perhaps by a foreign practitioner, or a research assistant at a foreign law school or research institute. One may take issue with such an adversarial perspective. But, assuming the Convention's procedures remain optional, this may ensure that they are unlikely to be employed in the English context.

Overall, therefore, the Convention may, in the English context, suffer from many of the same problems which affect the employment of independent, court-appointed experts. In difficult cases, where party experts are also involved, its procedures may increase the cost, complexity and duration of proceedings. But in simpler cases there are other, more straightforward mechanisms for handling the problem. This is not to deny, however, that the Convention is employed, to varying degrees, in

---

[142] Article 6(2).

many other signatory states.[143] But such states are those in which foreign law is customarily determined by means of single court-appointed experts and, in a sense, the Convention's procedures are but a transnational extension of that mechanism. Certainly, its procedures can be accommodated more easily in a system in which the responsibility for determining foreign law falls upon the court, and in which the objective determination of foreign law is perceived as more important than permitting the parties to put their case by introducing their own expert evidence. Indeed, where a court is ultimately responsible for determining foreign law the Convention may significantly assist in the discharge of that responsibility. Not least, it removes the difficulty of identifying a suitable expert within the court's own jurisdiction, which may be especially valuable where established institutes of comparative law may not exist, or where the foreign law concerned is not that of a system in which local experts are likely to have expertise. Moreover, although English lawyers may be puzzled that such a protracted procedure is apparently best suited to addressing relatively simple questions of law, this is to mistake how it may operate in other systems. For, in many countries, a court's only means of resolving questions of foreign law, difficult or straightforward, may be to appoint an independent expert. Certainly, such possibilities as determining foreign law, at the parties' request, on the basis of foreign legal materials may be seen as a surrender of judicial responsibility.

6. FOREIGN LAW WITHIN THE COURT'S PROVINCE

We have so far considered five ways of determining foreign law without employing expert evidence introduced by the parties. A further possibility is to rely on the principle that certain matters are within the province of the court by virtue of its inherent skill or expertise. As we have seen, English courts generally lack notice of unpleaded, unproved facts. Certain matters, however, are deemed to be within the specific knowledge or general competence of the court such that they need not be proved. In such cases it is not so that the proof of foreign law is possible without calling expert testimony. It is that proof of foreign law is not required at all.[144] Evidence of foreign law may be dispensed with, because the matter is within the court's province, in five situations:

1. When a court has notice of specific foreign laws, either because the English court is sitting as an appellate court from the foreign jurisdiction

---

[143] Rodger and van Doorn, above n. 121, 159–161.   [144] Dicey and Morris, 218–220.

concerned,[145] or because statute deems the English court to have notice of foreign law.[146]

2. When a disputed point of foreign law reflects a general, universal principle of law, common to all legal systems.[147]

3. When a disputed point of foreign law is a fact of a notorious kind, such that it is within the court's general knowledge.[148]

4. When determining foreign law is characterized as involving no more than the construction of a private instrument, such as a contract or deed.[149]

5. When an issue of foreign law can be determined merely by interpreting foreign legal texts.[150]

In the first three situations a court has judicial notice of foreign law, which is regarded as within the court's direct knowledge. In the fourth and fifth it is not that the court has knowledge of foreign law, but that the issue, being simply one of construction, is within the scope of its inherent skill and competence. Technically, the construction of foreign laws differs from the construction of private documents. In principle, an expert must inform the judge as to the former, while the latter is always for the court.[151] But the distinction collapses in practice. On the one hand, the construction of contracts, deeds, or other private documents may depend upon foreign rules of construction or technical terms which a court should follow. On the other hand, litigants may sometimes leave the interpretation of foreign legal texts to the court, unaided by expert evidence. Certainly, there are situations where, in effect, the determination of foreign law is simply a matter of construction for the court.

A related situation concerns those rare instances in which English law is regarded as applying directly in a foreign country. It has been held, for example, that the common law of England applied in Ireland,[152] and that the activities of English settlers in new colonies were governed by English law until such time as local legislation was passed to supersede it.[153] In such cases an English court had judicial notice of those aspects of English law applicable in the jurisdiction concerned. Such recondite and antique cases are not strictly exceptions to the general principle, however, as they involve an English court having notice of English law, hardly a surprising proposition. They require no further examination.

---

[145] See below, p. 246. [146] See below, p. 246. [147] See below, p. 247.
[148] See below, p. 248. [149] See below, p. 251. [150] See below, p. 257.
[151] *Trotter v. Trotter* (1828) 4 Bli. (NS) 502; *King of Spain v. Machado* (1827) 4 Russ. 225, 239–240; *Chattanay v. Brazilian Co.* [1891] 1 QB 79; *Rouyer Guillet & Cie. v. Rouyer Guillet & Co. Ltd.* [1949] 1 All ER 244 (CA); Dicey and Morris, 224; Howard, Crane and Hochberg, *Phipson on Evidence*, 14th edn, (London, 1990), 18–19, 841.
[152] *Re Nesbitt* (1844) 14 LJMC 30, 32; cf. *Limerick v. Limerick* (1863) 4 Sw. & Tr. 252, 253.
[153] *Cooper v. Stuart* (1889) 14 App. Cas. 286, 291–292; *Terrell v. Secretary of State for the Colonies* [1953] 2 QB 482, 492.

Each of the five devices listed above represents a means whereby litigants who wish to save time and costs in establishing points of foreign law may do so without calling expert evidence. In such cases, counsel's submissions as to the generality or notoriety of the facts in question, or as to construction, effectively replace expert testimony as the means of establishing points of foreign law. It must be emphasized, however, that none of these situations is particularly suited to situations in which complex questions of foreign law are involved, and each mechanism contains its own limitations which reduce its practical value.

(a) Judicial Notice of Specific Foreign Laws

A court sitting in England may have specific notice of foreign law, making its proof unnecessary in two situations. First, it may have appellate jurisdiction over other law areas, and so have knowledge of their laws. The House of Lords may sit as a court of appeal from Scotland and Northern Ireland. But it also takes judicial notice of the laws of those jurisdictions even when sitting in an appeal from England. Similarly, it takes judicial notice of English law when hearing appeals from Northern Ireland or Scotland.[154] So too, the Privy Council has knowledge of the laws of those countries over which it exercises jurisdiction.[155] There is also evidence that the House of Lords may assume knowledge of the laws of states over which the Privy Council has jurisdiction, even when sitting in an English appeal.[156] Although strictly incorrect, this reflects the fact that in practice the composition of both tribunals is similar. Secondly, an English court may be deemed by statute to have notice of specific foreign laws, although such statutory conferment of notice is rare. One example is section 22(2) of the Maintenance Orders Act 1950, which provides:

For the purposes of subsection (1) of this section, a court in any part of the United Kingdom may take notice of the law in force in any other part of the United Kingdom.

Not only are such statutory notice provisions rare, the courts are unwilling to regard more ambiguous legislation as having this effect. In *Re Helbert Wagg and Co.*[157] the question was whether Article 7(2) of the Distribution of German Enemy Property (No. 2) Order 1951 allowed a party to state a case to the High Court on a point of German law. The provision allowed such a course in the event of errors of law but was silent as

---

[154] *Elliott* v. *Joicey* [1935] AC 209, 236; *MacShannon* v. *Rockware Glass Ltd.* [1978] AC 795, 815, 821.
[155] Dicey & Morris, 219.
[156] *Attorney General of New Zealand* v. *Ortiz* [1984] AC 1 (HL); Hartley, (1996) 45 *ICLQ* 271, 280–281.
[157] [1956] Ch. 323, 355–356.

to whether that included foreign law. Upjohn J held that the draftsman could not have intended to allow a court to treat foreign law as law in the absence of 'clear and unmistakeable language'.[158]

A related matter, of potentially greater importance in practice, concerns section 4(2) of the Civil Evidence Act 1972 which, in effect, allows a court to accord the same precedent value to a previous finding as to foreign law as it would to a finding as to domestic law.[159] The section recognizes the special status of foreign law by allowing the court to take notice of a previous foreign-law finding notwithstanding that it is strictly a finding of fact.[160] The effect of this transformation of fact into law is, however, limited in so far as contrary evidence may always be adduced to rebut the presumption that the foreign law as previously found is correctly stated.

(b) General Principles of Law

That general principles of law do not require formal proof was recognized in *Di Sora* v. *Phillipps*.[161] The case concerned the respective roles of the judge and expert witnesses in construing the terms of a marriage settlement governed by foreign law. The Vice Chancellor required evidence of 'principles peculiar to foreign law', but did not require proof of 'any general rule of law which is not peculiar to one code or another, but which is co-extensive with every system of jurisprudence'.[162] He offered a somewhat unimaginative instance of such a universal rule, one chosen no doubt with the task of construing a document in mind: 'effect is to be given to every word in a contract, if possible'.[163] He summed up his powers, however, in the widest terms, indicating a broad area in which formal proof of foreign law may be unnecessary: 'General principles are within my province'.[164]

For all its width, such language may only have been intended to embrace general principles of construction, not principles of a substantive nature. It is also unclear what such general principles might be and how they might be identified. Nonetheless, judges recognize the existence of such principles, even where more than documentary construction is involved. In *The Tolten*,[165] for example, Scott LJ, conscious of the objection that foreign laws require proof, nonetheless sought to apply 'the general law of the sea' in determining his jurisdiction in admiralty actions *in rem*. Similarly, in *Adams* v. *Cape Industries plc*,[166] the trial judge resolved a conflict of expert evidence as to the law of Texas by appealing to the principles underlying all common law systems. The notion that a court might

[158] Ibid., at 356.   [159] See further, above, p. 223.
[160] Section 4(2)(b).
[161] (1863) 33 LJ Ch. 129 HL; but see, Miner, (1995) 43 *Am Jl Comp L* 581, 585.
[162] At 130.   [163] Ibid.   [164] At 130–131.   [165] [1946] P 135, 148–149 (CA)
[166] [1990] 2 WLR 657, 714 (Scott J); affd. (without consideration of the point), [1990] 2 WLR 657 (CA).

assess damages without evidence of loss offended his 'understanding of the role and function of a judge in a common law jurisdiction'.[167] Again, it might be counted a general principle of law, requiring no proof, that an arbitrator in one country is not bound by the procedural laws of another.[168]

(c) Notorious Foreign Laws

It is well-accepted that notorious matters require no formal proof, being within the knowledge of the judge.[169] Indeed, it is hard to imagine a viable legal system whose courts do not take some facts for granted as being generally known. Where the doctrine of notoriety applies, it is insufficient that the fact in question is within the judge's own private knowledge[170] where it is not also within the comprehension of any person of ordinary intelligence and experience.[171] A fact's notoriety is objectively judged.

The doctrine's application is uncertain in connection with foreign law. There ought to be no objection to treating facts *about* foreign law as notorious because to do so does not impinge on the principle that points of foreign law are facts, requiring proof accordingly. Indeed, this may explain the decision in *Re Turner*,[172] sometimes cited as illustrating how foreign laws can be notorious, in which it was accepted as a commonplace that the laws of various parts of the German Empire differed considerably. More controversial is the possibility of treating the content of foreign law as notorious, which amounts to a genuine exception to the normal principle that foreign laws are facts. A proposition of foreign law was treated as notorious in the well-known case of *Saxby* v. *Fulton*[173] in which both the trial judge and the Court of Appeal took for granted that roulette is lawful in Monte Carlo. That the Court of Appeal did so is less interesting because by that stage of the proceedings the parties had agreed to this course but the trial judge's handling of the matter is more arresting. Although no evidence as the legality of gambling in Monte Carlo had been tendered he declined to apply the usual presumption that the law of Monaco should therefore be assumed to be the same as that in England. He took it to be well known that gambling was legal there. Again, the doctrine may explain a number of situations in which particular tribunals have specialist knowledge and expertise in foreign law. It has long been accepted that

---

[167] At 714.
[168] See, e.g. the remarks of Mustill LJ in *The Eras EIL Actions* [1992] 1 Lloyd's Rep. 570, 611.
[169] *Commonwealth Shipping Representative* v. *P & O Branch Service* [1923] AC 191, 212 (HL).
[170] *Palmer* v. *Crone* [1927] 1 KB 804; *Reynolds* v. *Llanelly Associated Tinplate Co. Ltd.* [1948] 1 All ER 410 (CA).
[171] *R* v. *Aspinall* (1876) 2 QPD 48, at 61; 62 (CA); *Morgan* v. *London General Omnibus Co.* (1884) 13 QBD 832, 833 (CA).
[172] [1906] WN 27.
[173] [1909] 2 KB 208, 211.

arbitrators appointed from within a trade may take cognisance of facts which are known within that trade, if not to the general public.[174] And in commercial cases it is commonplace to assume that certain facts, known to commercial parties, may be taken for granted.[175] Although examples where matters of foreign law have been treated in such a way by specialist tribunals are rare it appears to be the case that the Immigration Appeal Tribunal, and the parties before it, may accept certain frequently recurring facts without question and without proof. Facts relating to the marriage laws of Pakistan and Bangladesh, for example, seem never in practice to be put to formal proof in cases involving a spouse's right of entry, no doubt because it is a commonplace amongst Tribunal members that polygamous marriage is lawful in those countries.[176] Similarly, Cairns J in *Jasiewicz* v. *Jasiewicz*,[177] having accepted evidence that the Indian Christian Marriage Act 1872 was still in force in 1962, took a robust approach to the requirements of the fact doctrine. He declared that in future cases before him he would consider the point as settled:

I may add that having now been satisfied on this point in relation to Pakistan I shall in future cases assume that the law remains the same there unless there seems some good reason for supposing otherwise. It would be pedantic to require this matter to be proved afresh in every case.[178]

Again, the House of Lords is treated as knowing the laws of other parts of the United Kingdom, even in cases on appeal from a different part. In English appeals, for example, it has notice of the laws of Scotland and Northern Ireland.[179] Although normally explained in terms of judicial notice alone, the rationale for the House of Lords having such notice implies a wider principle. Because it hears appeals from each part of the United Kingdom, and has notice of their laws for that purpose, it has a knowledge of those laws which it can hardly disclaim simply because an appeal arises from a different part. A similar principle may also explain the otherwise difficult decision in *Attorney General of New Zealand* v. *Ortiz*.[180] There the House of Lords apparently assumed a knowledge of New Zealand law, notwithstanding the existence of expert evidence. No doubt it did so because the Privy Council has notice of the laws of those Commonwealth countries from which it hears appeals. Although having a different jurisdiction, the similar composition of the Privy Council and

---

[174] *Port Sudan Cotton Co.* v. *Govindaswamy Chettiar & Sons* [1977] 1 Lloyd's Rep. 166, at 179.
[175] e.g. judicial notice has been taken of the fact that the standard form Lloyd's SG Policy is used throughout the world: *Amin Rasheed Shipping Corp.* v. *Kuwait Insurance Co.* [1984] AC 50, at 64–65 (per Lord Diplock) (HL).
[176] e.g. *ECO, Dhaka* v. *Ranu Begum* [1986] Imm. AR 461; *R.* v. *Immigration Appeal Tribunal, ex parte Rafika Bibi* [1989] Imm. AR 1.
[177] [1962] 1 WLR 1426. [178] At 1428. [179] See above, p. 246.
[180] [1984] 1 AC 1.

the House of Lords may have led the latter to assume *de facto* knowledge of matters known to the former. It may be, therefore, that foreign laws may be notorious whenever a judge in fact has expertise in a particular area.

But the possibility that foreign law may be notorious has been doubted. In *Hartmann* v. *Konig*[181] the Court of Appeal had taken a view of German law because 'it is commonly known that the Continental jurists adopt a wider interpretation of surrounding circumstances than we allow for the purpose of a contract in England'.[182] This approach was firmly rejected by the House of Lords because there was no expert evidence to support that view. More recently, in *El Ajou* v. *Dollar Land Holdings plc*[183] Millett J expressly denied that a court could take notice of foreign law 'though it be notorious'.[184] As such, the defendant failed in its argument that the claimant's alleged title to certain monies could not be established once the monies passed into the hands of recipients in jurisdictions which had no concept of equitable ownership.

Neither decision, however, is conclusive. *Hartmann* might be confined to its facts. It was a case in which expert evidence was available and as such may not affect whether foreign laws may be treated as notorious where it is not. Nor does it appear that *Saxby*, despite its prominence, was considered or cited in *El Ajou*. Nor does *Lazard Bros.* v. *Midland Bank Ltd.*,[185] the case on which Millett J relied in *El Ajou*, actually support the proposition that notice cannot be taken of notorious foreign laws. It was not concerned with notoriety, but with whether a court could rely on a previous English decision on a point of foreign law, in the absence of fresh evidence.[186]

The conflicting case law once again reflects the ambiguous status of foreign law in English courts.[187] If treated strictly as an issue of fact there should be no room to determine it except by expert evidence.[188] On such a view, short of formal proof, no means exist to determine foreign law and the court's province is restricted, confined perhaps to matters of construction. As such, even if a foreign rule is indeed notorious, this is irrelevant, its determination being solely a matter of evidence. The contrary view is that issues of foreign law have a hybrid character. This explains why appeals are possible on points of foreign law[189] and justifies the readiness of courts to rely on their general legal expertise to save the proof of foreign law from failure.[190] Approached in this way foreign laws may certainly be proved as facts, but they may also be determined by such other means as courts have at their disposal.

---

[181] (1933) 50 TLR 114 (HL).   [182] Ibid., at 117.   [183] [1993] 3 All ER 717.
[184] Ibid., at 736.   [185] [1933] AC 289.   [186] See below, p. 223.
[187] See above, p. 5, below, p. 257.
[188] In *El Ajou* v. *Dollar Land Holdings plc*, Millett J doubted that foreign laws could be notorious by appealing directly to their status as facts, and to the need as such for expert evidence: above, n. 183, 736. But contrast *Jasiewicz* v. *Jasiewicz* [1962] 1 WLR 1426, 1428 (per Cairns J).
[189] See above, p. 201.   [190] See above, pp. 194–201.

In principle, it is hard to justify a view of foreign law so narrow as to exclude the possibility that foreign laws may be notorious. It is formalism indeed to insist that foreign laws are facts, and must be proved as such, when plausible authority and sound policy suggest other means to determine their content. Certainly, at a time when considerations of cost and proportionality of response are to the fore, it is curious to require foreign law to be determined only by expert evidence when cheaper, quicker alternatives exist.[191] In practice, however, it may seldom happen that foreign laws will be treated as notorious. There is no secure benchmark of notoriety, which makes the technique hard to use. And, if nothing else, the very fact that a point of foreign law is contested between the parties gives the lie to its being so obvious as to be common knowledge. Overall, although possible in principle, there may be few cases in which it will be necessary or possible to treat foreign law as a notorious fact.

(d) The Construction of Documents

The next section examines how far an English court may dispense with expert proof of foreign law by construing foreign legal materials, in the form of law reports, statutes, and commentaries. We are now concerned with the possibility that foreign law may be determined, albeit indirectly, by treating the issue as one involving the construction of a private document, such as a contract or a will. This does not strictly concern the proof of foreign law, nor even perhaps its determination in any wider sense. It involves treating such questions of foreign law as may be raised in interpreting a contract or deed merely as matters of construction. In charting the extent of the parties' freedom to ignore issues of foreign law we have already seen that a court may insist that evidence of foreign law is supplied where this is necessary for the meaningful construction of a contract or a deed.[192] We may now consider more closely the extent to which litigants may handle what are in effect issues of foreign law by characterising the issue as one of construction.

This possibility arises whenever, in drafting a document, the parties employ terms of art, or words or phrases which have a distinct meaning under foreign law, or which allude to aspects of foreign law. In one case, for example, a bill of lading exempted a shipowner from liability if goods were shipped 'from a port in the United States'.[193] Because the goods in

---

[191] It was the strict treatment of foreign laws as facts, and the constraints that placed on the proof of foreign law, which prompted reform in the United States: Federal Rules of Civil Procedure, Rule 44.1; Wright and Miller, *Federal Practice and Procedure: Civil 2d*, para. 2441; Miller, (1967) 65 *Mich L Rev* 613.

[192] See above, pp. 135–138.

[193] *Stafford Allen & Sons Ltd.* v. *Pacific Steam Navigation Co.* [1956] 1 Lloyd's Rep. 105, affd. [1956] 1 WLR (CA).

question were shipped from a court in the Panama Canal Zone the meaning of the phrase raised a question of US Maritime Law. In another case, one party promised to indemnify the other against liability to 'Argentine Maritime Pensions Tax'.[194] In both the meaning of those phrases was contested and the question was whether this was a matter of construction or of foreign law. Other cases concern the common practice of incorporating aspects of foreign law into commercial contracts, notably in charter-parties or bills of lading. It frequently happens, for example, that such documents, although governed by one law, are also made expressly subject to the laws of another country. This is typically achieved by means of a clause paramount whereby the contract is explicitly made subject to the provisions of a particular foreign statute. The intention of the parties in such cases is normally to ensure that their liability shall be no greater than that under the law which is incorporated, although in every other respect the contract is governed by its applicable law in the usual fashion.

In such cases there is no doubt that the document must be interpreted in accordance with its governing law, and that the words of any foreign statute whose terms have been incorporated will be interpreted merely as contractual terms in accordance with that governing law. This fundamental principle originates in *Dobell v. Steamship Rossmore Co.*,[195] which concerned aspects of US maritime law which the parties had expressly incorporated into a bill of lading. The Court of Appeal without pause determined the meaning of the US Harter Act by construing its provisions as it would have construed any other contractual terms. Lord Esher MR expressly declined to construe it 'as an Act'[196] but merely as 'words occurring in the bill of lading'.[197]

But it is important not to mistake the proper analysis of such cases. The question is not, for example, whether English law or foreign law governs the construction of the document or of the term in question. As we have seen, it is clear that the applicable law of the contract, whatever that might be in a given case, governs even the construction of incorporated foreign laws. The question, whatever the applicable law might be in a particular case, is whether the court is able to construe a provision which alludes to foreign law without evidence of that law. This arises only where the construction of the contract falls to be determined under English law. Certainly, the choice in the cases is always between adopting an English approach to the parties' intentions or seeking evidence of foreign law. But

---

[194] *The Glenbank* [1959] 1 Lloyd's Rep. 133; [1960] 1 Lloyd's Rep. 178 (CA), [1961] 1 Lloyd's Rep. 231 (HL). See also *Di Sora v. Phillipps* (1864) 10 HLC 624, above p. 136.
[195] [1895] 2 QB 408 (CA); Dicey and Morris, 1222–1223. The 1980 Rome Convention on the Law Applicable to Contractual Obligations, Article 10, provides that a contract's construction is governed by its applicable law.
[196] At 413. [197] Ibid.

this is not to deny that in theory the problem may occur as much when the applicable law is foreign as when it is English. More precisely, it might occur either where it is English, or where it is foreign but no evidence is introduced, or where foreign law evidence has been introduced but is inadequate. Given that in all such cases an English court will be required to apply English canons of construction, the issue is whether, in a given case, the construction of the words in question is within the court's province. Can a court resolve it merely by employing its inherent interpretative skill, and in particular by establishing the parties' presumed intentions? That this is the correct analysis is confirmed by the approach adopted by Rix J in *The Stolt Syndess*.[198] There the court was invited to consider whether a question of construction under the Hague Rules, in so far as they had been incorporated into an English charter-party by a US clause paramount, was a matter for English or US law. But, on inspection, Rix J considered that this was not truly the issue:

In the course of considering that question I believe that it has been shown to offer a false choice . . . Of course ultimately the question of construction must be answered as a matter of the proper law of the contract. But along the path of finding that answer, it may well be that English law may have to refer to the foreign law, to assist it in discovering the parties' presumed intentions.[199]

Nor is the question whether the meaning of a foreign-related provision is either a matter of construction or one of foreign law. As Rix J implies, it is always a matter of construction, although reference might have to be made to foreign law in order to make such construction possible.

The issue in practice, therefore, is whether in a given case it is necessary to introduce evidence of foreign law in construing a contractual term. Conversely, how far is it possible to treat what are, in truth, questions of law as if they are questions of construction? As we have seen, it is possible that a court might, in effect, oblige the parties to secure such evidence where the construction of a document would otherwise be pointless. A court may decline to treat the matter as one purely of construction and direct that expert evidence of foreign law be produced,[200] unless perhaps the parties are in agreement that the matter should be handled in that fashion.[201] But the parties may have a practical reason for not wishing to do so, and in treating the question merely as one of construction, in so far as it removes the need to call expensive evidence. In the *Pacific Steam* case,[202] for example, the parties requested Sellers J to treat as a matter of construction

---

[198] [1997] 1 Lloyd's Rep. 273.   [199] At 282.
[200] *Stafford Allen & Sons Ltd.* v. *Pacific Steam Navigation Co.* [1956] 1 Lloyd's Rep. 105, 119 (Sellers J).
[201] Ibid.
[202] *Stafford Allen & Sons Ltd.* v. *Pacific Steam Navigation Co.*, above n. 193. See also, *The Merak* [1964] 2 Lloyd's Rep. 527, 537 (CA).

the question whether the port of Cristobal in the Panama Canal Zone was a US port for the purposes of American legislation, apparently to avoid calling expert evidence. Alternatively, a party who might be disadvantaged by any reference to foreign law might seek to argue that the question is one of construction.

Whether evidence of foreign law was required for the meaningful construction of a contract was directly in issue in the *Pacific Steam* case.[203] This concerned an attempt by the defendant shipowners to escape liability for damage suffered to the plaintiff's goods during carriage. Their case relied on the fact that the US Carriage of Goods by Sea Act 1936 did not govern. But by a clause paramount in the bill of lading, which was expressly governed by English law, the 1936 Act applied 'with respect to shipments from a port in the United States'. Everything turned on whether Cristobal, the port of shipment in the Panama Canal Zone, was such a port. Neither the trial judge nor the Court of Appeal doubted that it was and that the defendants were liable. But the interest of the case lies in the different lines of reasoning used to achieve that result. The parties were content to treat Cristobal's status as a matter of construction. For them the issue was simply the meaning of the bill of lading, which they said depended on how ordinary business men would regard it.[204] But Sellers J did not see the issue purely as one of construction. Indeed, he may not have regarded it as a question of construction at all. He took the unusual step of requiring the parties to produce authoritative evidence as to the status of Cristobal under United States law.[205] One reason was his concern that he might arrive at a result different from that which the United States government might take.[206] The other was the difficulty of knowing what ordinary business men might make of such a recondite issue. As he said:

> If ... the Court should properly look at the contract and construe it, I find the question of pure construction very difficult ... The shipowners who are regular traders may know a great deal about the United States' position in Cristobal and the Canal Zone generally, but whether the importers of a small parcel of ipecacuanha roots would know very much, I cannot conjecture.[207]

The Court of Appeal did not share Sellers J's concern that the question was not truly one of construction.[208] Importantly, however, they relied on evidence as to Cristobal's status in determining the parties' intentions. As such the decision confirms that the true question in such cases is not whether the issue is one of construction or of foreign law, but whether evidence of foreign law is necessary to construe the contract at all.

A further example is *The Glenbank*.[209] This concerned a charterer's agreement to indemnify a shipowner against liability to 'Argentine Maritime

---

[203] Above n. 193. [204] At 119. [205] Ibid. [206] Ibid. [207] At 120.
[208] [1956] 1 WLR 629, 632; 635; 637. [209] Above n. 194.

Pensions Tax'. The charterers had refused to reimburse the owners for the full amount which the latter had paid on the ground that the sum claimed by the Argentine authorities exceeded the amount lawfully due. This turned on whether the owners were entitled to reimbursement for the (higher) amount which they had actually paid. That in turn depended on whether the meaning of 'Argentine Maritime Pensions Tax' was to be determined by reference to Argentine law, as to which there was some dispute, or solely by reference to the parties' intentions. There was some difference of view as to whether the question was one of construction or of law. Straightforwardly, Diplock J saw the question as one of construction.[210] By contrast, at least some members of the House of Lords seem to have assumed as a matter of principle that a reference in a contract to a foreign tax or impost should be viewed strictly as one of foreign law.[211] But the position which best conforms with orthodoxy is perhaps that of Lord Guest. His view appears to be that some questions may ultimately have to be treated as questions of foreign law. But that is only because otherwise the construction of a contract may be impossible. As he expressed it, in remarks not free from ambiguity:

The question stated is, in my view, properly a question of law, the question being whether the owners had a right of recovery from the charterers under Clause 42 of the charterparty. But the meaning of 'Argentine Maritime Pensions Tax to be for the Charterer's account' involves the ascertainment of a question of fact, namely: 'What is the tax according to Argentine law?' A British court uninstructed cannot, in the absence of evidence, construe this expression.[212]

A contrasting illustration is provided by *The Stolt Sydness*.[213] There, as we have seen, US maritime law was incorporated into an English charterparty by virtue of a US clause paramount. The court accepted that US law did not apply as a matter of law but that its effect on the parties was a matter of construction. In particular, given that the US version of the Hague Rules was incorporated into the contract, was it necessary to interpret the relevant article relating to the limitation of actions in accordance with US law? Rix J observed that in cases such as *Pacific Steam* the construction of a contract might be 'profoundly affected' by relevant provisions of foreign law.[214] This was presumably because there was no meaningful answer to whether the US Carriage of Goods by Sea Act operated in respects of shipments out of the Panama Canal Zone except under US law. By contrast, an English court would have no difficulty interpreting the provisions of the Hague Rules in a meaningful way. They were as much part of English law as of US law. As such, even if English law and US law might differ in their interpretation of those rules, information was at least available such that

---

[210] At 140.   [211] At 243 (Lord Radcliffe); cf. *The Hamlet* [1924] P. 224 (CA).
[212] At 246.   [213] Above, n. 198.   [214] At 282.

an English court could interpret them without reference to foreign law. Where foreign law is incorporated into a contract there is no need to introduce evidence of foreign law where its provisions are also part of English law by virtue of an international convention.[215]

Whether evidence of foreign law is required in construing a private document therefore depends on the circumstances. Where the parties' intentions can sensibly be discerned by reference to a contract's applicable law, or where the parties might reasonably have a view on the meaning of the words in question, there may be no need for such evidence. But this may not always be the case. And, as *Pacific Steam* and *The Glenbank* imply, questions concerning foreign public policy or illegality are inherently more likely to be referred to foreign law. Certainly, in such cases comity might not be served if an English court were, in effect, to resolve legal questions in which a foreign state is closely interested without reference to the law in question. But the implications of the case law are ambiguous. Arguably, Sellers J's doubts about taking such a course in *Pacific Steam* were peculiarly connected with the facts of the case, so concerned was he about the case's awkward diplomatic dimension, and so alive to the unreality of discerning the parties' true intentions in any meaningful way. Similarly, it is clear that the House of Lords in *The Glenbank* found it hard to ignore the arbitrator's previous finding of fact that the tax paid had been unlawfully demanded.[216] How could they depart from a definitive ruling on Argentine law? Again, the reliance on expert evidence on appeal in *Pacific Steam* and in *The Glenbank* may owe something to the fact that such evidence was already available. Would they have been decided differently if no such evidence had been introduced?

But where does principle suggest the line should be drawn? On the one hand, it may seem inherently odd that questions of law should be referred merely to the parties' intentions. It may reflect an extreme application of the principle that foreign laws are facts, as well as a somewhat formalistic adherence to the rule that the construction of a document is a matter for its governing law. Some may also see in the practice insufficient respect for comity, not least because the effect of dispensing with foreign law is in effect that English law is applied. But several considerations favour the English approach. It may be preferable in principle not to treat questions of construction as implicating issues of foreign law, save in exceptional cases. It is simpler and cheaper to treat such questions as answerable by reference to the parties' intentions, without recourse to foreign legal evidence. It also respects principle not to refer to one law aspects of a contract which is governed by that of another, not least where the applicable law has been expressly chosen by the parties. Indeed, to do otherwise is effec-

[215] Ibid.   [216] At 245.

tively to change such a contract's substantive applicable law, at least for the limited purpose of reading such of its terms as may refer to foreign law.

But, in the end, the question whether evidence of foreign law may be required in construing a document has wider implications. At the level of theory, the authorities are richly suggestive, the differences of view which they disclose reflecting some familiar tensions. Should foreign laws be treated strictly as facts requiring evidence, or more flexibly, permitting other means of ascertainment? And if contracting parties, by express choice or by omitting to plead foreign law, evince a wish that a particular law shall govern their dealings, why should a court disturb their choice?

(e) Reading Foreign Materials

We have seen that English courts may dispense with expert testimony, and may form their own view of foreign law, by reference to those materials, typically legislative texts, on which an expert may have relied.[217] We are now concerned with a different but related question: might courts determine foreign law merely by reading such materials in the absence of expert evidence? It is commonly supposed that they cannot do so as a matter of principle,[218] and some familiar judicial statements are often deployed in support of this strict position. It has been said, for example that:

It is not sufficient to prove a foreign statute or code by a translation, and then leave the Court to place its own construction on it. The code must be interpreted by an expert in the foreign law.[219]

Again,

The evidence it is clear must be that of qualified experts in the foreign law. If the law is contained in a code or written form, the question is not as to the language of the written law, but what the law is as shown by its exposition, interpretation and adjudication.[220]

But such sweeping pronouncements are apt to mislead unless placed in context and set against the rather different practice revealed in the case

---

[217] See above, p. 194. Although expert evidence is generally employed in US Federal practice, there are cases where courts have determined foreign law by reference exclusively to foreign legal materials: *In Re Fotochrome, Inc.*, 377 F.Supp. 26, 29 (DCNY 1974); *Burnett v. Trans World Airlines, Inc.*, 368 F. Supp 1152 (DCN Mex. 1973); *Ramirez v. Autobuses Blancos Flecha Roja*, 486 F.2d. 493, 497 (5th Cir. 1973); Sass, (1981) 29 *Am Jl Comp L* 97, 108–10; Wright and Miller, *Federal Practice and Procedure: Civil 2d*, 645–646.

[218] Hodgkinson, 294; Howard, Crane and Hochberg, *Phipson on Evidence*, 14th edn., (1990), 837; Furmston, (1959) 22 *MLR* 317.

[219] *Buerger v. New York Life Assurance Co.* (1927) 96 LJKB 930, 940 (CA) (per Atkin LJ).

[220] *Lazard Brothers and Co. v. Midland Bank* [1933] AC 289, 297 (HL) (per Lord Wright).

law. For just as courts are able to replace expert testimony with their own assessment of foreign legal materials, so they are able to determine foreign law on the basis of such materials alone.[221] Indeed, it would be anomalous if a court were able to form a view of such materials for the purposes of rejecting the opinion of a qualified expert, but not in the absence of such an opinion. Strict adherence to the principle that foreign laws are facts, as such unknown and unknowable without assistance, would certainly prevent courts from determining foreign law on textual materials alone. But we have seen how elastic the fact doctrine is when applied to foreign law, making such a fundamentalist view inaccurate and uncompelling.[222] Indeed, to insist upon it is perhaps to place too much weight on some early cases of great authority which pre-date a more flexible approach.[223] To do so is also to misunderstand the scope of some familiar propositions by not locating the often expansive language of the courts in context. Take, for example, the cardinal principle that foreign laws, being facts, must be proved as such by expert evidence.[224] This properly describes the position where a court is otherwise unable to determine foreign law. But it need not foreclose the possibility of employing other techniques when a court is able to do so, as where the matter is within its inherent skill and competence.[225] Similarly, it is true that one who offers an opinion as to foreign law must be a qualified expert.[226] It is also true that when such testimony is offered it is primarily upon that, and not upon written materials, that a court should rely.[227] But neither principle implies that such evidence is always necessary. It is also clear that courts may not research foreign law themselves.[228] This prohibits them from finding foreign law entirely unaided, but not from examining for themselves such materials as may be in evidence. Consider, again, the principle that a court cannot weigh expert testimony by reference to material on which the expert who offers it has not relied.[229] That need not prevent a court from examining written material, where it has been tendered, and where it is the only evidence of foreign law, no experts having been called.

---

[221] O'Malley & Layton, 235. [222] See above, p. 66.
[223] The decision in *The Sussex Peerage Case* (1844) 11 Cl & F 85, which is apparently hostile to dispensing with expert evidence, pre-dates the developments described in this section and throughout the present chapter.
[224] e.g. *The Sussex Peerage Case*, op. cit., 114; *Nelson v. Bridport* (1845) 8 Beav. 527, 536; *Lazard Brothers and Co. v. Midland Bank* [1933] AC 289 (HL); *El Ajou v. Dollar Land Holdings plc* [1993] 3 All ER 717, 736.
[225] *Nelson v. Bridport*, op. cit., 536; *A/S Tallinna Laevauhisus v. Estonian State Steamship Line* (1947) 80 Ll L R.99, 108 (CA).
[226] *The Sussex Peerage Case*, above n. 223, 114; *Baron de Bode's Case* (1845) 8 QB 208, 250, 265; *Nelson v. Bridport*, op. cit.
[227] *Baron de Bode's Case*, op. cit., 250, 265.
[228] *Di Sora v. Phillipps* (1863) 10 HLC 624, 640.
[229] *Bumper Development Corp. Ltd. v. Comr. of Police* [1991] 1 WLR 1362, 1369 (CA).

Moreover, it may be that evidence of foreign law must be in the form of expert opinion. But foreign law may be established without formal evidence. More precisely, proof of foreign law may be dispensed with if the matter is within the scope of the court's inherent knowledge and competence. It should be unnecessary in principle in so far as a party's allegations are confined to matters of reasoning and construction. At least in straightforward cases this means that the interpretation of, say, foreign legislative texts ought to be permissible without the need for expert evidence. As we shall see, this does not depend, as might be supposed, on the agreement of the parties. It merely reflects the fact that courts are inherently skilled in legal reasoning and construction. Certainly, in so far as the determination of foreign law is exceptionally within a judge's knowledge or competence strict proof is unnecessary. This important principle was first recognized in *Nelson v. Bridport*,[230] the source of the English approach to foreign law. As Lord Langdale said, albeit in the context of how expert testimony should be assessed:

... the foreign law and its application ... must be proved, as facts are proved, by appropriate evidence, i.e. by properly qualified witnesses ... Such I conceive to be the general rule: but the cases to which it is applicable admit of great variety. Though a knowledge of foreign law is not to be imputed to the Judge, you may impute to him such a knowledge of the general art of reasoning, as will enable him, with the assistance of the Bar, to discover where fallacies are concealed, and in what cases he ought to require testimony more or less strict. If the utmost strictness were required in every case, justice might often have to stand still; and I am not disposed to say, that there may not be cases, in which the Judge may, without impropriety, take upon himself to construe the words of a foreign law, and determine their application to the case in question, especially if there should be a variance or want of clearness in the testimony.[231]

Vice Chancellor Wood makes the same distinction between matters of general reasoning and matters of foreign law in *Di Sora v. Phillipps*.[232] Having confirmed that expert evidence was required so as to establish propositions which were unique to the foreign system in question he said:

... then it is my province to apply ... any general rule of grammatical construction which may exist, or any general rule of law which is not peculiar to one code or another, but co-extensive with every system of jurisprudence.[233]

The scope of the court's competence is suggested by several decisions. Some concern the law of former colonies. *Re Baker's Trusts*[234] involved the construction of the Colonial Lunacy Acts 1867 and 1869, both Victorian statutes. No expert evidence was introduced but the court ruled on the law

---

[230] Above, n. 224.   [231] At 536.   [232] 33 LJ Ch. 129.   [233] At 130.
[234] (1871) LR.13 Eq. 168. This and the following cases were within the scope of the Colonial Laws Validity Act 1865 and the Evidence (Colonial Statutes) Act 1907, although those statutes are not referred to.

of Victoria entirely on counsel's oral submissions, assisted by copies of the Acts. This procedure was endorsed in later cases, most clearly in *Bonhote v. Bonhote*,[235] concerning the restitution of conjugal rights under the law of the Bahamas. The petitioner's counsel, in undefended proceedings, sought to prove the local statute without calling expert evidence, which the court permitted without comment.[236] Such informal determination of foreign law is especially appropriate where Commonwealth statutes are involved—or may have been at the time such cases were decided. But it has been applied to the laws of other common law countries. *Beatty v. Beatty*[237] turned on the status of a New York judgment for the payment of alimony. Rather than seek expert evidence the parties invited the court to refer to the judgment and a US Supreme Court decision. The court agreed, although Bankes and Sargent LJJ went further by relying also on a deposition obtained in New York which was included in the bundle of documents.[238] Scutton LJ was clearly concerned that this represented a departure from principle.[239] But, significantly, he complied with the parties' wishes because the alternative was a re-trial with expert evidence, at great expense to the parties. He reassured himself, as did Sargent LJ, by resorting to the fiction that, in ruling on foreign law without formal proof, the court's members were acting as arbitrators.

A decision involving the law of a civil law country is *Re Cohn*,[240] which turned on the nature of the presumption of death in German testamentary law. Uthwatt J apparently assumed that he could rule on an English translation of the German rule despite the absence of expert testimony. He concluded directly from its terms and its location in the relevant legislation that the disputed presumption was a matter of substance not evidence. *Re Cohn* was treated as authority for such an informal approach in *F & K Jabbour v. Custodian of Israeli Absentee Property*.[241] There both parties wished the court to apply Israeli law in the absence of expert evidence, on the basis only of an English translation of the local regulations. Pearson J, clearly concerned that he might not have the power to dispense with expert proof, considered the matter at length, consulting a range of authorities.[242] He concluded that he was entitled to do so, and construed the Israeli texts accordingly, assuming in the process that the Israeli canons of construction were the same as those of England.[243]

---

[235] [1920] WN 142; see also, *Re Barlow's Will* (1887) 36 Ch.D. 287 (CA); *Roe v. Roe* (1916) 115 LT 792; *L v. L* (1919) 36 TLR 148.

[236] At 142. [237] [1924] 1 KB 807 (CA). [238] At 813.
[239] At 814–815. [240] [1945] Ch. 5. [241] [1954] 1 WLR 139.

[242] Including a passage from *Dicey on Conflict of Laws*, 6th. edn, 868 (cited above, p.221), absent from the present edition, advocating flexibility in establishing foreign law, and *Lazard Brothers and Co. v. Midland Bank*, above n. 224, which is normally thought to be hostile to such an approach.
[243] At 144.

As such cases imply, it is usual to dispense with expert evidence only where relatively simple issues are involved, typically where no more is required than interpreting a statute. But the technique has been used in more difficult circumstances, as exemplified by *Stafford Allen & Sons Ltd.* v. *Pacific Steam Navigation Co.*[244] As we have seen,[245] this concerned whether goods were shipped from 'a port in the United States' for the purposes of the US Carriage of Goods by Sea Act. Sellers J allowed the parties to dispense with oral testimony in proving the scope of the Act,[246] reference being made instead to an extensive range of secondary sources in the form of textbooks, law reports and the written opinion of a US official. This was despite Sellers J's reservations about the adequacy of the evidence, given the diplomatic sensitivity of the question and the need for accuracy.[247] It was also a point of first impression on which US maritime law was unclear.[248] Difficult questions of foreign law were also in dispute in *Krajina* v. *Tass Agency*,[249] a case which turned on the Agency's juridical status under Russian law. Although a certificate from the Russian ambassador was in evidence this was limited in its scope and was not treated as conclusive. Despite encouragement from the court to introduce better evidence, no experts in the usual sense were called and the court was required, in effect, to determine Russian law on the basis of a translation of the statute creating the Agency.[250] As such, like *Pacific Steam*, *Krajina* illustrates how even difficult questions of foreign law may be addressed without expert testimony, although such a course is hardly satisfactory.

It is sometimes said that foreign materials may only be introduced without expert testimony with the agreement of the parties. It is certainly true that nothing precludes the parties from agreeing to dispense with formal proof of foreign law, and thus with expert evidence.[251] And such agreement, express or implied, is invariably present in the cases discussed above. It is also highly unlikely that one party would contest the opinion evidence of the other without calling an expert. Not least there is a risk that the court would inevitably favour the expert's opinion. But is such agreement necessary in principle? What if one party introduces expert evidence

---

[244] [1956] 1 Lloyd's Rep. 105, affd. [1956] 1 WLR 629 (CA).   [245] See above, p. 254.
[246] At 119.   [247] At 114, 119.   [248] At 116.
[249] [1949] 2 All ER 274 (CA). The paucity of evidence in *Krajina* may be explained by the difficulty of identifying suitable Russian law experts. In the circumstances, the ambassador's certificate was 'probably the best kind of evidence that can be produced', op. cit. 281.
[250] At 282–283.
[251] *Re Baker's Trusts*, above n. 234; *Bonhote* v. *Bonhote*, above n. 235; *Beatty* v. *Beatty*, above n. 237; *F. & K. Jabbour* v. *Custodian of Israeli Absentee Property*, above n. 241; *Stafford Allen & Sons Ltd.* v. *Pacific Steam Navigation Co.*, above n. 244; *Re Marshall* [1957] Ch. 507 (CA); *Re Sebba* [1959] Ch. 166; *Wilson, Smithett & Cope Ltd.* v. *Terruzzi* [1976] QB 683; *Dalmia Dairy Industries Ltd.* v. *National Bank of Pakistan* [1978] 2 Lloyd's Rep. 223 (CA). See also those cases in which such agreement may be implicit: *Re Barlow's Will*; above n. 235; *Re Cohn*, above n. 240. Dicey and Morris, 227–229.

but the other relies merely on foreign legal materials? Many cases imply that agreement is necessary,[252] and there is apparently clear authority that such informal evidence cannot be used to rebut the opinion of an expert, suggesting that both parties must employ informal evidence for it to be admissible.[253] But this is hard to reconcile with those cases in which a judge has rejected the uncontradicted opinion of an expert by reference exclusively to documentary material.[254] And if, as we have seen, the source of the court's power in all cases involving documentary evidence is their inherent ability to interpret foreign materials it ought to be irrelevant whether the parties have agreed to such a course. The true position may be that one party cannot express an opinion concerning foreign law, and thus seek to counter the evidence of an expert called by the other, without calling an expert. But there ought to be no reason why one party, without calling an expert, should not take issue with the reasoning of an expert called by the other, nor such an expert's interpretation of written materials. Such matters are within the province of the court, such that evidence of foreign law is not required.

Care must be taken with some of the decisions which illustrate how foreign law may be established on the basis of written materials. The colonial cases, all of which are old, may be special to a period when it was legitimate to assume that colonial statutes, although foreign, could be construed exactly as if they were English.[255] And in others, such as *Beatty* and *Pacific Steam*, the court derived assistance from specialist opinion as to foreign law, albeit that party experts were not called. But the informal determination of foreign law, by inviting a judge to rule directly on textual material, is an alternative to proof by expert testimony. It is cheaper and faster than proof by formal means. And it may be effective from the parties' perspective in establishing points of foreign law. This may not be so in complex cases, however, and the fact that most cases involving foreign law are relatively complex suggests why the procedure is seldom used.

7. CONCLUSION

This chapter, like the last, begs a question. The proof of foreign law by party-led expert testimony is notoriously costly and protracted, its deficiencies attracting frequent complaint from litigants and lawyers. Yet,

---

[252] Most prominently, *Beatty* v. *Beatty*, above n. 237, 815; *F. & K. Jabbour* v. *Custodian of Israeli Absentee Property*, above n. 241, 153; *Dalmia Dairy Industries Ltd.* v. *National Bank of Pakistan*, above n. 251, 236. Cheshire and North, 108.

[253] *Buerger* v. *New York Life Assurance Co.*, above n. 219, 940–941 (per Atkin LJ).

[254] See above, p. 194.

[255] But for a related example, see *Attorney-General of New Zealand* v. *Ortiz* [1984] AC 1, above, p. 249.

despite the existence of means of expediting or replacing proof by party experts, such alternatives are rarely, if ever, employed. Why is this so? Perhaps it is not always appreciated that such alternatives exist, so prevalent being the assumption that only expert proof is permitted. Or perhaps the reason is that expert evidence is undoubtedly treated by practitioners as the 'industry standard', the normal means of proof. This being so, it would be a bold adviser who employed a novel technique (however efficacious), with the attendant risk that such originality might be more costly, or might alienate the court, or might simply be ineffective, calling into question the decision to try something new. Certainly, market norms and the *opinio juris* are powerful constraints on legal practice and inhibitors of change. Or perhaps the reason lies in the dynamics of litigation. For, long before trial, the parties' advisers are likely to have obtained expert opinion on relevant questions of foreign law, if only to see whether reliance on foreign law is necessary or desirable. But, if a claim or defence is founded on a particular expert's view, it is almost inevitable that an adviser would seek to rely on that opinion in establishing the content of foreign law. Moreover, the obvious fact that English lawyers are unlikely to be familiar, or sufficiently familiar, with foreign law suggests that some form of expert opinion will always be relied upon in framing the proceedings. Granted, the cost of examining an expert is especially expensive. But if an expert will have to be employed anyway, why add delay and expense by employing another method of establishing foreign law?

The almost invariable use of expert testimony is also a tribute to its many advantages, or to the disadvantages of the alternatives. Such a technique which is, in a sense, inherently adversarial and combative is a perfect vehicle for allowing each party to present its case under foreign law. Certainly, to allow each party to mould how its case is put, and to cross-examine the other's expert, affords a greater degree of control over the presentation of evidence than any other mechanism. Resort to expert evidence also has less tactical benefits. It is a process of proof which is inherently suited to the argumentative nature of legal reasoning. As such its use may contribute to the accurate and effective determination of foreign law. It is also a just procedure, allowing litigants the opportunity to contest the contestable in a way which, say, the employment of an independent expert would not. Certainly, it is an important truth that English law does not compel the use of party experts in cases concerning foreign law, as the existence of the alternatives described in this chapter reveals. Litigants rely upon their own experts through choice, despite the existence of alternatives, a conclusion with important consequences for whether the English approach to foreign law requires reform.

But it remains important that it is possible to establish foreign law informally. It once again confirms how unwise it is to take too literally the principle that foreign laws are facts. More practically, such an informal approach offers a means to prove foreign law inexpensively in simple cases. This is especially valuable given the cost of civil proceedings and the need to identify procedures which offer a proportionate response to relatively straightforward disputes, thereby eliminating needless cost and delay. It is true, as we have seen, that this may mean less in practice than it promises. It may be true that complex issues of foreign law are best resolved by experts. But this does not mean that easier cases do not occur. Some of these, presumably, are resolved at needless expense in the traditional way. And many may never come to court precisely because it is assumed that experts must be employed, a procedure so inappropriate in such cases that the parties settle or desist. Certainly, it is hard to resist the suspicion that such informal techniques are under-exploited because it is wrongly assumed, as a matter of law, that experts must always be called. In reality, there may well be straightforward cases in which foreign law might be resolved without experts. But such cases will only become visible once it is appreciated that this is possible.

IX
Comparative Excursus

A comprehensive survey of national approaches to foreign law is beyond the scope of this discussion.[1] But it is necessary to draw selectively on the experience of other systems, the better to assess the English approach and to identify possible patterns for its reform. In doing so, whether foreign law must be applied (which is properly part of the choice of law process) must be separated from how it is established (which is a procedural matter).

1. THE APPLICATION OF FOREIGN LAW

In principle, any given legal system might belong to one of three categories, in terms of its approach to whether, if the governing law is foreign, that law must be introduced and established. It might adopt a mandatory model, in which the application of foreign law is always required, or a voluntarist model, in which it is invariably optional. Or, like most systems, it might assume a hybrid position, requiring it in some cases but not in others.

In the first category the application of foreign law is invariably required whatever the parties' wishes. In principle, this might oblige a party whose case depends upon foreign law to plead and prove that law, a failure to do so resulting in dismissal of the claim or defence. In this form the doctrine has sometimes been endorsed in common law jurisdictions.[2] Indeed, it should not be assumed that the mandatory introduction of foreign law is confined to civil law systems. But a mandatory approach is certainly more commonly associated with those civil law systems in which a court is

---

[1] See Zajtay, 'The Application of Foreign Law', Vol. III, Ch. 14, *International Encyclopedia of Comparative Law* (1972); Sass, (1968) 16 *Am. Jl. Comp. L.* 333; Kahn-Freund, *General Problems of Private International Law*, 2nd edn., (1976), 276–280; Kerameus, 'Revisibilitat Ausländischen Rechts, Ein Rechtsvergleichender Überblick', 99 *Zeitschrift für Zivilprozess* 116 (1986); Hartley (1996) 45 *ICLQ* 271; De Vos and Rechtberger, 'Transnational Litigation and the Evolution of the Law of Evidence', *General Report to the International Conference on Procedural Law*, Taormina, 1995.

[2] As formerly in the United States: *Cuba R. R. Co. v. Crosby*, 222 US 473 (1912); *Walton v. Arabian American Oil Co.*, 233 F.2d. 541 (2d. Cir. 1956), cert. den. 352 US 872 (1956); Sass, (1981) 29 *Am. Jl. Comp. L.* 97, 102–107.

obliged (perhaps with the parties' assistance) to introduce (and ascertain) foreign law on its own motion. This approach may depend on the scope of judicial notice in the system concerned. It may reflect an expansive application of the doctrine *iura novit curia*, perhaps originating in the theory that foreign and domestic law belong equally to the community of the law of nations, permitting no discrimination between them.[3] Or it may express a particular concept of adjudication and the judicial role. It may reflect the principle that a court should always adjudicate on the objectively correct legal basis, adjudication being viewed as more than merely the accommodation of private interests.[4] Alternatively, it may reflect the theory that the rules for choice of law are, or are generally, mandatory in character, such that they cannot be ousted by a mere omission to plead any foreign law which might be applicable thereunder.[5] Again, a mandatory approach to foreign law may reflect—or may once have reflected—the vested rights theory which at one time dominated the theory of private international law.[6] By holding that persons have certain rights enshrined in the governing law this implies that those rights must be strictly enforced.[7] Finally, such an approach may be a function of the forensic procedures available in a given system. In a procedural regime which confers wide investigatory powers upon a judge, there is no reason why these should not be applied to foreign law as to any other aspect of a case—a court introduces and establishes foreign law *ex officio* simply because it can. Conversely, in a system such as that in England, where it is traditionally for litigants to control the shape and nature of disputes, and to establish facts, a court may be procedurally disabled from establishing foreign law *ex officio*. Certainly, it may be thought that there is little point in a court requiring the introduction of foreign law if, in the end, it lacks the power or the means to establish its content without the parties' co-operation.[8]

---

[3] Savigny, VIII *System des heutigen Römischen Rechts* (1849), 24–28; Gierke, *Deutsches Privatrecht* (1895), 212.

[4] Sass, above n. 1, 358.

[5] This view finds support in the French literature, but has not apparently prevailed in the courts: Cass. civ. 2 March 1960, 49 *Rev. cr. dr. int. pr.* 97 (1960). See, Maury, 'La condition de la loi étrangère en droit français', *Travaux du Comité français de droit international privé*, IXe–XIII (1948–1952) 17 (1953); Motulsky, 'L'office du juge et la loi étrangère', 1 *Mélanges offerts à Jacques Maury* 337 (1960).

[6] As some early US cases suggest. Above, n. 2.

[7] In practice the logic of the vested rights theory is easily subverted, either by insisting that whether a foreign right exists at all is a question of fact, to be pleaded and proved, or by relying on the fiction that foreign law always 'applies', whether or not it is pleaded, although its content is presumed to be identical with that of the *lex fori*. See further, Sass, above n. 1; 338–339.

[8] Although this problem may be overcome. A court may enforce co-operation by threatening to dismiss a claim or defence which does not contain relevant arguments concerning foreign law. See above, p. 68.

But it would be wrong to seek, in any legal system, the master key which unlocks its approach to foreign law. Why a given system might adopt a mandatory approach to foreign law is seldom simply explained. Such an approach need not depend upon whether a court generally adopts an interventionist or a passive role in civil litigation, upon whether the system is, to speak loosely, 'adversarial' or 'inquisitorial'. In England, for example, where the course of proceedings has traditionally been shaped by the parties, the introduction of foreign law might still be obligatory if the relevant choice of law rule so requires. Admittedly, a litigant could not be required to rely upon foreign law, still less would the court research foreign law and apply it *ex officio*. But a litigant's omission to plead and prove foreign law might nonetheless lead to dismissal of the claim. Conversely, even a judge in the most case-managed of systems would not have to apply foreign law if the relevant conflicts rule is optional. Nor does a mandatory approach depend upon treating foreign laws as laws rather than facts, or on granting courts judicial notice of foreign laws. For even if a court must (or may) take judicial notice of all laws (local and foreign), it may be legitimate to allow litigants to waive such rights as they have thereunder by omitting to rely upon them. Moreover, even if a court has notice of foreign law this is irrelevant unless the law concerned is applicable. Whatever the scope of judicial notice, the application of foreign law is only compulsory if the appropriate choice of law rule is mandatory in nature. Nor is it enough that a court has a general duty to decide upon the correct legal basis. This simply begs the question of what that basis may be. In particular, it depends upon what is required by the relevant rules for choice of law. This important truth is illustrated by the recent French experience. Article 12 of the New Code of Civil Procedure might be understood as invariably requiring the introduction of foreign law by imposing a general requirement that a court must decide a case 'in accordance with the rules of law applicable to it'. Although the *Cour de Cassation* initially interpreted this as rendering all choice of law rules mandatory[9] it has since made clear that the application of such rules is only compulsory in specific situations.[10]

---

[9] Cass. civ. 11 and 18 October 1988, *Clunet* 1989.349, note Alexandre; *JCP* 1989.II.21327, note Courbe; *Rev. crit. dr. int. pr.* 1989.368.

[10] In cases involving unwaivable rights and choice of law rules contained in international conventions. Cass. civ. 4 December 1990, *Clunet* 1991.371, note Bureau; *Rev. crit. dr. int. pr.* 1991.558, note Niboyet-Hoegy; Cass. civ. 10 December 1991, *Rev. crit. dr. int. pr.* 1992.316, note Muir-Watt. See also previous attempts by the Cour de Cassation to define the scope of mandatory choice of law: Cass. civ. 25 Nov. 1986, *Rev. crit. dr. int. pr.* 1987.383, note Ancel and Laquette; JCP. 1988.II.20967, note Courbe; Cass. civ. 25 May 1987, *Clunet* 1987.927, note Gaudemet-Tallon; *Rev. crit. dr. int. pr.* 1988.60, note Lequette. See generally, Battifol and Lagarde, *Droit international privé*, 8th edn., (Paris, 1993), vol. 1, 531 ff; Loussouarn and Bourel, *Droit international privé*, 4th edn., (Paris, 1993), Ch.1; Mayer, *Droit international privé*, 5th edn., (Paris, 1994), 106–111; Ponsard, 'L'office du juge et l'application du droit étranger', *Rev. crit.*

Again, even when the application of the rules for choice of law is in principle mandatory, this does not mean that the introduction of foreign law is necessarily required. That a court must apply the relevant conflicts rule says nothing about the content of that rule and particular choice of rules may be either optional or compulsory. They may themselves permit litigants to select the *lex fori* as an issue's governing law, if only in limited types of case. This achieves the same result as an English court would obtain by applying the *lex fori* in default of foreign law being pleaded. But, in substituting local law for an otherwise applicable foreign law, such a technique employs choice of law methodology. In so doing it preserves the principle that the *lex causae* must be introduced and applied, in theory if not in practice. But it may also erode that principle to a considerable degree if the category of cases in which a choice of the *lex fori* is permitted is widely drawn.[11]

On the other hand, even if foreign laws are treated as facts it is possible to treat them effectively as if they are laws by embracing them within an expanded concept of judicial notice.[12] And even if the content of foreign law is treated as an issue of fact there is no reason why litigants should not be obliged to introduce and to prove that law. The factual status of foreign law may certainly condition how it is pleaded and proved, but not whether it should be pleaded and proved at all. That foreign laws are facts in France, for example, is no obstacle to the requirement that foreign law must sometimes be introduced.[13] Equally, as we have seen in Chapter III, foreign law may occasionally have to be pleaded and proved in English law despite its factual character. Indeed, even if foreign laws are facts, the question whether or not foreign law applies in a given case is one of law. Whether the introduction of foreign law is mandatory is ultimately not a

dr. int. pr. 1990. 607; Bureau, 'L'application d'office de la loi étrangère, Essai de synthese', *JDI*. 2, 1990, 317; Pedone, ed., *Droit international privé, Travaux du Comité français de droit international privé*, Annees 1990–1991, (Paris, 1992), 19; Lagarde, *Rev. crit. dr. int. pr.* 1994. 332.

[11] Party autonomy may be respected, even in cases not involving a contractual dispute. It is possible in the Netherlands with regard to all patrimonial matters: Hoge Raad, 19 November. 1993, NJ 1994, 622; NILR 1994, 363, note Duintjer Tebbens. It is permitted in tortious disputes in Switzerland, provided the *lex fori* is selected (Swiss Law on Private International Law 1987, Art.132; Symeonides, (1989) 37 *Am. J. Comp. L.* 187), as it may be in Germany (BGH 26 March 1964, IPrax 1964, 201; Kahn-Freund, (1974) *Recueil des Cours*, 139, 341 n. 44).

[12] A characteristic technique for departing from strict adherence to the fact doctrine in common law systems is to extend judicial notice to foreign law. See, e.g., the state practice in the United States described by Miller, (1967) 65 *Mich LR* 615, 624 ff; Sass, above n. 1, 341–346; Schlesinger, (1973) 59 *Cornell LR* 1, 16–23. For a recent example see the Quebec Civil Code of 1994, Article 2809: 'Judicial notice may be taken of the law of other provinces or territories of Canada and of that of a foreign state, provided it has been pleaded . . .'. In the United States Rule 44.1 of the Federal Rules of Civil Procedure eradicates the effects of the fact doctrine without reference to the scope of judicial notice; see below, p. 315.

[13] Battifol and Lagarde, above n. 10, 531–534; Loussouarn and Bourel, above n. 10, 244–248.

procedural matter but one of private international law. It turns on whether the rules for choice of law, or any such rules in particular, are imperative in nature.[14] The introduction of foreign law may be required even in systems where foreign laws are designated as facts if that is what the relevant conflicts rule ordains. As this confirms, there are several alternative justifications for requiring the introduction and proof of foreign law. Indeed, in many systems a combination of factors explains this result. But the ultimate question, whatever the conceptual basis for the answer, is whether any particular choice of law is mandatory, such that the application of a foreign applicable law cannot be avoided.

At first sight, German law classically exemplifies a mandatory approach to foreign law.[15] Indeed, its stance is reinforced by several assumptions each of which might, by itself, lead to such a position. Foreign law is regarded as law,[16] which, by virtue of the doctrine *iura novit curia*, imposes a duty on the court to apply it.[17] Although this does not imply actual knowledge of foreign law the court's duty is made effective by its accompanying power to determine foreign law with or without the parties' co-operation.[18] It does not know the content of foreign law but it has the means to know it. But merely to equate foreign law with domestic law need not compel the introduction and application of foreign law. Such a result assumes either that all rules of domestic law must always be applied or, more probably, that the rules of private international law are treated as mandatory. The rules of private international law are therefore treated as mandatory in German law, except in so far as they themselves permit litigants to choose the governing law. This ensures that a court, having notice of German conflicts rules, has no choice but to give effect to them.

A second possibility is that a system might regard the introduction of foreign law as invariably voluntary. This is commonly associated with

---

[14] The position in France, whereby a court is under no general duty to apply foreign law *ex officio*, originates in the view, endorsed in the famous *Bisbal* case, that the rules of private international are not mandatory, not being *d'ordre public*: Cass. civ., 12 May 1959, *Rev.crit.dr.int.pr.* 1960.62. This has been confirmed as the general rule: Civ. 4 Dec. 1990, *Clunet* 1991.371, note Bureau; *Rev. crit. dr. int. pr.* 1991.558, note Niboyet-Hoegy; Lagarde, *Rev. crit. dr. int. pr.* 1994.332.

[15] For expositions of the German approach see, Stein & Jonas, *Kommentar zur Zivilprozessordnung*, 21st edn., (Tübingen, 1997), Vol. III, Section 293 (Leipold); Zöller, *Zivilprozessordnung*, 19th edn., (Cologne, 1995), Section 293 (Geimer); Sass, above n. 1, 357–359; Schlesinger, Baade, Damaska, and Herzog, *Comparative Law*, 5th ed., (Mineola, 1988), 224–228; Hartley, above n. 1, 275–276.

[16] The equation between the two may be implied by the terms of § 293, *Zivilprozessordnung* (ZPO), which refers both to foreign law and 'customary law and municipal ordinances', the latter being a reference to the laws of Germany. The theory of non-discrimination between foreign and local law is associated with Savigny; above n. 3.

[17] Kralik, 'Iura novit curia und das ausländisches Recht', 3 *Zeitschrift fur Rechtsvergleichung* (1962) 75, 83.

[18] See below, p. 278.

common law systems and with the idea that the pleading of foreign law is a matter of procedure. To reduce the application of foreign law to a procedural issue is itself a feature of the characterization of foreign laws as facts,[19] which implies that the application of foreign law is no more than a question of evidence. Taken literally this suggests (improbably) that the rules of private international law can never require the introduction of foreign law because *procedurally* litigants are always free to ignore the relevant choice of law rule. As we have seen, however, it is unlikely that this analysis is correct even in English law.[20] Not least it may confuse the question *how* foreign law is pleaded—in what form, using what language—with *whether* it must be introduced. The former may be a matter of procedure, but the latter is properly a choice of law issue and depends on whether the relevant conflicts rule is mandatory in form. Certainly, although English law is commonly assumed to adopt a voluntarist approach, and largely does so in practice, it is unlikely that it (or any other system) actually does so without qualification. True, it may start with the assumption that the *lex fori* is the applicable law unless foreign law is relied upon and proved.[21] But this position is modified in so far as the relevant choice of law rule may be mandatory, requiring the introduction and application of foreign law. Possible examples of such mandatory conflicts rules may be those concerning contracts under the 1980 Rome Convention, and those concerning jurisdiction under the Brussels and Lugano Conventions. It is also not beyond argument that it is required in defamation claims, and in matters involving status, illegality and foreign limitation periods. Whatever their merit, that such possibilities exist at all implies that the English principle of voluntary pleading is far from being an immutable rule.[22]

The third category comprises legal systems which adopt a hybrid approach, the introduction of foreign law being required in some cases but not in all. As the foregoing discussion suggests, most countries employ such a mixed regime, although those that do so may differ significantly in where and why the line is drawn. English law, as we have seen, cleaves to the doctrine that foreign laws are facts, which combines (importantly) with the principle that facts are unknown to the court and so must be pleaded and proved. In consequence, it is only in those rare cases in which a choice of law rule is mandatory, such that the *lex causae* must be applied, that foreign law must be introduced.[23] Moreover, in the absence of a

---

[19] This came about in English law for pragmatic reasons. As English courts inevitably lacked knowledge of foreign laws such laws were equated with facts, of which a judge equally lacks knowledge in the absence of pleading and proof. Moreover, lacking knowledge of foreign laws their application was only possible at all by allowing them to be put in evidence as facts: *Mostyn* v. *Fabrigas* (1774) 1 Cowp. 161, 174.

[20] See above, p. 70.

[21] Currie, (1958) 58 *Col. L. Rev.* 964; Ehrenzweig, (1960) 58 *Mich. L. Rev.* 637.

[22] See above, Chapter III.   [23] See above, Chapter III.

choice of law rule which is expressly mandatory, no other justification exists for requiring the introduction of foreign law. As well as lacking the doctrine *iura novit curia*, English law lacks those general principles which might also justify such mandatory introduction in other systems. Notably, it has no general doctrine of unwaivable personal rights which might otherwise require the introduction of foreign law in cases involving personal status or capacity.[24] Indeed, this suggests an important contrast between English law and many other systems. The mandatory status of any particular choice of law rule depends in most civil law systems upon some ulterior explanation, such as a conception of the court's role or the view that certain rights are indefeasible. But in English law the mandatory nature of any particular choice of law rule is simply a matter of interpretation, depending on the wording and purpose of the rule in question.

Other systems define the area where mandatory introduction is required somewhat differently—and far more widely. Sometimes the line is drawn by reference to a general judicial discretion to introduce foreign law whenever desirable.[25] The decision whether foreign law must be considered is thus left to the court to judge on a case-by-case basis. In many systems, however, doctrine draws a sharper distinction between situations where the introduction of foreign law is mandatory and those where it is not. Typically, the line is drawn by creating an exception to the mandatory introduction of foreign law where, in certain types of case, the parties are allowed to agree to the *lex fori* as the applicable law.[26] This may

[24] See above, p. 119.
[25] As in certain US states and, possibly, under Rule 44.1 of the Federal Rules of Civil Procedure, although it is unlikely that a court would act unless foreign law is introduced by one of the parties. Rule 44.1 is silent on the matter. Its accompanying commentary contemplates discretionary introduction: *Notes of Advisory Committee on Rules, Fed.Civ. P. 44.1*. See Kaplan, (1968) 81 *Harv. L. Rev.* 591, 616; Miner, (1995) 43 *Am. Jl. Comp. L.* 581, 582. See, *Bartsch v. Metro-Goldwyn-Mayer Inc.*, 391 F.2d. 150, 155 n. 3 (2d. Cir.), cert. denied, 393 US 826 (1968). The power was assumed (but not exercised) in *Vishipco Line v. Chase Manhattan Bank NA*, 660 F.2d 854, 860 (2d Cir. 1981), cert. denied., 459 US 976 (1982). *Vishipco* was applied in *Kleartex (USA), Inc. v. Kleartex*, SDN BHD, 1994 WL 733688, at *15 n. 5 (SDNY June 9, 1994), cited in Miner, op. cit., 583. An example of state practice is the rule in force in New York which provides that 'Every court may take judicial notice without request of . . . the laws of foreign countries or their political subdivisions': *NY Civ. Prac. Law. R.* 451(b) (McKinney, 1963). See further, Schlesinger, above n. 12, 20–21; Sass, above n. 1, 102–107. The French courts formerly adopted a discretionary approach, being permitted but not required to introduce and research foreign law *ex officio*: Cass. civ., 2 March 1960, *Rev. crit. dr. int. pr.* 1960.97, note Battifol; Sass, above n. 1, 354–356. They still do so where the introduction of foreign law is not required. See the *Société Damart* case, Cass. civ. 5 October 1994, *Rev. crit. dr. int. pr.* 1995.60, note Bureau.
[26] As in the Netherlands, which starts from a mandatory position similar to the German but allows litigants to agree to the application of the *lex fori* in disputes concerning patrimonial matters (*vermogensrechtelijke zaken*): Hoge Raad, 19 Nov. 1993, NJ 1994, 622; NILR 1994, 363, note Duintjer Tebbens. An implicit choice of Dutch law is also permitted in divorce proceedings: Law of 25 March 1981, Arts. 1(2) and 1(4); Van Rooij and Polak, *Private International Law in the Netherlands* (Deventer, 1987), 216.

be a simple reflection of their general freedom to choose the applicable law, or it may represent a special concession permitting selection of the law of the forum.[27]

Alternatively, some legal systems adopt the position that, even if not universally required, the mandatory introduction of foreign law is obligatory in certain cases. In jurisdictions of the latter type it is not necessarily—or not merely—the principle *iura novit curia* which conditions their response, nor (as in England) the existence of specific, mandatory choice of law rules. Rather it is the theory that certain species of individual rights, such as those concerning personal status, are indefeasible. Being unwaivable, even at the instance of the affected party, rights of this type arising under foreign law may not be abrogated by an omission to rely upon that law. In France, for example, a court has no general obligation to apply foreign law *ex officio*, apparently because rules for choice of law are not generally treated as *d'ordre public*, as such not demanding mandatory application.[28] But, as we have seen, the introduction of foreign law is required in cases where the rights in dispute have an unwaivable character, as they generally would if they concerned personal status or capacity, or where they otherwise have a non-economic nature.[29] It is also required where the relevant choice of law rule is contained in an international convention.[30]

The category of legal systems which require the introduction of foreign law in some cases, but not in all, may be further subdivided into those in which its introduction in non-mandatory cases is exclusively a matter for the parties,[31] and those in which a court always retains a discretion to introduce foreign law *ex officio*.[32] In the former case the treatment of such situations mirrors that in England, the *lex fori* applying in default of foreign law being introduced by the parties. In the latter there is a possibility, more or less real depending on the jurisdiction, that a court may introduce foreign law on its own motion.

A particularly subtle approach, which warrants special mention, is contained in the 1987 Swiss Law on Private International Law.[33] This

---

[27] As e.g. in Switzerland in connection with actions in tort: Swiss Law on Private International Law 1987, Article 132.

[28] This would seem to follow from the *Bisbal* case, above n. 14.

[29] Cass. civ. 4 Dec. 1990, *Clunet* 1991.371, note Bureau; *Rev. crit. dr. int. pr.* 1991.558, note Niboyet-Hoegy; Lagarde, *Rev. crit. dr. int. pr.* 1994.332.

[30] Ibid.

[31] In Switzerland the Law on Private International Law 1987, Art. 16(2), provides that *'Le droit suisse s'applique si le contenu du droit etranger ne peut pas etre establi'*.

[32] As in France, where difficulty has arisen as to whether a court should determine foreign law *ex officio* where it has introduced foreign law although not required to do so: see the *Société Damart* case, Cass. civ. 5 October 1994, *Rev. crit. dr. int. pr.* 1995.60, note Bureau.

[33] See further, Symeonides, (1989) 37 *Am. Jl. Comp. L.* 187; Samuel, (1988) 37 *ICLQ* 681; North, *Essays in Private International Law* (Oxford, 1993), 188.

combines three principles with some sophistication. It adheres to the doctrine that the application of foreign law is generally mandatory, but respects the parties' right to choose the applicable law, yet also protects those legal rights of an unwaivable nature. It begins with the assumption that foreign law must generally be applied.[34] But it defines three categories of case in which this is unnecessary. In two situations the exclusion of the law which would otherwise apply is achieved by adopting choice of law methodology. Where the general rules of private international law permit an express choice of law, such as in connection with contract, the parties may at the time of proceedings vary their choice by selecting the *lex fori*.[35] Again, in tortious disputes, where necessarily no choice of law will have been made before the wrong is done, the parties may agree that the *lex fori* (but only the *lex fori*) may be applied.[36] But in a third type of case the exclusion of foreign law is achieved procedurally, as it would be in English law. Provided the rights in question are of a patrimonial character the *lex fori* will be applied in default of its being relied upon and proved.[37] By this means the 1987 Law expresses a particular conception of the judicial role, a theory of indefeasible rights and a view on the scope of party autonomy in choice of law. But it also reinforces an important truth. There is nothing particular about the question when the introduction of foreign law is required or not. The answer depends partly on general principles of private international law, for in so far as litigants are free to select the applicable law they should be free to choose the law of the forum. And it depends partly on the extent to which a given legal system treats rights of a certain type as indefeasible, for if a species of right may not be waived in domestic law, nor should it be waived if it arises under foreign law.

As these observations suggest, it is not necessarily an easy matter to allocate particular jurisdictions to one category or another, such is the awkward tension between theory and practice. Germany, for example, belongs in principle firmly to the first category,[38] but, as occurs in other systems, compulsory resort to foreign law may be avoided, at least in proceedings in contract and tort, if the parties' omission to argue foreign law is understood as a choice of German law as the applicable law.[39] Although this leaves the principle of mandatory introduction untouched, by turning the issue into one of choice of law rather than of procedure, it nonetheless

---

[34] Article 16(1): '*Le contenu du droit etranger est establi d'office*'.   [35] Ibid.
[36] Article 132.
[37] Article 16(2); Bucher, *Droit International Privé Suisse* (1995), Vol. I/2, Section 375 ff.
[38] Section 293 ZPO.
[39] BGH 15.1.86; BGH 18.1.1988, NJW 1988, 1592. This position is controversial (see Schack, 6 IPRax 292, 272 (1986), Von Bar, *Internationales Privatrecht*, vol. II (Munich, 1987–1991), 341, but is consistent with the 1980 Rome Convention on the Law Applicable to Contractual Obligations, Article 3. In France such an agreement would presumably take effect as a procedural agreement within Article 12(3), New Code of Civil Procedure.

amounts to a practical threat to its stability. By contrast, as we have seen, English law is normally thought of as belonging to the second category, although there may be situations in which foreign law must be pleaded even in England. Again, Federal Courts in the United States are apparently empowered, but not required, to introduce foreign law although neither party has invoked it, illustrating the third model described above.[40] In reality, however, they seldom, if ever, exercise their discretion to do so, bringing their practice into line with that in England.[41] Finally, although in France the introduction of foreign law is required in cases involving indefeasible rights, the category of cases in which the waiver of legal rights is permitted is potentially large, possibly embracing cases affecting property, contract and tort, although not those affecting personal status and capacity.[42] The effect is to allow litigants not to introduce foreign law in a significant number of cases.

As this implies, the key question is not whether the introduction of foreign law is mandatory or optional. Nor is it whether a given system expresses its position procedurally, by defining the consequences of a failure to establish foreign law, or substantively, by describing the scope of choice in the conflicts process. The result may be the same however achieved. The fundamental question is not *how* the line between choice and compulsion is drawn, but *where*. The foregoing outline reveals a diversity of treatments and doctrinal assumptions, but also a marked similarity in the outcomes achieved. Certainly, those systems which favour the compulsory introduction of foreign law also recognize the importance of party autonomy. Some allow the parties to choose the *lex fori* as the governing law, some permit them not to introduce foreign law in a potentially wide area of law in which rights of a personal and indefeasible nature are not involved, others which allow courts to introduce foreign law in their discretion reveal little evidence that this is ever done. These exceptions to the mandatory application of foreign law are sometimes wide in their scope, effectively approximating some very different approaches with the English practice.

Overall, therefore, the English approach to the introduction of foreign law is somewhat closer to its foreign counterparts than might be supposed, in practice if not in theory. Like most systems it provides for the compulsory introduction of foreign law in some cases but not in others, albeit that this seldom, if ever, occurs. And, as in any system, foreign law will be introduced by the parties where this is necessary. The practical

---

[40] See, above, n. 25.

[41] Sass, (1981) 29 *Am. Jl. Comp. L.* 97, 102–107; 9; Wright and Miller, *Federal Practice & Procedure: Civil 2nd*, para. 2247 (1995).

[42] The introduction of foreign law is voluntary if the case concerns '*une matiere ou les parties ont la libre disposition de leurs droits*': Lagarde, *Rev. crit. dr. int. pr.* 1994.332, 337.

difference between English law and others is thus a matter of degree. As such, the question to which comparative law might offer a solution is not whether the introduction of foreign law should be made compulsory in England for, in practice, few systems (if any) insist on this with unwavering strictness. Rather, it is whether the balance, which in English law so dramatically favours party choice, may be regarded as the right one. This involves a consideration not of general principles but of specific cases. Should foreign law be pleaded in contractual disputes, for example, because the 1980 Rome Convention so requires? Must it be introduced in any case involving personal status because public policy is involved? As we shall see,[43] it is likely that English law survives the charge that it leans too far towards party choice in the introduction of foreign law. Largely, this is because of sound, independent reasons for favouring such a course, reasons recognized in other systems to the (often considerable) extent to which they achieve the same result. But the justification lies also in comparative law. For the voluntarism revealed in the English approach is true to English law's most basic assumptions about the court's role in litigation, assumptions absent in many other systems. So too, the element of compulsion visible in other systems is a proper and necessary reflection of elements which English law lacks, such as the expansive doctrine of *iura novit curia*, or the idea of non-defeasible personal rights enshrined in many civil law systems.[44] In an important sense, therefore, to criticize the English approach to foreign law is merely to condemn its attitude to civil procedure, its concept of judicial notice and its lack of a distinction between patrimonial and non-patrimonial rights. English law treats foreign law as it does because, given its underlying assumptions, it has to do so. More tellingly, it does not handle foreign law as other legal systems do because, lacking their distinctive features, it cannot, and need not do so.

But three notes of caution must be sounded. First, English law may be similar to other systems in the overall shape of its response, sometimes requiring the application of foreign law, sometimes not. But the mandatory introduction of foreign law remains firmly an exception to the basic rule that the *lex fori* applies, the opposite being true of many other systems. Such mandatory rules are also rare. Secondly, common law and civil law systems are likely to differ in an important sense in their treatment of foreign law. In some countries the fact that foreign law must be introduced imposes a duty on the court, not on the parties, to establish foreign law.[45] In others, although the responsibility for introducing foreign law may rest with the parties, a court may cure the defect by determining foreign law *ex*

---

[43] See below, p. 292.
[44] See e.g., Lagarde, *Rev. crit. dr. int. pr.* 1994.332, 337 (France); Bucher, above n. 37, paras. 375–379 (Switzerland).
[45] As in Germany.

officio. In English law, however, it is likely that the effect of a failure to comply with a requirement to plead foreign law is simply that the defective claim or defence will be dismissed.[46] English courts do not possess the investigative power to apply foreign law *sua sponte*.[47] Thirdly, it should not be imagined, merely because the pleading of foreign law is generally voluntary, that English litigants normally omit to introduce foreign law. This often occurs, as Chapter V reveals, but there are numerous cases in which foreign law is pleaded for the obvious reason that a claim or defence would otherwise fail. This further reduces the practical difference between the common law approach and its civil law counterparts, in so far as any litigant is bound to rely on foreign law in such cases. Admittedly, many systems deny the parties a general freedom to assess the efficiency and tactical benefit of introducing foreign law where it is not essential to their case, which is a singular feature of the common law approach. But even in such systems a claimant has an obvious, if drastic, remedy—they need not sue at all. Certainly, it is wrong to assume that English litigants invariably try to avoid a case's foreign dimension, just as it is simplistic to suppose that, say, German litigants are regularly required to consider foreign law against their will.

2. ESTABLISHING FOREIGN LAW

Inevitably, examination of the methods of proving foreign law in other countries reveals a diversity of approaches, reflecting deep-rooted differences between contrasting systems of procedure and evidence. Indeed, there is a risk that in comparing how foreign law is established we merely repeat familiar truths about the fabric of civil procedure in different countries. But three questions yield particularly illuminating information about the handling of foreign law. First, whose responsibility is it to establish foreign law? Secondly, what is the nature and value of expert assistance in different systems? Thirdly, what are the consequences of a failure in proof?

(a) Who Establishes Foreign Law?

Consider first who bears responsibility for establishing foreign law, the court or the parties. It is easy to assume that the answer lies in some fundamental assumptions about the conduct of litigation. In most common law systems it is the parties, and in many civil law systems it is the court. But this conceals a more intriguing picture. It has long been the case in

---

[46] See above, p. 68.   [47] But see above, p. 153.

French law that the burden of establishing foreign law is upon the parties, although this has become more controversial now that the introduction of foreign law has become mandatory in certain cases.[48] There is also no reason why a court in a common law system should not conduct its own research into foreign law. The possibility is implicit in Rule 44.1 of the American Federal Rules of Civil Procedure which dispenses with the traditional notion that foreign law must be strictly proved as a question of fact.[49] Even English courts may do so in a limited sense, in so far as they may dispense with expert evidence which they consider to be inadequate and establish foreign law on the basis of such written material as may be before the court.[50] Conversely, the parties are seldom prohibited from assisting the court in establishing foreign law in those system in which the responsibility is primarily with the judge.[51] Indeed, it is in their interests to do so, and so persuade the court that their version of foreign law is correct. But this is not to deny that real differences exist between approaches which are traditionally party-led and those which are not. It is apparent that American courts seldom if ever exercise their power to research foreign law,[52] and this may be unlikely unless the parties have themselves failed adequately to do so. And even when litigants in civil law systems assist the court in establishing foreign law the court is not confined—as it would be confined in, say, English law—to the issues and the material introduced by the parties. Certainly, their role is to assist the process, not to manage it. Moreover, whatever the relative roles of court and litigant in technical terms, the assumptions of those involved as to whose task it is to establish foreign law may differ significantly between different systems.

(b) The Role of Experts

Most legal systems provide, to varying degrees and with variable results, a range of optional techniques for establishing foreign law. Contrary to what is commonly supposed, few insist that a single method should be employed in all cases. This encourages, if it does not always ensure, proportionality between the sophistication of the mode of proof employed and the difficulty of the case.[53] The point emerges strongly from a comparison of four contrasting systems, the English, the German, the French, and the American. As we have seen, it is erroneous to imagine that English law allows foreign law to be established only by taking evidence from party-led experts.[54] This method is the most commonly used. And it may

---

[48] De Boer, 'Facultative Choice of Law', (1996) *Recueil des Cours*, vol. 257, 265.
[49] Wright and Miller, above n. 41, 648–650, and material cited at n.14 thereto.
[50] See above, pp. 194–200.   [51] As in Germany: Stein & Jonas, above n. 15, paras. 47–48.
[52] Pollack, (1974) 26 *Am. Jl. Comp. L.* 470, 471.
[53] For consideration of the concept of proportionality see, below, p. 299.
[54] See above, Chapter VIII.

be incorrect to speak of the *proof* of foreign law by other means. But resort might be made to foreign legal materials to establish foreign law. It may also be possible to avoid the strict requirements of proof by characterizing the matter as one of construction, or as falling within the court's inherent knowledge or expertise.

In a similar way it is wrong to suppose that German law, often seen as the best exemplar of this approach, invariably proves foreign law by employing court experts.[55] The basic rule is widely drawn:

> The law in force in another country, customary law and municipal ordinances require proof only in so far as they are unknown to the court. In ascertaining these legal rules the court is not confined to the evidence adduced by the parties; it is authorised to use such other sources of information and to make such orders as may be necessary for that purpose.[56]

In practice it is in the court's discretion to decide which mode of proof best suits any particular case.[57] Where the law of another German-speaking country is in dispute, but seldom otherwise, personal research by the judge is possible. In other cases of a simple nature resort may be had to authoritative certification by a foreign embassy, or to foreign legal materials, or to previous German decisions, or the published opinions of experts employed in other proceedings.[58] In more complex cases, some German courts—unlike most other European courts—are prepared to resort to foreign assistance under the 1968 European Convention on Information on Foreign Law,[59] although commentators tend not to favour this method.[60] Most commonly, however, foreign law is proved in German courts by independent, court-appointed experts. The parties may agree on such an expert, an agreement which binds the court, but, absent such agreement, the court will nominate its own expert.[61] The expert may, at a party's request, be required to attend the hearing and be questioned,[62] although it is unclear what use is made of this possibility.[63] Traditionally, such court experts were normally German academics, often from one of the leading university institutes of comparative law. It is now clear, however, that the evidence of local scholars may not be employed in matters involving a

---

[55] For accounts of German practice see, above, n. 15. [56] § 293, ZPO.

[57] Stein and Jonas, above n.15, paras. 37–38.

[58] A collection of such opinions is published annually: Ferid, Kegel and Zweigert, eds., *Gutachten zum internationalen und ausländischen Privatrecht*.

[59] Bülow-Böckstiegel, *Internationaler Rechstverkehr in Zivil- und Handelssachen*, (Munich, 1990), § 380; Rodger and van Doorn, (1997) 46 *ICLQ* 151, 160.

[60] Stein & Jonas, above n. 15, paras. 42, 81.

[61] § 404(4) ZPO. The remuneration of the expert is set by statute: Section 3, Gesetz über die Entschädigung von Zeugen und Sachverständigen. For a critical account of this procedure see, Ehrenzweig, *Private International Law* (1967), 191.

[62] § 441 ZPO; BGH 1975, NJW 2142, 2143; Stein and Jonas, above n. 15, paras. 43–44; Thomas and Putzo, *Zivilprozessordnung*, 17th edn., (1991), para. 411, No. 3.

[63] Stein and Jonas, above n. 15, paras. 43–44.

practical knowledge of foreign law. In such cases a foreign expert is appropriate.[64]

Far from adopting a single approach, therefore, German law offers a finely calibrated set of evidential techniques, each appropriate to cases of different levels of complexity, the decision as to which should be used lying with the court. Additional flexibility is also supplied by the likelihood that the parties will assist the court in its task,[65] and by the possibility that the matter may be referred to a judge with particular expertise in handling foreign law.[66] French law also offers some flexibility, although to a lesser extent.[67] The normal method of proof is by means of written submissions from a qualified person (*certificats de coutume*), on which—in accordance with general principle—cross-examination is not possible.[68] From the parties' perspective, however, this method is regarded as expensive and cumbersome, such that litigants may simply ask a court to determine foreign law by its own researches.[69] Moreover, the tendency for *certificats de coutume* to be seen as unreliable and overly partial means that they are often perceived as an ineffective source of evidence. Certainly, they are designedly argumentative in a way in which, say, English opinion evidence is not. As such, French courts sometimes appoint an independent expert to provide objective evidence of foreign law.[70]

Several techniques for establishing foreign law also exist in the United States, each suited in principle to different types of case. In the Federal Courts this flexible approach is underwritten by Rule 44.1 of the Federal Rules of Civil Procedure which expressly frees the courts from the limitations imposed by the formal rules of evidence.[71] It provides that the court, 'in determining foreign law may consider any relevant material or source, including testimony, whether or not submitted by a party or admissible under the Federal Rules of Evidence'. This accommodates a wide range of evidential techniques. Resort may be had to the court's own knowledge,[72]

---

[64] BGH 21.1.1991, NJW 1991, 1418, 1419; Samtleben, 'Der unfähige Gutachter und die ausländische Rechtspraxis', NJW 1992, 3057, 3058.
[65] See above, p. 277.
[66] Siehr, (1977) 25 *Am. Jl. Comp. L.* 663.
[67] See generally, Battifol and Lagarde, above n. 10, 537 ff; Mayer, above n. 10, 127–138; Herzog, (1978) 18 *Virginia J. Int. L.* 658.
[68] Mayer, op. cit., 132 ff.
[69] Hartley, above n. 1, 282.
[70] Art. 232, New Code of Civil Procedure, Civ. 19.10.1971, 62 RDCIP. 70 (1973), note Simon-Depitre; Paris 3 March 1994, *Rev. cr. dr. int. pr.*, 532, 536; Mayer, above n. 10, 133. France is also a party to the 1968 Convention on Information on Foreign Law: Mayer, op. cit., 133–134. Although relatively rarely used, there is an increasing awareness of the Convention amongst practitioners, many of whom favour it, at least in relatively straightforward cases: Rodger and van Doorn, (1997) 46 *ICLQ* 151, 159–160.
[71] See generally, Wright and Miller, above n. 41, para. 2441 ff.
[72] Sass, above n. 1, 109.

to foreign legal materials,[73] to unsworn, unexamined opinions[74] and, very commonly, to expert affidavits unaccompanied by oral testimony.[75] Although this may be less common than an English lawyer would expect, experts may also give oral testimony in addition to their affidavit evidence.[76] It is also possible, where party experts radically disagree, for a court to appoint an independent expert, at the parties' instigation or on its own motion, who may be cross-examined by the parties, who bear the costs of the appointment.[77]

As the foregoing summary suggests, relatively easy cases concerning foreign law may be resolved in most legal systems without undue formality. In others, however, it is generally accepted that the determination of foreign law may be hard to achieve without resort to expert assistance, although residual concern about the impartiality and reliability of party-led experts is not uncommon.[78] Systems may differ, however, in the status of such assistance and the manner in which expert evidence is presented. In France, Germany and the United States the tendency is to rely (to different degrees in each country) on written expert evidence, whereas in England oral testimony is regarded as of paramount importance. Such trends are not, however, without exceptions. In England affidavit evidence is sufficient in interlocutory proceedings[79] and, in each of the other systems under discussion, some questioning of an expert may be possible—a court appointed expert in the case of French and German law.[80] In French and German law anything resembling the common law practice of cross-examining party experts in open court is prevented as a matter of general principle. It is instructive, however, that some debate surrounds the desirability of this course in US Federal practice. Some commentators are reluctant to encourage oral testimony, and this is commonly perceived as an exceptional course.[81] Others, however, consider that the 'most expensive but probably the most effective method of presenting informa-

---

[73] *In Re Fotochrome, Inc.*, 377 F.Supp. 26, 29 (DCNY 1974); *Burnett v. Trans World Airlines, Inc.*, 368 F. Supp. 1152 (DCNMex. 1973); *Ramirez v. Autobuses Blancos Flecha Roja*, 486 F.2d 493, 497 (5th Cir. 1973).

[74] *Kalmich v. Bruno* 553 F.2d 549, 555 n. 4 (7th Cir. 1977).

[75] Sass, above n. 1, 108; Miner, above n. 25, 588.

[76] e.g. *Ramsay v. Boeing Company*, 432 F.2d 592, 600 (5th Cir. 1970); Miner, above n. 25, 588–589; Schmertz, (1978) 18 *Virginia J. of Intl. L.* 697, 707.

[77] Federal Rules of Evidence, Rule 706 provides that a court 'may on its own or on the motion of any party enter an order to show cause why expert witnesses should not be appointed, and may request the parties to submit nominations'; see Miner, above n. 25, 588–589.

[78] Mayer, above n. 10; Merryman, (1983) 19 *Stan. J. Intl. L.* 151, 157.

[79] See above, p. 206.

[80] A court-appointed expert may be questioned in Germany by the parties (Section 411 ZPO).

[81] Miner, above n. 25, 588; Sass, (1981) 29 *Am. Jl. Comp. L.* 97,108; cf. Merryman, (1983) 19 *Stan. J. Intl. L.* 151, 157.

tion about foreign law is through live examination . . .'[82] Systems may also differ as to the role given to court-appointed experts. In English law neither the court nor a party has ever apparently sought the appointment of an independent expert in a dispute concerning foreign law.[83] In France and the United States, as we have seen, this may be possible, and in Germany it is the normal course in cases of any complexity.

(c) FAILURE TO ESTABLISH FOREIGN LAW

Difficulty also occurs when foreign law is introduced but inadequately proved. Two issues arise from the problem of *non liquet*. One concerns how a court should respond when the point is reached at which proof of foreign law has failed. The other concerns how best to prevent this situation from occurring. The first issue has most exercised scholars, a variety of solutions having been advocated in the literature.[84] One possibility is to dismiss the claim altogether.[85] Others include applying the *lex fori*,[86] or the law of a similar legal system,[87] or a novel rule based on the court's researches in comparative law.[88] But it is unsurprising that so many legal systems, common law or civil law, would apply the law of the forum in the event of a failure in proof.[89] In some jurisdictions, where the application of foreign law is mandatory and a court is obliged to establish the applicable law, this is a doctrinally awkward solution. It involves a surrender of responsibility by the court and leads to a legally incorrect answer which principle cannot permit. These difficulties are perhaps most acutely felt in Germany. There, under the doctrine of *Ersatzrecht*, courts are required, where possible, to apply the law of another but related legal system rather than apply German law by default.[90] By contrast, resort to the *lex fori* is a natural response where foreign laws are viewed as facts, because such a failure amounts to no more than a failure to establish one of the facts in the case. But there is much to commend it even where they are not. Where it is the court's task to research foreign law there would be an element of unfairness in dismissing the claim, in so far as the responsibility for the failure in proof lies not with the parties but with the judge. And if dismissal is not the solution there are reasons of convenience for applying the

---

[82] Schmertz, (1978) 18 *Virginia J. of Int. L.* 697, 707. [83] See above, p. 232.
[84] Kahn Freund, *General Problems of Private International Law*, 2nd edn., (1976), 278–280; Cappelletti (1970) *CILSA* 60.
[85] Kahn Freund, op. cit., 278; Spiro (1976) *CILSA* 65.
[86] Kahn Freund, op. cit., 279–280. [87] Kahn Freund, op. cit., 278, 308.
[88] Cappelletti, op. cit., 60.
[89] BGH 23.12.1981, NJW 1982, 1215, 1216; Cass. Civ. 8 Jan. 1991, *Rev. cr. dr. int. pr.* 1991.569, note Muir Watt; Loussouarn and Bourel, above n. 10, 256–257; Zatjay, 1968 *Riv. di Dir. Internaz. e Process* 233, 269–270.
[90] BGH 23.12.1981, NJW 1982, 1215; Von Bar, above, n. 39, 329.

law of the forum. Moreover, if the proof of foreign law has failed, whichever law a court applies is plainly not the foreign law which in principle should govern. Being merely a default position, relying to some extent on a fiction, it may not, in truth, matter which law applies.

But in reality, how to respond to a failure in proof may be less important than how such a failure is to be prevented. Certainly, English lawyers might be less troubled by the problem of a failure in proof than others.[91] They may tolerate more readily the imperfect determination of foreign law on unsatisfactory evidence, or the pragmatic application of the *lex fori* in default. They are perhaps more easily persuaded that a workable solution which is fair between the parties is more important than deciding a case 'correctly'. This is not to say that English lawyers are more pragmatic than others, or less concerned with legal accuracy. But they are inclined to view the legal process as a means for resolving particular disputes, as opposed to a vehicle for excavating legal truth. It must also be remembered that foreign laws are viewed as facts, which implies that they are subject to a lower expectation of accuracy than issues of domestic law. Certainly, although propositions of law may perhaps be regarded as true it is tempting to treat propositions of fact as merely true *given the evidence*. Whatever the reason, however, the problem of defective proof will loom larger, and will occur more often, in a system where a judge expects to determine foreign law accurately than in one where the task is to resolve it fairly on the basis of the evidence provided.

Moreover, it may not simply be practical but doctrinally consistent that the law of the forum should apply by default. In any system, such as the English, which treats the application of the *lex fori* as the basic rule it is natural that it should govern if no other law is proved.[92] Indeed, no further rationale is required to explain why this occurs. Where the evidence has failed the principal pre-condition for the application of foreign law—that its content should be known—has not been satisfied. Indeed, this ensures not so much that the *lex fori* applies by default, but that it continues to govern, never having been displaced.

But it is probably far less likely than scholars sometimes suppose that a total failure of proof will occur. Courts in different countries—certainly in England—often display a remarkable ability to determine the hardest questions of foreign law.[93] Moreover, over-sensitivity to the problem may betray an ignorance of the reality of adjudication. It may certainly happen that a judge will be unable to determine foreign law exactly as a foreign court would. But there is no test for telling when this point is reached, such that the judge may surrender. Indeed, whether or not foreign law is actually determined in such a case, a finding as to its content will, practically

[91] But see, Loussouarn and Bourel, above n. 10, 256.
[92] See above, p. 70.   [93] See above, pp. 190–191.

speaking, always be possible. In this light, the question is not so much what happens when proof fails. It is whether English courts—and those elsewhere—are able and willing to make findings as to foreign law without too often resorting to application of the law of the forum.

(d) Establishing Foreign Law

Several lessons emerge from this brief survey. None, however, poses a significant challenge to the English approach to proving foreign law, for reasons which appear more fully in the following chapter. First, who bears the responsibility for establishing foreign law depends on procedural assumptions which are not unique to the treatment of foreign law. Secondly, it is apparent that English law, like most legal systems, provides techniques of varying formality and complexity, each suited to proving foreign law in different cases. But it remains to ask whether the choice offered by English law is adequate, whether each technique is effective in its own terms, and whether means exist to ensure that the appropriate method is employed in particular cases. The last issue is of special importance, going to the degree to which litigants or the courts should regulate matters of evidence. It especially invites the question whether it should be for the parties or the court to determine the method whereby foreign law is proved. As we shall see in Chapter X, English law may be judged largely satisfactory in each of these respects, particularly in the light of the changes currently occurring in the English law of civil procedure. Thirdly, English law also differs from some legal systems by making extensive use of the oral testimony of experts, and from others by largely dismissing a role for court-appointed advisers. Might English law be improved by making greater use of written opinions and of independent experts? Once again, whatever value there is in having such options available, it may be unlikely that the proof of foreign law would be improved by making greater resort to such independent assistance.[94] Finally, the inadequate proof of foreign law is a recognized problem in all legal systems, presenting courts with the awkward prospect of applying foreign law inaccurately or resorting to the application of the *lex fori*. In the light of the experience of other systems, it must be asked whether English law responds adequately to the problem of defective proof? But, as we have seen, English courts, like those in other countries, display remarkable tenacity and flexibility in ensuring that this problem seldom, if ever, arises.

[94] See above, pp, 211; 232.

3. COMPARATIVE LESSONS

Foreign comparisons need cautious handling. That another system is different does not make it better. Nor does English law's similarity with others validate its approach. As the foregoing account suggests, however, a comparative approach illuminates the debate concerning English law's treatment of foreign law. In principle, it invites consideration of whether institutions employed abroad may be of value at home. More importantly, as we have seen, it reveals how similar is the English approach to that which has evolved elsewhere. Behind the facade of doctrinal and idiomatic differences it is apparent that all systems face comparable problems and respond, in general, with similar solutions. But this is not to say that English law can learn nothing from its counterparts. In particular, the foregoing discussion highlights three areas in which its approach might be questioned.[95] Why does English law not require the introduction of foreign law in cases involving personal status, as other systems do? Why does it make no use of court-appointed experts in proving foreign law? Should the courts adopt a more pro-active role in ensuring proportionality between the mode of proof and the difficulty of the case in hand? Each of these important questions is addressed in the following. None, as we shall see, is without an answer.

But, in the end, the challenge to English law's approach to foreign law from overseas comparisons may be more general, concerning the remarkable lack of debate in England about the subject's success and its future. Indeed, one of the most striking features of any comparison with other systems does not concern the law itself, but the extent to which English lawyers take the law for granted, seldom considering its implications, still less its conceptual basis. By contrast, judicial activism in Germany has called aspects of German law's traditional approach into question. One important decision narrowed the permissible scope of academic expert evidence, treating it as inappropriate where practical knowledge is involved.[96] Others evoked controversy by allowing the parties to ignore questions of foreign law, the omission amounting to a choice of German law as the applicable law.[97] Similarly, a succession of decisions in the *Cour de Cassation* has radically reshaped French law's approach to foreign law.

---

[95] At first sight it might also seem troubling that English law does not explicitly protect the application of foreign law where this is required by an international convention, as is the case, for example, in France. But, as we have seen, the application of foreign law may be obligatory in English law where the relevant choice of law rule is mandatory, which would include such rules as may be contained in international conventions.

[96] BGH 21.1.1991, NJW 1991, 1418, 1419; Samtleben, NJW 1992, 3057, 3058.

[97] BGH 15.1.1986, 6 IPRax 292 (1986), criticized by Schack, ibid., 272; BGH 18.1.1988, NJW 1988, 1592, criticised in Von Bar, above n. 39, 341.

Rejecting the traditional view that the introduction of foreign law was for the parties, the court first ruled that it was mandatory in certain cases.[98] Then it decided that a court should always invoke foreign law *ex officio*.[99] Soon after, it reverted to a hybrid position, requiring *ex officio* application of foreign law only in cases concerning the parties' indefeasible rights.[100] Again, United States Federal practice, and that of almost all states, has for some time rejected the English approach, itself a striking challenge to the English position.[101] In preferring simply to give courts notice of unpleaded or unproved foreign law these developments began a debate on the correct approach to foreign law which has continued unabated.[102] Finally, and most arrestingly, a distinguished school of thought has in recent years come to question the fundamental notion, central to the approach of many civil law systems, that the application of foreign law is generally mandatory. By espousing the theory of 'facultative choice of law' commentators have advocated an approach which closely resembles the traditional common law position in its methodology and consequences.[103] It is striking, however, that they should do so, and in the process consider both the merits of the English system and its conceptual structure, when such reflection is in England almost entirely lacking.

Viewed in the light of such judicial and scholarly activity in other jurisdictions the stability of English law, and the dearth of critical commentary, is anomalous. But it is also challenging. By comparison with other countries, can it be that the English approach to foreign law is so clear as to require no examination, so perfect as to admit of no reform? As we have seen, English law, on inspection, is less clear than might be supposed. Indeed, it is somewhat different from what might be imagined. Whether it requires reform is a matter to which we must now turn.

---

[98] Cass. civ. 25 November 1986, *Rev. crit. dr. int. pr.* 1987.383, note Ancel and Lequette; *JCP* 1988.II.20967, note Courbe; Cass. civ. 25 May 1987, *Clunet* 1987.927, note Gaudemet-Tallon.

[99] Cass civ. 11 and 18 October 1988, *Clunet* 1989.349, note Alexandre; *JCP* 1989.II.21327, note Courbe; *Rev. crit. dr. int. pr.* 1989.368.

[100] Cass. civ. 4 December 1990, *Clunet* 1991.371, note Bureau; *Rev. crit. dr. int. pr.* 1991.558, note Niboyet-Hoegy.

[101] For an American critique of the traditional common law approach see, Miller, (1967) 65 *Mich. L. Rev.* 613, and works cited in Wright and Miller, above n. 41, 634–635.

[102] See generally, Wright and Miller, above n. 41.

[103] Flessner, 'Fakultatives Kollionsrecht', *Rabels Zeitschrift*, 1970, 547; *Interessenjurisprudenz im internationalen Privatrecht*, (Tübingen, 1990), 119 ff; De Boer, above n. 48.

X
Principle, Policy, and Reform

It remains to ask whether English law's treatment of foreign law is justified. This is a matter of concern on a number of levels. The success or otherwise of the English approach affects the expense, duration and fairness of litigation. Its deficiencies may discourage legitimate claimants from proceeding under foreign law, to their possible disadvantage; or from doing so at all, denying them access to justice; or from doing so in England, to the detriment of the market for legal services. That foreign law may be misapplied subverts the purpose of the choice of law process and distorts the legal rights and duties of litigants. It also casts doubt on the viability of that process, affecting the direction of law reform and the nature of future harmonization.[1] Whether litigants are always free to ignore a dispute's foreign elements is also of concern. It affects the scope of the conflicts process, by determining the extent to which they may select the *lex fori* as the applicable law. And it bears on the effectiveness of mandatory conflicts rules, especially those in international conventions, which may be subverted if the principle of voluntary pleading is strictly enforced.[2]

This chapter examines the case for amending English law's treatment of foreign law. It considers the difficult issue of whether foreign law must sometimes be applied, and examines the available means by which it may be established. It concludes by suggesting how legislation may eradicate some persistent faults in both areas. But it must begin by reprising the principal arguments of the previous chapters. For whether change is required turns on the state of the law. And the state of the law is not free from doubt.

1. FOUR PRINCIPLES REVISITED

How we understand English law's approach to foreign law determines whether reform is required. As we saw in Chapter I, the conventional wisdom is clearly delineated and may be expressed in four familiar principles. First, a question of foreign law is a question of fact. Secondly, being a question of a specialist, technical type, it must be proved by expert evidence.

[1] See above, pp. 13–16.　　[2] See above, p. 71.

Thirdly, whether foreign law is pleaded is voluntary, a matter for the parties' choice. Fourthly, in the event that foreign law is not pleaded, or is not satisfactorily proved, it is presumed to be the same as English law. But as we have seen, none of these propositions—not even the first—is as secure as might be supposed. Indeed, taken literally and unreflectively, each is misleading in principle and may be damaging in practice. This is not to say that orthodox accounts do not recognize that the subject's fundamental tenets must be qualified. Indeed, questions of foreign law are known to be facts 'of a peculiar kind'.[3] But the true extent to which the traditional position has been eroded is less well appreciated and the conventional wisdom has proved to be improbably durable.

Take, first, the cardinal rule that foreign laws are facts. This is so obvious to English lawyers as to require no justification. Yet its implications have been rejected entirely in the United States and the doctrine has been condemned as anachronistic, unsatisfactory, even 'primeval'.[4] And its accuracy has been doubted even in English law. It has been said that the treatment of foreign law 'is closer to that of a question of law and to regard it merely as a question of fact may therefore be misleading'.[5] Indeed, one commentator would reverse the usual presentation by regarding matters of foreign law not as unusual facts, but as laws of a special kind:

> Though the foreign law which the court has to apply remains law, it is in some respects treated very differently from a court's own law. This is because the judge cannot be expected to know it as he knows his own law.[6]

Certainly, the traditional fact doctrine is now subject to exceptions of such significance as to place it in jeopardy. The legal character of foreign law, affecting the rights and liabilities of the parties, is reflected in the preparedness of appellate courts to reconsider issues of foreign law.[7] It is also implicit in important rules of procedure. Under statute, previous findings on foreign law, unlike true findings of fact, are presumed to be correct.[8] It also underlies the rule that questions of foreign law are for a judge to answer, not a jury,[9] a reform described as a 'first step on the way to a better system, a recognition of the true nature of foreign law as law'.[10]

Most importantly, perhaps, the notion that foreign laws are merely facts is persistently challenged by the readiness of courts to establish foreign law other than by formal proof. Indeed, the second of the subject's ruling

---

[3] *Parkasho* v. *Singh* [1968] P. 233, 250.
[4] Miller, (1967) 65 *Mich.L.Rev.* 615, 628; Wright and Miller, *Federal Practice and Procedure: Civil 2d*, (1995) para. 2441.
[5] O'Malley and Layton, 230.   [6] Wolff, *Private International Law*, (Oxford, 1950), 218.
[7] *Parkasho* v. *Singh* [1968] P. 233, 250; *Dalmia Dairy Industries Ltd.* v. *National Bank of Pakistan* [1978] 2 Lloyd's Rep. 223, 286 (CA); *Bumper Development Corp.* v. *Comr. of Police* [1991] 1 WLR 1362, 1370 (CA).
[8] Civil Evidence Act 1972, s. 4(2); above, p. 223.
[9] Supreme Court Act 1981, s. 69(5).   [10] Wolff, above n. 6, 221.

principles—that such proof is necessary—is equally insecure. For, if foreign law is strictly regarded as factual, it is doubtful that a court can rely on its own expertise to establish its content without expert assistance. Contrary to strict doctrine, however, courts have rejected expert testimony, although uncontradicted, because it was at odds with their reading of the documentary evidence.[11] They are also prepared to establish foreign law by relying on their own knowledge and competence. Foreign laws have been treated as notorious,[12] or as reflecting general principles of law[13] and, even before statute legitimised the practice, courts would rely on their previous findings in similar cases.[14] Importantly, they have also dispensed with proof by experts when all that is in issue is the construction of documents.[15]

This is not to deny that foreign law is most commonly established by formal proof, nor that the use of other means is rare. But this merely confirms the practical value of proof by expert evidence, not that it is doctrinally required. And it cannot disguise the important truth that such alternatives exist in principle, whether or not their use is common. True, it cannot be ignored that courts sometimes enforce the fact doctrine strictly.[16] But this is simply to recognize its tenacity, not its correctness. Nor is it impossible to neutralize decisions of a flexible nature, perhaps by classifying them as cases where foreign law, although established, is not formally proved.[17] But it is hard to see why principle or policy justifies such fundamentalism. Merely because a court is almost always ignorant of foreign law is no reason to insist that it is when it is not.[18] If foreign law is notorious, or if common sense and sound reasoning can determine its content, why deny it? Such a denial is excessively formalistic, doing no service to the law. It is also hard to reconcile with the courts' preparedness to take account of foreign materials as an aid to developing English law.[19] Certainly, they may resort to foreign law for the purposes of comparison, if not for the purposes of decision. Why should a court effectively have notice of foreign law in one type of case but not another?

If strict adherence to the fact doctrine is conceptually unsatisfying, it is also of practical concern. It threatens the courts' ability to assess defective evidence of foreign law, and limits its ability to establish foreign law

---

[11] See above, pp. 194–199.   [12] See above, p. 248.   [13] See above, p. 247.
[14] See above, p. 233.   [15] See above, pp. 257–262.
[16] A recent example may be *El Ajou* v. *Dollar Land Holdings plc* [1993] 3 All ER 717, 736 (doubting that foreign law may be notorious).
[17] Dicey and Morris, 227–229.
[18] As Lord Langdale apparently recognized in *Nelson* v. *Bridport* (1845) 8 Beav. 527, 537–538, quoted, above, p. 259; see also, *A/S Tallina Laevauhisus* v. *Estonian State Shipping Line* (1947) 80 LILR 99, 108 (CA).
[19] Wolff, above n. 6, 220; O'Malley and Layton, 231. As Blackburn J said: 'Though the civil law is not authority in an English Court, it affords great assistance in investigating the principles on which the law is grounded': *Taylor* v. *Caldwell* (1863) 32 LJQB 164, 166–167.

cheaply and quickly by informal means. To cleave strictly to the traditional account is also to misunderstand the true reason for equating foreign laws with facts. For, as the early cases reveal, foreign law need be factual only to the extent that its determination is actually beyond the knowledge and competence of the court.[20] Indeed, even when such questions were remitted to a jury, it was recognized that the judge had a role in assisting the determination of foreign law.[21] To assume, because they are facts, that courts can never establish them by other means is to draw an inference that may never have been intended. It should also be noticed that historically the reason for classifying foreign laws as facts was to enable courts to establish and apply them.[22] Having committed itself to the concept that only English laws are laws it was only by treating foreign laws as facts that they could be applied at all. It would be an unfortunate irony if the application of foreign law were hindered by adopting a dogmatic view of the fact doctrine.

So we must be circumspect with the principle that foreign laws are facts, and its corollary that they must be proved as such by expert evidence. Indeed, the better view may be that, although historically and technically foreign laws are facts in English doctrine, this may count for less in practice than might be supposed. We must also be cautious in assuming, as the third basic principle requires, that the pleading of foreign law is invariably voluntary. It is not the case that whether foreign law is introduced is always for the parties to decide. Although it is relatively unusual, there are situations where the pleading of foreign law is required by the relevant choice of law rule.[23] Nor should we suppose, merely because questions of pleading are procedural, that whether foreign law must be introduced is also a procedural issue. In truth, there is a distinction between how and when foreign law should be pleaded (which are procedural matters), and whether it should be pleaded at all (which is substantive, going to the identity of the applicable law).

This important error of classification itself derives from the fact doctrine. If foreign laws are facts the ascertainment of such laws may seem to belong to the law of evidence, and thus to the realm of procedure.[24] But the error also depends on a mistaken analysis of what it means to plead, or not to plead, foreign law. When a party declines to rely upon foreign law the effect is not that the rules of pleading thus exclude the choice of law process. Such an omission is an integral part of that process, being the mechanism whereby that party selects the *lex fori* as the applicable law. As such, whether in a given case a mere omission to rely upon foreign law is an effective choice of the *lex fori* depends on the prevailing choice of law

[20] *Nelson* v. *Bridport* (1845) 8 Beav. 527, 535–539; above, p. 259.
[21] *Mostyn* v. *Fabrigas* (1774) 1 Cowp. 161, 174.   [22] Ibid.   [23] See above, Chapter III.
[24] Schlesinger, (1973) 59 *Cornell L.Rev.* 1, 5.

rule. Generally, it will be effective. But there are situations where it is not, because the relevant choice of law rule is mandatory. This is not to say, however, that the principle of voluntary pleading is redundant. It signifies—except where the relevant conflicts rule is mandatory and the applicable law is foreign—that litigants may select English law merely by omitting to plead it. Such a choice of the *lex fori* apparently need not be established with any formality, for example by an agreement in writing. This analysis of the dynamics of selecting the law of the forum is of more than theoretical importance. It bears, for example, on whether the Brussels and Rome Conventions can impose mandatory conflicts rules in the context of English law.[25] For, even if certain of their rules purport to require the application of foreign law, these may be undermined if the issue of whether foreign law must be introduced is characterized as procedural rather than substantive. This is because, if procedural matters are untouched by such rules, so is the principle of voluntary pleading.

Finally, there is the presumption of similarity between English and foreign law. We have considered already the deficiencies of this artificial doctrine.[26] Granted that legal fictions may have value, such a presumption is strikingly unreal, except perhaps where the laws of some other common law jurisdictions is involved, at least where that law has not been superseded by local practice. It also conceals the true basis of English law's approach to choice of law which, it is suggested, is that the *lex fori* always applies unless the contrary is shown.[27] It is certainly difficult to see a meaningful sense in which foreign law 'applies' where it has not been relied upon. It is less troublesome to say that foreign law applies where it has been relied upon, but has not been proved, or its proof was unsatisfactory. At least in such cases a court may have identified the applicable law as a matter of law. But there is a more direct and less counter-intuitive route to the application of English law in default of pleading and proof. It is that English law applies unless a foreign applicable law has been identified and its content established. Certainly, it seems a reasonable precondition for the application of such a law that its content should be known.[28] This is not to say, however, that it is proper to apply English law when foreign law has been relied upon but no evidence introduced. Indeed, the misleading width of the presumption of similarity appears to have given spurious justification to this practice. As we have seen, however, it may never have been apt to apply the presumption in such a case.[29] Certainly, there are reasons of policy and principle for not doing so.

As these reflections suggest, English law's approach to foreign law must be carefully understood. The four principles on which it may be thought

---

[25] See below, pp. 80–97; 126–130.
[27] See, Ehrenzweig, (1960) 58 *Mich. L.Rev.* 638, 232–233.
[29] See above, p. 146.

[26] See above, pp. 146; 184.
[28] See above, p. 184.

to rest must be significantly qualified if they are not to mislead. Certainly, there have been many cases in which one or the other has been taken at face value, with unfortunate consequences in practice. But this, and the distortion to the law's conceptual base, are not the only reasons for re-establishing the principles on which the subject depends. Another is that, whether and to what extent reform is required depends upon how the present law is viewed. Certainly, if the fact doctrine operates in its full vigour in English law the case for reform is compelling. The point may be highlighted by reference to the sweeping reforms introduced into American practice by Rule 44.1 of the Federal Rules of Civil Procedure.[30] This was intended precisely to eradicate the effects of the common law fact doctrine. As such it poses an arresting question for English lawyers: is its equivalent necessary here? It seems that it is not, but only if we recognize that the solutions which it offers to the fact doctrine's shortcomings are already available in English law. Both systems now accept the possibility of appellate review of foreign law findings.[31] Neither would any longer submit questions of foreign law to a jury.[32] More importantly, Rule 44.1's objective of allowing foreign law to be established without formal proof is also achievable in English law. This is not to say that every technique available in one system exists in the other. Nor is it to deny that proof by expert opinion is the favoured method in both. But, as we have seen, English courts are more liberal than is commonly supposed in allowing the determination of foreign law other than by formal proof.[33]

The existence of such similarities between English and American law does not imply that the former is not in need of change. But it reinforces the point that the fact doctrine may not be the source of the difficulty, provided it is clear how attenuated it has become. But this is to beg the question. For the issue does not so much concern what English law is, as what it is perceived to be. The difficulty is no longer the fact doctrine itself, which may no longer exist in its traditional form, but in the tendency to ignore its demise. Certainly, it endures in the conventional wisdom of courts and commentators alike, for all its faults, and for all the cases which betray it. Indeed, although in one sense such reform is unnecessary if the law is properly depicted, the tenacity of the fact doctrine may yet compel statutory change in this area. Its death knell has sounded, but it may rule us from the grave.[34]

---

[30] Wright & Miller, above n. 4, paras. 2441–2447.
[31] Ibid., 656–657.
[32] Ibid., 654–655.
[33] See above, Chapter VIII.
[34] Miller, (1967) 65 *Mich. L.Rev.* 613.

2. THE APPLICATION OF FOREIGN LAW

How satisfactory is English law's normally voluntarist approach to the application of foreign law? To express the point differently, how desirable is it that the rules for choice of law should generally be optional in character? There is no doubting the consistency of such an approach with general principle. Certainly, it is true to the familiar principle that litigation should be shaped so far as possible by litigants themselves. For, as has been said:

> If civil procedure is to serve any purpose in society . . . the law which provides the necessary institutions and which regulates the actual process of litigation must start from the proposition that civil litigation is voluntary . . . it follows from this that rules of civil procedure operate mainly by the creation of choices for the parties . . .[35]

This might occasion surprise in those systems which adopt a more interventionist posture. But it is fruitless to suggest that English law should adopt a conceptual basis entirely different from its own. Indeed, to suggest as much is not to criticise English law's approach to foreign law, so much as its conception of adjudication. It is, however, ultimately misleading to found the voluntary pleading of foreign law on general procedural principles. For whether (or when) litigants are free to ignore foreign law, and so have English law applied, is a choice of law issue.[36] It turns on their freedom to select the applicable law in general and the *lex fori* in particular. As such, English law's liberal approach to foreign law reflects the essentially voluntarist character of English private international law. And as such it derives strength from those considerations which justify voluntarism in the conflicts process. It finds its justification in the principle of party autonomy and in the certainty which derives from respecting the parties' choice of law. Indeed, permitting choice in choice of law is not simply a matter of reflecting the parties' legitimate expectations concerning the applicable law. It introduces stability into a world of legal diversity. For to select the governing law is not merely to identify the applicable legal regime. It is also to exclude any conflict of laws, together with the doubt and uncertainty such conflicts occasion. As has been said:

> Ease of travel and communication mean that the lives of far more people are touched by transnational problems than ever was the case a few decades ago. Wisely, the majority wish to avoid the difficulties which may arise and which private international rules are designed to resolve. They certainly wish to avoid the

---

[35] Jolowicz, 'On the Nature and Purposes of Civil Procedural Law', Scott, ed., *International Perspectives on Civil Justice*, (1990), 43.
[36] See above, p. 70.

cost and anxiety of the litigation process. Choice of law rules should be designed to fulfil this prophylactic role. This is why choice in choice of law is so important.[37]

Moreover, this principle might be reflected even in English law's approach to whether particular choice of law rules are mandatory, removing the possibility of party choice. The point here is not merely that English law supports party autonomy by so seldom conferring mandatory effect upon its conflicts rules. It is that its approach to whether a given rule should have this effect is able in principle to capture those factors which favour allowing the parties to choose the *lex fori*. For, even if a given rule might otherwise be mandatory, it is open to ask whether its purpose would be served forcing the parties to dispute points of foreign law in an English court.

As this suggests, a voluntary approach to the application of foreign law has advantages beyond those normally associated with party autonomy in choice of law. Some are procedural. As we saw at greater length in Chapter V, it encourages cost-efficiency. It mitigates the cost and delay of litigation by allowing litigants to assess the advantages and disadvantages of introducing foreign law.[38] It gives each party the opportunity to gauge the delay and expense associated with embarking upon a choice-of-law dispute and with the proof of foreign law itself. By placing no reliance on foreign law they may escape the uncertainty and expense associated with the conflicts process. In particular, they may avoid inherently open-ended disputes concerning classification, and the uncertainty which afflicts the formulation and application of so many choice of law rules. Voluntary pleading also allows litigants to avoid the uncertainty, delay and expense of establishing foreign law. For even the best evidential techniques have cost implications, and however perfect they might be, cases involving the proof of foreign law are more expensive than those which do not. But, importantly, such considerations are not merely matters of efficiency. They serve the important goal of encouraging access to justice by allowing litigants to minimise the cost and delay of proceedings. Indeed, in a system such as that in England in which the cost of litigation falls almost entirely upon the parties, and in which the cost can be considerable, it is highly desirable that the parties should be able to reduce their possible exposure.

But there are further reasons to implement the parties' implicit choice of the *lex fori* through an omission to plead any other. Although the point should not be overstated, it encourages the just resolution of disputes by reducing the risk that the parties' rights and liabilities might be misapplied. It also reflects the fact that, merely through being the forum, an

---

[37] North, *Essays in Private International Law*, (Oxford, 1993), 200.
[38] See above, pp. 170–172.

English court immediately acquires at least some connection with, an interest in, any dispute for choice of law purposes.

Nor is English law greatly at odds with other systems in its approach, at least in principle. Even those which treat choice of law rules as generally mandatory may exceptionally allow litigants to select the *lex fori* as the applicable law.[39] Some civil law commentators also support the theory of 'facultative choice of law', which closely resembles the traditional common law position that the introduction of foreign law is a procedural matter.[40] In an attempt to circumvent the mandatory character of choice of law rules in many legal systems, this holds that the selection of the law of the forum is not a choice of law matter but reflects the freedom of litigants to define the terms of their dispute. But, although in this sense the theory of facultative choice of law differs from that proposed in the present discussion, its underlying basis is the same. It rests on the belief that here are sound reasons, reflecting the legitimate autonomy of the parties and the efficiency of applying the *lex fori*, for permitting litigants the greatest freedom to escape the application of foreign law.[41]

But this is not to say that the English approach exactly mirrors that in such countries. Indeed, even if there is broad agreement in many jurisdictions about the procedural advantages of a voluntarist approach, English law is singular in the scope which it affords to the parties' freedom of choice. Many systems, for example, allow the parties to select the *lex fori* only in certain cases.[42] Typically, it cannot be done where the protection of individuals or the preservation of inalienable rights are involved. Such systems may also assume, because the application of the *lex fori* involves a choice of law, that it should be subject to such limitations as affect such a choice, which in some countries may be greater than in English law.

That English law does not apparently restrict the parties' choice to the same extent may at first seem surprising. But it may be no cause for concern that English law may not respect, for example, rights in personal status, at least not in the present context.[43] The protection of such rights in other systems generally depends on the theory that they are inherently unwaivable, whether in the conflict of laws or domestic law. Lacking such a generalised theory of inalienable rights it is explicable that they should find no place in English conflicts practice. Whether English law should adopt a different general perspective is another matter, but one far beyond its approach to foreign law. Again, it is possible in most cases affecting

---

[39] See above, p. 268.
[40] Flessner, 'Fakultatives Kollisionsrecht', *Rabels Zeitschrift*, 1970, 547; *Interessenjurisprudenz im internationalen Privatrecht*, (Tubingen, 1990), 119 ff; Sturm, 'Fakultatives Kollisionsrecht: Notwendigkeit und Grenzen', Bernstein, Drobnig and Kotz, eds., *Festschrift fur Konrad Zweigert zum 70 Geburtstag* (Tubingen, 1981), 329; De Boer, 'Facultative Choice of Law', 1996 *Hague Recueil*, vol. 257, 227.
[41] De Boer, op. cit., Ch. III.   [42] See above, p. 270.   [43] See above, pp. 119–121.

personal status that the governing law is the *lex fori* according to the rules for choice of law. This may certainly be so in those cases concerning nullity in which the omission to plead foreign law is most troublesome.[44] If so, there is no sense in which an omission to introduce foreign law subverts the objectively applicable law. Indeed, the very opposite is true. Similarly, the English approach apparently undermines the application of mandatory foreign rules which render acts invalid or illegal. But this is hardly surprising given the uncertainty of the relevant English conflicts rules. The suggestion that an English court might insist unprompted on applying a foreign rule concerning illegality is also distinctly impractical given that it cannot, without the parties' evidence, know that any such foreign rule has been infringed. Nor could it discern unaided the bad faith on which the enforcement of foreign law may depend.[45] Moreover, if English law differs in practice from some other systems by not invariably enforcing foreign rights affecting status, or foreign mandatory rules, it resembles them in principle. For, if the principle is that litigants may only select the *lex fori* (by an omission to plead) where the general rules for choice of law permit, this is precisely what English law appears to do. It is merely that it does restrict party choice as other systems might.

But difficulty occurs where, by virtue of English private international law, courts are apparently required to respect foreign mandatory rules. Here the problem is not whether the relevant choice of law rule allows such rules to be displaced by choice, for it does not. It is whether by classifying the pleading of foreign law as procedural such rules may be subverted. Doubt surrounds, for example, Articles 5 and 6 of the 1980 Rome Convention. We have seen how these provisions may require the application of foreign law in defence, respectively, of the rights of consumers and employees.[46] It is unclear whether the risk to such persons is as great in practice as might be supposed. But the problem begs squarely a question of fundamental principle: is the introduction of foreign law an issue of substance or procedure? If the latter, English law's voluntarist approach should be untouched by the Convention, which expressly excludes procedural rules from its scope. But if the introduction of foreign law is substantive this is not the case. Whether foreign law should be introduced depends on the prevailing choice of law rules, which in the present context are contained in Articles 5 and 6 of the Rome Convention. We have argued that whether foreign law must be applied in a given case is a substantive question, although how it should be pleaded is procedural.[47] As such, where the application of foreign law is required any omission to plead and prove its content should result in the dismissal of the claim or

---

[44] See above, p. 116.   [45] See above, p. 113.   [46] See above, pp. 92–94.
[47] See above, pp. 70–74.

defence. Any fear is removed that the Convention might be undermined by a trick of pleading.

Even where the rules of any relevant foreign law are not themselves mandatory, the rules of English private international law may require the application of foreign law. We have seen how this may be the case with regard to Article 52 of the 1968 Brussels Convention.[48] Concerned with locating a defendant's domicile this provides that whether the party is domiciled in another Contracting State is a matter for the law of that State. Even where international conventions are not involved, the character of legislation may be equally problematic. Difficulty stems from the fact that English statutes seldom provide whether the introduction of foreign law should be mandatory, any more than they usually state whether English law has this effect. Because it is barely recognized that conflicts rule may be mandatory, requiring the application of the objectively applicable law, no learning has developed on this question. In principle, however, the basic rule in English private international is that the *lex fori* applies.[49] This generally means that, unless litigants argue otherwise, foreign law will not govern. If this is the starting place, the mandatory application of foreign law should be required only by virtue of express words in a statute, or by necessary implication. This approach is consistent with the reality that statutory conflicts rules are unlikely to be accorded mandatory status. To take three prominent examples, the Foreign Limitation Periods Act 1984 has been interpreted in this way in the courts.[50] Nor is it likely that Part III of the Private International Law (Miscellaneous Provisions) Act 1995 requires a foreign *lex loci delicti* to be applied, preserving the traditional English approach.[51] There is some doubt as to the import of section 72 of the Bills of Exchange Act 1882, but even here principle suggests that it should not be mandatory.[52]

Greater difficulty arises where a possibly mandatory rule has its source at common law, for here no refuge is possible in the canons of statutory interpretation. There is ambiguity, for example, as to whether foreign law must be introduced when this is required for the meaningful construction of a statute.[53] If it exists, does this override the counter-principle that, if foreign law is not pleaded or proved, its content is deemed to be that of English law? In practice, little may turn on the point. More problematic are the problems which arise in defamation proceedings.[54] In such cases it is sometimes assumed that the double actionability rule of liability is mandatory, such that it requires a claimant to plead actionability under the *lex loci delicti*. This leads to the associated difficulty that claimants, in an effort to avoid the burden of proof, may do so but introduce no evidence as to

[48] See above, p. 126.
[49] See above, p. 75.
[50] See above, p. 129.
[51] See above, p. 97.
[52] See above, p. 130.
[53] See above, pp. 135–138.
[54] See above, pp. 99–106.

foreign law. By relying on the presumption of similarity between English law and foreign law they may shift to the defendant the burden of rebutting the presumption. But, as we saw in Chapter IV, it is doubtful that the presumption of similarity justifies invoking foreign law but not also proving it. Indeed, the problem brings into sharp relief the somewhat doubtful status of that unlikely presumption.

Overall, therefore, English law's voluntarist approach to foreign law conforms with principle and has practical benefits. Those respects in which it differs from other legal systems teach little about the adequacy of that approach, although they illustrate some radical differences between English law and its civil law neighbours which originate in assumptions far beyond the pleading and proof of foreign law. Indeed, as we saw in Chapter IX, the difficulties which arise in this area are far from being special. They reflect, for example, the fact that English law lacks a clear taxonomy of mandatory rules of a type familiar in most civil law systems. Such questions as whether and to what extent a rule is imperative are seldom articulated in English law, whether in the conflict of laws or elsewhere, which is not to say that the problem may not arise. Still less does English law possess the conceptual equipment with which to answer them. Nor does it make use of the distinction between waivable patrimonial rights and unwaivable non-patrimonial rights on which the civil law approach to this area often depends. Nor do English lawyers tend to think in terms of particular areas of law being *d'ordre public*, having a public policy character which limits the extent to which litigants may freely regulate their affairs. Nor do they generally reflect on the extent which, outside the law of contract, it is possible to replace the objectively applicable law by choice.

Lacking such conceptual resources, the English approach to identifying the mandatory quality of rules for choice of law has a somewhat *ad hoc* appearance, often amounting to nothing more than an exercise in statutory interpretation. Indeed, without such conceptual tools it is not merely hard to discern the extent to which the pleading of foreign law is truly voluntary, it is sometimes easy to forget that such a possibility even exists. But, if English law has not articulated an approach to such questions, they do not raise issues which cannot be answered by careful analysis. In particular, the solution would seem to lie first in recognizing that the application of the *lex fori* is the general rule in English law; secondly, in properly classifying an omission to plead foreign law as having choice of law implications; and, thirdly, in enquiring whether, in its terms or by implication, any given choice of law rule excludes the possibility of party choice.

But, if it is generally satisfactory, complacency about the present law is not justified. There is much uncertainty about the status of several prominent choice of law rules, mostly statutory in origin. Only if such statutes clearly stated whether and to what extent they are mandatory would such doubts be resolved—or resolved without litigation. Again, the view that foreign law may be invoked yet not proved, which depends on a generous application of the presumption of similarity, is relatively widespread. It is one of many difficulties which may be eradicated finally only once the uncertain scope of that presumption is recognized.[55] Continued adherence to the presumption of similarity is not, however, the only obstacle to clarity in understanding the present law. More fundamentally, it is commonly assumed that whether foreign law must be introduced concerns the pleading of foreign law and is thus procedural. If this view is accepted, this at once obscures the important question whether any given choice of law rule is mandatory in character. One consequence is that tension is immediately created between English law and international instruments such as the Rome and Brussels Conventions. Indeed, if such a view is taken to its limits no English conflicts rule could be mandatory, in the sense that it would always be subverted by reference to procedural rules of pleading. As the persistence of such conceptual difficulties suggest English law currently rests on ambiguous doctrinal foundations. This is not to say that legislation is necessarily required, provided that the subject's inherent logic is kept firmly in mind, and provided that the proper limitations to be imposed upon some familiar notions are clearly understood. But, given the resilience of the conventional wisdom in this area, legislation may be the only way to dislodge some prevalent but misleading assumptions and to correct the law's trajectory.

3. ESTABLISHING FOREIGN LAW

How is any procedural institution to be assessed?[56] It might be supposed that access to justice is the measure, although it is unclear that such a benchmark is sufficient by itself. Certainly, access to justice cannot be an absolute good, for it cannot be that every prospective claimant should have such access without qualification. The most we can expect is that good reasons must exist where claimants are prevented from proceeding. It may be, for example, that the expense of proving foreign law is an obstacle to ill-funded parties. But this is a true objection only if such expense is unjustified, or if no cheaper means exist to achieve the same end. Again, as this suggests, access to justice is ultimately a matter of the cost of litigation. If so, the true measure of a procedure is its cost—or, more precisely, whether its cost is justified given the purpose it is designed to serve. But it

---

[55] See above, p. 143.
[56] See further, Jolowicz, above n. 35; Lord Woolf, *Access to Justice, Interim Report to the Lord Chancellor*, (London, HMSO, 1995), Ch. 1.

is not simply the accessibility of the legal process which matters. It is the fact that, once accessed, the process is just. This is partly a matter of procedural fairness, in so far as legal institutions must be impartial. But it is also a substantive matter. For, if, say, the procedures for proving foreign law are inadequate, this may be unjust if it prevents a proper determination of the parties' rights and liabilities. Justice apart, those procedures must also serve the purposes of substantive law. It would, for example, defeat the objectives of the choice of law process if the means of establishing the content of foreign law are deficient. There is, then, no single benchmark of acceptability in judging procedural institutions. They must be accessible. But they must also be procedurally fair, encourage just outcomes, and serve the purposes of substantive law. We should not suppose, however, that every procedural institution should (or could) satisfy all these requirements in equal measure. As we shall see, it is more likely, and more realistic, that a given procedure's success will depend on a trade-off between these important but challenging aspirations.

How are English law's procedures for establishing foreign law to be judged? In principle, English law provides a range of optional methods of establishing foreign law. In relatively easy cases, perhaps involving no more than the construction of a foreign statute, a court might determine foreign law without expert evidence.[57] But this is very unusual, and is subject to control by the courts, who may request expert testimony if they are unable to proceed in a meaningful way without it. The accuracy of this method is also suspect except, perhaps, where the statutes of other common law countries are involved. In cases of somewhat greater difficulty, the affidavit evidence of experts might be employed.[58] Those involving the written laws of civil law countries, or matters involving the effect of case law, might be examples. But the courts have deprecated the use of this method[59] and the lessons to be derived from interlocutory proceedings (where affidavit evidence is normal) are not encouraging.[60] As this implies, the majority of cases may be too complex to submit to streamlined treatment. Disputes about foreign law, which involve conflicts of opinion, also lend themselves naturally to the oral examination of experts.[61] It is therefore unsurprising that this method is almost invariably adopted in practice.

As this suggests, the central issue is whether employing party-led experts is a desirable and effective means of proving foreign law. In principle it has many advantages. It is a singularly appropriate way of handling foreign law disputes. It captures the argumentative, dialectical

---

[57] See above, pp. 257–262. [58] See above, pp. 204–210. [59] See above, p. 204.
[60] See above, pp. 206–210.
[61] This is the experience in the United States, where Federal practice encourages a choice in methods of proof: see above, p. 279.

nature of legal reasoning and may put the judge as nearly as possible in the position of one in a foreign system by offering the court alternative perspectives on the law in question. It is particularly effective because it depends upon forceful argument and counter-argument, reflecting the vigour and ingenuity which only those profoundly interested in the outcome may bring to such a contest. As has been said, truth 'is best discovered by powerful statement on both sides of the question'.[62] Again, as a prominent theorist of legal reasoning has said, to similar effect:

> Every practical man is thoroughly convinced that the proper method of legal reasoning is an argumentation through which we discuss, with regard to each problem, reasons for or against an attitude or decision.[63]

Just as the adversarial nature of the process makes proof by party experts effective, so it makes it fair, by allowing each party the opportunity to put its case and press it to the fullest extent. This is certainly the view of the courts. In a recent case, not involving foreign law, the question arose whether a court expert might be appointed instead of those of the parties. The argument for doing so was that such a course would be more efficient and less costly. The Court of Appeal responded with caution to that utilitarian argument and emphatically affirmed the right of litigants to introduce their own evidence on grounds of fairness:

> Limitations on expert evidence, although permissible under the rules, have rarely if ever been so strictly applied in a case of this kind ... It would be most unfortunate if the Court of Appeal were to block reasonable attempts to mitigate the effects of established practice. At the same time of course, both trial judge and Court of Appeal must be constantly alert to the paramount requirements of justice; justice to the plaintiff and justice to the defendant. To expedite the just despatch of cases is one thing; merely to expedite the despatch of cases is quite another. The right of the parties to a fair trial of the issues between them cannot be compromised.[64]

The employment of party experts is also likely to attract the confidence of litigants by allowing them considerable control of the presentation of their case, in the selection of experts, in examination and cross-examination. It thus offers what the parties most prize in an adversarial system. But this common practice is not free from difficulty. For all the virtues of an adversarial approach there may be doubt that proof by experts is, or can be, effective. Indeed, the adversarial nature of the process may be regarded as the source of difficulty in so far as party-led experts may be partial, and

---

[62] *Ex.p. Lloyd* (1822) Mont. at 72n., cited in *Jones* v. *NCB*. [1957] 2 QB 55 (per Lord Denning MR); see also, Andrews, *Principles of Civil Procedure* (London, 1994), 34–35.
[63] Perelman, *Justice, Law and Argument* (Dordrecht, 1980), 148.
[64] *Abbey National Mortgages plc* v. *Key Surveyors Nationwide Ltd.* [1996] 3 All ER 184, 186–187 (CA); see above, p. 237.

thus unreliable. Again, resort to party experts, compared perhaps with using a single independent expert, may seem unnecessarily costly.

(a) INEFFECTIVENESS

It is reasonable to suppose that any mechanism for proving foreign law must be effective in two senses. It must prosecute the principal purpose of the conflicts process, namely the application of the governing law, which implies that foreign law (when it governs) must be applied as accurately as possible. But any procedural institution must be effective in another way. It must encourage the resolution of the parties' differences in a way which has their confidence. For the application of foreign law, and the success of the conflicts process, are not ends in themselves, but merely means whereby disputes are fairly disposed of. Even if the proof of foreign law is inaccurate it may serve a useful function.

Expert proof might be ineffective if the evidence is incomplete.[65] But in the English experience, expert evidence is seldom criticized for its insufficiency.[66] At least in cases involving foreign law, it is a valuable means of supplying comprehensive information to the court and acquainting it with alternative points of view. A more important criticism is that such an adversarial approach to legal reasoning obstructs the search for legal truth by distorting the enquiry in favour of the partisan interests of litigants. But partiality, although widely perceived as a problem, is less troublesome than might appear. On the one hand, contrary to supposition, lawyers normally counsel their experts against lack of objectivity, partiality correctly being perceived as counter-productive.[67] A party's adviser is more likely to seek out evidence which is objective (but favourable) than rely on that which is partial, even if this means rejecting a number of unsatisfactory opinions.[68] A second reason why partiality is not especially problematic in proving foreign law concerns the nature of legal reasoning.[69] An expert's opinion, like any expression of opinion on a point of law, necessarily involves taking and arguing for a position. In a sense, it is bound to be partial in so far as it seeks to make a case. This does not mean that it should be intellectually dishonest, or omit to deal with contrary evidence, for it must at least conform to the accepted standards of ethical legal argument.[70] But it ensures that it will be, in a strict sense, rhetorical. Indeed, given the wide variety of conflicting views which may be held on any

---

[65] Wright and Miller, above n. 4, para. 2444.
[66] The opposite may be the case: *Macmillan Inc.* v. *Bishopsgate Investment Trust plc* [1995] 1 WLR 978, 1014.
[67] Hodgkinson, 85–88. [68] Hodgkinson, 86.
[69] For consideration of the rhetorical nature of legal reasoning see, Perelman, above n. 63; *The New Rhetoric* (Notre Dame, 1969).
[70] Ormrod, (1968) 92 JP 65, 67; Hodgkinson, 90–91.

point of law (English or foreign), it is especially hard to see in practice when an expert's opinion is illegitimately partisan, as distinct from properly persuasive. It is no coincidence that the most common defect which English judges detect in evidence as to foreign law is not that it is 'incorrect' but that it is 'unconvincing'.

It is clear, therefore, that opinions concerning foreign law must not suffer from bias or distortion, nor must they be merely hortatory. But, in an important sense, to criticize such opinions for their partiality may be to mistake the nature of legal reasoning. It may assume that foreign law can be established in some objective sense, as if by scientific demonstration. But to do so may also mistake the nature of the foreign law problem. Certainly, the traditional characterization of foreign laws as facts distracts attention from the reality that the determination of foreign law is, in effect, a matter of legal argument.

But special problems of effectiveness arise when expert evidence is required in interlocutory proceedings. In such cases, where affidavit evidence is normal, it may be necessary to determine foreign law on unsatisfactory evidence. We have seen how reluctant courts are in such cases simply to apply the burden of proof and find against one who has relied on foreign law.[71] Because such proceedings are interlocutory it is possible to take account of foreign law without resolving it finally.[72] It may also be possible to avoid having to determine foreign law on limited evidence. The court might do so, for example, by directing a defendant to waive any advantage it might have in a foreign forum under foreign law.[73] Again, it might be possible, although only perhaps if both parties agree, to call experts for examination, thereby removing the difficulty.[74] As many cases imply, real difficulty may be caused when a court is required to determine foreign law in interlocutory proceedings. But as they also suggest, an impressive range of strategies has been developed in response.

Problems of a different sort occur at trial. Here it must be emphasized that not all cases where expert evidence is required are of the same type. Indeed, in assessing the strength of the present system different situations must be segregated. Often the process of proof may be time-consuming and costly but neither the parties nor the court may doubt that an effective (or acceptable) determination is achievable. Indeed, the courts in such cases display considerable facility in resolving the most difficult questions, inevitably in the light of conflicting testimony.[75] On other occasions, however, the nature of the question of law involved may be such that the very effectiveness of the process is in doubt. Cases where everything turns on an intimate acquaintance with the underlying policies, principles and habits of thought in the foreign system may be of this type.[76] Particular

[71] See above, p.209.
[74] See above, p. 207.
[72] See above, p. 207.
[75] See above, p. 190.
[73] See above, p. 208.
[76] See above, p. 47.

problems arise, for example, when different sources of law—case law, statute, public policy, religious law—must be weighed against each other.[77] Given that relatively few cases concerning foreign law are easy, and that most will require expert evidence, the real question is how this final category of truly hard case may be dealt with. Do English courts possess techniques sophisticated enough to handle such situations?

One response is to prevent such proceedings from coming to trial at all. As we have seen, it is precisely in such cases of real difficulty, where the effectiveness of the process of proof may be compromised, that proceedings are sometimes stayed under the doctrine of *forum non conveniens*.[78] But this is not a complete solution, not least because the doctrine is not always available. Nor is it desirable simply to find that the burden of proof has not been discharged in cases of extreme difficulty. The courts are markedly reluctant to allow the proof of foreign law to fail and it may be unfair to penalise a party for failing to establish something which, in a sense, is beyond determination.[79] In truth, in cases such as this it may be necessary to augment the process of proof. One possibility is to use the European Convention on Information on Foreign Law, although doubts may surround the identity of the designated expert in such cases.[80] The appointment of a court expert is also possible, although it is unclear that merely obtaining a third expert opinion will always assist matters.[81] A better option may be to seek the appointment of an assessor whose task is to assist the court by supplying precisely the expertise and intimate acquaintance with the foreign system which is required.[82] The identity of the assessor may be problematic, however, and the cost of such proceedings may become daunting.

It may be hoped, especially in a more managed procedural climate, that courts and litigants will experiment with such techniques, at least in cases of extreme difficulty. But it is also clear that such methods have serious shortcomings and it would be wrong to exaggerate their potential. Indeed, the problem of proving foreign law in truly hard cases suggests that it may be inevitable that foreign law is sometimes determined ineffectively. This is not to say that there is a meaningful sense in which a foreign court is bound to get the right answer while an English court is not. But it is to recognize that the likelihood of a foreign court obtaining an accurate solution is higher. This does not mean, however, that the process of proof is without virtue, to be rejected. For, paradoxical as it may appear, it may sometimes be acceptable to determine foreign law ineffectively. Provided, that is, that it is done in a way which is acceptable to the parties and which facilitates the resolution of their dispute. Certainly, a likely response to such cases in practice is that litigants will place a higher value on an

[77] See above, p. 47.   [78] See above, p. 45.   [79] See above, p. 186.
[80] See above, p. 239.   [81] See above, p. 211.   [82] See above, p. 215.

authoritative if flawed result achieved without further delay and expense. The logic of the situation suggests as much. The extreme difficulty of the case may become apparent, at least to the court, only at trial as the examination of witnesses progresses. At that stage it may be preferable to resolve the matter finally, without further delay, rather than do so perfectly. Such a pragmatic solution cannot conceal the fact that, at least in the hardest case, the proof of foreign law may be unable to secure the proper application of foreign law. But it ensures that the process is not altogether devoid of purpose or meaning.

But the problem of the truly hard case should not be exaggerated, not least because courts display remarkable confidence in handling the most difficult questions of foreign law. Lord Langdale in *Nelson* v. *Bridport*[83] regarded all cases involving foreign law as intractable:

... there is, in every case of foreign law, an absence of all the accumulated knowledge and ready associations which assist him in the consideration of that which is English law, and of the manner in which it ought to be applied.[84]

But he also assumed that expert evidence was adequate in such situations. Certainly, the practice of the courts confirms that most cases involving foreign law are resolved without difficulty. As has been said:

It is part of the stock-in-trade of the practitioner and judge in the Commercial Court to deal with this kind of dispute and the volume of business in the court would give the lie to any suggestion that the court is seen by its users as incapable of dealing with any but characteristically English disputes...[85]

Even in cases of the most severe difficulty the range of strategies depicted above may permit a workable solution in most cases. And the parties may retain confidence that their dispute is being fairly handled, however inaccurate the process of determination becomes. Moreover, we should not employ too narrow a conception of what counts as an acceptable determination of foreign law. As we shall see in the following section it is simplistic to assume that a foreign court is empowered to secure the right answer while an English court is not. What matters is that the process of proof replicates as far as possible the circumstances in which a foreign court would decide. This might include familiarising the English court with the style of reasoning, the cultural assumptions and the underlying principles which are the context of the foreign court's approach. Nor is it appropriate to ask whether the English court thus equipped would arrive at the same result as a foreign court. For that is to assume that only one answer is correct. What matters is that the English court achieves a result which is

---

[83] (1845) 8 Beav. 527.   [84] At 534–535.
[85] *Muduroglu Ltd.* v. *T C Ziraat Bankasi* [1986] 3 WLR 606, 625 (per Mustill LJ)(CA); see also, the remarks quoted in Lord Woolf, above n. 56. But contrast the position in the United States: Zweigert (1973) 44 *Colorado L. Rev.* 283, 298.

within the range of options properly available to the foreign court. Judged by this less stringent, but more realistic, test the number of cases in which the proof of foreign law is truly ineffective is less than might be supposed.

But in the end, the question is not so much whether English law is deficient in such cases, as whether any better alternative exists. In this respect, it is hard to see how the current approach could be materially improved given the range of alternatives. The use of expert evidence is perhaps the most effective means of supplying the greatest range of information and opinion in such cases.[86] And, as we have seen, the opposing nature of such testimony comes close to reflecting the inherently argumentative character of legal reasoning. Merely because the technique is sometimes imperfect in hard cases does not mean that the application of foreign law in such cases should not be attempted. Moreover, that the proof of foreign law has its limits is not to say that the English approach is inadequate or easily replaceable. Certainly, it is doubtful that viable alternatives exist to the current English approach—none, at least, which do not attract other problems. We have already seen the disadvantages associated with foreign judicial assistance and court-appointed experts.[87] Neither mechanism in its pure form is likely to be fair or effective, except in simple cases, unless the parties call their own experts in addition. But in most situations that will add to the delay and expense without necessarily improving the court's knowledge or understanding. And in easy cases it will be pointless to use such devices when simpler means exist to establish foreign law. Resort to assessors to assist the court in matters of special difficulty has a particular attraction. It is peculiarly an assessor's function to compensate for a judge's inexperience in technical matters,[88] which may be especially valuable in cases which call for an intimate grasp of a foreign system's assumptions. But the expense, and the difficulty of identifying a suitable person, weigh against the possibility in practice.

(b) Excessive Costs

A common charge is that the use of expert opinion, and the examination of experts, is time-consuming and (which is the same point) costly. It can deter litigation, or cause litigants to proceed under English law. Its expense may also prejudice the less well-funded party who must gamble on the chance of success if the costs are to be recovered. But English law responds in several ways to the inevitable cost and delay of proving

---

[86] Schmertz, (1978) 18 *Virginia Jl. of Intl L.* 697, 707 (1978); Wright and Miller, above n. 4, para. 646.
[87] See above, pp. 232; 238.
[88] Cf. *Baldwin and Francis v. Patents Appeal Tribunal* [1959] AC 663, 691 (per Lord Denning MR) (CA).

foreign law. First, it is very often the case that proceedings in England under foreign law might alternatively be brought in the forum whose law is in question. A defendant in such a case might rely on such cost and delay in obtaining a stay of English proceedings. And the plaintiff has the opportunity to weigh such factors in deciding whether to proceed in England or in the country concerned. Secondly, English law generally allows both parties to dispense with a dispute's foreign elements altogether by not pleading foreign law. Indeed, a significant, if paradoxical, feature of English law's voluntary approach to pleading foreign law is that it commonly allows litigants to avoid its proof. Thirdly, there is a growing trend towards limiting the time taken in the oral examination of expert witness, thereby reducing the significant cost of this process. It is unlikely, save in the simplest cases, that it would be appropriate to contemplate excluding such evidence altogether.[89] But it is now clear that courts may exercise their discretion more readily to limit the duration of oral examination.[90]

Finally, and most importantly, even if proof by party experts is costly, it may be cost-effective, justifying the expense. Cost-effectiveness in this context means, first, that the use of experts is proportionate to the difficulty of the case in hand; secondly, that it is an effective means of proof; and, thirdly, that it was actually necessary in the case in hand to address questions of foreign law at all. The foregoing discussion implies an answer to the first and second points. English law encourages proportionality by making available a range of techniques for proving foreign law. In most cases, however, expert evidence will be required, which ensures that it is normally a proportionate method of proof. True, courts will not insist that litigants should prove foreign law other than by expert evidence, even if a case might be suitable for a less cumbersome approach. This is partly because, historically, they have never been able to exclude expert evidence. But it may also reflect the reality that litigants will normally want to introduce such evidence. Certainly, where the parties wish to employ less formal techniques—typically in the form of foreign legal materials—courts will normally accede to their request.[91] They will not require expert evidence where the parties want otherwise, and where it is unnecessary. Again, in the majority of cases this method is probably effective as a means of establishing foreign law authentically. In exceptional cases its success in doing so may be questioned, but the technique may be no less effective than any alternative mechanism.

The third point arises because there may be cases where expert evidence is introduced although no real issue of foreign law divides the parties. The difficulty in such a case is not that the proof of foreign law is inherently

---

[89] At the time of writing this is not permitted.
[90] Practice Direction [1995] 1 All ER 385, para. 2.   [91] See above, pp. 257–262.

costly, but that the expense of proving foreign law is unnecessary. At first sight it may seem surprising that such cases might exist but they are, in reality, a feature of adversarial approaches to litigation, in which courts have limited powers to control the framework of proceedings. Certainly, cases may arise in which conflicts issues are needlessly taken, or in which there is no real dispute between the parties as to foreign law. Indeed, the true solution to the problem of proving foreign law may lie not so much in altering the techniques for doing so, as in restricting, by such means, the number of cases in which it is required. It is therefore important that courts may exercise some control over the number of cases in which the proof of foreign law is required at all. Certainly, English law is gradually developing mechanisms whereby litigants are encouraged to reduce the issues which require expert proof, whether of foreign law or other matters. Meetings between the parties' experts[92] and the mutual disclosure of reports in advance of trial[93] are but examples of a growing trend.[94] Moreover, it is now clear that the introduction of needless expense, especially by taking unnecessary points which turn on expert evidence, may be penalised by 'appropriate orders for costs, including wasted costs orders'.[95] As a recent Practice Direction expresses it:

In advance of trial parties should use their best endeavours to agree which are the issues or the main issues, and it is their duty so far as possible to reduce or eliminate the expert issues.[96]

As such reflections imply, the cost of proving foreign law may not be quite the problem that is supposed. Certainly, if the cost of such proof is unjustified this may not be directly attributable to the use of party experts, but to the circumstances in which such experts are used. For, if an element of cost is recognized (as it must be) as an inescapable feature of litigation, the real issue is whether a given procedure is cost-effective. And, as we have seen, this may be said of many cases in which expert evidence is employed to prove foreign law. This is not to say that excessively costly cases may not arise. But it means that the proof of foreign law by party experts is not inherently flawed by reason of its expense.

(c) CONCLUSION

In conclusion, the success of English law's approach to proving foreign law depends on several factors. Like any procedural institution the regime

---

[92] RSC Order 38, r. 38.   [93] RSC Order 38, r. 37.
[94] Lord Woolf, above n. 56, 183–184; *Access to Justice, Final Report to the Lord Chancellor*, 147–149.
[95] Ibid.; see also *Macmillan Inc. v. Bishopsgate Investment Trust plc (No. 3)* [1995] 1 WLR 978, 1013–1014.
[96] Practice Direction [1995] 1 All ER 385, para. 4.

must offer proportionality between the technique employed and the case in hand. It must be effective in serving the objectives of substantive law—in this case in ensuring the application of foreign law. It must be fair, notably by allowing each party to put its case. It must also attract the confidence of litigants, the consumers of the legal system. Not least, it must be cost-effective, its inevitable expense justifiable. By these standards, as we have seen, the English approach is in principle satisfactory. But as always in the law, its success ultimately depends on the skill and good sense of the courts and those who argue before them. And, as the following section suggests, it is still possible to harbour doubts about the very practice of proving foreign law, and about how the English approach is commonly understood.

4. REMAINING DOUBTS

However satisfactory the English approach to foreign law, two lingering doubts remain. The first concerns whether the conflicts process, and the determination of foreign law, can ever be effective, however sophisticated the methods employed.[97] If not, only the harmonization of the world's legal systems will solve the problem of conflicting laws. And application of the *lex fori* may be preferable, on grounds of cost and convenience, to devising choice of law rules which may lead to the application of foreign law. The point here is not whether the English approach is as good as can be, it is whether the application of one country's law in another's courts is ever appropriate. The second cause for unease is that, although the English approach may be acceptable, it is too often depicted in a misleading fashion which masks its virtues and encourages its vices.

On inspection, scepticism about the very idea of applying foreign law may be unfounded. It is not to the point, for example, to say that the resolution of disputes would be assisted were their foreign elements removed, because they would be quicker and cheaper to resolve. One may just as well say that proceedings in negligence would be improved were there no need to establish a duty of care, or that contractual disputes would be less expensive if the need to establish agreement were abolished. As with such examples, so a case's foreign elements are important because they allow courts to arrive at results which reflect a case's true nature. To apply foreign law may be sound in policy, if it has a particular claim to be applied. And it is just, by enforcing the rights and duties of the parties under the law which they may expect to govern.

[97] See above, pp. 13–16.

Again, as we have seen, in judging the effectiveness of applying foreign law, a degree of realism is required. It should not be imagined, in particular, that establishing foreign law is inherently inferior to determining the matter in the courts of the country concerned. Certainly, to say that an English court is bound to be wrong in applying foreign law implies that the relevant foreign court is bound to be right. But to hold that the 'correct' answer is available in the foreign forum is to make the jurisprudentially suspect assumption that answers to legal questions can ever be correct in some objective sense. It is implicitly to deny a more plausible, but more relativist, account of legal truth. This is that the adequacy of a finding of law lies partly in its approximation to the substantive principles and assumptions of the system concerned, and partly in the conformity of the court's reasoning with the prevailing, formal standards of argumentation.[98] Provided a court can be acquainted with these defining aspects of the foreign legal culture its approach may be no less acceptable than that in the relevant foreign court. Certainly, it is important to recognize that there is no uniquely correct solution to complex questions of law, whatever the nature of the legal system concerned. As such, there is no meaningful sense in which an English court might be criticised for not obtaining the result which a foreign court might achieve. Indeed, even if a foreign court were subsequently to differ from an English court's finding of foreign law, this may be no cause for complaint. The benchmark is whether the English court secures a result which the foreign court might plausibly have secured. For just as the foreign court has, in effect, a choice between equally sound solutions, so should the English court be allowed an equivalent choice.

If an English court is adequately informed, and if the court decides in accordance with that information, then, save in the hardest cases, it is unclear in what sense its ruling on foreign law should be seen as inherently inferior. It may be cheaper and more convenient to have the point resolved abroad, but it need not be better—certainly, the application of

---

[98] The literature on legal objectivity and the constraints on judicial choice is large. For accessible accounts see the papers collected in Cohen, ed., *Ronald Dworkin and Contemporary Jurisprudence* (London, 1983), especially those in Parts Two and Three. A relativist account of legal truth is implicit in several discussions of the difficulty of establishing foreign law. Writers sometimes doubt the efficacy of the process because evidence of a foreign system's standards of adjudication may be hard to acquire. As has been said:

Each rule of law must be considered from the point of view of its temporal applicability, its constitutional validity, its context, its qualifications whether statutory or judicial, its value when compared with other legal notions or fitted into a different legal system and its meaning under the foreign legal terminology and manner of thinking. The foreign legal thinking may be so different as to preclude the use of analogies with the domestic law . . .

Stern, (1957) 45 *Cal.L.Rev.*23, 40–41, considered in Schmertz, (1978) 18 *Virginia Jl. Intl. L.* 697, 699.

foreign law in England need not be worse. As a distinguished judge has remarked:

> ... it does not follow that the judge at first instance here is more likely to misunderstand or misapply the law than his counterpart abroad ...[99]

In the end, if we jettison the troubling notion of legal objectivity, we can never expect more of a court in applying its own law than that its decisions are true to the principles, assumptions, and standards of argumentation of the system concerned. If so, we can expect no more of a judge applying foreign law. The purpose of proving foreign law is not to deliver truth, but to reproduce the circumstances in which decisions are made in a foreign court. The point is not whether a court achieves the right answer under foreign law but whether it secures an authentic answer.

But suppose that the proof of foreign law is indeed ineffective, in the sense that a judge cannot hope to handle it as a foreign judge might. This might be so in those exceptionally hard cases where an understanding of foreign law depends on an intimate knowledge of local assumptions, conventions of reasoning or policy. But, even if we allow that such cases exist, they do not render the application of foreign law inappropriate in those which are less intractable. It is no argument against the application of foreign law altogether. Again, inaccuracy (in the sense of lack of authenticity) in the application of foreign law may be intellectually unsatisfying. But, as we have seen in the English context, it does not rob the process of all purpose or justification. Inaccurate as it may be, that process may be as sound as can be, and it may retain the confidence of litigants by contributing to the resolution of their differences without undue expense and convenience. If so, it serves an important function for any procedural institution. For the proof of foreign law is not an end in itself. It is a means to the fair resolution of disputes, a result which may not depend upon whether foreign law is correctly applied.

So the proof of foreign law may not be inherently flawed. And, as we have seen, English law has the capacity to achieve the necessary authenticity in applying foreign law. But a nagging doubt remains. Certainly, the law may be presented in an acceptable fashion. Indeed, the present work is an extended argument for the view that, on inspection, English law is broadly satisfactory, its defects depending on misunderstandings of principle. But this depends upon a departure from tradition. It requires the

---

[99] *Muduroglu Ltd.* v. *T C Ziraat Bankasi* [1986] 3 WLR 606, 625, per Mustill LJ (CA); *The Eleftheria* [1969] 1 Lloyd's Rep. 237, 246. Mustill LJ did, however, have reservations about the possible difference between the treatment an issue might receive on appeal. See also, Schurig, 'Interessenjurisprudenz contra Interessenjurisprudenz, Anmerkungen zu Flessners Thesen', *Rabels Zeitschrift*, 1995, 229, 241, cited in De Boer, above n. 40, 422, n. 187: 'The proposition that, *in general*, the application of foreign law by German courts is spectacularly inferior cannot be accepted'.

abandonment of the fact doctrine, or at least of its more troubling implications. If the role of mandatory conflicts rules is not to cause intolerable difficulty, for example, we must understand how the pleading of foreign law functions in the conflicts process. We must especially be aware that whether foreign law must be introduced in a given case is a matter of substantive private international law, not one of procedure. Again, if the flexibility inherent in the proof of foreign law is to be exploited, we must remove the inhibitions imposed by the fact doctrine, strictly enforced.

But if the success of the English approach requires abandoning the fact doctrine or, at the least, appreciating its numerous shortcomings, does this require legislative reform? One argument against legislation is that the traditional view is adequate in practice, however we might interpret the law's conceptual structure. This is surely untenable with regard to the introduction of foreign law, given especially the potential conflict between the Rome and Brussels Conventions and English law's procedural approach to pleading. But is it plausible in connection with the proof of foreign law? If proof by expert testimony is, in practice, the most likely means of proof, why trouble with exceptional cases? One answer is that undue adherence to the fact doctrine may cabin the courts' assessment of foreign law by questioning their power to depart from such evidence. Another is that cases do arise in which flexibility may be necessary. More importantly, it is hard to resist the thought that the adequacy of the traditional approach is to some extent self-justifying. True, foreign law is normally proved by expert evidence. But is that because litigants, concerned at the needless cost, simply do not submit easier questions of foreign law to proof at all, unaware that cheaper means exist? Or is it that such alternative methods are not employed, and expert evidence is needlessly used, because it is conventionally assumed that no other methods exist? In reality, we can never know how viable other alternatives may be until their existence is recognized, or confirmed by statute.

Another objection to legislation is that the courts may be relied upon to ensure that the present approach is satisfactory. Certainly, there are many cases in which courts have appreciated the limitations of the fact doctrine. Indeed, such decisions are the basis for the view that the law, properly understood, is satisfactory. But courts and commentators are as ready to apply the fact doctrine strictly. And to rely on a liberal reading of the cases is no guarantee that the law will progress along flexible lines. Certainly, the four principles described at the start of this chapter are often regarded as axiomatic, and the force of conventional wisdom in the conflict of laws should not be underestimated.[100] Indeed, given the relative infrequency of

[100] Fentiman, 'Legal Reasoning in the Conflict of Laws', Krawietz, MacCormick and von Wright, eds., *Prescriptive Formality and Normative Rationality, Festschrift for Robert S. Summers* (Berlin, 1994), 454–460.

cases having foreign elements, by comparison with those which are purely domestic, this is not surprising. Nor is it a matter of criticism. If the case law is sparse, and cases infrequent, any subject takes on a particular shape and character. Neither counsel nor the courts acquire experience in its ways, which may incline them to rely to a high degree on commentators and the *opinio juris*. And because cases are few, such dicta as do exist, perhaps in old authorities, acquire exaggerated importance, whether or not they remain appropriate. The consequence is that in private international law we cannot always rely on judicial self-reform to progress the subject and cure its deficiencies. It may be an unusual situation in whch legislation might be necessary, not simply to resolve practical problems, but to assert the law's conceptual basis.

With such considerations in mind, legislation may be the only secure route to abandoning the fact doctrine—or, at least, to ensuring that its limitations are clear. Uncertainty as to how the law should be understood, and the tenacity of the traditional view, might alone argue for such reform. Certainly, statute might be the only guarantee that the difficulties inherent in the fact doctrine will be avoided. In general terms, such legislation might reflect the following principles.

First, English law should be regarded as the applicable law except where the law of another country applies, and where the content of that law has been established to the satisfaction of the court. A statutory provision in such terms would define the relationship between English and foreign law without reference to any presumption of similarity[101] and would clarify the role of English law where foreign law is unpleaded or inadequately proved.[102] In such cases it is simply the applicable law.

Secondly, the role of mandatory choice of law rules should be clarified.[103] Attention might be given to three matters. Thus, it should be clear that a failure to invoke foreign law where this is required by the rules of private international law should result, not in the application of English law by default, but in dismissal of the claim or defence. In principle, an omission to give particulars of the law in question, or to introduce appropriate evidence at trial, should have the same effect. Moreover, where the relevant choice of law rule allows for the possibility that English law might be the applicable law it should be clear that a claimant may avoid the obligation to establish foreign law by demonstrating that English law applies. As we saw in Chapter III it is doubtful whether the rule of double actionability in defamation requires a claimant to show actionability under the *lex loci delicti*. But if it does so, no such obligation would exist were the claimant to demonstrate that English law is that which is most

---

[101] See above, pp. 146–153, 183–188.

significantly related to the wrong in question. Finally, as considerable doubt surrounds whether particular choice of law rules have a mandatory character, it is arguable that this should be expressly addressed. A statement might be included to the effect that a choice of law rule shall be presumed to be optional in character unless in its terms or by implication its effect is otherwise. It is doubtful, however, that such a provision, which may simply reflect current practice, is strictly required. An alternative strategy would be to ensure that any future statute which contains rules for choice of law should state expressly whether they are to be accorded mandatory status.

Thirdly, even a party who relies voluntarily upon foreign law should be required to provide particulars of the law in question, and to introduce appropriate evidence at trial. This should not be understood as implying that the relevant claim or defence should suffer dismissal if ultimately such evidence does not prevail. But it removes the risk that a defendant may be required to disprove what a plaintiff has deliberately failed to establish.[104] It has the effect of abolishing the presumption of similarity between English and foreign law in the context in which it is most troublesome.

Fourthly, where the application of foreign law is required by a rule of private international law, it should not be open to the parties to argue that the pleading of foreign law is voluntary on the ground that it is a matter of procedure. A provision to this effect would confirm that the introduction of foreign law is a substantive issue of private international law and thus prevent the evasion of the objectively applicable law.[105]

Fifthly, it should be possible to establish foreign law by the evidence of experts, or by reference to any relevant material or source submitted by the parties, or by any other means acceptable to the court. This removes any constraints which the fact doctrine might otherwise impose. It offers flexibility in the process of establishing foreign law[106] and in the assessment of evidence by the court.[107] Any provision in such terms, by not adumbrating the available methods, would allow the courts to develop a practice as to what is permissible. It leaves open, for example, whether foreign law may be notorious.[108] But it explicitly sanctions the practice of establishing foreign law by the construction of foreign legal texts, and confirms the court's power to substitute its own view of such material for that of an expert. If desired, a proviso could be added whereby a court is permitted to depart from expert testimony by reference to such material only in exceptional cases.[109] Provision might also be made to confirm the status in English law of the European Convention on Information on Foreign

[102] See above, p. 290.
[103] See above, pp. 66–67.
[104] See above, pp. 146–153.
[105] See above, p. 70.
[106] See above, pp. 262–264.
[107] See above, pp. 194–201.
[108] See above, p. 248.

Law. But we have seen that the Convention may not be of particular value in practice and this may be unnecessary.[110]

Sixthly, the operation of the foregoing principles should be without prejudice to the terms of any existing enactment or order. As this suggests, it should not be the purpose of any legislation to affect such statutes as already bear upon the proof of foreign law.[111] Nor does it affect general procedural rules, such as those providing for the appointment of an independent expert[112] or assessor.[113] As we have seen, the value of such advisers in the proof of foreign law is not so apparent that it is necessary to make special provision for them.[114]

If such principles were reflected in legislation this would remove the encumbrance of the fact doctrine as traditionally and strictly conceived. This would achieve that objective without resort to more sweeping legislative devices which might impact more radically on English law's conceptual foundations. There may be no need, for example, to go so far as to declare that a ruling on foreign law shall be treated as one of law.[115] This is unnecessary in the English context given that such issues are already for a judge alone,[116] and are subject to appeal.[117] Moreover, as we have seen, a legal system's approach to foreign law does not depend on how foreign law is classified, but on what that classification implies. Nor would it be desirable to confer upon courts a general discretion to introduce foreign law *ex officio*. This conforms to the current practice whereby a party may be required to plead foreign law but only when this is required by the rules of private international law. It is true to the principle that conflicts rules are not generally mandatory in English practice. Again, it may be undesirable and pointless to allow a court to determine foreign law *ex officio*, perhaps by consulting material which the parties have not submitted in evidence.[118] This conforms to general principle and reflects the fact that it is unreal, and would be impractical, to suppose that an English judge might do so.[119] Nor, finally, need reference be made to the elusive concept of judicial notice which need not be invoked to achieve the desired objective.[120] Strictly, the value of such an approach is that it ensures that ques-

---

[109] Cf. *Sharif* v. *Azad* [1967] 1 QB 605, 616 (CA).
[110] See above, p. 242.
[111] e.g. the British Law Ascertainment Act 1859; the Evidence Colonial Statutes Act 1907; Civil Evidence Act 1972; Supreme Court Act 1981.
[112] RSC Order 40.   [113] RSC Order 33, r. 6.   [114] See above, pp. 211; 232.
[115] Cf. Rule 44.1 Federal Rules of Civil Procedure; Wright and Miller, above n. 4, 634.
[116] Supreme Court Act 1981, s. 69(5).   [117] See above, p. 201.
[118] Wright and Miller, above n. 4, 643–651.
[119] This is regarded as a viable possibility in the United States, although it is unclear how often courts undertake unprompted research: Wright and Miller, above n. 4, 648–651.
[120] The concept was deliberately omitted from Rule 44.1 of the Federal Rules of Procedure on the ground that it was inappropriate to treat the application of foreign law as simply a matter of evidence: *Rule 44.1, Advisory Committee's Note*, 56 FRD207 (1972).

tions of foreign law are for a judge not a jury to determine. But in English law this is clear in any event. More importantly the concept of judicial notice is ambiguous—does it imply that a court actually knows the content of foreign law, or that it has the power to ascertain it *ex officio*, or merely that foreign law may be established otherwise than by formal proof? Certainly, if only the latter is intended, it may be preferable, as it would be sufficient, simply to state that clearly.

Such a measure as that suggested here would be straightforward in its objectives and simple in its terms. It would eradicate the most significant defects of the fact doctrine and clarify the law's conceptual basis. It would also provide a method of handling foreign law which is worthy of a sophisticated legal system and appropriate to modern circumstances. It is hard to disguise the antique and formalistic character of English law's traditional approach, at least when it is taken to its logical extent. This attests to the power of the familiar in English private international law. But it is puzzling given the topic's role at the subject's practical and conceptual heart. It is also surprizing in the light of London's prominence in the resolution of international commercial disputes. And it is uncomfortably at odds with the increasing modernization of English civil procedure, with its fresh emphasis on economy and proportionality. Certainly, it is cause for concern that, at the century's close, English law's treatment of foreign law is defined by a cluster of fictions of varying degrees of improbability, each one seemingly ordained by the fact doctrine. Granted that they are subject to qualification, it is particularly unfortunate that the subject's central tenets should so often be taken literally. Is it right that a court's legal knowledge and competence is suspended, by operation of the fact doctrine, where foreign law is concerned? Is it justifiable that whether English law should apply becomes procedural where the pleading of foreign law is involved? What confidence can we have in the presumption that English and foreign law are the same? Above all, in the modern legal world, how can we insist that foreign laws are nothing more (or little more) than facts?

Select Bibliography

The selected works cited below fall into four categories. Those in the first address directly the pleading and proof of foreign law. Little periodical literature exists in England or the Commonwealth, treatments being largely confined to accounts of the fact doctrine and its consequences in the leading texts on private international law or the law of evidence. But much work of a more analytical and critical nature exists elsewhere. The implications of the Swiss Law on Private International Law of 1987, which handles the foreign law problem with particular sophistication, deserve attention, while the French, German and American material is especially valuable. Taken together, the work of writers in those jurisdictions sets the agenda for discussion, and does much to illuminate even the English approach. Recent work in France is largely concerned with exploring the implications of several recent decisions which re-define the role of the court in enforcing compliance with the rules for choice of law. Discussion centres on establishing when the application of foreign law is required against a background in which, as in England, it is generally optional. The American literature is compelling in a different way. Much concerned with how foreign law may be established in the light of the abolition of the fact doctrine by Rule 44.1 of the Federal Rules of Procedure, it suggests what the consequences might be were English law also to emancipate itself from the traditional view that foreign laws are facts. The German experience is of interest because it represents, in most respects, an approach entirely opposite to that of English law. But the debate surrounding the controversial theory of optional choice of law (*Fakultatives kollisionsrecht*) is also important for exposing the extent to which choice of law rules may be voluntary even in a system where they are generally viewed as mandatory.

There are also several comparative treatments of the topic. These are of particular interest, partly by revealing the conceptual foundations of different national approaches, and partly by demonstrating that those approaches may have more in common than sometimes appears.

Although most material in England and the Commonwealth is descriptive, several important works in English serve to shape any discussion of the foreign law problem in a common law context. These, with their more conceptual and critical concerns, are listed separately. Several amongst them are especially illuminating. Wolff, in his compelling treatise, trenchantly exposes the ambiguities and failings of the fact doctrine in the English context. The seminal work of Currie and Ehrenzweig poses challenging questions about the respective roles of foreign law and *lex fori* in the conflicts process. North's 'Choice in Choice of Law' explores the role of party autonomy in choice of law, and considers the omission to plead foreign law in that context. Finally, the work of De Boer (echoing that of Flessner in Germany) explores the extent to which the rules for choice of law should be treated as mandatory in the light of both the common law and civil law experience.

Beyond such dedicated accounts of the foreign law problem several works deal in important ways with the general legal background to the subject. Some concern matters of private international law. They address such issues as the extent to which English law requires a court to police illegality in another legal system, or the role of choice of law considerations in establishing jurisdiction, or the importance for the conflicts process of the trend towards international legal harmonization. Other works examine problems in the law of procedure and evidence. Of these the most important concern the viability of expert evidence as a means of resolving conflicts of specialist opinion. The proof of foreign law by expert testimony is a matter of particular importance in English law given renewed interest in the use of court advisers and doubts about an adversarial approach to expert opinion. Indeed, in the English context, any discussion of the proof of foreign law must largely concern itself with the nature and value of expert evidence.

A final group of issues, of more theoretical significance, concern the nature of legal argument and adjudication. A proper understanding of legal reasoning is essential in understanding how foreign law can be established in English courts, and in assessing the effectiveness of that process. The essentially dialectical nature of legal reasoning may explain the particular advantages of an adversarial approach to establishing foreign law. And the possibility that there are no right answers to questions of law, only plausible solutions within a range of permissible options, may alleviate concerns that the proof of foreign law can never be effective. As such, any account of the proof of foreign law must ultimately commit itself to a view on a number of fundamental questions which have long been debated in the jurisprudential literature. Is legal reasoning a process of argument or discovery? In what sense can there be right answers to questions of law (local or foreign)?

1. THE PLEADING AND PROOF OF FOREIGN LAW

(a) COMMONWEALTH JURISDICTIONS

Anton, A. E., *Private International Law*, 3rd edn. (Edinburgh, 1990)
Baker, J.H., 'Ascertainment of Foreign Law: Certification to and by English Courts Prior to 1861', (1979) 28 *MLR* 141

Benjamin's Sale of Goods, 5th edn. (London, 1997), by A.G. Guest, with specialist contributors

Bullen and Leake and Jacob's Precedents of Pleading, 13th edn. (London, 1990), by Sir Jack Jacob and Iain S. Goldrein with specialist contributors

Castel, J.-G., *Canadian Conflict of Laws* (Toronto and Vancouver, 1994)

Cheshire and North's Private International Law, 12th edn. (London, 1992), by P. M. North and J. J. Fawcett

Collier, J. G. *Conflict of Laws*, 2nd edn. (Cambridge, 1993)

Cross, Sir Rupert and Colin Tapper, *Evidence*, 8th edn. (London, 1995)

Dicey and Morris, *The Conflict of Laws*, 12th edn. (London, 1993), by Lawrence Collins with specialist editors

Droz, Georges, *Competénce judiciaire et effets des jugements dans le Marché Commun* (Paris, 1972)

Fentiman, Richard, 'Foreign Law in English Courts', (1992) 108 *LQR* 142

Fleming, John G., 'Formal Validity of Foreign Marriages', (1951) 25 *ALJ* 406

Forsyth, C., *Private International Law*, 3rd edn. (Cape Town, 1996)

Hill, J., *The Law Relating to International Commercial Disputes* (London,1994)

Hirschfeld, Julius, 'Proof of Foreign Law', (1895) 11 *LQR* 241

Hodgkinson, Tristram, *Expert Evidence: Law and Practice* (London, 1990)

Kahn, Ellison, 'What Happens in a Conflicts Case When the Governing Foreign Law is not Proved?' (1970) 87 *SALJ* 145

Kahn Freund, Sir Otto, *General Problems of Private International Law*, 2nd. edn. (1976)

Kaye, Peter, *International Contracts*, (Chichester, 1993)

Keane, Adrian, *The Modern Law of Evidence*, 4th edn. (London, 1996)

Leslie, R. D., 'Domestic Law Rules', (1990) 35 *JLSS* 475

Morris, J. H. C., *The Conflict of Laws*, 14th edn. (London, 1993), by J. D. Mclean

Neil, Sir Brian, *Report of the Supreme Court Procedure Committee on Practice and Procedure in Defamation* (1991)

Nygh, P. E., *Conflict of Laws in Australia*, 4th edn. (Sydney, 1995)

O'Malley, Stephen and Alexander Layton, A., *European Civil Practice* (London, 1989)

Phipson on Evidence, 14th edn. (London, 1990), by M. N. Howard, Peter Crane and Daniel A. Hochberg

Sykes, Edward I., and Michael C. Pryles, *Australian Private International Law*, 3rd edn. (Sydney, 1991)

Tetley, William, *International Conflict of Laws* (Montreal, 1994)

Westlake, John, *A Treatise on Private Internatonal Law* (1858), and 7th edn. (1925), by Norman Bentwich

(b) France

Battifol, Henri and Paul Lagarde, *Droit international privé*, 8th edn. (Paris, 1993), vol.1

Bureau, Dominique, 'L'application d'office de la loi étrangère, Essai de synthese', *JDI*. 2, 1990, 317

Lagarde, Paul, 'Soc. Amerford et autre c. Air France ets autres', *Rev. crit. dr. int. pr.* 1994, 332

Lequette, Yves, 'L'abandon de la jurisprudence Bisbal (a propos des arrets de la Premiere chambre civile des 11 et 18 octobre 1988)', *Rev. crit. dr. int. pr.* 1989, 277

Loussouarn, Yvon and Pierre Bourel, *Droit international privé*, 4th edn., (Paris, 1993)

Mayer, Pierre, *Droit international privé*, 5th edn., (Paris, 1994)

Motulsky, H., 'L'office du juge et le droit étranger', *Melanges offert à Jacques Maury*, tome I (Paris, 1960)

Ponsard, Andre, 'L'office du juge et l'application du droit étranger', *Rev. crit. dr. int. pr.* 1990, 607

(c) Germany

Von Bar, Christian, *Internationales Privatrecht*, vol. II (Munich, 1987–1991)

Flessner, A. 'Fakultatives Kollisionsrecht', *Rabels Zeitschrift* (1970), 547

Flessner, A., *Interessenjurisprudenz im internationalen Privatrecht* (Tübingen, 1990)

Bülow, A. und K.-H. Böckstiegel, *Der Internationaler Rechtsverkehr in Zivil- und Handelssachen* (Munich, 1987)

Schurig, Fritz, 'Interessenjurisprudenz contra interessenjurisprudenz, Anmerkungen zu Flessners Thesen', *Rabels Zeitschrift* (1995), 229

Siehr, Kurt, 'Special Courts for Conflicts Cases: A German Experiment', (1977) *Am Jl Comp L* 663

Stein & Jonas, *Kommentar zur Zivilprozessordnung*, 21st edn., (Tübingen, 1993–), vol. III, Section 293, (Leipold)

Sturm, Fritz, 'Fakultatives Kollisionsrecht: Notwendigkeit und Grenzen', in Herbert Bernstein, Ulrich Drobnig, and Hein Kotz, eds., *Festschrift für Konrad Zweigert zum 70 Geburtstag* (Tübingen, 1981), 329

Zöller, *Zivilprozessordnung*, 19th edn. (Cologne, 1995), Section 293, (Geimer)

(d) Switzerland

Bucher, Andreas, *Droit international privé Suisse* (Bale, 1995), vol. I/2
Samuel, Adam, 'The New Swiss Private International Law Act', (1988) 37 *ICLQ* 681
Symeonides, Symeon, 'The New Swiss Conflicts Codification: An Introduction', (1989) 37 *Am Jl Comp L* 187

(e) The United States

American Law Institute, *Restatement, Second, Conflict of Laws* (1971)
Baade, Hans W., 'Proving Foreign and International Law in Domestic Tribunals', (1978) 18 *Virginia Jl Int L* 619
Merryman, John H., 'Foreign Law as a Problem', (1983) 19 *Stan Jl Int L* 151
Miller, Arthur R., 'Federal Rule 44.1 and the 'Fact' Approach to Determining Foreign Law: Death Knell for a Die-Hard Doctrine', (1967) 65 *Mich L Rev.* 613
Miner, Roger J., 'The Reception of Foreign Law in the U.S. Federal Courts', (1995) 43 *Am Jl Comp L* 581
Nussbaum, Arthur, 'The Problem of Proving Foreign Law', (1941) 50 *Yale L J* 1018 (1941)
Pollack, Milton, 'Proof of Foreign Law', (1978) 26 *Am Jl Comp L* 470
Sass, Stephen L., 'Foreign Law in Federal Courts', (1981) 29 *Am Jl Comp L* 97
Schlesinger, Rudolf B., 'A Recurrent Problem in Transnational Litigation: The Effect of a Failure to Invoke or Prove the Applicable Foreign Law', (1973) 59 *Cornell L R* 1
Schlesinger, Rudolf B., Hans Baade, Mirjan R. Damaska, and Peter E. Herzog, *Comparative Law*, 5th edn. (Mineola, 1988)
Schmertz, John R., 'The Establishment of Foreign and International Law in American Courts: A Procedural Overview', (1978) 18 *Virginia Jl Intl L* 697
Sommerich, Otto. C. and Benjamin Busch, *Foreign Law* (New York, 1959)
Spranking, John G. and George R. Lanyi, 'Pleading and Proof of Foreign Law in American Courts', (1995) 19 *Stan Jl of Intl L* 3
Stern, 'Foreign Law in the Courts: Judicial Notice and Proof', (1957) 45 *Cal L Rev* 23
Wright, Charles Alan and Arthur R. Miller, *Federal Practice and Procedure: Civil 2d* (St. Paul, Minn., 1995), vol. 9, section 2441

(f) Comparative Accounts

De Vos, Wouter, and Walter H. Rechtberger, 'Transnational Litigation and the Evolution of the Law of Evidence', *General Report to the International Conference on Procedural Law, Taormina*, (1995)

Hartley, Trevor, 'Pleading and Proof of Foreign Law: The Major European Systems Compared', (1996) 45 *ICLQ* 271

Kerameus, K., 'Revisibilitat Ausländischen Rechts, Ein Rechtsvergleichender Überblick (1986) 99 *Zeitschrift fur Zivilprozess* 116

Rodger, Barry J. and Juliette van Doorn, 'Proof of Foreign Law: The Impact of the London Convention', (1996) 46 *ICLQ* 151

Sass, Stephen L., 'Foreign Law in Civil Litigation: A Comparative Survey', (1968) 16 *Am Jl Comp L* 332

Zajtay, Imre, 'The Application of Foreign Law', Vol. III, Ch.14, *International Encyclopedia of Comparative Law* (1972)

(g) Conceptual Issues

De Boer, Th. M., 'Facultative Choice of Law', (1996) *Recueil des Cours*, vol. 257, 227

Cappelletti, Mauro, 'Mandatory Ex-Officio Application of Foreign Law: The Comparative Method as an Answer in Cases Where the Foreign Law Cannot be Ascertained', (1970) 3 *CILSA* 60

Currie, Brainerd, 'On the Displacement of the Law of the Forum', (1958) 58 *Col L Rev* 964

Ehrenzweig, Albert A. and Peter Kay Westen, 'Fraudulent Conveyances in the Conflict of Laws: Easy Cases Make Bad Law', (1968) 66 *Mich L Rev* 1679

Ehrenzweig, Albert A., 'The Lex Fori – Basic Rule in the Conflict of Laws', (1960) 58 *Mich L Rev* 638; 'A Proper Law in a Proper Forum: A 'Restatement' of the 'Lex Fori Approach', (1965) 18 *Oklahoma L Rev* 340

Lando, Ole, 'Lex Fori in Foro Proprio', (1995) *Maastricht Journal of European and Comparative Law* 359

North, P.M., 'Choice in Choice of Law', *Essays in Private International Law* (Oxford, 1993)

Wolff, Martin, *Private International Law*, 2nd edn. (Oxford, 1950)

Zajtay, Imre, 'The Application of Foreign Law: Science and Fictions', (1973) 6 *CILSA* 245

Zweigert, Konrad, 'Some Reflections on the Sociological Dimensions of Private International Law or What is Justice in the Conflict of Laws?', (1973) 44 *Colorado L R* 283

2. THE PRIVATE INTERNATIONAL LAW BACKGROUND

Briggs, A., 'How Soon is a Court Seised (Revisited)', [1994] *LMCLQ* 470
Carter, P. B., 'Choice of Law in Tort: The Role of the *Lex Fori*', (1995) 54 *CLJ* 38; 'Location of a tort for the purposes of service of process out of the jurisdiction', (1989) *BYIL* 485
Collier, J. G., 'Conflict of Laws', *All England Law Reports Annual Review 1989*
Contracts (Applicable Law) Act 1990, *1990 Current Law Statutes Annotated*, annotation by C.G.J. Morse
Diamond, Aubrey, (1986) IV *Recueil des Cours*, Ch. IV
Fawcett, J. J., 'Evasion of Law and Mandatory Rules in Private International Law', (1990) 40 *CLJ* 44
Fentiman, Richard, 'Il problema dell'armonizzazione nell'ottica di un internazionalprivatista', in Stein, ed., *Il futuro codice europeo dei contratti* (Milan, 1993)
Goode, Roy, *Commercial Law* (London, 1982), and 2nd edn. (London, 1995)
Hobhouse, J. S., 'International Conventions and Commercial Law: The Pursuit of Uniformity', (1990) *LQR* 530
Hogan, G.W., 'Contracting Out of the Rome Convention', (1992) 108 *LQR* 12
Mann, F. A., 'Proper Law and Illegality in Private International Law', (1937) 18 *BYIL* 107; 'The Proper Law of the Contract – An Obituary', (1991) 107 *LQR* 353
Morse, C. G. J., 'Letters of Credit and the Rome Convention', [1994] *LMCLQ* 560
Private International Law (Miscellaneous Provisions) Bill, Proceedings of the Special Public Bill Committee, HL Paper 36, (HMSO, London, 1995)
Reynolds, F. M. B., 'Illegality by the *Lex Loci Solutionis*', (1992) 108 *LQR* 553
Rubino-Sammartano, Mauro and C. G. J. Morse, eds., *Public Policy in Transnational Relationships* (Deventer, 1991)
Spence, Donald, 'Conflict of Laws in Automobile Negligence Cases', (1949) 27 *Can BR* 661
Yntema, Hessel E., review of J. L. Falconbridge, Essays on the Conflict of Laws, (1949) 27 *Can BR* 116

3. THE PROCEDURAL BACKGROUND

Andrews, Neil, *Principles of Civil Procedure* (London, 1994)
Basten, J., 'The Court Expert in Civil Trials: A Comparative Appraisal', (1977) 40 *MLR* 174

Dickey, Anthony, 'The Province and Function of Assessors in English Courts', (1970) 33 *MLR* 494

Eggleston, Sir Richard, *Evidence, Proof and Probability* (London, 1978)

Goldrein, Iain, 'Case Management and Experts', (1995) *NLJ* 381

Jack, Adrian, 'Lord Woolf and Expert Evidence', (1994) 144 *NLJ* 1099

Jacob, Sir Jack, *Fabric of English Civil Justice* (London, 1987)

Jolowicz, J. A., 'On the Nature and Purposes of Civil Procedural Law', *International Perspectives on Civil Justice*, ed. Scott (London, 1990)

Ormrod, Sir Roger, 'Scientific Evidence in Court', [1968] *Crim L R* 240

Pollock, Sir Frederick, *Expansion of the Common Law* (1904)

Rosenthal, Lloyd L., 'The Development of the Use of Expert Testimony', (1935) 2 *Law & Contemp. Prob.* 403

Woolf, Lord, *Access to Justice, Interim Report to the Lord Chancellor on the Civil Justice System* (London, HMSO, 1995); *Final Report* (London, HMSO, 1996)

Zuckerman, A. A. S. and Ross Cranston, eds., *Reform of Civil Procedure, Essays on 'Access to Justice'* (Oxford, 1996)

4. THE THEORETICAL BACKGROUND

Dicey, A. V., *Law and Opinion in England*, 2nd edn. (London, 1914)

Dworkin, Ronald, *Taking Rights Seriously* (London, 1977; *A Matter of Principle* (Cambridge, 1985)

Fentiman, Richard, 'Legal Reasoning in the Conflict of Laws', in Krawietz, MacCormick and von Wright, eds, *Prescriptive Formality and Normative Rationality in Modern Legal Systems, Festshrift for Robert S. Summers* (Berlin, 1994)

Perelman, Chaim, *Justice, Law and Argument* (Dordrecht, 1980)

Perelman, Chaim and L. Olbrechts-Tyteca, *The New Rhetoric* (Notre Dame, 1969)

Woozley, A. D., 'No Right Answer', (1979) 29 *The Philosophical Quarterly* 29, 25

Index

abuse of process
  where foreign law not pleaded
    see pleading foreign law
access to justice
  foreign law, and 1–2, 286, 298–9
    see also civil justice reforms
adversarial system
  does not explain English approach to foreign law 63, 267
  effect upon treatment of foreign law 63, 237, 266–7
  fairness of 237, 299–300
  survival of 157n, 174–5
  value in complex disputes 174–6, 237, 299–301
affidavit evidence of foreign law
  see expert evidence of foreign law
American law
  application of foreign law
    discretionary approach 271n, 274
    lex fori as basic rule 75
    mandatory approach supported 264
    theoretical basis 75
  establishing foreign law
    experts employed 175–6, 232, 280
    flexible approach 175, 279–80
    judicial notice, extension of 268n, 315
    judicial research possible 314
  fact doctrine rejected 220, 285, 287, 291
  forum non conveniens
    efficiency overrides accuracy 48
    foreign copyright claim, and 48, 50
    role of foreign law in determining 48
  interest in foreign law problem 11, 285
  literature on foreign law problem 11
appeals on questions of foreign law
  effectiveness 48–9, 201–2
    appropriate forum, relevance in determining 48–9
    special nature 201–2
      distinguishes foreign laws from other facts 201, 287
assessors
  appointment without parties' consent 158
  appropriateness in establishing foreign law 212–13, 233
    appointment with experts 212, 232
  difficulty of identifying assessor 215
  expense 214
  unnecessary for establishing foreign law 215
  unsuitable given legal nature of foreign law 216
  distinguished from experts 212, 232
assignment of debts
  under Rome Convention 1980 81, 84, 93
autonomy of the parties
  see choice of law

bills of exchange
  Bills of Exchange Act 1882
    party autonomy, and 130
    pleading foreign law, whether required 130–1, 151
    presumption of similarity, application to Act doubted 151
    relied upon without evidence of foreign law 131–2, 151
British Law Ascertainment Act 1859
  see Commonwealth laws; official assistance
Brussels Convention on Jurisdiction and the Enforcement of Judgments 1968
  'court first seised' under Article 21
    adjournment for decision by foreign court 55–7
    determining 55
    experts exceptionally employed 55
  domicile in another contracting state
    establishing under Article 52 126–30
    proof of foreign law required 126–30
  foreign law, role in establishing jurisdiction 52–5
    whether proof required 122–5
  interpretation of Convention not question of foreign law 52–3

case management
  foreign law, and 18–19, 156–8, 174–6, 267, 303, 306–7
certification
  expert evidence, distinguished from 221
  proving foreign law, as means of 221–2
    disadvantages 222
  German experience 278
  status as inconclusive evidence 222

choice of law
  facultative
    see facultative choice of law
  importance of
    continuing 23–4, 33–41, 58–9
    factors diminishing 24–33
    factors increasing 33–41
  lex fori, role of 75
  objective of securing application of
    governing law 2–3, 6, 187–8, 194,
    286, 301–305
  party autonomy, and
    lex fori chosen
      presumption that *lex fori* may be
        chosen 75
      special case, whether 76
      substantive choice, whether 70–4,
        92–4
      particular cases
        bills of exchange 130
        contract 83–4
        marriage 121
        tort 97–9
        trusts 132–3
        wills 132–3
      scope generally 77–8
  pleading and proof of foreign law, and
    6–11
choice of law rules
  bills of exchange, concerning
    see bills of exchange
  contract, in
    see contract
  opinio juris, role in shaping 22
  statutory
    see mandatory choice of law rules
  tort, in
    see tort
  trusts, in
    see trusts
  marriage, in
    see marriage
  unpredictability of, as reason not to plead
    foreign law 169–70
  voluntary
    assumption that all rules voluntary
      73–4
    effects of 64–6
  wills, and
    see wills
civil justice reforms
  Lord Woolf's proposals, impact on
    foreign law
    court experts, and 2, 212–18, 232–8
    no effect on choice of law 18–19
    party experts, and 18–19, 174–6
    proportionality, and 18–19, 299

comity
  does not require policing of foreign
    illegality 112
  justifies respect for foreign public laws
    256
Commonwealth law
  special provisions for establishing
    British Law Ascertainment Act 1859 4,
      238–9
    proof of marriage 228–9
    proof of official documents 225–6
    proof of statutes 224–5
conflicting evidence of foreign law
  see expert evidence of foreign law
construction of foreign legal terms
  see contract
contract
  construction of foreign legal terms
    alternative to proof of foreign law 251–7
      where agreed by parties 137, 253–4
    always a matter of construction 252–3
    contract may be governed by foreign law
      137, 252–3
    foreign statute incorporated in contract
      251–2
    maritime contracts typically affected 252
    proof of foreign law may be required
      135–8, 251–7
      illegality under foreign law 137, 255–6
      diplomatically sensitive issue 137,
        254, 257
      pure construction impossible 136–7,
        254, 257
    international convention applies in
      English law 257–8
  Rome Convention 1980
    Article 3(3), ambiguity of 84–5
    consumer protection, and 80–1, 83–4,
      87–8, 93
    employee protection, and 80–1, 83–4,
      87–8, 93
    'force of law', ambiguity of expression
      85–7
    judicial notice of 88
    mandatory nature of 83, 85–7
    mandatory language of 80–1, 89–90
    party autonomy, restricted scope of
      83–4
    pleading the applicable law
      whether required 80–96
      whether substantive issue 92–4
      omission to plead, whether choice of
        lex fori under Article 3(2) 83, 93, 94–5
      practical impact on English law 82,
        94–6
      procedural issues unaffected by 81,
        92–93

Index

procedural issues determined by *lex fori* 92
proof of applicable law required 93–4
purposive interpretation of 89–90
uniform interpretation of 88–90
conventions, international
see international conventions
copyright
English law limited to local infringements 147, 152
foreign infringements, presumption of similarity inapplicable to 147, 152
forum non conveniens, and 48, 50
corporate status
proof under foreign law
act of state doctrine irrelevant 231
expert evidence required 231
court documents
proof where foreign 225–6
court-appointed experts
see experts on foreign law
criminal proceedings
application of foreign law required 78
bigamy as example 78–9
not a special case 79
policy considerations 79
presumption of similarity inapplicable 79, 186
theft as example 79

defamation where publication abroad
see tort
documentary evidence of foreign law
alternative to expert evidence 257–62, 299
comparative context 278–81
conflicting expert opinion 200–1
courts' inherent power to interpret 194–8, 257–9
expert opinion not obtained 256–62
expert opinion obtained 188–9
unsatisfactory expert opinion 195–9
domicile
proof of foreign law required under Brussels Convention, Article 52
see Brussels Convention 1968
double actionability rule in tort
see tort

English decisions on foreign law
previous decisions, German practice concerning 278
proof, as means of 223
Ersatzrecht
concept in German law 281–2
evidence of foreign law

documentary
see documentary evidence of foreign law
expert
see expert evidence of foreign law; experts on foreign law
expert evidence of foreign law
advantages of 174–6, 299–308
affidavit evidence and 203–10
limitations of 207–10
difficulty of assessing 207–10
alternatives to
certification 221–2
construction of private documents 251–2
court advisers, appointment of 232–8
English decisions, reference to 222–3
foreign formal acts, proof of 224–32
foreign law as notorious fact 248–51
foreign materials, assessment of 257–62
foreign official assistance, where obtained 238–44
general principles of law, where relied upon 247–8
judicial notice of foreign law 246–7
justification for 219–21
American practice 175–6
appeals 201–2
assessment of 188–201
conflicting evidence 200–1
documents produced, court restricted to 188–9
improved evidence, court's power to seek 154–6
interlocutory proceedings 204–10
novel points arising 190
unsatisfactory evidence 195–9
weighting of evidence 191–3
construction of documents, role in 136, 178, 245
dialectical nature of legal reasoning, reflects 20, 235–8, 299–300
disadvantages of
concern failure to narrow issues 306–7
cost 13, 170–2, 175, 305–7
ineffectiveness 301–5
partiality 176–7, 301–2
distinguished from expert evidence generally 20, 177, 235–8, 299–300
examination abroad, obtained by 210–11
expert witnesses, and
see experts on foreign law
French experience of 279
generally employed 174–6, 262–4, 299–308

expert evidence of foreign law (*continued*)
German experience of 277-9
improving
assessor, by appointing 211-18
court expert, by appointing 211-18
examination abroad, by 210-11
obtaining better evidence, by 153-6
written evidence, by employing 203-10
limited by court 156-8, 306-8
supplementing
courts' powers 194-201
experts on foreign law
appointed by court
assessors, distinguished from 212, 232
adversarial system, and 237, 300
appropriateness of 213-18, 235-8, 303-4
difficulty of identifying expert 215, 235
expense 214, 235
unnecessary to establish foreign law 215
unsuitable given legal nature of foreign law 216
comparative context 237-8, 277-81
historical role 233-4
with party experts 211-18
without parties' consent 158
without party experts 232-8
effectiveness 235-8
fairness 235-8
difficulty of identifying 165, 181, 192
distinctive role of 177
employed before trial 42-4, 165
impartiality of 176, 301-2
difficulty of ensuring in foreign law disputes 176-7, 301-2
meetings between, importance in narrowing dispute 157, 306-7
oral examination of
abroad 210-11
cost and duration 8, 156, 171
difficulty of 8
exceptionally permitted at interlocutory stage 55, 207-8
not in determining *forum conveniens* 207-8
under Brussels Convention 55
importance in establishing foreign law 204-6, 280-1
limitation necessary 55, 209
qualifications of 178-82
academic 179-80
'knowledge or experience' 179-81
jurist from another system 180
jurist from system concerned 180
non-jurists 180
practical 180-1

reports by
exchange required 157, 306-7
fact doctrine
ambiguity of 5-6, 197, 250
described 3-6, 64, 66-7
detrimental consequences of 220, 287-91
exceptions to
appeals 201
choice of law rule mandatory 66-8
foreign law within court's province 194-5, 197-9, 245-62, 287-8
irrelevance to whether foreign law applicable 66-8
explains approach to failure in proof 281-2
explains procedural approach to choice of *lex fori* 74
foreign laws unlike other facts 8-9, 216, 218
mandatory application of foreign law, compatible with 66-8, 268-9
rejected in America 291, 314-15
strict application of
criticised 194-5, 197, 220, 251, 257-9, 287-91, 315
defended 196, 257,
illustrated 196, 250, 257
'facultative choice of law'
theory described 72-3, 294
reflects concerns of civil lawyers 73
supports traditional English approach 72-3
foreign marriage
see marriage
forum non conveniens
difficulty of proof relevant in determining
appeal, difficulty of 48-9
assumptions of foreign law different 46-7, 49, 309
effective proof unlikely 48-50
inconvenience of proof 45-6
nature of issue requires accuracy
foreign public policy 49
foreign intellectual property rights 50
proof ineffective but convenient 48
importance of foreign law in determining 44-52
proof of foreign law necessary in determining 51-2
affidavit evidence employed 51, 206
evidence often insufficient 51, 206
not always problematic 209-10
strategies for assessing evidence
determination without resolving foreign law issue 52, 207-8

examination of experts unlikely 207–8
presumption of similarity inapplicable 209
stay on condition English law applies abroad 208–9
fraud
presumption of similarity doubted where alleged 147, 151, 186
French law
application of foreign law
choice of law rules, status 267n, 269n, 274
sometimes discretionary 272n
international conventions, mandatory status 267
patrimonial rights 267n, 273–4
establishing foreign law
certificats de coutume, role of 279
experts, role of 279, 280
foreign laws as facts 268
transformation of 267n, 272, 285

general principles of law
construction of documents, and 247, 136–7
evidence not required to establish 247–8
within province of court 247–248
German law
application of foreign law mandatory 269
approach qualified by scope of party autonomy 273–4
establishing foreign law
with court experts 178, 280
without court experts 278–9
failure to establish foreign law 281–2
Ersatzrecht, principle of 281

homeward trend
diminishes role of foreign law 29–33
feature of English law 29–33
procedural issues governed by English law 29–30
scope of procedural category now reduced 35–41
substance governed by English law 30
because of party preference 30
because of structure of choice of law rules 30–1
voluntary approach to foreign law, and 32–3

illegality under foreign law
as illegality under English law 111
beyond judicial notice 111–12
mandatory pleading
generally not required 106–13
exception for foreign exchange controls 107–8
impractical 113
where amendment sought on appeal 107, 112
incorporation of foreign statute in contract
see contract
inherent powers of court
in matters of evidence 241–2
to appoint independent experts 158, 242
to police illegality under English law 106, 111
to seek foreign official assistance 241–2
interlocutory proceedings
importance in practice 51, 207
presumption of similarity inapplicable to 103, 185–6, 208–9
proof of foreign law, and
affidavit evidence employed 204–10
expert evidence exceptionally employed 207–8
see also forum non conveniens
international conventions
as source of choice of law rules
contract, and 80–97
jurisdiction, and 122–30
trusts, and 134
wills, and 133
French approach 272
mandatory status of 83, 85–7, 272
distinguished from status of particular rules 85–7
uniformity required by, as argument for excluding party choice 86–7, 134–5
iura novit curia
absence of doctrine in English law 18
need not compel application of foreign law 267
implications of doctrine 269, 272, 266
origins of doctrine 266

judicial notice of foreign law
ambiguity of 269, 314–15
scope of
extended in other jurisdictions 268
limited in English law 64–5, 244–7
jurisdiction
proof of foreign law required to establish
where mandatory choice of law rule 124–5
where matrimonial relief sought 114–15, 123
under Brussels Convention, Article 52 126–9
see also Brussels Convention 1968; Lugano Convention 1988; *forum non conveniens*

Index

law, foreign law as
  see fact doctrine
legal reasoning
  dialectical nature reflected in expert proof 20, 263, 300
  process of argument not discovery 20, 263
  realistic perspective required 20, 309
  right answer to question of law, whether possible 309
  theories of 20, 309
    importance in assessing treatment of foreign law 20, 309
  truth, meaning when applied to legal propositions 20, 282, 310
lex fori
  application of
    as basic rule in the conflict of laws 75, 290
    presumption of 75
    reasons to favour 71–2, 293–4
  choice of
    omission to plead foreign law, by 70–4
    no formality required 94–5
    reasons for
      see pleading foreign law
  special features of 71–2, 293–4
limitation of actions
  Foreign Limitation Periods Act 1984
    difficulty of establishing when period begins 129
    foreign limitation period, whether pleading required 129–30
    limitation period a matter of substance 38
  Rome Convention 1980
    limitation period a matter of substance 38
London Convention on Information on Foreign Law 1968
  see official assistance
Lugano Convention on Jurisdiction and the Enforcement of Judgments 1988
  'court first seised' under Article 21
    adjournment for decision by foreign court 55–7
    experts exceptionally used 55, 56
  domicile in another contracting state
    establishing under Article 52 126–30
    proof of foreign law required 126–30
  foreign law, role in establishing jurisdiction 52–5
  proof required, whether 122–5
  interpretation of Convention not a question of foreign law 56–57

mandatory application of foreign law
  at court's discretion
    under British Law Ascertainment Act 1859 134–5
  where necessary for documentary construction 135–8
  where choice of law rule mandatory
    see mandatory choice of law rules
mandatory choice of law rules
  effects of
    dismissal for non-compliance 66–78
    pleading and proof required 61
  examples of
    bills of exchange 130–2
    contract proceedings 80–97
    criminal proceedings 78–80
    documentary construction 135–8
    illegality under foreign law 106–13
    foreign exchange controls 107–8
    jurisdiction proceedings 122–9
      RSC Order 11, 123–5
      European Conventions 125–8
    limitation periods 129–30
    matrimonial proceedings 113–12
    meaning of 66–78
    tort proceedings 97–106
      at common law 99–106
      under statute 97–9
    trusts 132–4
    wills 132–4
  identification of
    depends upon construction 75–6, 140
    does not depend upon classification 119, 140
    peremptory language inconclusive 75–6, 89–90, 127, 129, 133
    permissive language inconclusive 98, 130
    presumption that *lex fori* may be chosen 75
    problematic unless statutory 76, 130, 140
    problematic where statute silent 75, 129–30, 130–2, 132–4, 140
mandatory rules
  consumer protection, and
    see contract
  employee protection, and
    see contract
  foreign law, of
    meaning under Rome Convention, Article 3(3) 84–5
  taxonomy of, lacking in English law 75, 139, 297
  see also mandatory choice of law rules

Index

marriage
  choice of law in
    uncertainty of English law 121
      explains why proof of marriage not required 121
    lex fori often governs 10, 30–1, 32–3, 117, 161–2
  proof under foreign law 226–30
    certificate, by 227–9
    contested, where 226
    requirement of 113–22
      comparative context 113–14, 119, 271, 275
      distinctiveness of English approach 113–14, 119, 271
      English approach explained 119–21
      formal validity, and 115–16
      limited scope of requirement 116–19
      practical considerations 120–1
      pre-condition of matrimonial relief 226
      where English law territorially limited 115–16, 118–19
    presumption, by 229–30
    uncontested, where 226–30

non liquet
  see proof of foreign law, failure of
notice, judicial
  see judicial notice of foreign law
notorious facts
  status of foreign laws as
    ambiguity of fact doctrine regarding 250
    justification for treating foreign laws as notorious 251
    scope of principle 128–50
    within specific tribunals 248–50

official assistance
  as means of establishing foreign law
    appropriateness in English context 243–4
    disadvantages 242–4
  British Law Ascertainment Act 1859
    as means of establishing foreign law 238–9
    disadvantages of procedure 239
    rarely employed 239
  London Convention on Information on Foreign Law 1968
    as means of establishing foreign law 239–44
      available although not ratified 240–2
      criticised 242–5
      described 240
      French experience 279n
      German experience 278

party autonomy
  see choice of law
patrimonial rights
  role of concept in defining civil law approaches 113, 114, 118–19, 267, 268, 271, 276, 273, 294–5
pleading foreign law
  abuse of process, and 151–2
  distinguished from allegation that foreign law applies 61–2
  omission to plead
    choice of *lex fori*, as 66–8, 70–8
    consequences of
      where choice of law rule voluntary 64–6
      where choice of law rule mandatory
        dismissal of claim 68–9
        court cannot research foreign law 68
        contempt order inappropriate 69
    examples of 159–61
    procedural issue, whether 70–4, 92–4
    reasons for
      assumption that *lex fori* governs 30, 161–2, 170
      choice of law rule uncertain 169
        bills of exchange 130–1
        illegality 109–10
        marriage 121
        Rome Convention, Article 3(3) 84–5
        tort 97–8, 102–3
        trusts 133
        wills 133
      classification uncertain 165–8
        Romalpa case as example 166–8
      cost 45–7, 170–2, 305–8
      English law insufficiently different 165
      foreign law uncertain 165
      preference for English law 170
      proof of foreign law uncertain 169
      tactical advantage 143–5
      unexceptional 161–2
  required in law
    where application of foreign law mandatory *see* mandatory application of foreign law
  required in practice
    English law inapplicable 147, 150–1, 162
  technical requirements of 65–6
presumption of similarity
  criticised 144–53, 184–8, 290
  exceptions to
    abuse of process 151–2
    application of foreign law mandatory 61
    English law statutory 147

Index

presumption of similarity (*continued*)
    English law territorially limited 147
    English law unconnected with dispute 151
    English law unique 147
    fraud alleged 147
    interlocutory proceedings 103, 209
    summary proceedings 147
  judicial support for 146, 184
  tactical advantages of 143–4
procedure and substance
  relative importance of categories in English law 35–41
  omission to plead foreign law, whether procedural
  see pleading foreign law
proof of foreign law
  burden of 182
  comparative context 281–283
  difficulty of
    illustrated 45–56
    interlocutory proceedings, in 103, 206–10
    perhaps exaggerated 13, 20–1
  effectiveness of
    interlocutory proceedings, in 206–10
    questioned 46, 48
    supported 20–1, 174–6, 301–5, 309–10
  exceptions to formal proof permitted 244
    construction of documents 251–7
    construction of foreign legal materials 247–62
    court's knowledge and competence, matter within 245, 251ff
    foreign law notorious 248–51
    general principles of law relied upon 247–8
    judicial notice of foreign law 246–7
  expert evidence by
    see expert evidence of foreign law; experts on foreign law
  failure of
    avoided by courts 186–8
    comparative context 281–3
    consequences 182–8
      English law generally applies 184
      subject to exceptions 185–6
    presumption of similarity
      doubtful role of 184–6
      exceptions to 185–6
      persistence of 184–5
      rarely occurs 186–8, 282
  necessary where foreign law relied upon 143–53
proportionality
  as objective of procedural law
  see civil justice reforms

public policy under foreign law
  inappropriateness of establishing in English courts 49
  presumption of similarity applies to 146, 184
reform
  civil justice, of
  see civil justice reforms
  private international law, of
    importance of foreign law problem to 13–16
  rules concerning foreign law, of
    need for 290–1, 307–8, 310–15
    perception of fact doctrine, depends upon 311
    proposals for 312–15
registers
  proof where foreign 225–6
Rome Convention 1980
  see contract

settlement
  frequency in practice 26–7
  role of foreign law problem in encouraging 26–7
similarity, presumption of
  see presumption of similarity
statutes
  English
    mandatory status of 85–7
      distinguished from status of provisions 86
    see also mandatory choice of law rules
    presumption of similarity inapplicable 115–16, 147, 185
    proof where foreign 224
    territorial scope, effect on pleading 115–16, 147, 150–1, 186
status
  see marriage
substance and procedure
  see procedure and substance
summary proceedings
  affidavit evidence employed in 185, 206
  presumption of similarity inapplicable in 206,
supplementing expert evidence
  courts' powers
  see expert evidence of foreign law
Swiss law
  Law on Private International Law 1987 272–3
    mandatory application of foreign law 273
    party autonomy, and 273
    unwaivable rights, and 273

tort
  double actionability rule
    abuse of process, and 151–2
    changed nature of 105–6
    continuing importance of 100–1
    copyright infringement under 151–2
    deters claims involving foreign law 34–5, 102–3
    defamation under 99–106, 143–53
    English law applicable under 101–2, 105–6
    jurisdictional rule, whether 104–5
    peremptory language of 104
    pleading and proving the *lex loci delicti* under 143–53
    reliance on the *lex loci delicti* not required 99–106
    tactical importance of 144
  Private International Law (Miscellaneous Provisions) Act 1995
    encourages claims involving foreign law 34–5
    existing law, limited effect upon 98–9
    party autonomy under 97–8
    reliance upon foreign law, whether required under 97–9
trusts
  Recognition of Trusts Act 1987
    existing approach to pleading not preserved 133
    party autonomy under 133
    pleading foreign law possibly required 133–4

uniformity of laws
  diminishes foreign law problem 24–6
  incidence of foreign law questions, effect upon 26
  significance in English law 25
  trend towards 24–6
United States law
  see American law
unsatisfactory evidence of foreign law
  see expert evidence of foreign law

vested rights theory
  consequences of, for treatment of foreign law 266
  explains English approach to foreign law 74–5

wills
  Wills Act 1963
    existing approach to pleading not preserved 133
    party autonomy under 133
    pleading foreign law, whether required under 132–3